Federal Courts

WEST'S LAW SCHOOL ADVISORY BOARD

JESSE H. CHOPER
Professor of Law, University of California, Berkeley

DAVID P. CURRIE
Professor of Law, University of Chicago

YALE KAMISAR
Professor of Law, University of Michigan
Professor of Law, University of San Diego

MARY KAY KANE
Chancellor, Dean and Distinguished Professor of Law,
University of California,
Hastings College of the Law

WAYNE R. LaFAVE
Professor of Law, University of Illinois

ARTHUR R. MILLER
Professor of Law, Harvard University

GRANT S. NELSON
Professor of Law,
University of California, Los Angeles

JAMES J. WHITE
Professor of Law, University of Michigan

BLACK LETTER OUTLINES

Federal Courts

by Richard D. Freer
Robert Howell Hall Professor of Law
Emory University School of Law

Martin H. Redish
Louis and Harriet Ancel Professor of Law and Public Policy
Northwestern University

THIRD EDITION

THOMSON
WEST

Mat #11641490

West, a Thomson business, has created this publication to provide you with accurate and authoritative information concerning the subject matter covered. However, this publication was not necessarily prepared by persons licensed to practice law in a particular jurisdiction. West is not engaged in rendering legal or other professional advice, and this publication is not a substitute for the advice of an attorney. If you require legal or other expert advice, you should seek the services of a competent attorney or other professional.

COPYRIGHT © 1985, 1991 WEST PUBLISHING CO.
© 2004 West, a Thomson business
   610 Opperman Drive
   P.O. Box 64526
   St. Paul, MN 55164–05261
   800–328–9352

ISBN 0-314-06771-X

DEDICATIONS

RDF: To Courtney and Collin

MHR: To Elisa and Jessica

ACKNOWLEDGMENTS

We are grateful to our colleagues and students, who have pushed us to new levels of understanding and keep these issues fresh and lively. We are especially grateful to Myra Mormile, Emory Law School class of 2004, for truly outstanding research and editorial assistance.

Summary of Contents

CAPSULE SUMMARY 1
PERSPECTIVE 43

■ PART ONE: FEDERAL COURTS AND POLITICAL BRANCHES OF THE FEDERAL GOVERNMENT

I. PROBLEMS OF JUDICIAL REVIEW 47
    I. Introduction 49
    II. The Institution of Judicial Review 49
    III. Federal Courts Cannot Issue Advisory Opinions 50
    IV. Standing 51
    V. Ripeness 65
    VI. Mootness 67
    VII. Political Question Doctrine 71

II. CONGRESSIONAL POWER TO REGULATE FEDERAL JURISDICTION .. 77
    I. Introduction 79
    II. Distinction Between Congressional Power Over the Jurisdiction of the Supreme Court and of the Lower Federal Courts 79
    III. Congressional Power to Regulate Lower Federal Court Jurisdiction 81
    IV. Congressional Power to Regulate Supreme Court Original Jurisdiction 85
    V. Congressional Power to Regulate Supreme Court Appellate Jurisdiction 87
    VI. Limitations on Congressional Power Deriving From Other Constitutional Provisions 89
    VII. Congressional Power to Vest Article III Courts With Non–Article III Powers 94

III. LEGISLATIVE COURTS 99
    I. Introduction 100
    II. Article III Courts and Legislative Courts 100
    III. Constitutional Limits on Congressional Power to Vest Article I Courts With Authority to Decide Article III Matters 101
    IV. Adjudication by "Adjuncts" to Article III Courts ... 109

■ PART TWO: THE STRUCTURE OF FEDERAL COURT JURISDICTION

IV.	FEDERAL QUESTION JURISDICTION	119
	I. Introduction	120
	II. Constitutional and Policy Bases for Federal Question Jurisdiction	120
	III. The Statutory Grant of Federal Question Jurisdiction	123
V.	DIVERSITY OF CITIZENSHIP AND ALIENAGE JURISDICTION	133
	I. Introduction	135
	II. Constitutional, Statutory, and Policy Bases for Diversity of Citizenship and Alienage Jurisdiction	135
	III. Determining Whether the Case Involves Appropriate Litigants	140
	IV. Determining Whether the Amount in Controversy Requirement is Satisfied	150
	V. Exceptions to Diversity of Citizenship and Alienage Jurisdiction	156
VI.	SUPPLEMENTAL JURISDICTION	159
	I. Introduction	160
	II. Policy Issues	160
	III. Historical Development of Supplemental Jurisdiction	162
	IV. The Supplemental Jurisdiction Statute	168
VII.	REMOVAL JURISDICTION	177
	I. Introduction	178
	II. General Principles of Removal Jurisdiction	178
	III. Grants of Removal Jurisdiction	180
	IV. Procedures for Removal and Remand	186
VIII.	SUPREME COURT JURISDICTION	189
	I. Introduction	191
	II. Constitutional and Statutory Structure	191
	III. Original Jurisdiction of the Supreme Court	194
	IV. Appellate Jurisdiction of the Supreme Court	196

■ PART THREE: FEDERAL COURTS, FEDERALISM AND THE STATES

IX.	STATE COURTS AND FEDERAL POWER	215
	I. Introduction	217
	II. The Role of the State Courts in the Federal System	217
	III. State Court Power to Adjudicate Federal Matters	219

	IV.	State Court Obligation to Adjudicate Federal Claims	222
	V.	State Court Power to Control Federal Officers	227
X.	**STATE SOVEREIGN IMMUNITY AND THE ELEVENTH AMENDMENT**	233
	I.	Introduction	235
	II.	Background and History of the Eleventh Amendment	235
	III.	Interpretation of the Eleventh Amendment	237
	IV.	Avoiding the Bar of the Eleventh Amendment: The *Ex Parte Young* Doctrine	242
	V.	Avoiding the Bar of the Eleventh Amendment: Waiver by the State	246
	VI.	Avoiding the Bar of the Eleventh Amendment: Congressional Abrogation	247
XI.	**ABSTENTION**	253
	I.	Introduction	254
	II.	Sources of the Abstention Doctrines	254
	III.	*Pullman* Abstention	256
	IV.	*Burford* Abstention	259
	V.	*Thibodaux* Abstention	263
	VI.	*Colorado River* Abstention	265
	VII.	Procedural Aspects of Abstention	269
XII.	**THE ANTI–INJUNCTION STATUTE**	273
	I.	Introduction	274
	II.	The Statute and Background	274
	III.	The Scope of the Statutory Exceptions	277
	IV.	Other Statutory Restrictions on Federal Injunctions Against State Activities	281
	V.	Injunctions of Federal Judicial Proceedings	282
XIII.	**"OUR FEDERALISM": THE DOCTRINE OF *YOUNGER V. HARRIS***	285
	I.	Introduction	287
	II.	Background	287
	III.	Historical Development	289
	IV.	The Timing of Federal Intervention	292
	V.	Applicability of *Younger* to Civil Proceedings	296
	VI.	Applicability of *Younger* to Non–Judicial State Action	297
XIV.	**ACTIONS TO VINDICATE FEDERAL CIVIL RIGHTS**	301
	I.	Introduction	303
	II.	Principal Civil Rights Statutes	303
	III.	Litigation Under § 1983	306
	IV.	Immunity From § 1983 Cases	320
	V.	Deprivations Under Color of Federal Law: *Bivens* Claims	325
	VI.	Civil Rights Removal Jurisdiction	330
XV.	**HABEAS CORPUS**	337

	I. Introduction	339
	II. Background, Origins of the Writ, and Overview of Current Statutory Provisions	339
	III. Habeas Corpus for State Prisoners	342
	IV. "Abortive State Proceedings"—The Problem of Independent and Adequate State Grounds	351
	V. Habeas Corpus for Persons in the Custody of the United States	355
XVI.	**FEDERAL COMMON LAW**	357
	I. Introduction	358
	II. Sources of and Justification for Federal Common Law	358
	III. Application of Federal Common Law in Specific Areas	360
XVII.	**CLAIM AND ISSUE PRECLUSION IN THE FEDERAL SYSTEM**	371
	I. Introduction	372
	II. Full Faith and Credit and Related Common Law Doctrines	372

APPENDICES

App.

A	Answers to Review Questions	381
B	Model Examination	395
C	Glossary	403
D	Text Correlation Chart	411
E	Table of Cases	413
F	Index	419

Table of Contents

CAPSULE SUMMARY 1
PERSPECTIVE 43

■ PART ONE: FEDERAL COURTS AND POLITICAL BRANCHES OF THE FEDERAL GOVERNMENT

I. PROBLEMS OF JUDICIAL REVIEW 47
    I. Introduction 49
    II. **The Institution of Judicial Review** 49
        A. Political Insulation of the Federal Judiciary 49
        B. Marbury v. Madison 49
    III. **Federal Courts Cannot Issue Advisory Opinions** 50
        A. The Case or Controversy Requirement 50
        B. Applications 51
    IV. **Standing** 51
        A. Sources and Purposes of the Standing Requirement ... 51
        B. Three Constitutional Requirements for Standing 52
        C. Additional "Prudential" Limitations on Standing 58
        D. Special Problems of Taxpayer Standing 62
        E. Standing in the Supreme Court to Review State Court Decisions . 64
    V. **Ripeness** 65
        A. Sources and Purposes of the Ripeness Requirement ... 65
        B. Requirements and Application 65
    VI. **Mootness** 67
        A. Sources, Purposes, and Operation of the Mootness Doctrine 67
        B. Exceptions to the Operation of Mootness 68
    VII. **Political Question Doctrine** 71
        A. Sources and Purposes of the Political Question Doctrine 71
        B. Modern Explication of the Political Question Doctrine 73
        C. Categories of Cases to Which the Political Question Doctrine Has Been Applied and the Case Dismissed 74
        D. Areas in Which Application of the Political Question Doctrine Has Been Rejected 76

II.	**CONGRESSIONAL POWER TO REGULATE FEDERAL JURISDICTION**	77
	I. Introduction	79
	II. **Distinction Between Congressional Power Over the Jurisdiction of the Supreme Court and of the Lower Federal Courts**	79
	A. Article III Provisions About Establishment of the Supreme Court and Lower Federal Courts	79
	B. The Distinction Between Original and Appellate Jurisdiction of the Supreme Court	80
	C. Relevance of Other Constitutional Provisions	80
	III. **Congressional Power to Regulate Lower Federal Court Jurisdiction**	81
	A. The Traditional Theory of Broad Congressional Power	81
	B. Alternative Constructions of Article III	82
	C. Recent Congressional Regulation of Lower Federal Court Jurisdiction	84
	IV. **Congressional Power to Regulate Supreme Court Original Jurisdiction**	85
	A. Article III Self–Executing Regarding Some Cases	85
	B. Congressional Role Regarding Supreme Court Original Jurisdiction	86
	V. **Congressional Power to Regulate Supreme Court Appellate Jurisdiction**	87
	A. The Exceptions Clause	87
	B. *Ex Parte McCardle* and the Theory of Broad Congressional Power	87
	C. The "Essential Functions" Theory	88
	D. The Limitation–As–To–Fact Theory	89
	VI. **Limitations on Congressional Power Deriving From Other Constitutional Provisions**	89
	A. Equal Protection	89
	B. Due Process	90
	C. Separation of Powers	90
	VII. **Congressional Power to Vest Article III Courts With Non–Article III Powers**	94
	A. Characteristics of an Article III Court	94
	B. The Concept of "Non–Article III Powers"	94
	C. Article III Courts Performing Non–Judicial Functions	94
	D. Article III Courts Entertaining Cases Not Falling Within the Judicial Power of the United States	97
III.	**LEGISLATIVE COURTS**	99
	I. Introduction	100
	II. **Article III Courts and Legislative Courts**	100
	A. Article III Provides Protection for Article III Judges and Defines Judicial Power	100

		B. Article I Permits Congress to Create Legislative Courts	101
	III.	**Constitutional Limits on Congressional Power to Vest Article I Courts With Authority to Decide Article III Matters**	101
		A. Importance of the Issue	101
		B. Early Uncertainty About Whether Article I Courts May Adjudicate Article III Matters	102
		C. Modern Evolution: The "Inherently Judicial" Doctrine and Adjudication of Constitutional Facts	105
	IV.	**Adjudication by "Adjuncts" to Article III Courts**	109
		A. Background: The "Adjunct" Theory	109
		B. Administrative Agencies	109
		C. Bankruptcy Courts	111
		D. Magistrate Judges	112

■ PART TWO: THE STRUCTURE OF FEDERAL COURT JURISDICTION

IV.	**FEDERAL QUESTION JURISDICTION**	119
	I. **Introduction**	120
	II. **Constitutional and Policy Bases for Federal Question Jurisdiction**	120
	A. The Constitutional Grant of Judicial Power	120
	B. "Protective Jurisdiction"	121
	C. Policy Underpinnings for Federal Question Jurisdiction	123
	III. **The Statutory Grant of Federal Question Jurisdiction**	123
	A. Section 1331—The General Federal Question Statute	123
	B. Scope of the Statutory Grant: The Well–Pleaded Complaint Rule	125
	C. Scope of the Statutory Grant	129
V.	**DIVERSITY OF CITIZENSHIP AND ALIENAGE JURISDICTION**	133
	I. **Introduction**	135
	II. **Constitutional, Statutory, and Policy Bases for Diversity of Citizenship and Alienage Jurisdiction**	135
	A. The Constitutional Grants of Judicial Power	135
	B. The Statutory Grants of Diversity of Citizenship and Alienage Jurisdiction	136
	C. Policy Underpinnings for Diversity of Citizenship and Alienage Jurisdiction	138
	III. **Determining Whether the Case Involves Appropriate Litigants**	140
	A. The Complete Diversity Rule	140
	B. Determining Citizenship of Human Beings	143
	C. Determining Citizenship of Corporations	146
	D. Determining Citizenship of Non–Incorporated Associations	148

		E. Determining Citizenship in Cases by or Against Representatives	149
	IV.	**Determining Whether the Amount in Controversy Requirement is Satisfied**	**150**
		A. The Amount in Controversy Requirement and its Rationale	150
		B. Assessing the Amount in Controversy	151
		C. Aggregation of Claims	153
		D. Claims for Equitable Relief	155
	V.	**Exceptions to Diversity of Citizenship and Alienage Jurisdiction**	**156**
		A. Judge–Made Exceptions for Domestic Relations and Probate Cases	156
		B. Statutory Prohibition of Collusive Joinder to Create Jurisdiction	157
VI.	**SUPPLEMENTAL JURISDICTION**		**159**
	I.	**Introduction**	160
	II.	**Policy Issues**	160
	III.	**Historical Development of Supplemental Jurisdiction**	162
		A. Definitional Issues: "Pendent", "Ancillary," and "Supplemental"	162
		B. Until 1990, the Doctrine Was Developed by Case Law, Not Legislation	162
		C. The *Finley* Decision Led to Passage of the Supplemental Jurisdiction Statute in 1990	165
	IV.	**The Supplemental Jurisdiction Statute**	168
		A. Overview of the Statute	168
		B. The Grant of Supplemental Jurisdiction in § 1367(a)	168
		C. Restrictions on Supplemental Jurisdiction in § 1367(b)	170
		D. Discretionary Decline of Supplemental Jurisdiction Under § 1367(c)	172
		E. Tolling Provision of § 1367(d)	173
		F. Some Problems in Applying § 1367	174
VII.	**REMOVAL JURISDICTION**		**177**
	I.	**Introduction**	178
	II.	**General Principles of Removal Jurisdiction**	178
		A. Removal Contrasted With Remand	178
		B. Removal is Available Only to Defendants	178
		C. General Venue Provisions Do Not Apply in Removal Cases	179
		D. Generally, a Case is Removable Only if the Federal Court Would Have Subject Matter Jurisdiction Over it	179
		E. Case is Removable Even if State Court Lacked Subject Matter Jurisdiction	180
	III.	**Grants of Removal Jurisdiction**	180
		A. Removal is Governed by Statute	180
		B. The "General" Provision for Removal of Diversity and Federal Question Cases	181
		C. Special Considerations Regarding Removal of Federal Question	

		Cases	181
	D.	Special Considerations Regarding Removal of Diversity Cases	183
	E.	Specialized Grants of Removal Jurisdiction	185
IV.	**Procedures for Removal and Remand**		186
	A.	Defendant Files Notice of Removal in Federal Court	186
	B.	Timing of Removal	187
	C.	Remand to State Court	187

VIII. SUPREME COURT JURISDICTION ... 189

I.	**Introduction**		191
II.	**Constitutional and Statutory Structure**		191
	A.	Article III Draws Distinction Between Original and Appellate Jurisdiction of the Supreme Court	191
	B.	Relationship Between the Supreme Court's Original and Appellate Jurisdiction	192
III.	**Original Jurisdiction of the Supreme Court**		194
	A.	Cases Between Two or More States	194
	B.	Other Cases in Which a State is a Party	195
	C.	Cases Involving Ambassadors, Public Ministers, etc.	196
IV.	**Appellate Jurisdiction of the Supreme Court**		196
	A.	Statutory Provisions For The Supreme Court's Appellate Jurisdiction	196
	B.	Review Of State Court Decisions: Background	198
	C.	Review Of State Court Decisions: Highest State Court	199
	D.	Review Of State Court Decisions: The Final Judgment Rule	199
	E.	Review Of State Court Decisions: The "Independent And Adequate State Ground" Doctrine	203
	F.	Review of State Court Decisions: Findings of Fact	208
	G.	Review Of Decisions Of The Courts Of Appeals	208

■ PART THREE: FEDERAL COURTS, FEDERALISM AND THE STATES

IX. STATE COURTS AND FEDERAL POWER ... 215

I.	**Introduction**		217
II.	**The Role of the State Courts in the Federal System**		217
	A.	Constitutional Presumptions About State Courts	217
	B.	Statutory Scheme and the Concepts of Concurrent and Exclusive Subject Matter Jurisdiction	218
III.	**State Court Power to Adjudicate Federal Matters**		219
	A.	The Presumption of Concurrent Jurisdiction and the Doctrine of Implied Exclusivity	219

		B.	State Court Adjudication of Issues Falling Within Exclusive Federal Jurisdiction	221
	IV.		**State Court Obligation to Adjudicate Federal Claims**	222
		A.	The Traditional Rule	222
		B.	The "Valid Excuse" Doctrine	223
		C.	State Court Obligation to Employ Federal Procedures in Adjudicating Federal Claims	226
	V.		**State Court Power to Control Federal Officers**	227
		A.	Writs of Habeas Corpus	227
		B.	Mandamus and Injunctions	229
		C.	Relevance of Federal Officer Removal	230
X.			**STATE SOVEREIGN IMMUNITY AND THE ELEVENTH AMENDMENT**	233
	I.		**Introduction**	235
	II.		**Background and History of the Eleventh Amendment**	235
		A.	The Evolving Concept of Sovereign Immunity	235
		B.	The *Chisholm* Decision and Ratification of the Amendment	236
	III.		**Interpretation of the Eleventh Amendment**	237
		A.	Narrow Literal Terms Have Not Limited Application of the Amendment	237
		B.	The Amendment Does Not Bar All Suits Against States	237
		C.	The Amendment Bars Specified Suits in Federal Court Regardless of Jurisdictional Basis	238
		D.	Nature of the Eleventh Amendment Defense	239
		E.	What Constitutes the State?	240
		F.	Summary of Methods for Avoiding the Bar of the Amendment	242
	IV.		**Avoiding the Bar of the Eleventh Amendment: The *Ex Parte Young* Doctrine**	242
		A.	The *Ex Parte Young* Case	242
		B.	Development of Current Doctrine on Specific Issues	243
		C.	Development of Current Doctrine Concerning Remedies	244
	V.		**Avoiding the Bar of the Eleventh Amendment: Waiver by the State**	246
		A.	The Traditional Waiver Rule	246
		B.	Actions by the State Constituting Waiver	246
	VI.		**Avoiding the Bar of the Eleventh Amendment: Congressional Abrogation**	247
		A.	Background on the Concept of Congressional Abrogation	247
		B.	Direct Abrogation by Congress	247
		C.	Determining Whether Congress Intended Direct Abrogation Under § 5 of the Fourteenth Amendment	249
		D.	Indirect Abrogation by Congress (or "Constructive Waiver")	250

XI.	**ABSTENTION**	253
	I. Introduction	254
	II. Sources of the Abstention Doctrines	254
	A. The Concept of Judge–Made Abstention	254
	B. Comparative Aspects of The Different Forms of Abstention	255
	III. *Pullman* Abstention	256
	A. The *Pullman* Case	256
	B. Rationale and Requirements of *Pullman* Abstention	257
	C. Costs of *Pullman* Abstention	259
	IV. *Burford* Abstention	259
	A. The *Burford* Decision	259
	B. Rationale and Requirements of *Burford* Abstention	260
	V. *Thibodaux* Abstention	263
	A. The *Thibodaux* and *Frank Mashuda* Cases	263
	B. Rationale and Requirements of *Thibodaux* Abstention	264
	VI. *Colorado River* Abstention	265
	A. The *Colorado River* Case and Progeny	265
	B. Rationale and Requirements of *Colorado River* Abstention	268
	VII. Procedural Aspects of Abstention	269
	A. The *England* Doctrine—Procedure in *Pullman* Abstention	269
	B. Certification to State Court	270
XII.	**THE ANTI–INJUNCTION STATUTE**	273
	I. Introduction	274
	II. The Statute and Background	274
	A. The Statutory Provision	274
	B. History and Background	274
	III. The Scope of the Statutory Exceptions	277
	A. The "Expressly Authorized" Exception	277
	B. The "In Aid of Jurisdiction" Exception	278
	C. The "Relitigation" Exception	280
	IV. Other Statutory Restrictions on Federal Injunctions Against State Activities	281
	A. The Tax Injunction Act of 1937	281
	B. The Johnson Act of 1934	282
	V. Injunctions of Federal Judicial Proceedings	282
	A. Injunction by a Federal Court	282
	B. Injunction by a State Court	283
XIII.	**"OUR FEDERALISM": THE DOCTRINE OF *YOUNGER V. HARRIS***	285
	I. Introduction	287
	II. Background	287
	A. The Concept and Contours of "Our Federalism"	287
	B. Relationship to the Anti–Injunction Statute	288

III.	**Historical Development**	289
	A. Early Cases	289
	B. The *Dombrowski* Case	289
	C. *Younger v. Harris* and the Modern Concept of "Our Federalism"	290
	D. Exceptions to the Operation of *Younger*	291
IV.	**The Timing of Federal Intervention**	292
	A. The Distinction Between Future and Ongoing Prosecutions	292
	B. Post–Trial Intervention	295
V.	**Applicability of *Younger* to Civil Proceedings**	296
	A. Background	296
	B. Developments After *Younger*	296
VI.	**Applicability of *Younger* to Non–Judicial State Action**	297
	A. State Executive Actions	297
	B. State Administrative Actions	298
	C. State Legislative Actions	299

XIV. ACTIONS TO VINDICATE FEDERAL CIVIL RIGHTS — 301

I.	**Introduction**	303
II.	**Principal Civil Rights Statutes**	303
	A. Section 1983	303
	B. Contrast With Habeas Corpus	304
	C. Other Reconstruction–Era Civil Rights Statutes	305
	D. Modern Civil Rights Statutes	306
III.	**Litigation Under § 1983**	306
	A. Section 1983 Was Little–Used Until 1961	306
	B. *Monroe v. Pape* Invigorated the Statute	307
	C. Plaintiff Must be a Citizen or Person Within U.S. Jurisdiction	308
	D. Defendant Must be a "Person"	308
	E. Defendant Must Have Acted "Under Color" of "State Law"	310
	F. Defendant Must Have Deprived Plaintiff of a Federal Right	312
	G. Remedies, Including Attorney's Fees	316
	H. Miscellaneous Litigation Issues	317
IV.	**Immunity From § 1983 Cases**	320
	A. Background and Definitions	320
	B. Absolute Immunity	321
	C. Qualified ("Good Faith") Immunity	323
V.	**Deprivations Under Color of Federal Law: *Bivens* Claims**	325
	A. Section 1983 Does Not Apply to Federal Actors	325
	B. *Bivens* Recognizes a Right to Sue a Federal Actor for Damages for Deprivation of a Constitutional Right	325
	C. Limitations on the Scope of the *Bivens* Claim	327
	D. Procedural Issues in Cases Asserting a *Bivens* Claim	329
VI.	**Civil Rights Removal Jurisdiction**	330
	A. Background and the Provision for Civil Rights Removal	330

		B.	"Equal Rights" Interpreted Narrowly	332
		C.	The Distinction Between State Statutes and State Practices	333
		D.	The "Modern" Era	334

XV. HABEAS CORPUS 337

I. Introduction 339

II. Background, Origins of the Writ, and Overview of Current Statutory Provisions 339
   A. The Concept of Habeas Corpus 339
   B. History of the Writ 340
   C. Overview of Current Statutory Provisions, as Amended by the Antiterrorism and Effective Death Penalty Act of 1996 (AEDPA) .. 340

III. Habeas Corpus for State Prisoners 342
   A. Basic Statutory Provisions 342
   B. Statutory Requirement of Exhaustion of State Remedies 342
   C. Waiver by the State of the Exhaustion Requirement 344
   D. Review of State Court Findings 344
   E. Deprivations Cognizable in Federal Habeas Corpus Proceedings . 347
   F. Statute of Limitations and Limitations on Successive Applications for Federal Habeas Relief 349
   G. Appellate Review of Federal Habeas Decisions 350
   H. Special Provisions for Capital Cases 350

IV. "Abortive State Proceedings"—The Problem of Independent and Adequate State Grounds 351
   A. Background: Case Law Through *Wainwright v. Sykes* 351
   B. Subsequent Developments 353

V. Habeas Corpus for Persons in the Custody of the United States .. 355
   A. Statutory Provisions 355
   B. Some Specific Issues Concerning Habeas Corpus by Persons in Federal Custody 356

XVI. FEDERAL COMMON LAW 357

I. Introduction 358

II. Sources of and Justification for Federal Common Law 358
   A. Federal Common Law and the *Erie* Doctrine 358
   B. Federal Common Law and the Rules of Decision Act 359
   C. The Reach of Federal Common Law 360

III. Application of Federal Common Law in Specific Areas 360
   A. Use of Federal Common Law to Fill Statutory "Gaps" 360
   B. Federal "Proprietary" Interests 362
   C. International Relations 366
   D. Admiralty 367
   E. Interstate Disputes 369
   F. Interstate Pollution 369

	G. Enforcement of Constitutional Rights	370
	H. Claim and Issue Preclusion Effects of Federal Judgments	370

XVII. CLAIM AND ISSUE PRECLUSION IN THE FEDERAL SYSTEM **371**
    I. Introduction 372
    II. Full Faith and Credit and Related Common Law Doctrines 372
        A. Constitutional Provision 372
        B. Statutory Provision—The Full Faith and Credit Act 373
        C. Situations Covered by Neither Full Faith and Credit Provision ... 375

APPENDICES

App.

A	Answers to Review Questions	381
B	Model Examination	395
C	Glossary	403
D	Text Correlation Chart	411
E	Table of Cases	413
F	Index	419

Capsule Summary

■ CHAPTER 1: PROBLEMS OF JUDICIAL REVIEW

I. THE INSTITUTION OF JUDICIAL REVIEW

Article III, § 1, of the Constitution provides federal judges with lifetime tenure and ensures that their compensation cannot be reduced. It accords this extraordinary protection to ensure that federal judges can make decisions without fear of political reprisal. In *Marbury v. Madison*, 5 U.S. 137 (1803), the Supreme Court established that the federal judiciary has the constitutional power to declare acts of the other branches of government invalid if they violate the Constitution. This process of judicial review allows the judiciary to monitor the proper functioning of the government, but creates tension between it and the "political" branches. Several related doctrines limit the federal judicial power and, therefore, judicial review. They are known generically as doctrines of "justiciability."

II. FEDERAL COURTS CANNOT ISSUE ADVISORY OPINIONS

Article III, § 2, of the Constitution extends the judicial power of the federal courts to "cases" and "controversies" of various types. Thus, the judicial power can be exercised only if a true dispute exists, and cannot be used to render advisory opinions. Despite occasional requests for such advisory opinions from the other branches of government, the Supreme Court steadfastly has adhered to the prohibition against advisory opinions.

III. STANDING

A party may not litigate in federal court unless she has "standing" to bring suit. The "case or controversy" requirement of Article III imposes three requirements as "an irreducible minimum" for standing, which must be satisfied in every case. First, the plaintiff must show that she personally suffered actual or threatened injury as a result of putatively illegal conduct of the defendant. Second, injury to the plaintiff must be fairly traced to the challenged action. Third, the injury must be likely to be redressed if the plaintiff prevails in the litigation. These requirements promote separation of powers principles by confining the federal courts to the performance of the traditional judicial function of resolving disputes.

In addition to the three constitutional requirements for standing, the Supreme Court has imposed three "prudential" limitations on standing. First, the plaintiff must assert her own interest, and not that of a third-party. Second, the plaintiff's interest must fall within the "zone of interests" protected by the relevant law. Third, the plaintiff must not assert a "generalized grievance." These are imposed as a matter of prudent judicial administration, and can be overridden by Congress.

One subset of the standing problem concerns the extent to which taxpayers can sue to challenge the constitutionality of government spending programs. The Supreme Court has held that *federal* taxpayers have standing only if they can demonstrate a "necessary stake as taxpayers" to satisfy Article III. This stake is shown only in suits that challenge statutes passed pursuant to Congress' power under the taxing and spending clause of Article I, § 8, and only if the taxpayer can establish a nexus between that status and the nature of the constitutional infringement alleged.

IV. RIPENESS

The ripeness doctrine provides that the federal courts may not adjudicate when it is speculative whether the plaintiff will actually suffer injury. The dispute must have matured sufficiently to require adjudication. This doctrine reflects the Article III "case or controversy" requirement because until a dispute ripens, there is no case or controversy. It focuses on the fitness of the issues for judicial decision and the hardship to the parties of withholding a court determination.

V. MOOTNESS

Like ripeness, the doctrine of mootness is also concerned with the timing of litigation. It is concerned with whether the case is pending when it is too late for the court to act. For instance, if a challenged statute is repealed, the case becomes moot. The requirement that a case not be moot also reflects the Article III "case or controversy" requirement because if a change in circumstances means that judicial resolution would be meaningless, there would no longer be a justiciable controversy.

There are important exceptions to the mootness doctrine, including one that applies when a claim is "capable of repetition, yet evading review." This exception concerns harms that may pass before litigation can remedy them. Federal courts may hear such claims if there is a reasonable expectation or demonstrated probability that the same controversy will recur and if the harm is of such short duration that it will become moot before litigation can remedy it.

VI. POLITICAL QUESTION DOCTRINE

The political question doctrine is based upon the proposition that some issues of constitutional law are simply beyond the competence of the federal judiciary. It is undeniably based upon principles of separation of powers. By declining to adjudicate political questions, the federal bench avoids potentially dangerous confrontations between it and the other branches of the federal government. The Supreme Court has identified several factors as earmarks of a non-justiciable political question. They seem to embody (1) a constitutional commitment of the matter to another branch of the federal government, (2) a concern that courts should stay out of policy areas in which there are no clear judicial standards, and

(3) prudential concerns of comity for the coordinate branches of the federal government. As one example, the federal bench will not intervene in any aspect of impeachment, for which the Constitution vests sole responsibility in the House of Representatives and the Senate.

■ CHAPTER 2: CONGRESSIONAL POWER TO REGULATE FEDERAL JURISDICTION

I. DISTINCTION BETWEEN CONGRESSIONAL POWER OVER JURISDICTION OF THE SUPREME COURT AND OF THE LOWER FEDERAL COURTS

Article III, § 1, of the Constitution requires the existence of the Supreme Court of the United States and permits Congress to determine whether there will be any lower ("inferior") federal courts. As a matter of common sense, it seems clear that the power to create the lower courts carries with it broad power to regulate the jurisdiction of those courts. It also provides that the Supreme Court shall have original, meaning trial, jurisdiction over two types of cases (cases affecting ambassadors, other public ministers and consuls and cases in which a state is a party). In all other matters, it has appellate jurisdiction "with such Exceptions" that Congress shall make. This "exceptions clause" clearly gives Congress power to tailor the appellate jurisdiction of the Supreme Court.

II. CONGRESSIONAL POWER TO REGULATE LOWER FEDERAL COURT JURISDICTION

The traditional theory is that because Congress has the constitutional authority to create lower federal courts, it also has plenary power to regulate the jurisdiction of those courts. From time-to-time, other theories have been espoused concerning Congress's power to set the jurisdiction of the lower federal courts. Congress has recently limited jurisdiction of the district courts in the Antiterrorism and Effective Death Penalty Act and the Illegal Immigration Reform and Immigrant Responsibility Act.

III. CONGRESSIONAL POWER TO REGULATE SUPREME COURT ORIGINAL JURISDICTION

Because the Constitution requires the existence of the Supreme Court of the United States, Congress does not have authority to abolish that tribunal. As a consequence, it does not have the same plenary power to restrict jurisdiction that it has concerning the lower federal courts. The Constitution provides the Supreme Court with original (trial) jurisdiction over two types of cases: those "affecting Ambassadors, other public Ministers and Consuls" and those "in which a State shall be a party." These provisions are self-executing, so the Supreme Court has trial jurisdiction over such cases without action by Congress. On the other hand, the Constitution does not provide that the Supreme Court's original jurisdiction in such cases is *exclusive*. Thus, Congress has authority to grant concurrent original jurisdiction over such cases to the lower federal courts.

IV. CONGRESSIONAL POWER TO REGULATE SUPREME COURT APPELLATE JURISDICTION

After providing for original jurisdiction over two types of cases, the Constitution provides that the Supreme Court will have appellate jurisdiction in all other cases falling within the judicial power of the federal courts, but with such exceptions as Congress will make. This "exceptions clause" permits Congress to limit the appellate jurisdiction of the Supreme Court. In *Ex Parte McCardle*, 74 U.S. 506 (1968), the Supreme Court upheld a statute removing its appellate jurisdiction which Congress passed because it feared the result the Court might reach in the case. Though *McCardle* seems to imply nearly unfettered congressional authority to restrict the Supreme Court's appellate jurisdiction, some have argued against such expansive legislative power. One theory is that Congress may not make exceptions to appellate jurisdiction that would rob the Supreme Court of its essential role in the constitutional plan.

V. LIMITATIONS ON CONGRESSIONAL POWER DERIVING FROM OTHER CONSTITUTIONAL PROVISIONS

There are theories that Congress's power to regulate federal court jurisdiction is limited by other constitutional provisions. One theory is that the principle of equal protection prevents Congress from limited access to the federal courts for specific fundamental rights. Another is that due process requires that neither liberty nor property may be taken from an individual except in an independent judicial forum. This requirement, however, does not necessarily require a federal court for adjudication of constitutional rights; due process is satisfied by permitting litigation in a state court. Another theory, with more discussion in case law, is that separation-of-powers principles operate as a brake on Congress's authority to restrict federal court jurisdiction. Thus, Congress may not prescribe a rule for deciding a case in a particular way. *United States v. Klein*, 80 U.S. 128 (1871). Nor can Congress pass a statute that effectively converts an earlier Supreme Court holding into an advisory opinion. *Plaut v. Spendthrift Farm, Inc.*, 514 U.S. 211 (1995).

VI. CONGRESSIONAL POWER TO VEST ARTICLE III FEDERAL COURTS WITH NON–ARTICLE III POWERS

Article III courts are those whose judges possess the protections of life tenure and salary provided in Article III, § 1, of the Constitution. The federal district courts, courts of appeals, and the Supreme Court are Article III courts. Article III extends judicial power of the United States only to "cases" or "controversies." Congress has occasionally vested Article III courts with responsibilities beyond the adjudication of cases or controversies. For instance, the United States District Court for the District of Columbia performed administrative functions such as setting utility rates. The Supreme Court considered such tribunals "hybrid" courts; thus, they were Article III courts when they adjudicated cases or controversies and were not Article III courts when they performed non-judicial tasks. Congress ended the hybrid nature of these courts by creating a set of local courts for the District of Columbia, which are not Article III courts. Congress also clarified other situations by abolishing the Court of Claims and the Court of Customs and Patent Appeals and creating the Court of International Claims, the Court of Federal Claims and the Court of Appeals for the Federal Circuit. In sum, it seems clear that Congress can require an Article III court to perform some administrative tasks, though Congress has done so rarely.

But can Congress permit Article III courts to adjudicate cases that do not fall within the judicial power of the United States? The answer seems clearly to be no. Article III courts can adjudicate only those cases and controversies falling within the judicial power listed in Article III, § 2, clause 1, of the Constitution.

CHAPTER 3: LEGISLATIVE COURTS

I. ARTICLE III COURTS AND LEGISLATIVE COURTS

This Chapter discusses the converse of one of the issues discussed in Chapter 2. Here we address whether courts created by Congress under Article I of the Constitution can perform judicial tasks falling within Article III. Article I permits Congress to create "legislative courts" inferior to the Supreme Court. Because such courts are not created under Article III, none of the Article III protections for judicial tenure and salary applies. Also, none of the justiciability requirements of Article III applies. Examples of legislative courts include the territorial courts, military courts, the tax court, and the local courts for the District of Columbia.

II. CONSTITUTIONAL LIMITS ON CONGRESSIONAL POWER TO VEST ARTICLE I COURTS WITH AUTHORITY TO DECIDE ARTICLE III MATTERS

No one doubts that Congress can create legislative courts. There is serious debate, however, over whether those courts can be vested with authority to determine matters falling within the judicial power of the federal courts defined in Article III. If Congress can so vest the legislative courts, it can eviscerate a central goal of Article III—to ensure that such cases or controversies are heard by judges who are protected from political retaliation from the political branches of government. Early precedent suggested that there was no limit to Congress's authority to vest in Article I courts authority to decide Article III matters.

In recent years, however, the Supreme Court has indicated that there are two areas in which Congress may not place adjudicative power in Article I courts. First, private rights cases—involving disputes between private litigants—are "inherently judicial" and in the federal system must be determined by Article III judges. Public rights cases, in contrast—which are between the government and persons subject to its authority regarding the performance of the constitutional functions of the executive or legislative branches—need not be determined by Article III judges. Second, "constitutional facts"—which underlie a claim that a governmental act is unconstitutional—must be determined by Article III judges. *Crowell v. Benson*, 285 U.S. 22 (1932).

III. ADJUDICATION BY "ADJUNCTS" TO ARTICLE III COURTS

Legislative courts are created by Congress under Article I of the Constitution. They operate independently of the Article III courts. In contrast to such tribunals are various "adjuncts," often created by Congress, to assist Article III courts. These are also non-Article III officers or bodies. They can adjudicate even matters considered "inherently judicial," so long as their decisions are subject to substantial review by an Article III court.

Administrative agencies are created both by the executive and the legislative branches of the federal government. Typically, they have rulemaking and adjudicatory authority. Administrative finding of "constitutional facts" must be subject to Article III judicial review under *Crowell v. Benson*. In general, Congress has permitted a party to an administrative adjudication to petition for review in the Court of Appeals, which is, of course, an Article III court.

Bankruptcy judges are Article I officers, and serve as adjuncts to the district court in which they sit. Their jurisdiction is limited to core bankruptcy issues. The district court (an Article III court) retains jurisdiction over plenary matters.

Similarly, magistrate judges are not Article III judges. They are appointed by the district judges in the district and serve a term of years. The authority of magistrate judges is strictly defined by statute, which provides for appropriate review by the district judge. Magistrate judges can decide nondispositive matters subject to review by the district judge for "clear error." They can decide dispositive matters subject to de novo review. They can try cases only with the consent of the parties, who thereby waive their right to an Article III judge.

■ CHAPTER 4: FEDERAL QUESTION JURISDICTION

I. CONSTITUTIONAL AND POLICY BASES FOR FEDERAL QUESTION JURISDICTION

Article III, § 2, clause 1, of the Constitution extends the judicial power of the federal courts, *inter alia*, to cases "arising under this Constitution, the Laws of the United States, and treaties made, or which shall be made, under their authority." This branch of federal subject matter jurisdiction is known as "federal question" jurisdiction. The constitutional provision has been interpreted very broadly. So long as any issue of federal law "*might* form an ingredient" in a case, the constitutional basis for federal question jurisdiction is met. Thus any case in which a federal issue might arise—even if it does not in fact arise—is a "federal question" case under Article III. This broad interpretation opens the door to having federal courts determine cases involving state law, even in the absence of diversity of citizenship jurisdiction, as long as a federal issue could come up in the case. It has also opened the door to academic theories for expanding vastly the federal court's power to determine cases based upon state law.

"Protective jurisdiction" is the term used to describe two distinct theories to justify, under the federal question provision of Article III, the vesting of authority in the federal courts to hear cases involving solely issues of state law. Since Congress has never attempted to vest such authority in the federal courts, the legal validity of these theories has never been determined. One version of protective jurisdiction, associated with Professor Herbert Wechsler, suggests that if Congress possesses constitutional authority to legislate substantively in an area, it can take the lesser step of choosing not to enact substantive law but simply vesting jurisdiction in the federal courts to apply relevant state law. The other version of protective jurisdiction, developed by Professor Paul Mishkin, suggests that when Congress has a preexisting active and articulated policy in a substantive area, it may protect its program from being undermined by state court adjudication by allowing the federal courts to adjudicate even pure state law issues in areas related to the federal program.

The policy bases for the grant of federal question jurisdiction are clear and universally accepted. Federal judges can be expected to develop expertise in interpreting federal law, and might be sympathetic to policies underlying federal law. In addition, there seems to be no dispute, even in an era of overloaded dockets, that federal question jurisdiction is salutary. The adjudication and protection of federal rights is, arguably, the primary function of the federal courts.

II. THE STATUTORY GRANT OF FEDERAL QUESTION JURISDICTION

The federal question provision of Article III is not self-executing; federal courts only have the authority to determine federal question cases if Congress grants it in a jurisdictional statute. Congress has long done so. The present statute, § 1331, mirrors the constitutional grant of federal question jurisdiction by granting jurisdiction over cases "arising under" federal law. The Supreme Court has interpreted the statutory grant of federal question jurisdiction far more narrowly than the constitutional grant, despite the use of identical operative language. Though it creates some uncertainty at times, the narrow interpretation of the statutory grant of federal question jurisdiction serves the important function of docket control. The federal courts would be inundated if all cases satisfying the constitutional grant of federal question jurisdiction actually could be filed in federal court.

The Supreme Court has limited the reach of statutory federal question jurisdiction in two ways. First, the "well-pleaded complaint" rule provides that courts may look only to the plaintiff's claim itself in determining whether a case arises under federal law. That claim must be unadorned by anticipated federal defenses. Only if the plaintiff is asserting some right under federal law is § 1331 satisfied.

The second statutory limitation is more difficult to label, but concerns whether the federal law is a sufficiently important ingredient to the case. The Supreme Court has adopted different tests for this aspect of federal question jurisdiction. The decisions have not always been consistent, and the present state of the law is not clear in all particulars. As a general rule, if federal law creates the claim being asserted, the case will invoke federal question jurisdiction. A much more difficult situation is created when state law creates the claim being asserted, but incorporates federal law as its standard. In its most recent effort in this area, the Court ruled, in a five-to-four decision, that the incorporation of the federal standard in the state-law private action did not render the action one arising under federal law for purposes of § 1331.

CHAPTER 5: DIVERSITY OF CITIZENSHIP AND ALIENAGE JURISDICTION

I. CONSTITUTIONAL, STATUTORY, AND POLICY BASES FOR DIVERSITY OF CITIZENSHIP AND ALIENAGE JURISDICTION

Article III, § 2, clause 1 of the Constitution extends the judicial power of federal courts, *inter alia*, to cases between citizens of different states, which is known as "diversity of citizenship jurisdiction," and to cases between citizens of a state and foreign citizens of subjects, which is known as "alienage jurisdiction." These constitutional provisions are not self-executing, but require legislation to empower the federal courts to hear such cases. Congress has enacted diversity of citizenship jurisdiction in § 1332(a)(1) and alienage jurisdiction under § 1332(a)(2). As to each, however, the statutory grant of jurisdiction imposes a requirement that such cases involve an amount in controversy in excess of $75,000.

Historically, diversity of citizenship jurisdiction has been justified by a desire to provide a federal forum for cases involving citizens of different states, on the theory that state courts might be biased against out-of-state litigants. Federal judges are politically insulated, because they serve life terms and their pay cannot be reduced. State judges, in contrast, are often elected and are thus seen as susceptible to local political pressure. The continued need for diversity of citizenship jurisdiction is hotly debated.

Alienage jurisdiction, in contrast, is not controversial. It provides a federal forum for cases in which an alien is sued by or sues a citizen of a state of the United States. In part, the federal forum is intended to permit the alien to avoid any local bias of state courts. In part, it is intended to assure other countries that their citizens or subjects have ready access to the national courts.

II. DETERMINING WHETHER THE CASE INVOLVES APPROPRIATE LITIGANTS

Diversity of citizenship cases under § 1332(a)(1) must satisfy the "complete diversity rule," which requires that each plaintiff be of diverse citizenship from each defendant. An alienage case under § 1332(a)(2) must be between a citizen of a state of the United States, on the one hand, and a foreign citizen, on the other. In applying the rule, it is obviously important to be able to determine the citizenships of various types of litigants.

A human who is a citizen of the United States is deemed to be a citizen of the state in the United States in which she is domiciled. A person may have only one domicile at a time. Domicile is established by a requirement of physical presence in the state combined with the subjective intent to make that state one's permanent or fixed home. A United States citizen domiciled in a foreign country is not a citizen of a state, because she is not domiciled in one of the states of the United States. Neither is she an alien, because she is not a citizen of the foreign country; she is still a citizen of the United States. Such a person can neither sue nor be sued under diversity of citizenship or alienage jurisdiction.

The citizenship of a corporation is defined by § 1332(c)(1), and consists of all states in which the corporation is incorporated (usually there is only one such state) and the one state in which the corporation has its principal place of business. A corporation can only have one principal place of business. Courts tend to look at the totality of a corporation's activities to determine its principal place of business. Generally, they consider the state in which the corporation has its "nerve center"—where decisions are made—unless all of the corporate activity is in one state, in which case they tend to consider that state (the place of activities) as the principal place of business.

The citizenship of a non-incorporated association, such as a partnership, is not defined by statute. Rather, courts look to the citizenship of all the members of the association. For example, a partnership is deemed to be a citizen of all states of which its partners are citizens. In litigation by a fiduciary on behalf of decedents, minors, or incompetents, § 1332(c)(2) requires that the court look to the citizenship of the person being represented; thus, the citizenship of the fiduciary is ignored in assessing diversity of citizenship jurisdiction. On the other hand, § 1332(c)(2) does not apply to class action litigation; in those cases, the citizenship of the class is determined by looking only to the citizenship of the class representative(s).

III. DETERMINING WHETHER THE CASE SATISFIES THE AMOUNT IN CONTROVERSY REQUIREMENT

In addition to satisfying the complete diversity rule, § 1332 requires that a diversity of citizenship case (and an alienage case) involves an amount in controversy *exceeding* $75,000, not counting interest on the claim or recoverable costs of the litigation. The amount in controversy requirement serves a docket-control function of reducing the number of such cases in federal court and also ensures that federal courts not become small-claims tribunals. Whatever amount the plaintiff claims will control unless it is clear to a legal certainty that she cannot recover more than $75,000, which is difficult to show unless there is some legal limit on the amount recoverable in a particular case.

In determining the amount in controversy, courts will aggregate (add together) all claims asserted by a single plaintiff against a single defendant, even if the claims are unrelated legally or factually. Such aggregation is not permitted, however, if there are multiple plaintiffs or defendants. On the other hand, claims involving joint liability or joint rights are assessed by viewing the total value of the claim, regardless of how many parties there are.

Claims for equitable relief present special problems in determining the amount in controversy. Most courts consider such claims from the plaintiff's viewpoint, and deem the requirement satisfied if the defendant's behavior (to be modified by the equitable relief) harms the plaintiff by more than $75,000. Other courts consider the matter from the defendant's viewpoint, and deem the requirement met if it would cost the defendant more than $75,000 to comply with the equitable decree sought.

IV. EXCEPTIONS TO DIVERSITY OF CITIZENSHIP AND ALIENAGE JURISDICTION

Even if the requirements for a diversity of citizenship or alienage case are satisfied, federal courts have long refused to entertain cases involving the issuance of divorce, alimony, or child custody decrees, or to probate a decedent's estate. These exceptions to federal jurisdiction are based upon the fact that such cases historically were heard by ecclesiastical courts, and not common law courts. Thus, they are not within the grant of jurisdiction over "civil actions" in § 1332(a).

Section 1359 provides that parties may not be collusively joined or made to create subject matter jurisdiction. It is invoked most frequently in cases involving assignments of claims. If the plaintiff is an assignee of a claim and is merely a collection agent for the assignor, without any real interest in the case, § 1359 counsels courts to ignore the assignment for purposes of subject matter jurisdiction, and thus to consider only the citizenship of the assignor. The result is to preclude a would-be plaintiff from "manufacturing" diversity of citizenship jurisdiction by assigning her claim to someone who is of diverse citizenship from the defendant.

■ CHAPTER 6: SUPPLEMENTAL JURISDICTION

I. POLICY ISSUES

Supplemental jurisdiction permits federal courts to hear claims that do not invoke diversity of citizenship, alienage, federal question, or any other form of independent federal subject matter jurisdiction. They are permitted to do so only if the claim is so closely related to a dispute that did invoke federal subject matter jurisdiction as to be considered part of the same overall controversy with the jurisdiction-invoking claim. Supplemental jurisdiction is a discretionary doctrine, and the court has authority to refuse to exercise such jurisdiction under certain circumstances.

II. HISTORICAL DEVELOPMENT OF SUPPLEMENTAL JURISDICTION

What we now call supplemental jurisdiction is governed by statute—§ 1367. Before that statute was passed in 1990, supplemental jurisdiction was basically the creation of courts, not of Congress, and was referred to as "pendent" and "ancillary" jurisdiction. Federal courts long recognized that they could entertain claims that were closely related to a claim that invoked federal subject matter jurisdiction, even when that claim, by itself, did not invoke any independent basis of federal subject matter jurisdiction. The leading statement of the constitutional authority to exercise this form of jurisdiction was set forth in *United Mine Workers v. Gibbs*, 383 U.S. 715 (1966). That case, which is codified in § 1367(a), held that a federal court had power to hear claims that shared a "common nucleus of operative fact" with a jurisdiction-invoking claim.

Congress enacted § 1367 in 1990 in reaction to the unfortunate result and some loose language in the majority opinion in *Finley v. United States*, 490 U.S. 545 (1989). In addition to overruling the result in *Finley*, the statute adopted the generic terminology of "supplemental jurisdiction" in lieu of "pendent" and "ancillary" and purported to codify the entire area of supplemental jurisdiction as it existed before *Finley* was decided.

III. THE SUPPLEMENTAL JURISDICTION STATUTE

Section 1367 overruled the result in *Finley*, but has been plagued in some ways by poor drafting and unanticipated consequences. Section 1367(a) grants supplemental jurisdiction to the full extent of the Constitution, which clearly embodies the "common nucleus of operative fact" standard from *Gibbs*. The last sentence of that subsection makes clear that the grant applies even as to claims involving separate parties from that against whom the initial, jurisdiction-invoking, claim is asserted.

Section 1367(b) carves out exceptions from the grant of supplemental jurisdiction, but only in cases which invoked § 1332. In other words, the exceptions in § 1367(b) apply only in diversity of citizenship cases. These exceptions are intended to preserve the complete diversity rule and the limits of supplemental jurisdiction as they were recognized before *Finley*. Specifically, § 1367(b) removes supplemental jurisdiction over claims, in diversity of citizenship cases, asserted (1) by plaintiffs joined under Federal Rule 19, (2) by plaintiffs who seek to intervene under Federal Rule 24, and (3) by plaintiffs against parties joined under Federal Rules 14, 19, 20, and 24.

Section 1367(c) lists discretionary factors under which a court whose supplemental jurisdiction is invoked may nonetheless refuse to exercise such jurisdiction. The *Gibbs* opinion discussed the discretionary nature of supplemental jurisdiction and suggested factors counseling against the exercise of supplemental jurisdiction. Section 1367(c) codifies some of the factors discussed in *Gibbs*. For instance, if the federal question claim that forms the basis for invoking federal subject matter jurisdiction is dismissed early in proceedings, a court ordinarily will refuse to exercise supplemental jurisdiction over transactionally-related state law claims.

Section 1367(d) is a helpful provision that tolls the statute of limitations for any claim invoking supplemental jurisdiction under § 1367(a) "and for any other claim in the same action that is voluntarily dismissed at the same time as or after the dismissal" of a claim invoking supplemental jurisdiction. It tolls the statute of limitations for 30 days after the claim is dismissed. The subsection also provides that state law might permit a longer tolling of the limitations period. The Supreme Court upheld the provision in the face of a constitutional challenge in *Jinks v. Richland County, S.C.*, 123 S.Ct. 1667 (2003).

There are several serious interpretational problems with § 1367. One is whether the statute overturns the longstanding principle that each member of a diversity of citizenship class action must claim more than $75,000. To date, five courts of appeals have concluded that it does, and permit a class action to invoke diversity of citizenship (assuming the citizenship requirement is met) if the class representative's claim exceeds $75,000, regardless of the value of class members' claims. Three other courts of appeals have concluded that the longstanding rule remains in place, largely because of a single sentence in the legislative history of § 1367.

■ CHAPTER 7: REMOVAL JURISDICTION

I. GENERAL PRINCIPLES OF REMOVAL JURISDICTION

Removal permits a defendant in a case filed in state court to have the case transferred to a federal court. It operates only in that direction: from state to federal court. If a case is improperly removed, either procedurally or because the federal court lacks subject matter jurisdiction, the federal court will "remand" the case to state court. Thus, the combination of original jurisdiction statutes and removal statutes provide both the plaintiff and the defendant with a right to have an appropriate case decided in a federal court. Courts have concluded that all defendants served in the case in state court must join in the notice of removal. And, obviously, a defendant may remove the case only if the case would invoke some basis of federal subject matter jurisdiction, such as diversity of citizenship or federal question jurisdiction.

II. GRANTS OF REMOVAL JURISDICTION

There is no constitutional provision concerning removal; it is purely the product of statute. Most removal of civil cases is authorized by 28 U.S.C. § 1441(a), which permits the defendant to remove a civil action of which the federal district court would have original jurisdiction. The requirements for invoking diversity of citizenship and federal question jurisdiction as an original matter, such as, for example, the complete diversity rule in diversity of citizenship cases, apply in removed cases as well. Thus, because federal question jurisdiction is invoked only by plaintiff's claim that arises under federal law, removal of a federal question case cannot be based upon the presence of a federal defense or even of a counterclaim arising under federal law.

Congress can obviate removal even of cases that would otherwise arise under federal law and invoke federal question jurisdiction under 28 U.S.C. § 1331. It has done so in several particulars in 28 U.S.C. § 1445. For example, a case brought under the Federal Employers' Liability Act (FELA), which authorizes railroad employee negligence suits against employers, cannot be removed.

Under 28 U.S.C. § 1441(b), the defendant can remove a case based upon diversity of citizenship jurisdiction "only if none of the parties in interest properly joined and served as defendants is a citizen of the State in which such action is brought." Because of this restriction, cases in which the plaintiff could invoke diversity of citizenship jurisdiction if she sued in federal court cannot be removed to federal court. This restriction is consistent with the underlying purpose of diversity of citizenship jurisdiction: to protect out-of-state litigants from potential bias in state courts.

III. PROCEDURES FOR REMOVAL AND REMAND

Pursuant to 28 U.S.C. § 1446(a), the defendant files in the federal court a "notice of removal," which is signed under Federal Rule 11. The notice contains "a short and plain statement of the grounds for removal, together with a copy of all process, pleadings, and orders served upon [the defendant] in such action." Promptly after filing the notice of removal in federal court, the defendant must give written notice to all adverse parties. She must file a copy of the notice with the clerk of the state court. Such filing of the copy of notice "shall effect removal and the State court shall proceed no further unless and until the case is remanded." 28 U.S.C. § 1446(d). In a civil case, the defendant must file the notice of removal in federal court within 30 days after her receipt, "through service or otherwise," of a copy of the initial pleading or within 30 days "after the service of summons upon the defendant if such initial pleading has then been filed in court and is not required to be served on the defendant, whichever period is shorter."

If the plaintiff feels that the case was improperly removed, she can move to remand it to state court. She might do so either because the federal court lacks subject matter jurisdiction or because of a procedural defect in the defendant's removal. If the motion to remand is based upon "any defect other than lack of subject matter jurisdiction," the plaintiff must move to remand the case no later than 30 days after the defendant filed her notice of removal. 28 U.S.C. § 1447(c). In other words, defects in removal other than lack of subject matter jurisdiction are waivable. Obviously, however, lack of federal subject matter jurisdiction is not waivable, and the plaintiff or the court on its own motion may raised the issue at any time. If there is no federal subject matter jurisdiction, the federal court must remand the case to the state court from which it was removed. 28 U.S.C. § 1447(c).

CHAPTER 8: SUPREME COURT JURISDICTION

I. CONSTITUTIONAL AND STATUTORY STRUCTURE

Article III, § 2, of the Constitution provides that the Supreme Court shall have "original jurisdiction" over two kinds of cases: (1) those affecting Ambassadors, other public Ministers and Consuls" and (2) those in which "a State shall be a party." Original jurisdiction is trial jurisdiction, so the Constitution provided that the Supreme Court could try such cases. In all other cases falling with the judicial power of the United States, in Article III, § 2, paragraph 1, the Supreme Court "shall have appellate Jurisdiction. . . . " The Supreme Court's appellate jurisdiction may be over cases from the lower federal courts or from each state's highest state court.

II. ORIGINAL JURISDICTION OF THE SUPREME COURT

The Supreme Court has original jurisdiction over cases in which a state is a party. Congress has subdivided such cases and has provided that the Supreme Court's original jurisdiction is exclusive when the case is "between two or more states." 28 U.S.C. § 1251(a). Thus, when the dispute is between states (which usually, but not always, involve things like boundary disputes and water rights), only the Supreme Court can try the matter. Notwithstanding this fact, the Court on occasion has refused to hear such cases. In other cases in which a state is a party, Congress has provided that the Supreme Court's original jurisdiction is not exclusive. 28 U.S.C. § 1251(b). Thus, such disputes can be tried in a federal district court, assuming, of course, that they invoke federal subject matter jurisdiction.

The Supreme Court also has original jurisdiction over cases involving ambassadors and other public ministers or consuls. It has exercised this jurisdiction very rarely. One reason for this is that foreign ambassadors and public ministers (but not consuls) have diplomatic immunity from suit in the United States. Another is that the Court's original jurisdiction in such matters is not exclusive. Thus they can be heard in a federal district court.

III. APPELLATE JURISDICTION OF THE SUPREME COURT

The Supreme Court has jurisdiction by writ of certiorari to review final decisions of a state's highest court in cases in which the validity of a federal law is challenged on constitutional grounds, or in which a state statute is challenged as repugnant to federal law, or in which any title, right, privilege or immunity is claimed under federal law. 28 U.S.C. § 1257. In addition, the Court may use the writ of certiorari to review any decision of a federal court of appeals. 28 U.S.C. § 1254(1). Review by certiorari is discretionary.

Under § 1257, the Supreme Court can review only a decision by the highest court of the state in which review could be had. If review by that state court is discretionary, the case cannot be taken to the Supreme Court until a litigant has sought that discretionary review in the highest state court. In addition, under the same statute, the Supreme Court can review only "final" judgments of the state court. The Court has recognized limited exceptions to this requirement and has great discretion in determining whether a judgment in which review is sought was "final."

Further, the Court has long held that it lacks authority to review state-court decisions interpreting state law. It is not clear whether this rule is required by the Constitution, but it is clear in practice. The Court has established a corollary to this principle, pursuant to which it will not hear cases in which the decision is premised on "adequate and independent" state law grounds. Thus, if the state decision rests upon both federal and non-federal substantive grounds, the Court will not review if the non-federal ground, standing alone, would support the judgment. This rule ensures that the Supreme Court does not issue what is in essence an advisory opinion on federal law. In addition, if the state court refused to adjudicate a federal issue because the litigant failed to comply with a legitimate state procedural rule, the Court will not review the federal claim. This rule is based upon the Court's desire to avoid undermining legitimate state-court procedures. The Court has recognized several circumstances in which a state procedural bar will not preclude its appellate review. In *Henry v. Mississippi*, 379 U.S. 443 (1965), the Court seemed especially willing to ignore a state procedural rule and undertake appellate review, leading some to believe that it had diluted the procedural bar to review of state decisions markedly. More recent cases, however, indicate that this is not the case.

■ CHAPTER 9: STATE COURTS AND FEDERAL POWER

I. THE ROLE OF THE STATE COURTS IN THE FEDERAL SYSTEM

The Founders clearly envisioned that state courts would play a major role in adjudicating and enforcing federal law. The fact that the Constitution did not mandate the creation of lower federal courts indicates that they assumed state courts would be involved in such cases. Moreover, though Congress has always provided for lower federal courts, it did not vest them with general federal question jurisdiction until 1875. The Supremacy Clause ensures that the state courts are bound to enforce federal law.

II. STATE COURT POWER TO ADJUDICATE FEDERAL MATTERS

When Congress creates a right and provides that federal courts have jurisdiction to enforce it, but does not provide that federal jurisdiction is exclusive, courts generally will presume that jurisdiction is concurrent between the federal and state courts. Occasionally, state courts will adjudicate issues that appear to fall within the exclusive jurisdiction of federal courts, as when the exclusive federal issue is injected into the case by way of defense in a state-court proceeding.

III. STATE COURT OBLIGATION TO ADJUDICATE FEDERAL CLAIMS

When Congress creates a claim and does not provide for exclusive federal jurisdiction, state courts are under an *obligation* to enforce that claim, unless the state has a "valid excuse" not to do so. The "valid excuse" doctrine is not well-defined, and there are few examples of its application. One is when the state court has limited subject matter jurisdiction, and simply could not hear the federal claim. Another example is if the state courts would dismiss a state-law claim involving the same situation under the doctrine of *forum non conveniens*. In some circumstances, achieving congressional goals may require state courts to apply federal *procedural* provisions, such as the requirement of a jury trial in Federal Employers' Liability Act cases.

IV. STATE COURT POWER TO CONTROL FEDERAL OFFICERS

State courts have no power to issue writs of habeas corpus against federal officers. *In re Tarble*, 80 U.S. 397 (1871)(state court without power to order United

States Army officer to release enlisted man). Similarly, state courts cannot issue mandamus to a federal officer. The Supreme Court has not determined whether a state court may validly issue an injunction against a federal officer. By statute, a federal officer sued in her personal or official capacity for an act under color of office may remove the case to federal court.

■ CHAPTER 10: STATE SOVEREIGN IMMUNITY AND THE ELEVENTH AMENDMENT

I. BACKGROUND AND HISTORY OF THE ELEVENTH AMENDMENT

Article III, § 2, of the Constitution, which lists the classes of cases falling within the federal judicial power, includes cases "between a State and Citizens of another State." Though some framers felt that this clause did not envision cases in which a state would be defendant, the Supreme Court upheld federal jurisdiction in such a case in *Chisholm v. Georgia*, 2 U.S. 419 (1793). The decision led to public uproar and to the ratification of the Eleventh Amendment, which removes federal judicial power over cases "commenced or prosecuted against one of the United States by Citizens of another State, or by Citizens of Subjects of any Foreign State." The Supreme Court has interpreted it to bar cases by a citizen against the state of which she is a citizen as well. *Hans v. Louisiana*, 134 U.S. 1 (1890). For generations, the Supreme Court treated the Eleventh Amendment as ensuring that a state could not be held liable in federal court. More recently, however, the court has emphasized a broader notion of sovereign immunity—not immunity against liability, but immunity from being subjected to suit in the federal courts at all.

II. INTERPRETATION OF THE ELEVENTH AMENDMENT

Though the language of the Eleventh Amendment is narrow, the Supreme Court has interpreted it broadly. On its face, it bars suits against a state by citizens of another state or of a foreign country. As noted above, however, it is interpreted to bar suits by a citizen against the state of which she is a citizen. It also bars suits by Indian tribes, municipalities, and other states against a state. In addition, it bars suits against Puerto Rico and other territories, though they are not states. On the other hand, it does not bar suits by the United States against a state. And, of course, it does not apply to suits brought against a state in state court.

Though it was long debated whether the Eleventh Amendment barred suits in federal court brought under certain grants of federal jurisdiction, it is now clear that its bar operates regardless of the jurisdictional basis. Though the defense of the Eleventh Amendment seems to be jurisdictional in nature, the Supreme Court has sent conflicting signals on this point. If the defense were jurisdictional, the court would be required to raise it in appropriate cases sua sponte and the state could not waive it. The Court has permitted states to raise the issue at any time, but has not required appellate courts to raise the issue sua sponte. Moreover, the defense certainly can be waived. So its character as jurisdictional is not clear.

The Court has interpreted "state" broadly. The Eleventh Amendment bars suits in federal court in which a state is the named defendant. Moreover, it bars cases in which a state is the real party in interest, which requires the court to determine the essential nature and effect of the litigation to determine if it is truly against a state. Thus, a claim against a political subdivision or against an officer may be seen as one against the state, and thus barred. As a very rough rule of thumb, a state is the real party in interest if the suit seeks recovery from the state treasury. That test has been refined, however, and the Court seems now to emphasize the avoidance of legal liability for the state, rather than whether the plaintiff seeks to collect from the state treasury.

III. AVOIDING THE BAR OF THE ELEVENTH AMENDMENT: THE DOCTRINE OF *EX PARTE YOUNG*

Much of the important case law concerning the Eleventh Amendment addresses methods in which plaintiffs might avoid its bar. The holding of *Ex Parte Young*, 209 U.S. 123 (1908), provides an important avenue for plaintiffs challenging state action. There, the plaintiff sought an injunction against a state attorney general, prohibiting him from enforcing a state law that the plaintiff alleged was unconstitutional. If the federal court issued the requested injunction, it would have had the effect of stopping the state from enforcing its statute. Thus it seemed to be a case against the state, which would be barred by the Eleventh Amendment. The Court permitted the case to proceed, on a fictive theory: because the state officer acted in an illegal way, he was stripped of the immunity of the Eleventh Amendment; because he did not act for the state, the case was seen as being against a private individual, and not barred. The reasoning is faulty, because the allegedly illegal acts of the state officer are considered *not* to be state action for purposes of the Eleventh Amendment, but *are* considered to be state action for purposes of determining whether there was a constitutional violation.

Ex Parte Young remains vital despite the fictive quality of its reasoning. Generally, it applies if (1) the state officer sued has a duty to enforce the challenged state law, (2) the state action constitutes a violation of federal law, and (3) the federal law is the "supreme law of the land." But the Court has also held that the theory is not available if federal law provides such intricate remedies that it is clear that Congress did not intend for suit under *Ex Parte Young*. In addition, the theory is not available if it would interfere with special state sovereignty interests, such as those implicated by quiet title actions concerning real property.

Ex Parte Young cannot be used to support a claim for damages against the state. Rather, it permits equitable relief—such as injunctions or declaratory judgments—that are *prospective* in nature. That is, the relief must be forward-looking, rather than compensatory for past acts. Such relief is not rendered inappropriate by the fact that it will have an impact on the state treasury. This prospective-versus-retrospective distinction is criticized, but remains vital. Obviously, it requires that the suit concern an ongoing violation of federal law. If the violation has ceased, the only remedy would be compensatory damages, which are barred by the Eleventh Amendment.

IV. AVOIDING THE BAR OF THE ELEVENTH AMENDMENT: WAIVER BY THE STATE

A state may waive its Eleventh Amendment protection. Because it involves constitutional protection, however, waiver is not easily inferred. Waiver may result from express provisions of state law or from express consent to suit in federal court. The fact that a state consents to suit in state courts does not imply, however, that it has waived its protection against suit in federal court. A state may waive its Eleventh Amendment immunity by litigation conduct, such as removing a case from state to federal court, at least in certain instances.

V. AVOIDING THE BAR OF THE ELEVENTH AMENDMENT: CONGRESSIONAL ABROGATION

The preceding section dealt with the state's waiving its protection by taking some act. Here, the focus is whether Congress can abrogate the Eleventh Amendment protection. There has never been serious doubt that Congress may do so by proper legislation rendering states amenable to suit in federal court. The serious question, however, has been what parts of the Constitution permit Congress to do this. It is clear that Congress can override the Eleventh Amendment through legislation passed under § 5 of the Fourteenth Amendment. Though the Supreme Court earlier had found congressional abrogation under other constitutional provisions, it has now apparently limited the legislative power to enforcement of the Fourteenth Amendment. *Seminole Tribe of Florida v. Florida*, 517 U.S. 44 (1996). In other words, Congress cannot abrogate Eleventh Amendment protection by passing legislation under Article I. *Alden v. Maine*, 527 U.S. 706 (1999). It is not always easy, however, to determine whether Congress has acted under § 5 of the Fourteenth Amendment.

In earlier times, the Court recognized that Congress may abrogate Eleventh Amendment protection indirectly, by the doctrine of constructive waiver. The notion was that a state waived its immunity by participating in federal programs after Congress conditioned such participation upon amenability to suit in federal court. More recently, the Court has rejected this notion of indirect abrogation. *Florida Prepaid Postsecondary Education Expense Board v. College Savings Bank*, 527 U.S. 627 (1999).

■ CHAPTER 11: ABSTENTION

I. SOURCES OF THE ABSTENTION DOCTRINES

Abstention is a generic term that refers to judge-made doctrines by which a federal court refuses to exercise its subject matter jurisdiction. Despite a strong argument that federal courts should have no authority to abstain when their subject matter jurisdiction is properly invoked, abstention doctrines are well established, but invoked only in extraordinary circumstances. Mainly, abstention is justified by considerations of federalism, and display great deference to state decision-making bodies and courts in circumstances in which federal court involvement might be disruptive or disrespectful of state efforts. Each abstention doctrine has different requirements, however, and slightly different justifications. Procedures may vary for the different types as well.

II. *PULLMAN* ABSTENTION

The Supreme Court ordered a federal district court to abstain in *Railroad Commission of Texas v. Pullman*, 312 U.S. 496 (1941). In the case, plaintiffs challenged an order entered by a state administrative agency as racially discriminatory. There was a serious question as to whether state law gave the agency the authority to enter the order at all. If it did, there was a serious constitutional issue. If it did not, there was no constitutional issue. In such circumstances—when a constitutional issue could be obviated if an unclear state law were interpreted in a particular way—the Court held that federal courts should defer to state interpretation of the state law. The federal court should stay proceedings while the litigants go to state court to secure a definitive interpretation of the state law issue. If the party seeking abstention properly reserves the federal constitutional issue for the federal court, the litigation will return to federal court for ultimate determination of the case. This complicated procedure is required by *England v. Louisiana State Board of Medical Examiners*, 375 U.S. 411 (1964).

III. *BURFORD* ABSTENTION

Burford Abstention gets its name from *Burford v. Sun Oil Co.*, 319 U.S. 315 (1943). It stands for the proposition that a federal court should abstain when a state has established a complex regulatory scheme for dealing with an issue of local import. Abstention in such situations avoids federal disruption with state efforts to establish a coherent policy with respect to that issue. Thus, in *Burford* itself, the Court held that a federal court should not intervene into the allocation of oil drilling rights, which was subject to significant state regulation and oversight. The mere existence of a state mechanism for dealing with an important local issue is not usually enough to support abstention. The court must determine whether federal resolution of the particular claim asserted will enmesh the federal court into a complex area for which the state has established mechanisms for decision and review. If the federal court abstains under *Burford*, it dismisses the case, rather than stay proceedings (as it would in *Pullman*).

IV. *THIBODAUX* ABSTENTION

The basis and scope of this form of abstention is confused, in part because the Supreme Court was inconsistent in what it said in two cases decided on the same day—*Louisiana Power & Light Co. v. City of Thibodaux*, 360 U.S. 25 (1959) and *County of Allegheny v. Frank Mashuda Co.*, 360 U.S. 185 (1959). Each case involved a challenge to a municipality's exercise of eminent domain. In *Thibodaux*, the Court upheld abstention, and emphasized the "special nature of eminent domain proceedings," which it saw as intimately involved with a "sovereign prerogative." In *Frank Mashuda*, however, the Court did not uphold abstention, and said that eminent domain did not involve any particular "sovereign prerogative." Perhaps the cases can be reconciled by noting that in *Thibodaux*, but not *Frank Mashuda*, the state law was unclear.

V. *COLORADO RIVER* ABSTENTION

Unlike other forms of abstention, this one is not rooted in a concern for federalism. Rather, it is based upon "wise judicial administration" and a desire to avoid overlapping litigation in federal and state courts. It is thus potentially the most far-reaching and controversial type of abstention. In *Colorado River Water Conservation District v. United States*, 424 U.S. 800 (1976), the Supreme Court upheld dismissal of a federal case which concerned allocation of water which was already the subject of litigation in state court. It identified four factors as relevant to whether the federal court should dismiss under this form of abstention: (1)

whether either the federal or state court had assumed jurisdiction over property; (2) inconvenience of the federal forum, (3) the desirability of avoiding piecemeal litigation, and (4) the order in which jurisdiction was obtained by the federal and state court. The Court emphasized that abstention on the grounds of "wise judicial administration" was extraordinary, though many commentators thought the facts in the case itself were not extraordinary.

VI. PROCEDURAL ASPECTS OF ABSTENTION

As noted in § I above, *Pullman* abstention requires the federal court to stay its proceedings while the parties secure a definitive interpretation of state law in state court. This procedure, detailed in the *England* case, is cumbersome. It requires that the party seeking the state interpretation preserve his right to return to the federal court for determination of federal constitutional issues. In some states, a federal court may "certify" an issue of state law to the state's highest court for interpretation. This procedure, which is available in over half the states, can streamline *Pullman* abstention considerably by obviating the need for the parties to bring a separate action in state court.

■ CHAPTER 12: THE ANTI–INJUNCTION STATUTE

I. THE STATUTE AND BACKGROUND

The anti-injunction statute, 28 U.S.C. § 2283, has existed in some form since 1793. Today, it provides that a federal court cannot enjoin state-court proceedings, with three exceptions. The Supreme Court has recognized another exception for cases brought by the United States. If an exception applies, a party may seek an injunction from a federal court to enjoin other parties from litigating in state court. Though the original motivations for the statute are unclear, it is today understood to be a cornerstone of federalism—aimed at avoiding unnecessary friction between state and federal courts. Because the statute generally prohibits injunctions of state court "proceedings," it does not apply if a federal court issues an injunction before any state action is filed.

II. THE SCOPE OF THE STATUTORY EXCEPTIONS

First, Congress may "expressly authorize" injunctions against state-court proceedings. There are several examples, including statutory interpleader under 28 U.S.C. § 2361. The Supreme Court found such an exception with regard to cases brought to vindicate federal rights under 42 U.S.C. § 1983, notwithstanding the fact that Congress was silent in that statute as to whether federal courts should be able to enter such injunctions. *Mitchum v. Foster*, 407 U.S. 225 (1972). Second, federal courts may issue injunctions against state-court proceedings if "necessary in aid of their jurisdiction." This exception has been interpreted quite narrowly, and generally applies only in cases involving the federal court's seizure of property. Third, federal courts may enjoin parties from proceeding in state court to "protect or effectuate" their judgments. This "relitigation" exception also is narrow, and generally applies only to permit enforcement of federal judgments through claim preclusion or issue preclusion.

III. OTHER STATUTORY RESTRICTIONS ON FEDERAL INJUNCTIONS AGAINST STATE ACTIVITIES

Other statutes limit the power of federal courts to enjoin proceedings in state courts. One is the Tax Injunction Act of 1937, which prohibits federal district courts from enjoining, suspending, or restraining the assessment, levy, or collection of a tax under state law, provided a speedy remedy may be had in the state courts. The Johnson Act of 1934 restrains federal injunctive power in diversity cases concerning public utility rates set by a state or local administrative agency.

IV. INJUNCTIONS OF FEDERAL JUDICIAL PROCEEDINGS

The anti-injunction statute limits the power of a federal court to enjoin state-court proceedings. It does not apply to cases involving a federal injunction of other court proceedings. Such an injunction does not implicate concerns of federalism, because they do not affect state courts in any way. As a general rule, the federal district in which related *in personam* litigation is filed will have authority to enjoin litigants from proceeding in another federal district. A state court in which related *in personam* litigation is first filed has no authority to enjoin proceedings in federal court. But a state court that has jurisdiction over property may enjoin parties from federal proceedings concerning that property, if the federal proceedings would interfere with state-court jurisdiction over the property.

■ CHAPTER 13: "OUR FEDERALISM": THE DOCTRINE OF *YOUNGER v. HARRIS*

I. BACKGROUND

"Our federalism," espoused in *Younger v. Harris*, 401 U.S. 37 (1971), imposes a case law restriction on the power of federal courts similar to that imposed by the Anti–Injunction Statute. It is rooted not only in comity, but at least in part in a long-followed maxim that a court of equity will not act if a party has an adequate remedy. Thus, for example, a federal court should not issue an injunction or declaratory relief concerning an ongoing state criminal judicial proceeding. The criminal defendant who seeks federal equitable relief can raise his constitutional challenges to his prosecution in state court. Because the Anti–Injunction Statute does not apply to cases brought in federal court to vindicate federal rights under 42 U.S.C. § 1983, any restriction on federal court power in such cases comes from "our Federalism."

II. HISTORICAL DEVELOPMENT

In *Dombrowski v. Pfister*, 380 U.S. 479 (165), the Supreme Court authorized a federal court to enjoin a *threatened* state prosecution. Though usually the right to raise a constitutional defense during the state prosecution provides adequate protection of federal constitutional rights, the Court noted that on the facts of the case there was an allegation that the threatened prosecution was in bad faith and had a chilling effect on free speech. In *Younger*, however, the Court refused to allow a federal court to enjoin an *ongoing* prosecution, and distinguished *Dombrowski* on the grounds that no bad faith or harassment was alleged.

In *Younger*, the Court recognized that its bar on access to federal equitable remedies was not absolute. There are exceptions for cases in which state prosecution is brought in bad faith or is part of a series of harassing prosecutions, or if the federal issue simply cannot be raised in the state action, or other "extraordinary circumstances" such as prosecution under a state law that is flagrantly and patently unconstitutional.

III. THE TIMING OF FEDERAL INTERVENTION

Younger involved a request for a federal injunction against an *ongoing* state prosecution. Many observers conclude that federal relief in such a situation should be especially difficult, because it involves a greater intrusion upon state interests than relief against a *future* state prosecution. In *Steffel v. Thompson*, 415 U.S. 452 (1974), the Supreme Court held that *Younger* does not apply to the issuance of declaratory relief against future prosecutions. The Court did not comment on whether the same would be true concerning federal injunctive relief, but did note that declaratory relief is less intrusive of state interests than injunctive relief. In *Hicks v. Miranda*, 422 U.S. 332 (1975), a plaintiff sought federal injunctive relief against a future state prosecution after the state named him as a criminal defendant, but before the federal court actually issued an injunction. In these circumstances, the Court held that the federal court could not issue an injunction unless "proceedings of substance on the merits" had taken place in federal court before the state case was filed. The quoted phrase is ambiguous. The Court may have extended *Hicks* to the injunctive area in *Wooley v. Maynard*, 430 U.S. 705 (1977), in which it authorized permanent federal injunctive relief against a future state prosecution.

IV. APPLICABILITY OF *YOUNGER* TO CIVIL PROCEEDINGS

Though *Younger* concerned federal equitable relief against a state criminal prosecution, in subsequent cases the Supreme Court extended the doctrine to civil matters in some situations. In *Huffman v. Pursue, Ltd.*, 420 U.S. 592 (1975), the Court applied *Younger* concerning a state quasi-criminal proceeding concerning enforcement of a public nuisance statute. In *Pennzoil Co. v. Texaco, Inc.*, 481 U.S. 1 (1987), it applied *Younger* to bar federal injunctive relief against a state court civil proceeding between private parties.

V. APPLICABILITY OF *YOUNGER* TO NON–JUDICIAL STATE ACTION

The Supreme Court has employed *Younger* to avoid federal relief concerning review of state executive decisions. *Younger* may also play a role in some administrative contexts as well. For example, in one case the Court applied *Younger* to preclude a federal injunction concerning a bar disciplinary proceeding.

■ CHAPTER 14: ACTIONS TO VINDICATE FEDERAL CIVIL RIGHTS

I. PRINCIPAL CIVIL RIGHTS STATUTES

Following the ratification of the Thirteenth, Fourteenth, and Fifteenth Amendments, Congress enacted statutes designed to permit persons to enforce federal civil rights. Some of these Reconstruction-era statutes are quite specific. In addition, Congress has passed important civil rights statutes in recent times, including the Civil Rights Act of 1964 and the Voting Rights Act of 1965. The main focus of study here, however, is a broad Reconstruction-era statute now codified at 42 U.S.C. § 1983, which provides that "every person" acting "under color" of state law who "subjects, or causes to be subjected" a citizen of the United States or a person within the United States to "deprivation of any rights, privileges, or immunity secured by the Constitution and laws" shall be liable in civil suit. This important statute creates liability for one who has deprived another of her federal civil rights. It is to be contrasted with habeas corpus, which permits a prisoner to challenge the legality of her incarceration.

II. SECTION 1983 LITIGATION

Though § 1983 was passed shortly after the Civil War, it was little used until 1961, when the Supreme Court decided *Monroe v. Pape*, 365 U.S. 167. There, it upheld a man's right to sue municipal police officers for damages under § 1983 for violating his Fourth Amendment rights. It established two major points. First, a § 1983 plaintiff need *not* exhaust any state remedies (such as tort suits or administrative claims with the police department) before suing in federal court. Second, the police officers' actions were "under color" of state law, as required by § 1983, even though the actions constituted violations of federal and state law and were not authorized by superiors or the city that employed the officers.

The defendant in a § 1983 case must be a "person." This does not include a state or officers sued in their official capacities. On the other hand, it does include officers sued in their personal capacities. The Supreme Court had difficulty determining whether a municipality is a "person" under § 1983. Today it is clear that a municipality cannot be held liable on a theory of *respondeat superior*. It can be held liable, however, and thus is a "person" under the statute, for deprivations of federal rights caused by some municipal policy or custom. *Monell v. Dept. of Social Servs.*, 436 U.S. 658 (1978). In no case, however, may a municipality be held liable for punitive damages.

As noted above, the defendant must act "under color" of state law. *Monroe v. Pape* established that the "under color" requirement looks to whether the defendant acted under some badge of authority to enforce state law, rather than to whether the actions were authorized by state law. Private actors may be sued under § 1983 if they act under color of state law, as, for example, if they engage in joint activity with state actors to deprive the plaintiff of federal rights.

Section 1983 does not create substantive rights. Instead, it provides a vehicle for vindicating "rights, privileges, or immunities" secured by federal law. Not all constitutional provisions can be enforced through § 1983. The Supreme Court has likened the inquiry of what rights are enforceable to the inquiry into whether a statute creates a private right of action. Specifically, a statute can be enforced through § 1983 if Congress indicated that the statute created "an unambiguously conferred right" for enforcement. *Gonzaga University v. Doe*, 536 U.S. 273 (2002).

III. IMMUNITY FROM § 1983 CASES

Section 1983 is silent about immunity from suit. Nonetheless, courts have consistently recognized that certain individuals may be immune not just from liability, but from litigation under § 1983. Such immunity generally attaches only to suits for damages, and one immune from suit for that relief may not be immune to litigation for equitable relief. Some state actors have absolute immunity, which is thought to be necessary to permit them to perform their functions with requisite boldness. For example, judges simply cannot be sued for damages under § 1983 for acts taken in their judicial capacity. Similarly, prosecutors are immune for damages claims concerning the performance of traditional functions performed by advocates. Legislators enjoy absolute immunity for acts taken within the sphere of legitimate legislative activity.

Other officers, such as governors, mayors, and police officers, enjoy only "qualified" or "good faith" immunity. That is, they will not be held liable for damages if they acted in good faith. The question of good faith is measured objectively, by whether a reasonable official would have known—at the time of the alleged misconduct—that something constituted a violation of a clearly established right.

IV. DEPRIVATIONS UNDER COLOR OF FEDERAL LAW: *BIVENS* CLAIMS

Section 1983 does not apply to persons acting under color of *federal* law. There is no general statute analogous to § 1983 allowing suit against federal actors. The Supreme Court, however, recognized a common law right of action to sue federal officers for damages for deprivation of Fourth Amendment rights in *Bivens v. Six Unknown Federal Agents*, 403 U.S. 388 (1971). *Bivens* raises serious separation-of-powers issues, since it is arguably the role of Congress, and not the courts, to provide a right of action to enforce constitutional guarantees. A *Bivens* claim is against individual actors and seeks to impose liability for damages in their personal capacity. It has been expanded beyond the Fourth Amendment context to permit vindication of other constitutional rights as well. On the other hand, the Supreme Court has found instances in which Congress is deemed to have precluded a *Bivens* claim.

Generally, a plaintiff asserting a *Bivens* claim need not exhaust administrative remedies before filing suit. Immunities are recognized in *Bivens* litigation along the same lines as in § 1983 cases.

V. CIVIL RIGHTS REMOVAL JURISDICTION

The civil rights removal statute, 28 U.S.C. § 1443, has its roots in the Reconstruction era. It permits removal of a case from state to federal court, *inter alia*, by a defendant who "is denied or cannot enforce in the courts of such state a right under any law providing for the equal civil rights of citizens of the United States." This part of the statute thus permits removal when one fears that she cannot enforce in state court some federal provision for equal rights. In this and other provisions, the statute permits removal on a prediction of unconstitutional behavior by a state court, which obviously creates potential for friction between the federal and state court systems. Not surprisingly, the statute has been interpreted narrowly, and is rarely invoked.

■ CHAPTER 15: HABEAS CORPUS

I. BACKGROUND, ORIGINS OF THE WRIT, AND OVERVIEW OF CURRENT STATUTORY PROVISIONS

The writ of habeas corpus (known as "the Great Writ") permits a federal court to order the release of someone being held in custody of the government.

The release is justified only if the person is being held in violation of federal law, usually constitutional law. The writ developed in England, and is part of our constitutional heritage; Article I, § 9 provides that the privilege of the writ "shall not be suspended, unless when in cases of rebellion or invasion the public safety may require it." Several provisions of the Judicial Code relate to habeas corpus in the federal courts. Congress enacted restrictions on habeas corpus in the Antiterrorism and Effective Death Penalty Act of 1996 (AEDPA).

II. HABEAS CORPUS FOR STATE PRISONERS

28 U.S.C. § 2254 governs issuance of the writ of habeas corpus for persons in custody of a state court. Obviously, this use of habeas—by which a federal court reviews the legality of a person's confinement by state authorities—raises profound questions of federalism. Section 2254(a) imposes an exhaustion requirement on state prisoners seeking federal habeas. Such an applicant must have exhausted remedies available in state courts or else demonstrate that there is no state corrective process available. Exhaustion requires the state prisoner to present her federal argument to the highest state court once, either on appeal or collateral attack. Because of the exhaustion requirement, the federal court will review the constitutionality of incarceration after the state courts may have decided issues of fact. Under the AEDPA, fact findings by a state court are presumed to be correct.

Habeas is a vehicle for reviewing the legality of a state prisoner's conviction and deprivation of liberty. But not every constitutional violation can be remedied by federal habeas corpus. In *Stone v. Powell*, 428 U.S. 465 (1976), the Supreme Court held that a federal habeas court could not review a claim by a state prisoner that evidence used against him in his criminal trial was illegally seized and should not have been admitted. The state court had provided the prisoner an opportunity for full and fair consideration of the claimed illegal seizure. Despite concern that *Stone* would lead to other areas in which a state prisoner could not avail himself of federal habeas, the Court has not expanded *Stone* beyond cases involving claims based upon the exclusionary rule.

The AEDPA imposes a one-year limitations period on an application by a state prisoner for federal habeas relief. It also imposes important restrictions on successive applications for habeas relief by state prisoners. Repeat applications are not permitted without authorization of the court of appeals. There are clear waiver provisions for claims not set forth in a previous application.

III. "ABORTIVE STATE PROCEEDINGS"—THE PROBLEM OF INDEPENDENT AND ADEQUATE STATE GROUNDS

Some state prisoners seeking federal habeas corpus relief lost in their state proceedings because they failed to comply with state procedural rules. Such cases involve "abortive state proceedings." Whether the federal habeas court should address the merits of claims raised in such cases has been a difficult issue. Initially, the Supreme Court held that procedural default in state court barred federal habeas review, on much the same basis that the Supreme Court refuses to entertain appeals in cases in which there is an independent and adequate state ground for decision. Later, the Court held that a state prisoner's failure to comply with state procedural requirements would not preclude federal habeas review unless the prisoner had consciously by-passed his state judicial remedies. *Fay v. Noia*, 433 U.S. 72 (1963).

More recently, the Court has turned away from this approach. In *Wainwright v. Sykes*, 433 U.S. 72 (1977), the Court held that the state prisoner's failure to raise a contemporaneous objection to the admission of evidence at his criminal trial precluded Supreme Court review of his habeas proceeding. This was true even though his failure to raise the issue was not the result of a deliberate by-pass of a state judicial remedy. Only if the habeas applicant could establish cause for his failure to object and prejudice from the admission of the evidence could a federal court consider the issue in a habeas proceeding.

IV. HABEAS CORPUS FOR PERSONS IN THE CUSTODY OF THE UNITED STATES

A person in the custody of the federal government may seek habeas corpus relief from a federal court under 28 U.S.C. § 2241(c)(1). In addition, § 2255 allows a prisoner in federal custody to make a motion to vacate, set aside, or correct her sentence, based upon various grounds, including that the sentence was imposed in violation of the Constitution or federal statute.

■ CHAPTER 16: FEDERAL COMMON LAW

I. SOURCES OF AND JUSTIFICATION FOR FEDERAL COMMON LAW

The doctrine of *Erie Railraod v. Tompkins*, 304 U.S. 64 (1938), provides that federal courts exercising diversity of citizenship jurisdiction generally must apply state substantive law. It established that there is no "general federal common law." Nonetheless, the Supreme Court has made it clear that there are narrow areas in which federal common law does apply, and is binding upon both federal and state courts under the Supremacy Clause. Such areas of federal common law usually are justified by the need to effectuate congressional policy or to secure federal interests.

II. APPLICATION OF FEDERAL COMMON LAW IN SPECIFIC AREAS

One area in which federal common law is needed is to fill "gaps" in statutory schemes created by Congress. For example, sometimes Congress will enact a general regulatory scheme and provide expressly that the federal courts are to develop rules—through federal common law—for effectuating it. Other times, however, Congress is unclear on whether there is an individual right to sue to vindicate federal rights it creates. The federal courts in such situations must determine whether there is a private right of action.

Beyond such circumstances involving statutory gaps, federal courts will develop federal common law in specific substantive areas in which there is a particular federal interest. For example, when the federal government issues or holds commercial paper, enters a contract, or oversees a regulatory program, any dispute will involve a federal interest which may justify development and application of federal common law. For example, in *Clearfield Trust Co. v. United States*, 318 U.S. 363 (1943), the United States issued a check that was subsequently stolen and cashed. Because the power of the federal government to issue checks is founded in the Constitution, and because a uniform federal standard was necessary to ensure uniform rules for the government, the Supreme Court adopted federal common law as the rules of decision regarding liability on the check. The Court has not always been consistent on when to apply federal common law concerning such federal "proprietary" interests.

Another substantive area in which federal common law is applied is international relations, in which the need for a uniform federal standard is obvious. Similarly, federal common law applies to determine interstate disputes, concerning many issues in admiralty, for enforcement of federal constitutional rights, and concerning other relatively well-defined topics.

■ CHAPTER 17: CLAIM AND ISSUE PRECLUSION IN THE FEDERAL SYSTEM

I. FULL FAITH AND CREDIT PROVISIONS OF THE CONSTITUTION AND STATUTE

In Civil Procedure, you studied the doctrines of claim and issue preclusion (also known as res judicata and collateral estoppel). Under these doctrines, a valid, final judgment "on the merits" precludes parties from litigating various things in a second case. States are free to determine their own principles of claim and issue preclusion, and there is federal law on the point as well. The question here is what law of claim and issue preclusion should apply to determine the preclusive effect of a judgment. In the federal system, when the two cases might be adjudicated in the judicial systems of different states, or in federal and in state courts, the issue can become more complicated. The matter is addressed by full faith and credit—as to which there is both a constitutional provision and a statute—and by common law principles.

Article IV, § 1, of the Constitution provides, in part, that "Full Faith and Credit shall be given in each State to the . . . judicial Proceedings of every other State." This provision applies only to cases in state courts, and thus does not apply to proceedings in the federal courts. The requirement that the state courts in one state accord "full faith and credit" to the judgment of the courts of another state generally means that the court of the second state must apply the claim and issue preclusion rules (rules of res judicata and collateral estoppel) of the state that entered the judgment in the first case.

Section 1738, known as the Full Faith and Credit Act, provides, in part, that "judicial proceedings" of a "State, Territory, or Possession of the United States" shall have "the same full faith and credit in every court within the United States and its Territories and Possessions as they have by law or usage in the courts of each State, Territory, or Possession from which they are taken." This provision applies not only in the state-to-state situation addressed by the constitutional provision for full faith and credit, but also in the situation in which the first judgment is entered in a state court and the second case is pending in a federal court. The statute requires the federal court to give the state court judgment the same "full faith and credit" as would the state court that rendered the judgment, which generally means that the federal court of the second state must apply the claim and issue preclusion rules (rules of res judicata and collateral estoppel) of the state that entered the judgment in the first case.

II. SITUATIONS COVERED BY NEITHER FULL FAITH AND CREDIT PROVISION

Neither the constitutional nor the statutory provisions for full faith and credit applies when the initial judgment is entered in *federal* court. Both apply to define the credit due a judgment entered by a *state* court. But courts have established that a second court—state or federal—must apply federal claim and issue preclusion law if the first judgment was entered by a federal court in a federal question case.

A more difficult issue is whether a second court must apply federal claim and issue preclusion law if the first judgment was entered by a federal court in a diversity of citizenship case. The Supreme Court addressed this issue in *Semtek International, Inc. v. Lockheed Martin Corp.*, 531 U.S. 497 (2001). It held that the matter was governed by federal common law, but, on the facts of the case, that federal common law would adopt the state law of the state in which the federal court sat. By doing this, the Court retains the flexibility to adopt state law on preclusion in such cases when it wants to and to ignore it when it feels there is a justification.

*

Perspective

■ APPROACH TO FEDERAL COURTS

The study of federal courts includes consideration of the internal structure and operation of the federal judiciary, its relationship to the other branches of the federal government (separation of powers principles) and its interaction with the judicial and political segments of the state governments (federalism principles). The subject constitutes a unique blend of highly technical and detailed statutory analysis and the study of broad theoretical issues of federalism and separation of powers. It is this combination of very different modes of thought—of detail and of "big picture"—that makes the study of federal courts so interesting.

To gain the most from the course, the student should recognize the importance of both the intricate detail and the broad themes, and not emphasize one over the other. For example, the student must be able simultaneously to comprehend the highly theoretical issues surrounding the controversy over congressional power to regulate the jurisdiction of the federal courts and the technicalities of removal jurisdiction. Whatever area of the course is being studied, however, the student should always attempt to relate the practical legal doctrines to the policies behind the development of the federal judiciary and its role as part of a dynamic federal system, in which the often competing interests of state and federal governments must be reconciled.

The student will find available a number of resources to aid in understanding the complexities of the subject. Two multi-volume treatises are routinely consulted by judges and lawyers and are available in your law school's library: Wright & Miller, Federal Practice and Procedure and Moore's Federal Practice. In addition, very helpful single-volume resources include: Chemerinsky, *Federal Jurisdiction* (4th ed. 2003); Mullenix, Redish & Vairo, *Understanding Federal Courts* (1998); Wright & Kane, *The Law of Federal Courts* (6th ed. 2002); and Currie, *Federal Jurisdiction in a Nutshell* (4th ed. 1999).

■ APPROACH TO EXAMINATIONS

In deciding how to prepare for an examination in federal courts, a great deal may depend on whether the test will include short answers, or instead will consist exclusively of essay questions. If the examination contains numerous short answer questions, it is likely that the professor is interested in the students' knowledge and understanding of specific legal doctrines and statutory structure. A student preparing for such an examination should emphasize the details of the various jurisdictional statutes and judge-made principles, and should consider closely the specific elements of each. If the examination is open-book, perhaps less emphasis will have to be placed on rote memorization. Given the limited time generally available during an examination, however, a student should not to rely too heavily on access to the book.

If the examination is primarily or exclusively of the essay variety, the student should be prepared to deal with some of the many unresolved policy issues in the field. As in most law school exam questions of this variety, it is likely that there is no one "right" answer, and it is important both to explain why you have reached your conclusion and why you have rejected opposing arguments. But while it is important to include broad policy analysis in such questions, it is also important to demonstrate familiarity with detailed statutes and doctrines that are applicable. Particularly in an essay question, the two modes of analysis—detail and "big picture"—are not mutually exclusive.

PART ONE

Federal Courts and Political Branches of the Federal Government

■ ANALYSIS

1. Problems of Judicial Review
2. Congressional Power to Regulate Federal Jurisdiction
3. Legislative Courts

I

Problems of Judicial Review

■ ANALYSIS

I. Introduction
II. The Institution of Judicial Review
    A. Political Insulation of the Federal Judiciary
    B. *Marbury v. Madison*
III. Federal Courts Cannot Issue Advisory Opinions
    A. The Case or Controversy Requirement
    B. Applications
IV. Standing
    A. Sources and Purposes of the Standing Requirement
    B. Three Constitutional Requirements for Standing
    C. Additional "Prudential" Limitations on Standing
    D. Special Problems of Taxpayer Standing
    E. Standing in the Supreme Court to Review State Court Decisions
V. Ripeness
    A. Sources and Purposes of the Ripeness Requirement
    B. Requirements and Application
VI. Mootness
    A. Sources, Purposes, and Operation of the Mootness Doctrine

B. Exceptions to the Operation of Mootness
VII. **Political Question Doctrine**
  A. Sources and Purposes of the Political Question Doctrine
  B. Modern Explication of the Political Question Doctrine
  C. Categories of Cases to Which the Political Question Doctrine Has Been Applied and the Case Dismissed
  D. Areas in Which Application of the Political Question Doctrine Has Been Rejected

I. Introduction

The principle of judicial review permits the judicial branch to declare acts of the other branches of government (the executive and legislative) invalid because they are contrary to the United States Constitution. Judicial review is necessary to ensure the proper functioning of government, but creates tension because federal judges are not elected, and thus are not necessarily responsive to the will of the majority. Several doctrines serve to limit the judiciary's ability to engage in judicial review. Article III permits the federal courts to decide "cases" or "controversies," and thereby forbids advisory opinions. In addition, standing, mootness, ripeness, and the political question doctrine limit the sorts of disputes that can be decided by the federal judiciary. The proper balance between the need for judicial review and the need to restrain it is a subject of ongoing debate.

II. The Institution of Judicial Review

A. Political Insulation of the Federal Judiciary

1. Article III, § 1, of the Constitution provides that federal judges have lifetime tenure and that their pay cannot be reduced. The only way a federal judge can be formally removed from office is by impeachment; in the history of the country, fewer than ten federal judges have been removed.

2. The Constitution accords this extraordinary protection to federal judges to insulate them from political pressure. If federal judges were elected, they might lack the courage to rule in unpopular ways. If Congress could reduce their pay, judges might be reluctant to rule against the federal government.

B. Marbury v. Madison

1. In *Marbury v. Madison*, 5 U.S. 137 (1803), the Supreme Court established that the federal judiciary has the constitutional power to declare acts of the other branches of government invalid if they violate the Constitution.

    a. Chief Justice Marshall concluded that the executive branch had violated the rights of Mr. Marbury by failing to deliver to him a commission making him a justice of the peace.

    b. Marshall avoided direct conflict with the executive branch, however, by holding that although Mr. Marbury had been wronged and was entitled to a remedy, the Supreme Court was not the proper tribunal to grant it. This result was dictated by Article III, § 2, clause 1, which sets forth the limit of the judicial power of the federal courts. (We address that aspect of *Marbury* in Chapter 8, § I.B).

2. Judicial review allows the judiciary to monitor the proper functioning of government. But it creates tension precisely because it permits the nonelected branch of the federal government to invalidate the acts of the "political" or "representative" branches.

3. The remainder of this Chapter addresses doctrines that limit judicial power and thus limit judicial review. As a group, these limitations are known as doctrines of "justiciability."

III. Federal Courts Cannot Issue Advisory Opinions

A. The Case or Controversy Requirement

1. Article III, § 2, extends the judicial power of the federal courts to various "cases" and "controversies." Thus, the federal courts may not issue opinions giving advice to the other branches of the federal government. The judicial power is exercised only to decide actual disputes; their job is to decide cases, not to make general decrees about the propriety of government action.

   a. Thus, judicial review is possible only if an actual legal dispute presents a question concerning the constitutionality of an act by one of the political branches of government.

   b. No federal court can declare a statute unconstitutional—even if it is plainly so—until the issue is presented to the court in the context of litigation.

2. The case or controversy requirement serves related purposes.

   a. By leaving the political branches to act without prior intrusion by the courts, it promotes the separation of powers between the branches.

   b. The requirement also helps to ensure that the judiciary acts only when there is a true adversary dispute. The adversary system of litigation then acts to ensure that the issues are presented with "concreteness," rather than as hypotheticals. This concreteness is thought to ensure better decision-making.

c. Like other justiciability doctrines, this requirement serves as "docket control"—to conserve the resources of the federal judiciary by limiting the number of matters it will address.

B. Applications

1. When he was Secretary of State in the Washington administration, Thomas Jefferson asked the justices of the Supreme Court whether the United States could legally undertake certain acts while remaining neutral in the war between France and England. The justices refused to answer the question. They cited the roles of the three branches of government and found "strong arguments against the propriety of our extrajudicially deciding the questions."

2. Congress occasionally has set up schemes in which the federal courts would have mere advisory authority. These schemes violate the case or controversy requirement by reducing the role of the judiciary to mere advisor. *See, e.g., C & S Air Lines v. Waterman Corp.*, 333 U.S. 103, 113 (1948)(federal courts' review of administrative rulings concerning airline routes could be ignored by the President; scheme rejected as forcing federal courts to "render an advisory opinion in its most obnoxious form.").

3. Suits for declaratory judgments under 28 U.S.C. § 2201 present special problems. Because a declaratory judgment may decree the parties' rights prior to the relevant event's occurring, it can often appear to be an advisory opinion. The Supreme Court has upheld the constitutionality of declaratory judgments, "so long as the case retains the essentials of an adversary proceeding, involving a real, not a hypothetical, controversy." *Nashville, C. & St. Louis Ry. v. Wallace*, 288 U.S. 249, 264 (1933).

IV. Standing

A. Sources and Purposes of the Standing Requirement

1. A party may not litigate in the federal courts unless she has "standing" to bring the suit. The focus of standing, then, is whether the plaintiff is an appropriate person to assert a claim—"whether the litigant is entitled to have the court decide the merits of the dispute or of particular issues." *Warth v. Seldin*, 422 U.S. 490, 498 (1975).

2. The contours of the standing requirement have fluctuated over the years, and the Supreme Court has admitted that the concept "has not been defined with complete consistency in all of the various cases decided by this Court." *Valley Forge Christian College v. Americans United for Separation of Church and State*, 454 U.S. 464, 475 (1982).

3. Nonetheless, basically the concept of standing requires that a litigant have some direct, concrete interest in the outcome of the case—that the conduct of which the plaintiff complains has caused her some real injury. Such harm is usually obvious in litigation between private parties. Most problematic cases, as we will see, involve public law litigation, or suits by "ideological plaintiffs," those who challenge some governmental act on the basis of strongly held ideological views. Such cases on occasion give rise to the problem of "citizen" standing, or standing by a citizen to challenge government action.

4. As with other justiciability doctrines, the rules of standing raise tension about the proper role of the federal courts. If standing restrictions are lowered, judicial review is more readily available. If standing restrictions are raised, the courts will less readily review the other branches of government.

5. There are two sources of standing requirements. First, Article III imposes three absolute requirements, which can never be overridden by statute. Second, the Supreme Court recognizes additional "prudential" limitations on standing. These restrictions are not imposed by the Constitution, but by the courts, in the interest of judicial administration. These prudential limitations can be overridden by statute.

B. Three Constitutional Requirements for Standing

1. The "case or controversy requirement" of Article III of the Constitution imposes three requirements for standing. These three requirements constitute "an irreducible minimum" for standing, and must be satisfied in every case. They are (1) that the plaintiff "show he personally has suffered some actual or threatened injury as a result of the putatively illegal conduct of the defendant," (2) that "the injury fairly be traced to the challenged action," and (3) that the injury "is likely to be redressed by a favorable decision." *Valley Forge Christian College v. Americans United for Separation of Church and State, Inc.*, 454 U.S. 464, 472 (1982). Stated in more shorthand form, these are: (1) "injury in fact," (2) causation (that

the defendant's act caused the harm to the plaintiff), and (3) redressability (that if the plaintiff wins the case, her harm will be redressed). *See Bennett v. Spear*, 520 U.S. 154, 167 (1997).

2. "Injury in fact" may be satisfied by showing "an invasion of a legally protected interest which is (a) concrete and particularized . . . ; and (b) actual or imminent, not 'conjectural' or hypothetical." *Lujan v. Defenders of Wildlife*, 504 U.S. 555, 560 (1992).

   a. Demonstrating injury in fact is often a problem in cases brought by "ideological plaintiffs" to challenge government action. The results of cases are often difficult to reconcile, and often involve assessment of whether the plaintiff properly pleaded an injury.

   Example: To have standing, prospective tenants attempting to challenge restrictive zoning ordinances have to allege more than that the ordinances had prevented builders from constructing low-income housing. In addition, they must allege facts that demonstrate that, but for the restrictive zoning practices, it is probable that they would have been able to purchase or lease in the area. *Warth v. Seldin*, 422 U.S. 490 (1975).

   b. Injury in fact may be "economic or otherwise." *Association of Data Processing Service Organizations, Inc. v. Camp*, 397 U.S. 150, 152 (1970). Thus it can include non-economic harm to purely aesthetic interests. *United States v. SCRAP*, 412 U.S. 669 (1973)(upholding standing in case brought by students who alleged that increased railroad freight rates approved by the government would result in less use of recycled goods which, in turn, would lead to increased use of natural resources, harming their enjoyment of forests and streams in the Washington, D.C. area). On the other hand, the Supreme Court has been very strict in requiring allegations of direct injury to the plaintiff.

   Example: The Sierra Club sued to challenge a decision by the Secretary of the Interior to allow development of a ski resort in the Mineral King Valley in California. It alleged that it had a special interest in conservation and maintenance of parks, game refuges, and forests. The allegations failed to establish injury in fact, because there was no allegation that the Sierra Club or its members "use Mineral King for any purpose, much less that they use it in any way that would be significantly affected by the proposed actions of [the developers]." *Sierra Club v. Morton*, 405 U.S. 727, 735 (1972).

Example: Plaintiffs, including the National Wildlife Federation (NWF), challenged a government action that permitted increased mining on specific federal lands. Two members of the NWF stated in affidavits that they used land "in the vicinity" of the land on which mining was to be permitted, and that the mining would harm the environment there. The plaintiffs failed to demonstrate injury in fact because the "affidavit is ambiguous regarding whether the adversely affected lands are the ones she uses." *Lujan v. National Wildlife Federation*, 497 U.S. 871, 888 (1990). As a matter of pleading, the plaintiffs failed to allege that they used the precise federal land on which mining was to be permitted.

c. Some constitutional violations may injure no specific individual. In such areas, the requirement of an injury in fact may effectively preclude judicial review, even though the challenged legislation would be found unconstitutional on the merits.

Example: Former members of the Armed Forces Reserve opposed to United States involvement in Vietnam lacked standing to challenge the membership of congressional representatives in the Reserve as a violation of the Incompatibility Clause of Article I, § 6, cl. 2 of the Constitution. That clause provides that "no Person holding any Office under the United States shall be a Member of either House during his Continuance in Office." *Schlesinger v. Reservists Committee to Stop the War*, 418 U.S. 208 (1974). It is highly unlikely that *any* private plaintiff could claim to have suffered an injury in fact in such a situation. As the Court said: "The assumption that if [plaintiffs] have no standing to sue no one would have standing, is not a reason to find standing." *Id*. at 227. Thus, the issue is to be resolved by the political branches through the political process.

Example: By statute, the executive department of the federal government is allowed to turn over surplus government property to tax-exempt educational institutions free of charge. Plaintiffs, citizens dedicated to the separation of church and state, sued to challenge the donation of a former military hospital to a Christian college. Plaintiffs failed to allege an injury in fact: "Although

[they] claim that the Constitution has been violated, they claim nothing else. They fail to identify any personal injury suffered by the plaintiffs *as a consequence* of the alleged constitutional error, other than the psychological consequence presumably produced by observation of conduct with which one disagrees." *Valley Forge Christian College v. Americans United for Separation of Church & State, Inc.*, 454 U.S. 464, 485 (1982)(emphasis in original).

On the other hand, one who suffers an injury in fact does not lose standing just because others also suffered the same harm. Voters challenging a Federal Election Commission decision not to require the American Israel Public Affairs Committee to register as a "political committee" alleged an injury in fact. They suffered an "informational injury" because, they asserted, they were denied information that would help them in voting. *Federal Election Commission v. Akins*, 524 U.S. 11, 24 (1998).

d. The injury in fact may be to one's statutory rights. Thus, "Congress may create a statutory right or entitlement the alleged deprivation of which can confer standing to sue even where the plaintiff would have suffered no judicially cognizable injury in the absence of statute." *Warth v. Seldin*, 422 U.S. 490, 514 (1975).

Example: White tenants of an apartment complex alleged that their landlord discriminated by not renting to nonwhites. As a result, they alleged, they were robbed of the social and economic benefits of living in an integrated community. The plaintiffs alleged injury in fact, because the Civil Rights Act of 1968 had created a right to be free from the effects of racial discrimination. Concurring, Justice White stated that he would have had difficulty finding a case or controversy absent the direct authorization of that Act. *Trafficante v. Metropolitan Life Insurance Co.*, 409 U.S. 205 (1972).

Example: Under the Endangered Species Act (ESA), "any person may commence a civil suit on his own behalf" to enjoin a violation of the ESA. The ESA also requires the Secretary of the Interior to promulgate regulations listing endangered species and requires other agencies to ensure that its acts do not jeopardize such species or their habitat. If they do, the agency must consult with the Fish and Wildlife Service to find alternatives. The Bureau of Reclamation determined that its operation of the Klamath Project threatened protected species of fish, and ultimately it was decided that the Bureau would maintain higher reservoir levels. Irrigation districts and ranchers who receive water from the Klamath Project sued to challenge the determination of threat and the government action. They demonstrated injury in fact under the ESA. The Court concluded that under the ESA, "standing was expanded to the full extent permitted under Article III." *Bennett v. Spear*, 520 U.S. 154, 165 (1997).

Example: In *Lujan v. Defenders of Wildlife*, 504 U.S. 555 1992), the plaintiffs challenged a federal regulation providing that the ESA did not apply to federal government activities outside the United States. The plaintiffs did *not* have standing under the ESA. "To permit Congress to convert the undifferentiated public interest in executive officers' compliance with the law into an 'individual' right vindicable in the courts is to permit Congress to transfer from the President to the courts the Chief Executive's most important constitutional duty, to take care that the laws be faithfully executed." *Id.* at 577. Thus, apparently, Congress can create "statutory standing" only if there is also an Article III injury in fact, as there was in *Bennett*.

3. In addition to injury in fact, the plaintiff must show causation and redressability. Causation requires that the injury in fact was the result of the defendant's conduct. The redressability factor addresses whether a favorable ruling would remedy the harm the plaintiff has suffered. Courts tend to treat these two constitutional requirements together.

Example: Plaintiffs, low-income persons and their representatives, sued the Secretary of the Treasury to challenge an IRS regulation providing that hospitals can qualify as charitable institutions (to which donations would be tax deductible) even though they failed to provide service to indigents (except in emergency cases). Plaintiffs alleged an injury in fact, because they were denied medical care by such hospitals, and thus harmed. But they lacked standing, because there was no necessary connection between the IRS regulation and the harm they suffered. Moreover, even if the plaintiffs won the case, hospitals would not be compelled to provide service to indigents. Instead, they might forego charitable contributions to avoid having to take on that responsibility. *Simon v. Eastern Kentucky Welfare Rights Organization*, 426 U.S. 26 (1976).

Example: In *Allen v. Wright*, 468 U.S. 737 (1984), parents of black public school students sued to challenge the IRS's failure to deny tax-exempt status to private schools that discriminated on the basis of race. Their claim that their children suffered a stigma because the government permitted tax-exempt contributions to discriminatory schools failed to meet the injury in fact requirement because it was not concrete enough. Their claim that the children's ability to have an integrated school was harmed by the tax advantages to discriminatory schools failed to meet the causation requirement. "From the perspective of the IRS, the injury to [plaintiffs] is highly indirect and results from the independent action of some third party not before the court." *Id.* at 757. In short, the children's inability to obtain a desegregated education did not result from the IRS's violation of the law. This was one of the fairly rare cases in which causation and redressability were treated separately, as the Court was willing to assume that the relief requested by the plaintiffs "might have a substantial effect on the desegregation of public schools." *Id.* at 753 n.19.

Example: An arguably inconsistent decision is *Duke Power Co. v. Carolina Environmental Study Group, Inc.*, 438 U.S. 59 (1978). There, the plaintiffs, who were organizations and individuals who were located within close proximity to planned nuclear power facilities, sued the power company and others. They challenged the constitutionality of the provisions of the Price–Anderson Act that limited private liability in the event of a nuclear accident. The Supreme Court found that the plaintiffs had standing, noting that operation of the power plants had immediate harmful effects (such as the increase of thermal pollution of nearby lakes) and caused plaintiffs injury in fact, even though no accident had occurred. The Supreme Court accepted the lower court finding that, but for the protections of the Price–Anderson Act, the power plants would not have been built. Once the plants had been built, though, the question still remained whether winning the case would remedy the harms plaintiffs were presently claiming to suffer.

4. The three constitutionally-based standing requirements serve several purposes, mostly in common with other justiciability requirements.

   a. They promote principles of separation of powers by confining the federal courts to the performance of the traditional judicial functions of resolving individual disputes and adjudicating the rights of individuals. The Supreme Court has said, bluntly, that standing is "built on a single basic idea—the idea of separation of powers." *Allen v. Wright*, 468 U.S. 737, 752 (1984). Stated another way, standing "is founded in concern about the proper—and properly limited—role of the courts in a democratic society." *Warth v. Seldin*, 422 U.S. 490, 498 (1975).

b. Some commentators have criticized the Court for restricting standing excessively in recent years, and thereby effectively precluding judicial review of government action.

c. The requirement that the plaintiff suffer an actual injury is said to ensure that she has a personal incentive to litigate fully and to present issues with "concreteness," rather than as hypotheticals. This concreteness is thought to ensure better decisionmaking.

d. Some commentators have responded, however, that many institutional litigants possessing solely an ideological interest in the case are just as likely to provide vigorous litigation as are many individual litigants.

e. Standing also serves a "docket control" function to avoid inundation of the federal courts.

C. Additional "Prudential" Limitations on Standing

1. In addition to the constitutional requirements for standing discussed above, the Supreme Court has also imposed "prudential" limitations on standing. These are imposed as a matter of prudent judicial administration. The Court has identified three such limitations: (1) the plaintiff must assert her own interest, and not that of a third-party; (2) the plaintiff's interest must fall within the "zone of interests" protected by the relevant law; and (3) the federal courts will not hear "generalized grievances."

2. The prohibition against third-party standing is rooted in the notion that "one to whom application of a statute is constitutional will not be heard to attack the statute on the ground that impliedly it might also be taken as applying to other persons or other situations in which its application might be unconstitutional." *United States v. Raines*, 362 U.S. 17, 21 (1960).

a. In other words, generally, individuals do not have standing to assert the rights of others.

Example: A defendant is prosecuted for violating a law that he claims is so broad that it could be applied unconstitutionally to others, even though a narrower statute could be drafted that would constitutionally penalize the particular defendant. As a general rule, this defendant will not be allowed to have the law declared unconstitutional just because it could be unconstitutionally applied to others.

b. Again, the rule against third-party standing generally does not derive from Article III's "case or controversy" requirement.

c. Instead, the traditional third-party standing rule, at least in the context of a constitutional challenge, derives largely from prudential precepts about the judiciary's limited role: courts in a democratic society should not seek out statutes for constitutional perusal unless and until the statute has been directly applied in an unconstitutional manner.

d. Because the prohibition against third-party standing is subject to judicial exception, some courts and commentators have referred to it as "jus tertii" instead of a prong of standing.

e. The Supreme Court has recognized a limited exception to the rule against third-party standing when the constitutional challenge is premised on the First Amendment right of free expression. This exception is contained in what is known as the "overbreadth" doctrine.

f. The rationale for the overbreadth exception is that free speech rights are of paramount importance; if a law that violated the First Amendment remains in force, persons may be "chilled" from expressing their views. This chilling effect effectively insulates the law from constitutional challenge because people will not risk violating the law.

g. The Supreme Court has emphasized that the overbreadth exception is "strong medicine" and thus is rarely invoked. Thus, the Court will not allow one to whom a law may be constitutionally applied to challenge the law as overbroad unless the overbreadth is "substantial," meaning that the law must be unconstitutional in the large majority of its applications. *New York v. Ferber*, 458 U.S. 747 (1982); *Broadrick v. Oklahoma*, 413 U.S. 601 (1973).

3. The second prudential requirement is that the plaintiff's injury must be "arguably within the zone of interest to be protected or regulated by the statute or constitutional guarantee in question." *Association of Data Processing Service Organizations, Inc. v. Camp*, 397 U.S. 150, 153 (1970).

   a. This issue almost always is encountered in cases in which the plaintiff sues under the Administrative Procedures Act to challenge the action of an administrative agency. The requirement means that the plaintiff must be within the group which the violated statute was intended to benefit. *See Clarke v. Securities Industry Association*, 479 U.S. 388, 400 n.16 (1987)(zone of interest test "most usefully understood as a gloss" on § 10 of the Administrative Procedures Act and is "not a test of universal application.").

   Example: Section 10 of the Administrative Procedures Act allows judicial review of an agency action by one "aggrieved by agency action within the meaning of the relevant statute." The Bank Service Corporation Act of 1962 forbade bank service corporations from engaging in any activity other than providing bank services. The Comptroller of the Currency ruled that such corporations could provide data processing services for banks and their customers. The plaintiff, representing data processors, challenged the administrative ruling. The Supreme Court concluded that the plaintiff had standing. In addition to the Article III requirements for standing, the plaintiff was within the zone of interests Congress intended to protect with the Bank Service Corporation Act of 1962.

   Example: The Postal Express Statutes provide monopoly status for the United States Postal Service by preventing private competition on certain routes. The Postal Service issued an administrative ruling that exempted international remailing by private couriers, thus giving up its monopoly in that area. Postal workers challenged the ruling because they would likely be harmed by the resulting loss in business by the Postal Service. The Supreme Court held that they lacked standing because they were not within the zone of interests protected by the statutes. Rather, the statutes were intended to benefit the general citizenry by providing postal service to all communities. Neither the language of the Postal Express Statutes nor the legislative history supported the plaintiffs' contention that Congress had intended to protect employment with the Postal Service. *Air Courier Conference v. American Postal Workers Union*, 498 U.S. 517 (1991).

    b.   The Supreme Court has not been consistent in its application of the zone of interests requirement. Sometimes the Court finds standing without rigorous application of the test. *See, e.g., Clarke v. Securities Industry Association*, 479 U.S. 388, 399–00 (1987)(creating a presumption that agency action is reviewable; zone of interests "test is not meant to be especially demanding; in particular, there need be no indication of congressional purpose to benefit the would-be plaintiff.").

    c.   The Court itself has conceded that its opinions have not stated a clear rule for applying the restriction. *National Credit Union Administration v. First National Bank & Trust*, 522 U.S. 479, 486 (1998). In *National Credit Union*, it upheld standing, in a 5-to-4 opinion based upon a less rigorous application of the zone of interests—more like that used in *Clarke* than in *Air Courier Conference*.

4.   The third prudential limitation is that there is no standing "when the asserted harm is a generalized grievance shared in a substantially equal measure by all or a large class of citizens." *Warth v. Seldin*, 422 U.S. 490, 499 (1975). Thus, "even when the plaintiff has alleged redressable injury sufficient to meet the requirements of Art. III, the Court has refrained from adjudicating 'abstract questions of wide public significance' which amount to 'generalized grievances,' pervasively shared and most appropriately addressed in the representative branches." *Valley Forge Christian College v. Americans United for Separation of Church & State, Inc.*, 454 U.S. 464, 474–75 (1982). This requirement makes it difficult to bring suits simply as a citizen concerned with a particular issue.

    a.   Commentators have criticized this limitation as potentially shielding government action that blatantly violates constitutional rights of a large number of people. As applied, however, the Supreme Court seems to be saying that this limitation simply keeps out of federal court the general complaint of a citizen who sues to ensure that the federal government acts in compliance with the law. Indeed, the Court has made it clear that one who meets the constitutional requirements for standing will not be denied standing simply because she shares that harm with many others. *See, e.g., Federal Election Commission v. Akins*, 524 U.S. 11, 24 (1998), discussed at § IV.B.2.c, above.

  b. Thus, the rule against generalized grievances is very similar to the rules concerning taxpayer standing, discussed in § D., below.

  c. Examples of cases involving generalized grievances include *Valley Forge Christian College v. Americans United for Separation of Church & State, Inc.*, 454 U.S. 464 (1982) and *Schlesinger v. Reservists Committee to Stop the War*, 418 U.S. 208 (1974), both of which were discussed at § IV.B.2.c, above.

  d. More recently, the Supreme Court has indicated that the rule against generalized grievances is required by Article III, and is not simply a prudential limitation. *Lujan v. Defenders of Wildlife*, 504 U.S. 555, 575–76 (1992). In that case, discussed at § IV.B.2.d, above, the Court rejected standing under the Endangered Species Act, which permits "any person" to commence a suit to enjoin violations of the Act. Because the plaintiffs were asserting merely a generalized grievance, they failed to satisfy Article III standing requirements, and Congress was powerless to extend standing to them.

5. Because prudential limitations are self-imposed restrictions on the judiciary, and are not based in the Constitution, they can be overridden by Congress. Examples of cases in which Congress has done so, and prescribed standing based solely upon satisfaction of the three constitutional requirements, include *Bennett v. Spear*, 520 U.S. 154 (1997) and *Trafficante v. Metropolitan Life Insurance Co.*, 409 U.S. 205 (1972), both of which were discussed at § IV.B.2.d, above.

D. Special Problems of Taxpayer Standing

1. One subset of the standing problem concerns the extent to which taxpayers may sue to challenge the constitutionality of governmental spending programs. This set of cases is similar to those in which plaintiffs sue as citizens to challenge governmental acts. *See* § IV.C.4, above.

2. In *Massachusetts v. Mellon*, 262 U.S. 447 (1923), the Supreme Court held that federal taxpayers lacked standing to challenge the constitutionality of federal expenditures. As a pragmatic matter, the Court noted that

allowing standing would potentially swamp the federal courts with such challenges. To have standing, the Court held, a party "must be able to show not only that the statute is invalid but that he has sustained or is immediately in danger of sustaining some direct injury as the result of its enforcement, and not merely that he suffers in some indefinite way in common with people generally." *Id.* at 488.

3. Later, however, in *Flast v. Cohen,* 392 U.S. 83, 102 (1968), the Supreme Court held that federal taxpayers have standing if "they can demonstrate the necessary stake as taxpayers in the outcome of the litigation to satisfy Article III requirements." Such status can be established (a) only in suits challenging statutes enacted pursuant to Congress' power under the taxing and spending clause of Article I, § 8, of the Constitution, and (b) only if the taxpayer can establish a "nexus between that status and the precise nature of the constitutional infringement alleged."

    a. In *Flast*, the Court purported to distinguish *Frothingham* because the taxpayer there had failed to allege that Congress had breached a *specific limitation* upon its taxing and spending power.

    b. Commentators have long questioned, however, whether the two decisions are distinguishable in any meaningful sense. They also have questioned whether the two *Flast* factors are rationally related to the issue of standing in any way.

    c. Two concurring Justices in *Flast* expressed the view that taxpayer standing should be allowed only in cases challenging laws under the First Amendment's establishment-of-religion clause.

4. In *Valley Forge Christian College v. Americans United for Separation of Church and State Inc.,* 454 U.S. 464 (1982), the executive branch of the federal government, pursuant to statutory authorization, turned over surplus federal realty to a Christian college. The plaintiffs lacked standing as citizens (as discussed at § IV.B.2.c, above). In addition, they lacked standing as federal taxpayers. The Supreme Court held that taxpayer standing is not permitted when the challenge is not to a congressional action, but to a decision by an executive department, and when that property transfer was not an exercise of authority conferred by the taxing and spending clause of Article I, § 8.

5. Despite these limitations on the standing of federal taxpayers, the

Supreme Court has upheld standing of local taxpayers (e.g., state or municipal) to challenge a local expenditure.

  a. Thus, a municipal taxpayer could challenge the use of public funds to transport students to Catholic schools. *Everson v. Board of Education*, 330 U.S. 1 (1947).

  b. On the other hand, state and municipal taxpayers did not have standing to challenge a state statute that required a daily Old Testament reading in the public schools. They lacked standing because they were suing over religious differences. The case was not a "good-faith pocketbook action" involving an economic effect of the state law. *Doremus v. Board of Education*, 342 U.S. 429 (1952). *Everson*, in contrast, had concerned a direct appropriation or spending of funds because of the challenged activity.

  c. In a case decided the same day as *Doremus*, the Supreme Court ruled on the merits of a challenge brought by local taxpayers and others to a state statute that required that state school teachers advocating the overthrow of the United States government be fired. Although the local taxpayers, like those in *Doremus*, seemed to lack any economic injury, the Court, oddly, addressed the merits without even mentioning the issue of standing. *Adler v. Board of Education*, 342 U.S. 485 (1952).

E. Standing in the Supreme Court to Review State Court Decisions

  1. Article III applies to the federal courts, including the Supreme Court. Thus, the standing requirements of Article III apply to matters adjudicated in that Court, even when those matters may involve only a review of state court decisions involving federal law.

  2. Because state judiciaries are not governed by Article III, a state may allow its courts to issue advisory opinions or to resolve cases brought by individuals who would not have standing under Article III.

  3. In *ASARCO, Inc. v. Kadish*, 490 U.S. 605 (1989), the Supreme Court held that it had authority to review a decision of the Arizona Supreme Court, even though the plaintiffs would have lacked the standing to sue in federal court under Article III. The Arizona judgment was against the defendants, who then sought to invoke the appellate jurisdiction of the Supreme Court. The negative state court decision harmed the defendants sufficiently to constitute a cognizable injury to permit a federal court to determine the case.

V. Ripeness

A. Sources and Purposes of the Ripeness Requirement

1. While standing is concerned with whether the case is brought by an appropriate plaintiff, both ripeness and mootness (discussed in § VI, below) are concerned with timing. Put roughly, ripeness is concerned with whether the plaintiff has sued "too soon," and mootness is concerned with whether the plaintiff has sued "too late."

2. The ripeness doctrine provides that the federal courts may not adjudicate when it is speculative whether the plaintiff will actually suffer injury. The courts may not become involved before the dispute has matured sufficiently to require an adjudication.

3. To some extent, the requirement flows from the Article III case or controversy requirement. Until a dispute ripens, there is no real case or controversy, and thus nothing the federal courts can adjudicate. The determination may be affected by the level of hardship to be suffered by litigants if the judiciary does not act.

4. To some extent, the ripeness doctrine is also rooted in prudential considerations of when issues ought to be left for decision to the other branches of government. "We have noted that ripeness doctrine is drawn both from Article III limitations on judicial power and from prudential reasons for refusing to exercise jurisdiction." *Reno v. Catholic Social Services*, 509 U.S. 43, 58 n.18 (1993).

5. Without doubt, standing and ripeness concerns can overlap. If a plaintiff sued because she thought she might someday be harmed by the defendant, a court might say either that she lacks standing (because she has not suffered an injury in fact) or that her claim is not ripe (because any harm is still speculative).

6. Ripeness serves similar functions to standing: promotion of separation of powers, promotion of better judicial decision-making by providing concrete facts for decision, and docket control. *See* § IV.B.4, above.

B. Requirements and Application

1. Ripeness focuses on two points: "the fitness of the issues for judicial decision," and "the hardship to the parties of withholding court consideration." *Abbott Laboratories v. Gardner*, 387 U.S. 136, 149 (1967).

2. The "fitness" requirement is largely concerned with whether judicial action is appropriate given the development of the dispute.

   a. In *California Bankers Association v. Schultz*, 416 U.S. 21 (1974), for example, plaintiffs sought to enjoin enforcement of a federal law imposing various reporting requirements for banks, which they claimed would violate bank customers' First Amendment rights. The dispute was not fit for judicial decision, basically because not enough had happened to make clear whether the customers might actually suffer the harm they foresaw. "[I]n the absence of a concrete fact situation in which competing . . . interests can be weighed, [a court] is simply not in a position to determine whether an effort to compel disclosure of such records would or would not be barred." *Id*. at 56.

   b. Sometimes, the question presented is purely one of law, which is fit for review immediately. *See, e.g., Pacific Gas & Electric Co. v. State Energy Resources Conservation & Development Commission*, 461 U.S. 190, 201 (1983)("The question of preemption is predominantly legal, and although it would be useful to have the benefit of California's interpretation of what constitutes a demonstrated technology or means for the disposal of high-level nuclear waste, resolution of the preemption issue need not await that development.").

3. The "hardship" factor assesses the extent to which a delay in judicial action will harm the plaintiff. Thus, in some cases, the Court has allowed adjudication, even though no harm has yet been inflicted, because delay would likely harm the plaintiff.

Example: The Food and Drug Administration (FDA) required that all prescription medications indicate the generic drug names on labels. Drug companies challenged the regulation as being beyond the scope of FDA power. The Supreme Court found the case ripe even though no drug company had been prosecuted for violating the new regulation. The Court noted that violation of the regulation could be punished by civil and criminal penalties, and explained: "If [plaintiffs] wish to comply [with the new regulation] they must change all their labels, advertisements and promotional materials; they must destroy stocks of printed matter; and they must invest heavily in new printing type and new supplies. The alternative to compliance . . . would risk serious criminal and civil penalties. . . . " *Abbott Laboratories v. Gardner,* 387 U.S. 136, 152–53 (1967).

Example: The Court has not always been consistent in this regard. A labor union challenged the constitutionality of a federal statute declaring specified political activities of federal employees to be unlawful. The plaintiffs had not violated the law, and had not been charged under its terms. The Supreme Court held that the case was not ripe, because it was purely speculative whether any harm would result to plaintiffs. *United Public Workers of America v. Mitchell,* 330 U.S. 75 (1947). The problem with the Court's holding, of course, is that the only alternative means to challenge the law would be to risk criminal penalties by actually violating it.

Example: Teachers challenged a provision of a New York statute prohibiting the employment as teachers of those advocating overthrow of the government by force and violence. They did not allege that they had engaged in the proscribed conduct or that they had any intention to do so. The Supreme Court decided the case on its merits, without raising the ripeness issue. *Adler v. Board of Education,* 342 U.S. 485 (1952), discussed at § IV.D.5.c, above. Justice Frankfurter dissented, arguing that the case was not ripe: "The allegations in the present action fall short of those found insufficient in the *Mitchell* case [noted as the preceding *Example*]. These teachers do not allege that they have engaged in proscribed conduct or that they have any intention to do so. They do not suggest that they have been, or are, deterred from supporting causes . . . for fear of the [statute]." *Id.* at 504.

VI. Mootness

A. Sources, Purposes, and Operation of the Mootness Doctrine

1. The doctrine of mootness, like that of ripeness (§ V, above) concerns timing. While ripeness is concerned, roughly, with whether the plaintiff has sued "too soon," mootness addresses whether circumstances have changed so that there is no longer a live dispute between the parties. The inquiry, then, is essentially whether the case is pending when it is "too late" for the court to act.

2. It is not uncommon that cases become moot. For example, if the parties settle their dispute, if a challenged regulation expires, or if a challenged

statute is repealed, the parties' dispute—once live and needing judicial action—is now moot. Other cases, as we will see below, are not as easy.

Example: Plaintiff challenged the constitutionality of a state law school's admissions process. He won in the trial court, and that court ordered the school to admit him to the law school. By the time the case reached the United States Supreme Court, the plaintiff was nearing completion of his final year in law school. The Supreme Court held that the case was moot, because its decision would not affect the plaintiff's interests. *DeFunis v. Odegaard*, 416 U.S. 312 (1974).

3. Mootness derives in part from the Article III case or controversy requirement. If the change in circumstances means that the judicial resolution will be meaningless, there is no case or controversy and the court cannot act. Judicial resolution at that point would constitute nothing more than an impermissible advisory opinion (*see* § III, above).

4. As is true throughout the topic of justiciability, there is a great deal of potential overlap between mootness and other topics, including standing. The Supreme Court, adopting a famous description by Professor Henry Monaghan, has said that mootness can be seen as the "doctrine of standing set in a time frame: The requisite personal interest that must exist at the commencement of the litigation (standing) must continue throughout its existence (mootness)." *United States Parole Commission v. Geraghty*, 445 U.S. 388, 397 (1980).

5. Mootness can serve similar functions to standing and ripeness: promotion of separation of powers, promotion of better judicial decisionmaking by providing concrete facts for decision, and docket control. *See* § IV.B.4, above.

B. Exceptions to the Operation of Mootness

1. The Supreme Court has recognized three major exceptions to the operation of mootness: (1) cases presenting issues "capable of repetition, yet evading review," (2) voluntary cessation, and (3) class actions.

    a. Each of these exceptions can be seen as avoiding mootness when it is expedient to do so.

    b. The problem, of course, is that if mootness is rooted wholly in Article III, expediency cannot be allowed to outweigh the requirements of Article III. Thus, some commentators criticize these exceptions as violating Article III. Others, however, argue that mootness is at least in part a prudential limitation on judicial power, and praise the exceptions as necessary to preserve the proper function of judicial review.

2. The "capable of repetition but evading review" exception recognizes that some harms may pass before litigation can remedy them. The exception requires (1) "a reasonable expectation or a 'demonstrated probability' that the same controversy will recur involving the same complaining party," *Murphy v. Hunt*, 455 U.S. 478, 482 (1982), and (2) that the harm complained of is of such short duration that it will become moot before litigation can remedy it. *Southern Pacific Terminal Co. v. Interstate Commerce Commission*, 219 U.S. 498, 514 (1911).

Example: A state law denied bail before trial to those accused of violent sex crimes. A criminal defendant challenged the law, but was convicted before the challenge was completed. The Supreme Court concluded that this particular defendant was unlikely to be prosecuted and denied bail under this law again, so the exception did not apply. The challenge to the law was moot. *Murphy v. Hunt*, 455 U.S. at 478.

Example: Plaintiff, a pregnant woman, challenged the constitutionality of a state law prohibiting her from getting an abortion. By the time the case reached the Supreme Court, she was no longer pregnant. The Supreme Court agreed to adjudicate the case, however, because it fell within this exception. The limited time of pregnancy effectively precludes any similar case from reaching the Supreme Court for review before the gestation period ends. *Roe v. Wade*, 410 U.S. 113, 125 (1973).

Example: The exception applied to a suit, brought under the Education of the Handicapped Act, brought by an emotionally disturbed 20 year-old who was expelled from a California public school for violent and disruptive behavior. The Act limits eligibility for its protections to disabled children between the ages of three and 21. "Although at present he is not faced with any proposed expulsion or suspension proceedings . . . he remains a resident of California and is entitled to a 'free appropriate public education' within that State. . . . Given [the student's] continued eligibility for educational services under [the Act], the nature of his disability, and [defendant's] insistence that all local school districts retain residual authority to exclude disabled children for dangerous conduct, we have little difficulty concluding that there is a 'reasonable expectation' that [the student] would once again suffer the consequences of defendant's allegedly unlawful conduct." *Honig v. Doe*, 484 U.S. 305, 318–20 (1988).

3. The "voluntary cessation" exception holds that a case will not be considered moot when the defendant has refrained from the challenged conduct if the defendant is free "to return to his old ways" and there is a strong public interest in resolving the legal issue. *United States v. W.T. Grant Co.*, 345 U.S. 629, 632 (1953).

   a. This exception means that a defendant cannot escape judicial action simply by stopping the challenged behavior while remaining free to continue it later.

   Example: The United States sued several corporations, charging that their interlocking boards of directors violated the antitrust laws. After being sued, the defendants indicated that they had eliminated the interlocking directorships and that they had no intention of resuming them. The Supreme Court held that the case was not moot. The voluntary cessation exception did not apply precisely because the defendant was free "to return to his old ways." There was nothing stopping the defendants from reinstituting the practice. *United States v. W.T. Grant Co.*, 345 U.S. at 632.

   b. But the exception will not apply—and the case will be dismissed as moot—if there is no reasonable expectation that the defendant will resume the challenged activity. *County of Los Angeles v. Davis*, 440 U.S. 625 (1979)(interim injunctive relief ensured that county would not resume discriminatory hiring practices; case dismissed as moot). Recently, the Supreme Court held that the party asserting mootness has the burden of showing that it is "absolutely clear" that the behavior will not recur. *Friends of the Earth, Inc. v. Laidlaw Environmental Services*, 528 U.S. 167, 189 (2000).

4. The Supreme Court has been flexible in dealing with mootness in the class action context.

   a. If a class action is certified, the dispute will not be rendered moot even when the named representative no longer has an interest in the outcome. *Sosna v. Iowa*, 419 U.S. 393 (1975)(in class action challenging residency requirement for divorce, named representative satisfied the requirement during pendency of the case). So long as *some* member of the class has a live controversy, the class action may proceed. In effect, the class members—not just the named representative—are seen as plaintiffs for purposes of mootness.

    b. In *Sosna*, the class action had been certified before the representative plaintiff's claim was mooted. The Court has explained, however, that "[a]lthough one might argue that *Sosna* contains at least an implication that the critical factor for Art. III purposes is the timing of class certification, other cases, applying a 'relation back' approach, clearly demonstrate that timing is not crucial." *United States Parole Commission v. Geraghty*, 445 U.S. 388, 398 (1980). In *Geraghty*, the named representative's claim expired while the case was on appeal. The Court held "that an action brought on behalf of a class does not become moot upon expiration of the named plaintiff's substantive claim, even though class certification has been denied. The proposed representative retains a 'personal stake' in obtaining class certification sufficient to assure that Art. III values are not undermined." *Id*. at 404.

    c. Similarly, a named representative may continue to prosecute an appeal of the denial of class certification even if she has settled her individual claims. *Deposit Guaranty National Bank v. Roper*, 445 U.S. 326 (1980). And a member of a proposed class may intervene to appeal the denial of class certification. *United Airlines, Inc. v. McDonald*, 432 U.S. 385 (1973).

VII. Political Question Doctrine

A. Sources and Purposes of the Political Question Doctrine

1. The political question doctrine stands for the proposition that some issues of constitutional law are beyond the competence of the federal judiciary. If the Constitution commits a particular matter to one of the political branches of the federal government, the federal judiciary should decline to adjudicate it.

2. The doctrine shares this much with other principles of justiciability: it is undeniably based upon the concept of separation of powers.

3. But political question differs from the prohibition against advisory opinions, standing, ripeness, and mootness in a fundamental way: it holds that certain disputes—no matter how live, concrete, and ripe—are simply not judicially cognizable; they are, rather, simply beyond the competence of the federal judiciary.

4. By declining to adjudicate political questions, the bench avoids potentially dangerous confrontations between it and the coordinate branches of the federal government. By doing so, it may also funnel decisionmaking to the branch of government with the greatest expertise on the matter.

5. Because the doctrine concerns separation of powers among the branches of the federal government, it does not apply to clashes between the federal judiciary and branches of state governments. Such clashes are justiciable, assuming the other requirements of justiciability are satisfied.

6. The political question doctrine has deep judicial roots. In *Marbury v. Madison*, discussed at § II.B, above, Chief Justice Marshall noted that there are "political act[s], belonging to the executive department alone, for the performance of which entire confidence is placed by our constitution in the supreme executive; and for any misconduct respecting which, the injured individual has no remedy." 5 U.S. at 164. Although Marshall spoke of acts reposed in the executive department alone, the doctrine applies to acts that are the sole responsibility of the legislative branch as well.

7. Although each area of justiciability is plagued by uncertainty, as seen above, commentators seem to feel that the lack of meaningful guidance and principle is worse here than in other areas. Moreover, the name "political question" is misleading. Not all questions dealing with political rights fall within the doctrine.

8. More important than the ubiquitous criticism of the doctrine's lack of certainty is the argument by some commentators that the doctrine has no place in American government. Invoking the political question doctrine, they argue, constitutes an abdication of the judiciary's responsibility to interpret and enforce the Constitution. Interpretation of the Constitution is a responsibility vested by that document in the unelected federal judiciary. The Founders intended that function to be performed by the nonpolitical branch. Contrary to that intent, the political question doctrine funnels the control back to one of the majoritarian branches.

B. Modern Explication of the Political Question Doctrine

1. *Baker v. Carr,* 369 U.S. 186 (1962), contains the leading explication of the political question doctrine. The Supreme Court held that a claim that state legislative apportionment violated equal protection did not come within the political question rule and thus was justiciable. In the course of the discussion of that doctrine, the Court listed six relevant factors in assessing whether a case presents a political question. The presence of any one of these factors may trigger application of the doctrine and counsel the federal court to dismiss the case. *Id.* at 217.

   a. A "textual commitment of a matter to another branch of the federal government."

   Example: The "Republican form of government" clause, or "Guaranty Clause," Article IV, § 4, of the Constitution, provides that "[t]he United States shall guarantee to every State in this Union a Republican form of Government." Claims arising under this clause present political questions that the federal courts will not adjudicate, in part because by its terms the provision may be deemed to commit enforcement to another branch of the federal government. *Luther v. Borden,* 48 U.S. 1 (1849)(refusing to determine which competing group constituted the legitimate government of Rhode Island).

   b. A "lack of judicially discoverable and manageable standards" for resolving the legal issue.

   Example: The "Republican form of government" clause is an example of such a provision.

   c. The "impossibility of deciding without an initial policy determination of a kind clearly for nonjudicial discretion. . . . "

   d. The danger of "expressing lack of the respect due coordinate branches of government . . . "

   e. An "unusual need for unquestioning adherence to a political decision already made. . . . "

   Example: The Court has invoked the political question doctrine to avoid deciding questions about the validity of the constitutional amendment process.

f. The "potentiality of embarrassment from multifarious pronouncements by various departments on one question."

2. Some commentators see these six factors as embodying three themes. First, the constitutional allocation of the matter to another branch. Second, a functional approach that counsels courts to stay away from policy areas in which there are no clear judicial standards. And third, prudential considerations involving comity, respect for a political decision that has already been made, and avoidance of embarrassment.

C. Categories of Cases to Which the Political Question Doctrine Has Been Applied and the Case Dismissed

1. Republican form of government clause.

   a. In *Luther v. Borden*, 48 U.S. 1 (1849), the Supreme Court refused to decide which of two competing factions constituted the legitimate government of Rhode Island, invoking the political question doctrine.

   b. In *Texas v. White*, 74 U.S. (7 Wall.) 700 (1869), the Court held that only Congress has the authority to reestablish and recognize governments in the states that had seceded during the Civil War.

2. Foreign affairs.

   a. In *Goldwater v. Carter*, 444 U.S. 996 (1979), a group of senators challenged the legality of the President's unilateral notice of termination of the nation's mutual defense treaty with the Republic of China. The Supreme Court summarily vacated the opinion of the court of appeals and ordered the case dismissed.

   b. Justice Rehnquist, speaking for four Justices in *Goldwater*, concurred separately, arguing that the case was non-justiciable because the Constitution was silent on how a treaty is to be terminated, and thus the issue should be left to the political process. Moreover, he noted, the case involved the authority of the President to conduct foreign affairs.

   c. In *Baker v. Carr*, 369 U.S. 186, 211 (1962), the Court noted that issues of foreign affairs frequently "turn on standards that defy judicial application, or involve the exercise of a discretion demonstrably committed to the executive or legislature." In the same breath, however, the Court added that "it is error to suppose that every case or controversy which touches foreign relations lies beyond judicial cognizance." *Id*.

3. Impeachment. The Constitution vests "sole"power of impeachment in the House of Representatives and "sole" power to try all impeachments to the Senate. Thus, the federal courts will not intervene in any aspect of impeachment. *Nixon v. United States*, 506 U.S. 224 (1993)(refusing to rule on challenge to procedures used in impeachment of federal district judge Walter Nixon).

4. Dates of duration of hostilities. In *Commercial Trust Company v. Miller*, 262 U.S. 51 (1923), the issue was whether a congressional proclamation had ended World War I and thus ended the applicability of the Trading with the Enemy Act. The Court concluded: "[T]he power which declared the necessity is the power to declare its cessation, and what the cessation requires. The power is legislative." *Id*. at 67.

5. Regulation of political parties. While in a number of cases the Supreme Court has demonstrated a willingness to review the constitutionality of the actions of political parties, in *Cousins v. Wigoda*, 419 U.S. 477, 483 (1975), the Court expressly left unresolved the question "whether or to what extent national political parties and their nominating conventions are regulable by, or only by, Congress."

6. Judicial review of the training and weaponry of the National Guard.

    a. In *Gilligan v. Morgan*, 413 U.S. 1 (1973), the Supreme Court held that constitutional challenges to the training and weaponry of the Ohio National Guard are non-justiciable.

    b. The Court found a conflict with a coordinate branch of the *federal* government, because Article I, § 8, clause 16 of the Constitution vests in Congress the power "[t]o provide for organizing, arming, and disciplining the Militia, and for governing such Part of them as may be employed in the Service of the United States, reserving to the States respectively the Appointment of the Officers, and the Authority of training the Militia according to the discipline *prescribed by Congress*." *Id*. at 6.

D. Areas in Which Application of the Political Question Doctrine Has Been Rejected

1. The constitutionality under the equal protection clause of state representational apportionment. The Court rejected the applicability of the doctrine to such cases in *Baker v. Carr*. That decision surprised some commentators, since it broke from past practice, under which the Court invoked the doctrine and refused to hear such cases. Justice Frankfurter, dissenting in *Baker*, argued that apportionment cases were in reality "republican form of government" cases, and therefore should be deemed non-justiciable. 369 U.S. at 289–92.

2. Exclusion of a member of Congress by one of the houses of Congress. In *Powell v. McCormack*, 395 U.S. 486 (1969), a congressman-elect challenged the House of Representatives' decision not to seat him. Because Article I, § 5, of the Constitution authorizes "each house [to] be the judge of the elections, returns and qualifications of its members," and, "with the concurrence of two thirds, [to] expel a member," there was a strong argument that the issue was committed to the legislative branch. Nonetheless, the Court noted that the congressman-elect met the "qualifications" set out by the Constitution, and held that his exclusion on other grounds was justiciable. Historically, the Court explained, the quoted provisions had not been intended to provide the houses of Congress such unreviewable authority to expel members.

3. Claims of executive privilege. President Nixon's claim of executive privilege regarding Watergate tapes did not present a political question. *United States v. Nixon*, 418 U.S. 683 (1974).

II

Congressional Power to Regulate Federal Jurisdiction

■ ANALYSIS

I. Introduction
II. Distinction Between Congressional Power Over Jurisdiction of the Supreme Court and of the Lower Federal Courts
   A. Article III Provisions About Establishment of the Supreme Court and the Lower Federal Courts
   B. The Distinction Between Original and Appellate Jurisdiction of the Supreme Court
   C. Relevance of Other Constitutional Provisions
III. Congressional Power to Regulate Lower Federal Court Jurisdiction
   A. The Traditional Theory of Broad Congressional Power
   B. Alternative Constructions of Article III
   C. Recent Congressional Regulation of Lower Federal Court Jurisdiction
IV. Congressional Power to Regulate Supreme Court Original Jurisdiction
   A. Article III Self-Executing Regarding Some Cases
   B. Congressional Role Regarding Original Supreme Court Jurisdiction

V. **Congressional Power to Regulate Supreme Court Appellate Jurisdiction**
   A. The Exceptions Clause
   B. *Ex Parte McCardle* and the Theory of Broad Congressional Power
   C. The "Essential Functions" Theory
   D. The Limitation-as-to-Fact Theory

VI. **Limitations on Congressional Power Deriving From Other Constitutional Provisions**
   A. Equal Protection
   B. Due Process
   C. Separation of Powers

VII. **Congressional Power to Vest Article III Federal Courts With Non–Article III Powers**
   A. Characteristics of an Article III Court
   B. The Concept of "Non–Article III Powers"
   C. Article III Courts Performing Non–Judicial Functions
   D. Article III Courts Entertaining Cases Not Falling Within the Judicial Power of the United States

I. Introduction

The issue here is what power Congress has to regulate the jurisdiction of the federal courts. The answer depends in part on Article III and perhaps other provisions of the Constitution. In addition, congressional power may be different for the Supreme Court than for the lower federal courts, and there is also an important distinction in this regard between the Supreme Court's appellate jurisdiction and its original (trial) jurisdiction. In several instances, there is little or no case guidance, but there are important academic theories. In some instances, there is case guidance, but its ultimate application is unclear. These issues are important because they determine the extent to which Congress can engage in "jurisdiction stripping"—removing certain types of disputes from the federal court docket, perhaps because Congress is displeased with the substantive rulings the judiciary has been rendering in specific areas.

II. Distinction Between Congressional Power Over the Jurisdiction of the Supreme Court and of the Lower Federal Courts

A. Article III Provisions About Establishment of the Supreme Court and Lower Federal Courts

1. Article III, § 1, of the Constitution provides that "[t]he judicial Power of the United States shall be vested in one Supreme Court, and in such inferior Courts as the Congress may from time to time ordain and establish."

2. This provision expressly mandates that there be a Supreme Court. Just as clearly, it vests in Congress at least the original decision of whether to create any lower ("inferior") federal courts. We will see below that all assumptions about congressional power to control the jurisdiction of the lower federal courts flow from this fact. As a commonsense notion, if Congress has the authority to create lower federal courts, it seems plausible that it should have broad power to regulate the jurisdiction of those courts.

3. Because the Supreme Court's existence is required, however, no similar conclusion may be drawn about congressional power over its jurisdiction.

B. The Distinction Between Original and Appellate Jurisdiction of the Supreme Court

1. Article III, § 2, clause 2 provides that "[i]n all Cases affecting Ambassadors, other public Ministers and Consuls, and those in which a State shall be Party, the supreme Court shall have original jurisdiction. In all the other Cases before mentioned [in Article III, § 2, clause 1], the supreme Court shall have appellate Jurisdiction, both as to Law and Fact, with such Exceptions, and under such Regulations as the Congress shall make."

2. This provision requires that the Supreme Court have original jurisdiction only in cases affecting ambassadors and other public ministers and consuls, and when a state is a party. Original jurisdiction means that the Supreme Court has trial jurisdiction. Such cases are fairly rare, but when they arise, the language of Article III is clearly mandatory: the Supreme Court will try the case.

3. Article III, § 2, clause 1 lists nine types of cases within the judicial power of the federal courts. Two of these types, as we just saw, are expressly vested in the Supreme Court for trial, though the Court's original jurisdiction has been held not to be exclusive.

4. The vast majority of the Supreme Court's workload concerns its appellate jurisdiction. As to this aspect of Supreme Court jurisdiction, Article III, § 2, clause 2 provides in all other cases—presumably the other seven types of cases that can be heard by the federal judiciary—the Supreme Court is to have appellate jurisdiction, as to law and fact, "with such Exceptions, and under such Regulations as the Congress shall make." This provision is known as the "Exceptions Clause." Clearly, it vests some power in Congress to tailor the appellate jurisdiction of the Supreme Court.

C. Relevance of Other Constitutional Provisions

1. In addition to considering the meaning of the language of Article III, those who debate congressional power over federal court jurisdiction also point to other provisions of the Constitution which might limit the legislature's power.

2. In particular, the Due Process Clause of the Fifth Amendment, the "equal

protection" component that has been read into that clause, and the largely implicit constitutional doctrine of separation of powers may prove relevant.

III. Congressional Power to Regulate Lower Federal Court Jurisdiction

A. The Traditional Theory of Broad Congressional Power

1. By its terms, Article III vests in Congress the original decision of whether to establish lower federal courts. *See* § I.A.1 & 2, above. According to the generally accepted historical analysis, the Framers reached an impasse between two groups. One group believed that the Constitution should mandate the creation of lower federal courts. The other believed the Constitution should prohibit lower federal courts and that state courts should be the only trial courts for the adjudication of federal law, with appellate supervision by the Supreme Court. The "Madisonian Compromise" resolved the deadlock. Under that agreement, the question of whether lower federal courts should be established was left to Congress.

2. Although Congress immediately established lower federal courts in the Judiciary Act of 1789, the historical assumption has been—and in large measure continues to be—that Congress did not have to do so. As a consequence, historically it has been assumed that if Congress did create lower federal courts, it could later abolish them. And if Congress may abolish lower federal courts, the long-held assumption has been that Congress may instead choose the less radical step of limiting their jurisdiction. In other words, the "greater" power (to abolish lower federal courts altogether) includes the "lesser" power (to curb their jurisdiction without abolishing them).

3. This logical principle—that the greater power includes the lesser power—underlies the Supreme Court's long-held conclusion that Congress has very broad power to limit the jurisdiction of the lower federal courts. *See, e.g., Lockerty v. Phillips,* 319 U.S. 182 (1943); *Sheldon v. Sill,* 49 U.S. 441 (1850).

4. Because the Framers vested discretion in Congress to choose not to create lower federal courts, it was apparently their assumption that Congress could choose instead to rely on state courts as the primary adjudicators of federal law and enforcers of federal rights. This conclusion is underscored by the Supremacy Clause of the Constitution, Article

VI, clause 2, which obligates the state courts to obey and enforce federal law as "the supreme law of the land . . . any thing in the Constitution or laws of any state to the contrary notwithstanding."

5. Thus, although Congress created lower federal courts in 1789, it was not until 1875 that it enacted a permanent general grant of federal question jurisdiction. Until then, Congress largely relied on the state judiciary as the original fora for the adjudication of federal law. *See* Chapter 4, § III.A.

B. Alternative Constructions of Article III

1. The traditional theory that Congress has plenary power to regulate the jurisdiction of the lower federal courts has dominated. But it is not the only theory. Other major notions concerning congressional control of lower court jurisdiction include: (a) Justice Story's mandatory theory, (b) the "changing circumstances" theory, and (c) the "two-tier" theory.

2. Justice Joseph Story argued in the early 19th century that Congress lacked any authority to regulate lower federal court jurisdiction. In dictum in *Martin v. Hunter's Lessee*, 14 U.S. 304, 328–31 (1816), Story noted that Article III states that the federal judicial power "*shall* be vested" in the Supreme Court and the lower federal courts that Congress may establish. He construed the mandatory word "shall" to require that the whole of federal judicial power be exercised *somewhere in the federal judiciary*. Because the Supreme Court only has appellate jurisdiction in many areas, Story reasoned that if no lower federal court existed there would be no original forum from which an appeal could be taken to the Supreme Court.

   a. Thus, Story opined, Congress was under a duty (1) to create lower federal courts and (2) to vest in them the full judicial power—all types of cases listed in Article III, § 2, clause 1 (except, of course, those two types of cases in which the Supreme Court has original jurisdiction). "If, then, it is the duty of Congress to vest the judicial power of the United States, it is a duty to vest the whole judicial power. The language, if imperative as to one part, is imperative as to all." *Id.* at 330.

   b. Although Congress has always provided for lower federal courts, it never has vested in them the entire judicial power. In Chapters 4 and 5, we will see statutory limitations, respectively, on federal question and diversity of citizenship jurisdiction, which make it obvious that Congress did not vest the whole constitutional grant of those two bases of jurisdiction.

c. Noting this fact, Story concluded that while the Constitution was mandatory on these points, it was not self-executing. Thus, if Congress failed to vest the whole of the judicial power in the lower courts, nothing could be done about it. *See White v. Fenner*, 29 Fed. Cas. 1015 (Cir.Ct.D.R.I. 1818)(Story, J., sitting as circuit judge).

d. Story's theory also ignores the possibility that state courts would be available to determine questions of federal law, subject to appellate review in the Supreme Court. That is, if Congress created no lower federal courts, the various types of cases within the appellate jurisdiction of the Supreme Court would be heard, in the first instance, in state court.

e. Some modern commentators have supported Story's theory, arguing that the Framers felt that state courts would fail to hear cases involving federal issues. On the whole, however, Story's theory has not fared well historically. The typical Supreme Court view long has been: "Congress is not bound, and it would, perhaps, be inexpedient, to enlarge the jurisdiction of the federal courts, to every subject, in every form, which the constitution might warrant." *Turner v. The President, Directors, and Co. of the Bank of North America*, 4 U.S. 8, 10 (1799).

f. One interesting case is consistent with the Story theory. Indeed, the language of the opinion is broader than the Story theory. In *Eisenstrager v. Forrestal*, 174 F.2d 961 (D.C. Cir. 1947), *rev'd on other grounds*, 339 U.S. 763 (1950), a prisoner of the American military in Germany sought habeas corpus relief from the federal court for the District of Columbia. The relevant statutes, however, required that federal habeas be sought only from a court in the district in which the petitioner is imprisoned. There was no such district, of course, in Germany. Moreover, no state court can grant habeas relief to one in federal custody. *See* Chapter 15, § II. The Supreme Court lacked original jurisdiction, so there appeared to be no court that could entertain the petition. The District of Columbia Circuit exercised jurisdiction over the case, holding that Congress has a duty to confer all of the judicial power on some *federal* court. The court held that the Constitution itself compelled this exercise of jurisdiction. Thus, the court went beyond Story, to conclude that the Constitution was self-enacting in this regard. Moreover, it noted, a lack of jurisdiction would effectively allow the government to suspend the writ of habeas corpus, in violation of Art. I, § 9, cl. 2 of the Constitution.

3. Several modern commentators have argued what can be called the "changing circumstances" theory. They assert that changing circumstances today render the original plan of the Framers unworkable. At the time of the drafting of the Constitution, the Framers could rely on the availability of the Supreme Court to unify federal law and to police state courts. The modern workload of the Supreme Court, and sheer numbers of cases in various trial courts, makes this assumption untenable today. This theory has not been tested in the courts, and it seems unlikely that it would win widespread acceptance.

4. Several modern commentators have also espoused a "two-tier" theory regarding congressional power to control lower court jurisdiction. Justice Story initially raised this idea, as an alternative to his mandatory theory discussed above. Proponents argue that some federal court—either a lower court or the Supreme Court—must be available to adjudicate cases arising under federal law, cases affecting ambassadors, and admiralty cases. These three categories are selected for special treatment because they are the only categories of cases listed in Article III, § 2, clause 1 preceded by the word "all." Thus, all cases falling within these three heads of jurisdiction must be tried by some federal court. There is little if any historical evidence to demonstrate that the Framers considered such an opinion.

C. Recent Congressional Regulation of Lower Federal Court Jurisdiction

1. Congress passed the Antiterrorism and Effective Death Penalty Act (AEDPA) and the Illegal Immigration Reform and Immigrant Responsibility Act (IIRIRA) in 1996. These Acts amended the Immigration and Nationality Act in significant ways and purported to restrict the power of federal courts to review certain immigration and deportation orders made by the Immigration and Naturalization Service (INS).

2. One part of the 1996 legislation limits judicial review in the deportation context to three issues: (a) the decision to commence proceedings, (b) adjudication of cases, and (c) execution of the deportation orders. The Acts clearly provided that this section was to apply even to deportation proceedings in effect at their effective date. Certain immigrants sued to

challenge the deportation proceedings against them, and contended that the government engaged in selective enforcement, targeting them because they were members of politically unpopular groups. In *Reno v. American–Arab Anti–Discrimination Committee*, 525 U.S. 471, 486 (1999), the Supreme Court upheld the restriction on jurisdiction and ordered the case dismissed for lack of jurisdiction. Because the plaintiffs did not raise one of the three issues within the limited grant of judicial review, the courts were powerless to hear the case.

    a.   The Court concluded that "protecting the Executive's discretion from the courts . . . can fairly be said to be the theme of the legislation."

    b.   A lower court, discussing one of the Acts, noted that it removed jurisdiction to review "not only a decision in an individual case *whether* to commence, but also *when* to commence, a proceeding [for removal of an alien]." Thus, the court lacked jurisdiction to review the petitioner's claim that the INS was under an obligation to commence deportation proceedings immediately upon learning that she was in the United States illegally. *Jimenez-Angeles v. Ashcroft*, 291 F.3d 594, 599 (9th Cir. 2002)(emphasis original).

IV. Congressional Power to Regulate Supreme Court Original Jurisdiction

A. Article III Self–Executing Regarding Some Cases

1.   As noted, Article III, § 1 of the Constitution requires that the Supreme Court be established. *See* § I.A, above. Thus, unlike the situation with the lower federal courts, Congress has no power to abolish the Supreme Court. Consequently, the "greater power includes the lesser power" theory that underlies the dominant view of congressional power over lower federal court jurisdiction cannot apply to Supreme Court jurisdiction. *See* § III.A, above.

2.   Article III, § 2, clause 2 provides that in two types of cases—(a) those "affecting Ambassadors, other public Ministers and Consuls," and (b) those "in which a State shall be a party"—the Supreme Court "shall have original Jurisdiction."

3.   The Supreme Court has held that this provision is self-executing. That is, the Constitution itself vests the Supreme Court with this trial jurisdiction, even in the absence of action by Congress.

a. The first case so holding was *Chisholm v. Georgia*, 2 U.S. 419 (1793), in which a citizen of South Carolina sued the state of Georgia. The Court concluded that the language of Article III clearly vested original jurisdiction in it. One justice dissented, arguing that in the absence of a statute, the Court should apply the common law rule precluding actions against a sovereign.

b. *Chisholm* inspired the Eleventh Amendment, which removes federal jurisdiction in actions against states. *See* Chapter 9.

B. Congressional Role Regarding Supreme Court Original Jurisdiction

1. Because the original jurisdiction of the Supreme Court with regard to two classes of cases is self-executing, all observers seem to agree that Congress cannot restrict it. Congress has never tried to do so expressly. *See Wisconsin v. Pelican Insurance Company of New Orleans*, 127 U.S. 265, 300 (1888).

2. In *South Carolina v. Katzenbach*, 383 U.S. 301, 357 n. 1 (1966), Justice Black, dissenting, suggested that a provision of the Voting Rights Act of 1965 would be unconstitutional if it were interpreted to limit the Supreme Court's original jurisdiction in actions by the United States against a state. The Act was not interpreted in that fashion.

3. Article III does not provide that the original jurisdiction of the Supreme Court is *exclusive*. Accordingly, Congress does have the power to grant original jurisdiction over these types of cases to a lower federal court. *United States v. California*, 297 U.S. 175 (1936).

4. In *Marbury v. Madison*, 5 U.S. 137 (1803), the Supreme Court held unconstitutional Congress' effort to expand its original jurisdiction by vesting it with jurisdiction to issue mandamus to federal officers. It concluded that issuance of mandamus to the Secretary of State was a function of original, not appellate jurisdiction. Chief Justice Marshall noted that Article III prescribes only two classes of cases as falling within the original jurisdiction of the Supreme Court, and that *Marbury* did not fall within either of them. Because Article III provides that in all other cases the Supreme Court "shall have appellate Jurisdiction," the effort to vest original jurisdiction in the Court was unconstitutional. Marshall said: "If congress remains at liberty to give this court appellate jurisdiction, where the constitution has declared their jurisdiction shall be original; and original jurisdiction where the constitution has declared it

shall be appellate; the distribution of jurisdiction, made in the constitution, is form without substance." *Id.* at 174.

5. The Supreme Court has discretion to refuse to hear a case invoking its original jurisdiction, and is reluctant to hear cases between a state and a private litigant when another forum is available for trial. *See Ohio v. Wyandotte Chemicals Corp.*, 401 U.S. 493 (1971)(claim based on common law nuisance theory better tried in another court, with the possibility of Supreme Court appellate review).

V. Congressional Power to Regulate Supreme Court Appellate Jurisdiction

A. The Exceptions Clause

1. After delineating the Supreme Court's original jurisdiction, Article III, § 2, clause 2 provides in "all the other Cases [within the judicial power of the United States], the supreme Court shall have appellate jurisdiction, both as to Law and Fact, with such Exceptions, and under such Regulations as the Congress shall make."

2. Clearly, the "Exceptions Clause" vests some power in Congress to tailor the appellate jurisdiction of the Supreme Court.

B. *Ex Parte McCardle* and the Theory of Broad Congressional Power

1. *Ex Parte McCardle*, 74 U.S. 506 (1868), involved an extraordinary set of facts. McCardle was incarcerated in Mississippi under Reconstruction statutes. After the federal trial denied his petition for habeas corpus, he appealed to the Supreme Court. A recent statute had created that appellate jurisdiction. McCardle argued that he was entitled to habeas corpus because the Reconstruction statutes under which he was held were unconstitutional. After oral argument at the Supreme Court, members of Congress, fearful that the Supreme Court would invalidate the challenged parts of the Reconstruction legislation, repealed the statute that had created appellate jurisdiction in the Supreme Court.

   a. The Supreme Court refused to reach the merits of the case, and held that Congress' repeal of its appellate jurisdiction was effective. The repealer was a legitimate exercise of the legislative power under the Exceptions Clause. The fact that the case was pending on appeal when Congress acted was irrelevant.

b. The repeal of appellate jurisdiction is an archetypal example of "jurisdiction stripping." Congress took the act precisely because it feared how the Court would rule on the merits of the challenge to the Reconstruction statutes.

2. The opinion in *McCardle* contains broad language implying nearly unfettered congressional authority under the Exceptions Clause. Indeed, through the years, many people have, in the words of Professor Henry Hart, read *McCardle* "for all it's worth"—as a signal that Congress has essentially plenary power over the Supreme Court's appellate jurisdiction.

3. In recent years, however, many have argued that *McCardle* should not be read as giving such expansive power to Congress. They point out that just one year after the decision in *McCardle*, the Supreme Court held that it had the authority to issue *original* writs of habeas corpus. *Ex Parte Yerger*, 75 U.S. 85 (1869). Thus, although Congress removed the Supreme Court's appellate jurisdiction to review habeas cases, another statute allowed the Court to issue original writs. In view of this fact, commentators argue, *McCardle* may stand for the proposition that Congress may remove Supreme Court appellate jurisdiction so long as Supreme Court review of the question is available by other means.

4. The important 1996 amendments to immigration law—the AEDPA and IIRIRA—are noted at § III.C, above. One part of the AEDPA prohibits prisoners in state custody from filing successive petitions for habeas corpus unless the United States Court of Appeals approves such repeat petitions. In addition, the Act precludes any review by the Supreme Court of a Court of Appeals decision concerning a state prisoner's petition to file successive habeas petitions. The Supreme Court unanimously upheld the restriction on its jurisdiction, but emphasized that the legislation did not completely preclude Supreme Court review of the denial of permission to file successive petitions, because the Court retains the authority to entertain original petitions for habeas corpus relief. *Felker v. Turpin*, 518 U.S. 651 (1996).

C. The "Essential Functions" Theory

1. Several commentators have argued that Congress may not make exceptions to the Supreme Court's appellate jurisdiction that will destroy the essential role of the Supreme Court in the constitutional plan. The asserted functions of the Court deemed to be "essential" are to provide

a uniform interpretation of federal law and to police state court interpretation and enforcement of federal law. They note the fact discussed at § B.3, above, that the congressional restriction upheld in *McCardle* did not completely remove the Supreme Court from reviewing habeas corpus matters. Thus, the statute in *McCardle* did not totally block access to the Supreme Court in a case involving the supremacy of federal law.

2. While there is neither a linguistic nor firm historical basis upon which to support this theory, its advocates find it implicit in our constitutional structure. The theory has never been tested in the courts.

D. The Limitation–As–To–Fact Theory

1. Several commentators have focused on the phrase immediately preceding the Exceptions Clause. Article III, § 2, clause 2 states that the Supreme Court shall have appellate jurisdiction, "both as to law and fact," with such exceptions and regulations as Congress shall make. These commentators argue that the Founders intended to limit Congress' authority under the Exceptions Clause to the power to limit Supreme Court review of factual determinations.

2. While there is historical evidence that the Framers were concerned with the Supreme Court's review of lower court findings of fact, the language of the clause simply does not lend itself to such a limited interpretation. In addition, the broader grant of the Supreme Court's appellate jurisdiction in the Judiciary Act of 1789 is a strong indication that the Framers did not intend such a narrow scope of appellate review. Finally, *McCardle* at least implicitly rejected this theory, since the limitation on the Court's appellate jurisdiction upheld there was not confined to review of factual findings.

VI. Limitations on Congressional Power Deriving From Other Constitutional Provisions

A. Equal Protection

1. Although the Fifth Amendment contains no express equal protection provision, the Supreme Court has construed that Amendment's Due Process Clause to include such a requirement. Thus, it is clear that Congress cannot employ its Article III power, for example, to prohibit racial or religious minorities from gaining access to the federal courts.

2. In fact, some commentators argue that the equal protection component extends further, to prevent Congress from limiting access to the federal courts for specific fundamental rights, because such a limitation would discriminate on the basis of a fundamental right. This theory has not yet been tested in the courts.

B. Due Process

1. The Supreme Court has held that the Due Process Clause requires that neither liberty nor property may be taken absent some form of hearing before an independent adjudicator. It has even been suggested that due process may require an independent *judicial* forum, although the status and contours of this requirement have not been fully defined. *See, e.g., Bartlett v. Bowen*, 816 F.2d 695 (D.C. Cir. 1987); *Battaglia v. General Motors Corp.*, 169 F.2d 254 (2d Cir. 1948), *cert. denied*, 335 U.S. 887 (1948).

2. It is unlikely, however, that this constitutional requirement imposes significant limits on congressional authority to regulate the jurisdiction of the lower federal courts or the appellate jurisdiction of the Supreme Court. As to the former, while due process may prevent Congress from denying access to *any* judicial forum for the adjudication of a constitutional right (*see Bartlett* and *Battaglia*), traditionally Congress has been able to satisfy the due process requirement by allowing the *state* courts to serve as the ultimate protector of federal constitutional rights. Congress is justified in this conclusion because—as reflected in the Madisonian Compromise and the Supremacy Clause—state courts are both empowered and obligated to vindicate federal rights. *See* § III.A.1. & 4, above.

3. A limitation of the Supreme Court's appellate jurisdiction will not violate due process, because due process has never been construed to require any level of appellate review.

C. Separation of Powers

1. While Congress may well retain broad power to limit the jurisdiction of the federal courts, the implied constitutional doctrine of separation of powers has been construed to confine that power. This doctrinal limitation arises even if one accepts the proposition that the "Exceptions Clause" would permit Congress to remove the Supreme Court's appellate jurisdiction altogether.

2. *United States v. Klein*, 80 US. 128 (1871), involved a statute passed during the Civil War. It permitted persons whose property had been seized to recover it, or its monetary value, if they could show that they had not aided the rebellion. The Supreme Court held in 1869 that a presidential pardon constituted proof for purposes of this statute that someone had not aided the rebellion. *United States v. Padelford*, 76 U.S. 531 (1869). In reaction to numerous presidential pardons, Congress then passed a statute providing that such a pardon was proof that the person *had* aided the enemy and that once a pardon was proved, "the jurisdiction of the court shall cease" and the case for recovery of property would be dismissed.

   a. The Court held the statute unconstitutional. "What is this [law] but to prescribe a rule for the decision of a cause in a particular way?" the Court asked. "We must think that Congress has inadvertently passed the limit which separates the legislative power from the judicial power." *Klein*, 80 U.S. at 146, 147.

   b. Commentators have long debated the scope of the holding in *Klein*. Some interpret *Klein* broadly to mean that Congress cannot restrict jurisdiction to direct a particular substantive outcome. Others argue for a narrower reading. These commentators note that the statute at issue in *Klein* was itself an unconstitutional interference of the President's pardon power under Article II, § 2, of the Constitution, and that it arguably effected a denial of property without just compensation, in violation of due process. Thus, they see *Klein* as holding only that Congress cannot limit jurisdiction by using a statute that violates other provisions of the Constitution.

   c. In 1980, the Supreme Court described *Klein* as having held the statute unconstitutional in two respects: "it prescribed a rule of decision in a case pending before the courts, and did so in a manner that required the courts to decide a controversy in the Government's favor." *United States v. Sioux Nation of Indians*, 448 U.S. 371, 404 (1980).

   d. This interpretation in *Sioux Nation* supports a relatively broad reading of *Klein*, because it does not require that the congressional act itself be unconstitutional. In the narrower interpretation, noted in § b, above, *Klein* would apply only if the statute violates some other constitutional provision, such as the President's pardon power.

3. The Supreme Court revisited *Klein* in 1992. The case involved an appropriations statute that required the Bureau of Land Management to offer certain land for sale and to restrict other land from harvesting. The Act then took note of two actual cases and set out Congress' determination that if the specific land involved in those two suits were managed according to certain substantive provisions of the Act, that would constitute "adequate consideration for the purpose of meeting the statutory requirements that are the basis for [the two pending cases]." The Supreme Court upheld the law in *Robertson v. Seattle Audubon Society*, 503 U.S. 429 (1992).

   a. The Ninth Circuit had held that *Klein* applied and rendered the statute unconstitutional, but the Supreme Court reversed that decision, and found *Klein* distinguishable.

   b. According to the Supreme Court, *Klein* applies when Congress dictates to the courts a substantive decision under an extant law. In contrast, *Robertson* involved Congress' adoption of a new substantive law. Thus, *Klein* did not govern.

   c. Some commentators have found the Court's effort to distinguish the two fact patterns unconvincing.

4. Even more recently, the Supreme Court indicated, albeit in a different context, that principles of separation of powers limit congressional power in this general area. After the Supreme Court had held that certain securities fraud cases must be brought within a specific (relatively short) period, Congress amended the securities laws to allow cases to proceed if they were filed before the Supreme Court decision and would have been timely under the law as it had been thought to exist. The Court held that this statute violated separation of powers and thus was unconstitutional. *Plaut v. Spendthrift Farm, Inc.*, 514 U.S. 211 (1995).

   a. The statute was unconstitutional because it robbed the judiciary of its power to "render dispositive judgments." The statute would have permitted a party to proceed and seek relief after the federal judiciary had held that that party was entitled to no relief. In effect, the congressional act would have converted the earlier Supreme Court holding into an improper advisory opinion. *See* Chapter 1, § III.

   b. Although the statute did not involve a congressional effort to remove jurisdiction of the federal courts, it clearly indicates that separation of powers principles limit congressional power to dictate substantive results in federal litigation.

5. The important 1996 amendments to immigration law—the AEDPA and IIRIRA—are discussed at § III.C, above. Before passage of those Acts, a statute expressly vested the Attorney General with discretion to waive deportation of resident aliens who were convicted of specific crimes. AEDPA and IIRIRA repealed that provision. Before that repeal, a resident alien entered a guilty plea to a crime that made him deportable. By the time the government commenced deportation proceedings, however, the two Acts had been enacted. The government claimed (1) that the Attorney General no longer had the authority to waive deportation, because the repeal contained in the two Acts would apply retroactively, and (2) that the jurisdiction-stripping provisions of both Acts precluded any judicial review of the legal question of whether the Attorney General retained discretion to waive deportation. In *Immigration and Naturalization Service v. St. Cyr*, 533 U.S. 289 (2001), the Supreme Court rejected both of the government's contentions.

    a. The Court held that the Acts' restrictions on jurisdiction did not repeal habeas corpus jurisdiction. Thus, the resident alien was entitled to raise the legal question of the Attorney General's discretion to waive deportation in a habeas corpus proceeding. In other words, the restrictions on jurisdiction applied to judicial review of deportation orders, and not to block habeas review.

    b. The strong presumption in favor of judicial review of administrative action and the requirement of a clear legislative statement of intent to repeal habeas corpus jurisdiction supported the conclusion that habeas corpus review remained available to the petitioner.

    c. Moreover, a construction of the Acts "that would entirely preclude review of a pure question of law by any court would give rise to substantial constitutional questions." Specifically, the Court noted the Suspension Clause, Article III, § 9, clause 2 of the Constitution, which provides that "the privilege of the Writ of Habeas Corpus shall not be suspended, unless when in Cases of Rebellion or Invasion the public Safety may require it." According to the Court, "a serious Suspension Clause issue would be presented if we were to accept the INS's submission that the 1996 statutes have withdrawn that power from federal judges and provided no adequate substitute for its exercise." The Court avoided that constitutional question by concluding that Congress had not repealed habeas corpus jurisdiction.

    d.   On the merits, the Court concluded, as a matter of statutory interpretation, that the repeal of the Attorney General's discretionary power to waive deportation did not apply retroactively.

VII. Congressional Power to Vest Article III Courts With Non–Article III Powers

A. Characteristics of an Article III Court

1. Article III courts are the federal courts whose judges possess the protections of life tenure and salary provided in Article III, § 1 of the Constitution. *See* Chapter 1, § II.A.

2. The federal district courts, courts of appeals, and the Supreme Court are Article III courts.

B. The Concept of "Non–Article III Powers"

1. Traditionally, the Article III courts hear cases falling within the categories listed in Article III, § 2, clause 1, which lists the cases to which the Constitution extends the federal "judicial power."

2. Occasionally, however, Congress has attempted to expand the "business" of Article III courts to handle a broader array of responsibilities. It has done so in two ways. First, it has allowed some Article III courts to entertain disputes that do not fall within the judicial power of Article III, § 2, clause 1. Second, it has required some Article III courts to engage in tasks other than the adjudication of disputes.

3. In lieu of vesting Article III courts with such non-Article III powers, Congress could establish non-Article III courts. Such "legislative" courts—or Article I courts—are discussed in Chapter 3. There we will address whether non-Article III courts may entertain Article III matters. Here we are concerned with whether Article III courts may discharge non-Article III powers.

C. Article III Courts Performing Non–Judicial Functions

1. Article III extends the federal judicial power only to "cases" or "controversies." *See* Chapter 1, § III.A. Starting in the 1920s, Congress vested the

United States District Court for the District of Columbia and the Court of Appeals for the District of Columbia with responsibilities beyond adjudicating cases or controversies. For instance, they were required to assume some administrative and even some legislative functions concerning setting utility rates in the District of Columbia.

   a. The Supreme Court held that these courts were created under Congress' power to legislate regarding the District of Columbia under Article I, § 8 of the Constitution. Thus, they could perform, in addition to adjudication, the various non-judicial functions Congress gave them. The Supreme Court, however, being an Article III tribunal, could not entertain appeals from a matter that was non-judicial. *Keller v. Potomac Electric Power Co.*, 261 U.S. 428 (1923). *See also Federal Radio Commission v. General Electric Co.*, 281 U.S. 464 (1930)(reaching same conclusions regarding review of Federal Radio Commission orders).

   b. In dictum, the Supreme Court later declared that the courts of the District of Columbia were not Article III courts. *In re Bakelite Corporation*, 279 U.S. 438 (1929).

   c. Next, the Supreme Court held that these were "hybrid" courts. They were Article III courts when they adjudicated cases or controversies under Article III, but were Article I courts when they performed non-judicial tasks. *O'Donoghue v. United States*, 289 U.S. 516 (1933).

   d. The District Court for the District of Columbia upheld a statute requiring it to appoint school board members for the District. It relied on the "hybrid" theory to do so. *Hobson v. Hansen*, 265 F. Supp. 902 (D. D.C. 1967). The statute was amended to take this responsibility from the judiciary by providing for an elected school board.

2. Congress ended the hybrid nature of the United States District Court for the District of Columbia and the Court of Appeals for the District of Columbia in 1970 by establishing a set of local courts, which clearly are not Article III courts. These tribunals function as state courts do in the states, and, because they are not limited by Article III, clearly can perform non-judicial tasks. Thus, today, there is no doubt that the United States District Court for the District of Columbia and the Court of Appeals for the District of Columbia are Article III courts.

3. Similarly, the Court of Claims and the Court of Customs and Patent Appeals presented difficult issues. These courts performed non-Article

III functions, including the issuance of what essentially were advisory opinions, which an Article III court simply cannot do. *See* Chapter 1, § III.

    a. In *In re Bakelite Corporation*, 279 U.S. 438 (1929), the Supreme Court held that the Court of Customs Appeals was not an Article III court. Four years later, the Court reached the same conclusion regarding the Court of Claims. *Williams v. United States*, 289 U.S. 553 (1933).

    b. In 1953 and 1956, Congress passed statutes declaring these two courts to be Article III courts.

    c. Finally, in *Glidden Company v. Zdanok*, 370 U.S. 530 (1962), the Court held that they were Article III courts. The justices split badly on the question of why this is so, however, and there is no definitive explanation for the holding. The Court instructed these bodies to avoid performing non-Article III functions, which they did.

4. Congress largely alleviated the difficulties, however, by removing the advisory function from the Court of Claims and giving it only to the chief commissioner of that court. In addition, it removed judicial involvement until after the President had acted in certain matters, thereby deleting another aspect of the advisory nature of the Court's function.

5. Today, the Court of Claims and the Court of Customs and Patent Appeals no longer exist as such. They have been merged into the United States Court of Appeals for the Federal Circuit, which is plainly an Article III court. In this reorganization, the trial functions of the Court of Claims and other matters were vested in what is now called the United States Court of Federal Claims, which is not an Article III court. The Customs Court is now called the Court of International Claims, and is an Article III court.

6. More recently, the Supreme Court has on occasion upheld congressional direction to Article III judges to perform functions other than the adjudication of cases or controversies.

    a. In *Morrison v. Olson*, 487 U.S. 654 (1988), the Supreme Court upheld use of a specially-created Article III court to perform certain administrative tasks as part of the creation and implementation of the system for appointing and overseeing the operation of an independent counsel, appointed to investigate and prosecute high-ranking government officials. Under Article II, Congress has the authority to vest in an Article III court the appointment of some officers. The power to appoint also carries with it appropriate related powers.

    b.   The Court reasoned that the functions of an Article III court were not inherently executive, and were "directly analogous to functions that federal judges perform in other contexts. . . . " Moreover, the Court found that the court's power to terminate the independent counsel did not unduly interfere with executive discretion.

    c.   In *Mistretta v. United States*, 488 U.S. 361 (1989), the Supreme Court upheld the statutory requirement that several Article III judges sit on the United States Sentencing Commission, created by Congress to promulgate binding sentencing guidelines. The Court reasoned that breaches of separation of powers were to be invalidated only when they "either accrete to a single branch powers more appropriately diffused among separate branches or . . . undermine the authority and independence of one or another coordinate branch."

    d.   The Court further noted that the judiciary had long performed the function of determining sentences in the course of specific adjudications. It also relied on the fact that no specific "court" had been delegated the power to promulgate sentencing guidelines. Rather, the statute directed that individual Article III judges were to be made members of the Commission. The Court cited the long tradition of Supreme Court Justices' service in non-judicial capacities, and noted that "[t]he text of the Constitution contains no prohibition against the service of active federal judges on independent commissions such as that established by the Act."

7.   Thus it seems clear that Congress can require Article III courts to perform some administrative tasks, but such acts are rare.

D. Article III Courts Entertaining Cases Not Falling Within the Judicial Power of the United States

1.   From the earliest days, the Supreme Court has made it clear that Article III courts cannot adjudicate disputes that do not fall within the judicial power as prescribed in Article III. In *Marbury v. Madison*, 5 U.S. 137 (1803), the Court rejected Congress' effort to permit the Supreme Court

to issue a writ of mandamus, because such original jurisdiction did not fall within Article III. In *Hodgson v. Bowerbank*, 9 U.S. 303 (1809), the Court struck a legislative grant of jurisdiction over cases in which an alien was a party because it would permit suit by an alien against an alien; the judicial power defined in Article III does not reach such cases. *See* Chapter 5, § II.A.3.

2. A majority of the Supreme Court rejected the notion that Congress could grant jurisdiction to an Article III court in excess of the judicial power as defined in Article III in the famous case of *National Mutual Insurance Co. v. Tidewater Transfer Co.*, 337 U.S. 582 (1949). The decision is also discussed at Chapter 5, § III.A.7. In that case, the Supreme Court upheld legislation vesting the Article III federal courts with diversity of citizenship jurisdiction over suits between citizens of a state and those of the District of Columbia. The statute provided that citizens of the District of Columbia were to be treated as citizens of a State for diversity purposes. The statute flew in the face of an old Supreme Court holding that the District was not a State for diversity purposes. *Hepburn & Dundas v. Ellzey*, 6 U.S. 445 (1804).

    a. Although a majority of the Supreme Court upheld the statute, it did so on the basis of two separate theories, none of which commanded a majority. Thus, there is no rationale for the holding.

    b. Of most interest is the opinion of Justice Jackson, in which two other justices joined. They concluded that Congress has the authority to vest the federal courts with jurisdiction over non-Article III cases, by means of its legislative powers under Article I.

    c. This potentially wide-reaching theory was rejected, however, by six justices, who expressed concern about federalism and separation-of-powers factors.

    d. Two of those six justices concurred, however, in upholding the jurisdictional statute, on the ground that the District should properly be deemed a "state" for diversity purposes; they would overrule the old Supreme Court authority to the contrary.

3. Thus it seems clear that Congress cannot expand the jurisdiction of the federal courts to adjudicate beyond the judicial power in Article III, § 2, clause 1.

III

Legislative Courts

■ ANALYSIS

I. Introduction
II. Article III Courts and Legislative Courts
    A. Article III Provides Protection for Article III Judges and Defines Judicial Power
    B. Article I Allows Congress to Create Legislative Courts
III. Constitutional Limits on Congressional Power to Vest Article I Courts with Authority to Decide Article III Matters
    A. Importance of the Issue
    B. Early Uncertainty About Whether Article I Courts May Adjudicate Article III Matters
    C. Modern Evolution: The "Inherently Judicial" Doctrine and Adjudication of Constitutional Facts
IV. Adjudication by "Adjuncts" to Article III Courts
    A. Background: The "Adjunct" Theory
    B. Administrative Agencies
    C. Bankruptcy Courts
    D. Magistrate Judges

I. Introduction

In Chapter 2, § VII, we considered whether Article III courts could be given non-Article III powers, consisting either of non-judicial functions or of the adjudication of cases not falling within the judicial power of the federal courts. In this chapter we address the converse situation—whether courts created by Congress under Article I can perform judicial tasks falling within Article III. It is helpful in this context to distinguish between such legislative courts, on the one hand, and officers or bodies that act as adjuncts to Article III courts, on the other. Legislative courts (such as the territorial courts, military courts, the local courts in the District of Columbia, and the tax court) act as independent adjudicatory bodies; they enter final judgments, which might be subject to appellate review in the Supreme Court. Adjuncts to Article III courts (such as administrative agencies, bankruptcy courts, and magistrate judges) adjudicate various matters, but their decisions are subject to review by an Article III court. Both situations involve the problem of vesting Article III business in non-Article III decision-makers.

II. Article III Courts and Legislative Courts

A. Article III Provides Protection for Article III Judges and Defines Judicial Power

1. Article III, § 1, of the Constitution declares that the "judicial Power of the United States shall be vested in one supreme Court, and in such inferior Courts as the Congress may from time to time ordain and establish." It then provides that Article III judges shall serve during good behavior (which means they have lifetime tenure, subject to removal only for impeachment) and that their compensation cannot be reduced. As we discussed at Chapter 1, § 2.A, these incidents provide the Article III judges with great job security. They are insulated from retaliation by the political branches and the populace, and thus are free to rule in ways that may be unpopular.

2. Article III, § 2, then defines the "judicial power of the United States" by listing those sorts of cases or controversies that can fall within federal subject matter jurisdiction.

3. These provisions seem to make it clear that the "judicial power of the United States"—as defined in Article III, § 2—can only be exercised by Article III courts. Thus, the judicial power is only to be exercised in courts having the constitutional protections given to Article III judges.

B. Article I Permits Congress to Create Legislative Courts

1. Article I of the Constitution lists Congress' enumerated powers. Pursuant to those powers and the Necessary and Proper Clause of Article I, Congress has the authority to create courts not bound by the restrictions of Article III. These tribunals are called "Article I courts" or "legislative courts."

    a. While the Supreme Court might have held that Congress cannot create courts other than pursuant to Article III, the Court reached the contrary conclusion. As early as *American Ins. Co. v. Canter*, 26 U.S. 511 (1828), it upheld Congress' right to create legislative courts.

    b. Because legislative courts are not created under Article III, none of the Article III case or controversy limitations apply to them. Thus, for example, legislative courts can issue advisory opinions.

    c. More importantly, because legislative courts are not created under Article III, the judges who serve on them are not protected by Article III's guarantees of lifetime tenure and freedom from salary reduction.

2. Examples of legislative courts include the territorial courts, military courts, the tax court, and local courts for the District of Columbia.

3. Originally, the Supreme Court held that the Court of Claims and the Court of Customs Appeals were legislative courts. As discussed in Chapter 2, § VII.C.3, however, the Court overturned that holding in 1962 and concluded that both the Court of Claims and the Court of Customs and Patent Appeals were Article III courts. More recently, Congress has replaced those courts with the United States Court of Appeals for the Federal Circuit and a trial forum known as the United States Claims Court. These are Article III courts.

III. Constitutional Limits on Congressional Power to Vest Article I Courts With Authority to Decide Article III Matters

A. Importance of the Issue

1. While no one today denies Congress' right to create legislative courts, *see* § B.1, above, there is a serious question about whether those courts ought to be entitled to entertain matters falling within the "judicial power of the United States," as defined in Article III, § 2, of the Constitution.

2. If Congress can permit legislative courts to hear cases falling within Article III, then Article III cases will be heard by judges who do not have the protections of lifetime tenure and salary guaranty provided by Article III.

   a. Such a result would eviscerate a central goal of Article III—that Article III cases be heard by judges who are protected from retaliation by the political branches.

   b. If Congress can divert cases from Article III courts to Article I courts, it can place such cases before judges whose pay and tenure Congress controls.

3. This fear might counsel that Article I courts should not be allowed to hear Article III cases. Though the Supreme Court seems to have embraced this position at one time, it has since departed from it.

B. Early Uncertainty About Whether Article I Courts May Adjudicate Article III Matters

1. The first important case concerning legislative courts was *American Ins. Co. v. Canter*, 26 U.S. 511 (1828). The case arose in Florida, which was then a territory, not a state. Congress had created the superior court in the territory, the judges of which served a limited term. The territorial legislature then created courts inferior to the superior court, one of which was the wreckers court. The wreckers court entered a judgment in favor of Canter, which an insurance company later challenged in a separate action in an Article III court. The question was whether the judgment of the wreckers court was valid. The Supreme Court held that it was.

   a. The insurance company argued that the wreckers court judgment was void because the case fell within admiralty jurisdiction, and thus could only be heard in an Article III court.

   b. The Supreme Court noted that neither the wreckers court nor the superior court was an Article III court, because the judges of neither enjoyed the tenure protections given to Article III judges.

   c. The Supreme Court then said that neither court could entertain an admiralty case. Admiralty cases fall within the judicial power of the federal courts under Article III. Legislative courts "are not Constitutional courts, in which the judicial power conferred by the Constitution . . . can be deposited. They are incapable of receiving it." *Canter*, 26 U.S. at 546.

    d. The case heard by the wreckers court was not an admiralty case, and thus did not fall within the Article III judicial power. Rather, the wreckers court jurisdiction "is conferred by Congress, in the execution of those general powers which that body possesses over the territories of the United States." *Id.*

2. *Canter* established at least three things: (a) Congress has the authority to create legislative courts; (b) the territorial courts are legislative, not Article III, courts; and (c) legislative courts are "incapable of receiving" Article III judicial power.

3. The notion that legislative courts are "incapable of receiving" Article III judicial power was problematic even at the time.

    a. Before the Supreme Court decided *Canter*, it had held that it had appellate jurisdiction to review judgments entered by the territorial courts. *Durousseau v. United States*, 10 U.S. 307 (1810).

    b. The Supreme Court appellate jurisdiction, however, extends only to cases within the judicial power of Article III, as we discuss in Chapter 8.

    c. It is completely inconsistent to say, on the one hand, that the territorial courts do not hear Article III cases yet, on the other, that the Supreme Court has appellate jurisdiction over their judgments.

    d. The Supreme Court has never addressed this inconsistency, and territorial courts are to this day considered Article I courts.

4. The Supreme Court early characterized military courts as Article I tribunals: "Congress has the power to provide for the trial and punishment of military and naval offenses in the manner then and now practiced by civilized nations. . . . [T]he power to do so is given without any connection between it and the 3d article of the Constitution." *Dynes v. Hoover*, 61 U.S. 65, 79 (1858).

    a. Military courts can deprive military personnel of their personal liberties.

b. The judges of military courts are military officers, and, thus are not independent of the military that is prosecuting the defendant.

5. The Supreme Court has never recognized any constitutional problem with having Article I military courts enter orders depriving military personnel of their personal liberty.

   a. The Court has noted practical considerations: "[E]xigencies of military discipline require the existence of a special system of military courts in which not all of the specific procedural protections deemed essential in Art. III trials need apply." *O'Callahan v. Parker*, 395 U.S. 258, 261 (1969).

   b. Some commentators question why the need for military discipline should preclude having an independent adjudicator in military cases.

   c. Some observers have argued that the Framers intended military courts to be independent of Article III requirements, but the Court has never embraced this argument expressly.

6. In Chapter 2, § III.C.3, we discussed two cases in which the Supreme Court held, respectively, that the Court of Customs Appeals and the Court of Claims were Article I courts. The cases were *Ex Parte Bakelite Corp.*, 279 U.S. 438 (1929), and *Williams v. United States*, 289 U.S. 553 (1933). As also discussed there, both of the cases were overruled, and the courts involved have since been restructured and renamed, and are today Article III courts.

7. Nonetheless, the two opinions are noteworthy for their treatment of whether Article I courts may entertain Article III cases.

   a. In *Bakelite*, the Court seemed to assume that Article I courts can entertain cases falling within Article III.

   b. In *Williams*, however, the Court indicated that an Article I court simply cannot adjudicate matters falling within Article III.

   c. In *Bakelite*, the Court indicated that there are "inherently judicial" matters that Article I courts simply may not hear. The Court did not, however, define that term.

8. The Supreme Court overruled *Bakelite* and *Williams* in *Glidden Co. v. Zdanok*, 370 U.S. 530 (1962). *Glidden* held that the courts involved were

Article III courts. In the plurality opinion, Justice Harlan expressly rejected the *Williams* notion that Article I courts may not hear Article III cases.

    a. *Glidden* made it clear that Congress can give Article III business to Article I courts, but it failed to delineate how much.

    b. In addition, *Glidden* left open the possibility, suggested in *Bakelite*, that there are "inherently judicial" matters that cannot be given to Article I courts.

9. In *Palmore v. United States*, 411 U.S. 389 (1973), the defendant was convicted of a felony by the local District of Columbia Superior Court, which is an Article I court. The Supreme Court held that that court had the authority to deprive a defendant of personal liberty. The holding is ambiguous, but seems premised on the unique relationship between Congress and the District of Columbia.

10. In addition to upholding the ruling by the local District of Columbia court, the Supreme Court in *Palmore* cited three situations in which Congress had properly vested non-Article III courts with Article III power.

    a. The three situations are: (1) territorial courts, (2) military courts, and (3) state courts. The holding in *Palmore*, of course, adds the local courts of the District of Columbia to that list.

    b. Of these, note that only state court judges are independent of political retaliation by a branch of the federal government. In other words, while state courts judges certainly lack Article III tenure protection, neither Congress nor the executive branch of the federal government may reduce their pay or remove them from office. This is not the case with territorial and military courts.

    c. Thus, at least in separation-of-powers terms, it is easier to justify vesting Article III matters in state courts than in territorial and military courts. With regard to the latter two, the judge is subject to oversight by one of the political branches of the federal government.

C. Modern Evolution: The "Inherently Judicial" Doctrine and Adjudication of Constitutional Facts

1. In recent years, the Supreme Court has indicated that there are two areas

in which Congress may not place adjudicative power in Article I courts: "inherently judicial" cases involving private rights and determination of constitutional facts.

2. In *Northern Pipeline Construction Co. v. Marathon Pipe Line Co.*, 458 U.S. 50 (1982)(*Marathon*), the Supreme Court struck down part of the 1978 Bankruptcy Reform Act. Specifically, it held that the Article I judges of the bankruptcy courts could not hear claims involving the bankrupt that arose under state law. In his plurality opinion, Justice Brennan distinguished between cases involving "public rights" and those involving "private rights."

   a. Public rights cases are those that arise "between the Government and persons subject to its authority in connection with the performance of the constitutional functions of the executive or legislative departments." The Court relied upon *Crowell v. Benson*, 285 U.S. 22, 50 (1932), for this definition.

   b. Private rights cases are disputes between private litigants.

   c. Public rights cases are not "inherently judicial" and thus need not be adjudicated by Article III judges.

   d. Private rights cases are "inherently judicial" and thus must be determined by Article III judges.

   e. Because the Bankruptcy Reform Act of 1978 allowed non-Article III judges to determine private rights disputes—state common law claims between private litigants—it violated Article III.

3. Congress responded by revamping bankruptcy jurisdiction substantially. In response to *Marathon*, it converted bankruptcy courts into "adjuncts" of the federal district courts, as we will see at § IV.C, below.

4. The notion that public rights cases (cases involving the federal government) are not "inherently judicial" is based upon sovereign immunity. Because the federal government may only be sued if Congress waives its sovereign immunity, Congress may take the lesser step of permitting suit against the government only in an Article I court.

   a. Commentators have criticized the public rights/private rights dichotomy on various grounds. Most note that it deprives litigants of the protection of an Article III decision-maker in the types of cases in which an independent judge is especially important.

b. Many "public rights" disputes—such as an individual's claim that the government wrongfully denied a statutory benefit—would seem to call for adjudication by a judge with the political insulation granted by Article III. Yet, according to this doctrine, such cases can be heard by Article I bodies.

c. On the other hand, many "private rights" disputes—such as those in *Marathon*—involve state law claims between private citizens. It is difficult to see why such disputes must be decided by politically-insulated judges. Yet, according to the public rights/private rights dichotomy, they must be.

d. Dissenting in *Marathon*, Justice White argued for a balancing process that would weigh the interest in salary and tenure protections against the governmental interest in maintaining flexibility.

5. More recent Supreme Court decisions, while not overruling *Marathon*, suggest a move toward a balancing test championed by Justice White's dissent in that decision.

   a. For example, in *Thomas v. Union Carbide Agricultural Products Co.*, 473 U.S. 568 (1985), the Supreme Court upheld a constitutional challenge to a provision of a federal statute providing for binding arbitration with only limited judicial review as the mechanism for resolving disputes among participants in a congressional scheme for the registration of pesticides.

   b. *Thomas* rejected the notion (adopted in *Marathon*) that the public rights/private rights dichotomy always "provides a bright line test for determining the requirements of Article III." The Court cited Justice White's balancing test as the basis for deciding what issues must be heard by Article III courts.

   c. In *Commodity Futures Trading Commission v. Schor*, 478 U.S. 833 (1986), the Supreme Court upheld an administrative regulation that allowed the Commodity Futures Trading Commission to adjudicate a counterclaim arising out of the same transaction as the complaint filed before the Commission, even though the counterclaim involved a state-created "private right." Though the decision could probably have been rationalized in terms of the *Marathon* Court's recognition of the legitimate use of non-Article III adjuncts, *see* § IV, below, the Court's opinion relied heavily on Justice White's balancing analysis.

6. The Supreme Court held that the dispute in *Thomas v. Union Carbide Agricultural Products Co.*, involved a public right, even though the federal government was not a party to the case. The right involved was "so closely integrated into a public regulatory scheme as to be a matter appropriate for agency resolution." This conclusion represents an extension of the definition of "public rights" in *Marathon*.

7. In addition to holding that public rights cases must be determined by Article III courts, the Court in *Marathon* recognized that cases involving the assertion of constitutional rights must be determined by independent tribunals. The leading case is *Crowell v. Benson*, 285 U.S. 22 (1932). There, the Court held that Congress cannot constitutionally take away from the judiciary the final authority to find, *de novo*, "constitutional facts." These are facts that form the underlying basis for the claim that a governmental act is unconstitutional.

    a. Under the holding in *Crowell*, such constitutional issues must be decided by a court independent of the political branches of the federal government, whether an Article III federal court or a state court (whose judges' salary and tenure are not subject to federal regulation).

    b. The Court was not entirely clear as to the basis of its decision. In part, it was separation of powers, but the opinion also appeared to include a due process element.

    c. Justice Brandeis dissented, and asserted that because Congress could choose to close off the federal courts and instead have these findings made in state courts, it could also provide that non-judicial administrative agencies may make final determinations on them as well. He concluded that the only time judicial review of factual findings was required was when personal liberty was at stake and due process would require such review.

8. The Supreme Court later modified *Crowell* to this extent: when judicial review is required, it need not be *de novo* review. In other words, judicial review of fact-finding by a non-judicial body need not entail a judicial

hearing; the court may simply review the record created by the non-judicial body. *St. Joseph Stock Yards Co. v. United States*, 298 U.S. 38 (1936).

9. Many commentators have attacked *Crowell*, and some even assert that the doctrine is dead. The Supreme Court has never overruled *Crowell*, however, and more recent cases clearly indicate that its doctrine survives, at least in cases involving personal liberty.

Example: In a prosecution for obscenity, a court must retain the final authority to determine whether books or films are legally obscene. The question of obscenity is a constitutional fact. *Jacobellis v. Ohio*, 378 U.S. 184 (1964).

IV. Adjudication by "Adjuncts" to Article III Courts

A. Background: The "Adjunct" Theory

1. Legislative courts, which we discussed above, operate independently of the lower federal courts. They enter final judgments in the matters before them, subject ultimately to appellate review by the Supreme Court.

2. In addition to legislative courts, there are several other non-Article III federal bodies and officers involved in the adjudication of disputes. The most important of these are administrative agencies, bankruptcy courts, and magistrate judges.

3. We discussed at § III.C, above, the requirement that certain "inherently judicial" functions cannot be performed by Article I decision-makers. Notwithstanding that limitation, administrative agencies, bankruptcy courts, and magistrate judges may adjudicate regarding "inherently judicial" matters, but only if their decisions are subject to substantial review in an Article III court.

4. This scheme is constitutional because the non-Article III decision-maker does not function independently; it is considered merely an "adjunct" to an Article III court. Because the Article III court makes the final decision, the "judicial power" remains in that court.

B. Administrative Agencies

1. The political branches of the federal government, both executive and legislative, have created myriad administrative agencies, which have

varying authority over matters addressed by legislation. Typically, an agency will have both rulemaking and adjudicatory authority.

    a. An example of rulemaking authority is the Security and Exchange Commission's promulgation of Rule 10b–5 under the Securities Exchange Act of 1934. Rule 10b–5 has become the principal federal tool for addressing insider trading in securities.

    b. Agencies adjudicate a wide variety of issues. For example, the Social Security Administration, through administrative law judges, makes findings about whether eligible employees have been injured and, if so, regarding the appropriate compensation; the Department of Veterans Affairs renders decisions concerning veterans' benefits, including reimbursement for medical expenses; the Immigration and Naturalization Service adjudicates applications for permanent resident alien status; and the Customs Service assesses forfeitures and penalties.

2. As we discussed at § III.C, above, the Supreme Court held in *Crowell v. Benson*, 285 U.S. 22 (1932), that administrative findings must be subject to judicial review of constitutional facts. The Court readily recognized "the utility and convenience of administrative agencies for the investigation and finding of facts," but noted that Congress cannot vest in agencies the power to make all determinations "with finality. . . . That would be to sap the judicial power . . . and to establish a government of a bureaucratic character alien to our system." 285 U.S. at 57.

    a. In *Crowell*, the Federal Employees' Compensation Commission made an award in favor of an employee and against Benson. The Commission found that the employee was injured while employed by Benson and while working upon the navigable waters of the United States.

    b. The Supreme Court characterized the case as one involving "private rights," in which a non-Article III body cannot make binding determinations. *See* § III.C, above.

    c. The Court also noted, however, that Article III courts often delegate fact-finding to others, such as juries and special masters, whose findings are not disturbed if supported by the evidence. Similarly, Congress can delegate fact-finding to an administrative agency, subject to judicial review. Congress thus "relieve[es] the courts of a most serious burden [of hearing thousands of cases in the first instance] while preserving their complete authority to insure the proper application of the law." 285 U.S. at 54.

  d. *Crowell* also held that a court must determine "constitutional" facts. Such facts underlie a constitutional claim but also encompass jurisdictional facts. For example, in *Crowell* itself, Benson claimed that the injury was not suffered upon navigable waters. Because the legislation under which the employee made his claim would not apply unless the injury were suffered on navigable waters, the issue presented a jurisdictional fact. Thus, the court must determine not only whether a compensation order is in accordance with law but "the fact . . . which underlies the operation of the statute." 285 U.S. at 62.

3. Although Congress has adopted different schemes from time to time, the typical provision permits a party to an administrative hearing to file a petition for review in the Court of Appeals for the Circuit where that party resides or in the Court of Appeals for the District of Columbia Circuit. (Of course, these are all Article III courts.)

  a. The reviewing court gives no deference to the agency's interpretation of law; it is the province of the court, of course, to determine matters of law with finality.

  b. The reviewing court defers to the agency's findings of fact only if they are supported by the record; the determination of whether the agency's findings are supported by sufficient evidence is itself a legal issue.

C. Bankruptcy Courts

1. In *Northern Pipeline Construction Co. v. Marathon Pipe Line Co.*, 458 U.S. 50 (1982)(*Marathon*), discussed at § III.C.2, above, the Supreme Court invalidated portions of the 1978 Bankruptcy Reform Act. The Act was unconstitutional to the extent it permitted non-Article III judges to determine disputes involving private rights. Such disputes, as we saw at § III.C, above, cannot be determined by Article I bodies or officers.

2. In 1984, in response to *Marathon*, Congress revamped the bankruptcy courts. Bankruptcy judges are Article I officers, and serve as adjuncts to the federal district court in which they sit. (The federal district court, of course, is an Article III court.)

3. Bankruptcy judges' jurisdiction is closely circumscribed to core bankruptcy issues. The district court retains jurisdiction over plenary matters.

D. **Magistrate Judges**

1. In 1968, Congress created the office of the federal magistrate, the name of which was changed in 1993 to magistrate judge. These officers serve a term of years, and clearly are not Article III judges.

2. Congress was motivated by the increase in complex litigation in the federal courts, and intended that magistrate judges assist federal district judges in processing cases.

3. The authority of magistrate judges is strictly defined by 28 U.S.C. § 636, which is structured to require that the ultimate decision in a case be made by the district judge, who is, of course, an Article III judge. The district judge may refer various matters to a magistrate judge.

    a. Without consent of the parties, the district judge may refer "nondispositive" pretrial matters to a magistrate judge. The magistrate's orders on such matters may be reviewed by the district judge on the record for "clear error."

    b. Without consent of the parties, the district judge may refer "dispositive" pretrial matters, such as a motion for summary judgment, to the magistrate judge. The magistrate enters findings and recommendations on such matters, which are reviewed by the district judge de novo.

    c. The parties may consent to trial before the magistrate judge. If they do, they have waived the right to have the matter tried by an Article III judge; the final judgment of the magistrate judge in such a case may be appealed to the court of appeals.

REVIEW QUESTIONS (PART I; CHAPTERS 1–3)

True or False Questions

1. **T or F** A private individual hears that the parents of a deformed infant in conspiracy with the doctors of a county hospital are not feeding the infant properly. The individual files suit in federal court to protect the federal civil rights of the infant. The private individual has standing to bring the suit.

2. **T or F** A state indicts one of two individuals distributing political leaflets at a shopping center, and threatens the second individual with prosecution if she continues to distribute the materials. The second individual files suit in federal court, seeking a declaratory judgment that her future prosecution would violate her constitutional rights, and seeking an injunction against prosecution. The second individual's case is not ripe for adjudication.

3. **T or F** Blacks file suit in federal court, challenging the constitutionality of the operation of a major political party's primary in their state, on the grounds that blacks are improperly excluded from participation. The defendants contend that the federal court may not adjudicate the dispute because of the political question doctrine. The federal court determines that the political question doctrine does *not* preclude it from adjudicating the suit. The federal court is correct.

4. **T or F** Because Congress retains power under Article III to regulate the jurisdiction of the lower federal courts, it may prohibit certain racial and religious groups from gaining access to those courts.

5. **T or F** Because the Supreme Court's existence is mandated by Article III of the Constitution, while that of the lower federal courts is not, Congress possesses no power to control Supreme Court jurisdiction.

6. **T or F** Though Congress retains power to regulate the jurisdiction of the federal courts, it cannot order those courts to convict an individual without allowing the courts to inquire into the constitutionality of the law under which the prosecution has been brought.

7. **T or F** In light of the Supreme Court's decision in *Northern Pipeline Construction Co. v. Marathon Pipe Line Co.*—which invalidated por-

tions of the 1978 Bankruptcy Reform Act to the extent that the Act permitted non-Article III judges to determine disputes involving private rights—it logically follows that federal administrative agencies are unconstitutional.

8. **T or F** A soldier about to be transferred to duty in the Middle East sues in federal court, claiming that the military involvement in the Middle East is unconstitutional because it does not follow a declaration of war by Congress, and seeking an injunction against his transfer. The federal court may refuse to hear the suit because of the political question doctrine.

9. **T or F** Under accepted principles of standing, an organization with a special interest in an area of social concern may bring an action to challenge governmental interference in that particular area.

10. **T or F** Application of the mootness doctrine can be influenced by the degree of public interest in having the particular legal issue resolved.

11. **T or F** Though Congress is authorized to circumvent the Article III federal courts by creating legislative courts, issues of constitutional interpretation must be finally resolved by an Article III court.

12. **T or F** The decision in *Ex Parte McCardle* definitively upholds plenary congressional authority to limit the Supreme Court's appellate jurisdiction.

13. **T or F** A Congressional exclusion of Supreme Court appellate jurisdiction in constitutional cases would violate the Due Process Clause of the Fifth Amendment.

14. **T or F** Congress may require Article III federal courts to adjudicate cases falling outside the scope of the judicial power, which is described in Article III, § 2 of the Constitution.

15. **T or F** Congress may not require Article III federal courts to issue advisory opinions.

Essay Question

You are a legal assistant to a United States Senator who is unhappy with the Supreme Court's decision holding prayer in public schools unconstitutional. He would like to learn your views on the constitutionality of various legislation he is considering proposing:

(1) A statute requiring the federal courts to hold that prayer in public schools is constitutional.

(2) A statute prohibiting any federal court from adjudicating cases concerning the constitutionality of prayer in the public schools.

(3) A statute prohibiting any court, state or federal, from adjudicating cases concerning the constitutionality of prayer in the public schools.

(4) A statute similar to proposal 3, except that in addition the law would create a new federal legislative court to adjudicate finally all such cases, in lieu of the existing federal or state courts.

Prepare a memorandum in response to the Senator's request.

*

PART TWO

The Structure of Federal Court Jurisdiction

■ ANALYSIS

4. Federal Question Jurisdiction
5. Diversity of Citizenship and Alienage Jurisdiction
6. Supplemental Jurisdiction
7. Removal Jurisdiction
8. Supreme Court Jurisdiction

*

IV

Federal Question Jurisdiction

■ ANALYSIS

I. Introduction
II. Constitutional and Policy Bases for Federal Question Jurisdiction
    A. The Constitutional Grant of Judicial Power
    B. "Protective Jurisdiction"
    C. Policy Underpinnings for Federal Question Jurisdiction
III. The Statutory Grant of Federal Question Jurisdiction
    A. Section 1331—The General Federal Question Statute
    B. Scope of the Statutory Grant: The Well–Pleaded Complaint Rule
    C. Scope of the Statutory Grant

I. Introduction

Federal question jurisdiction (sometimes called "arising under" jurisdiction) is a staple of the federal court docket. Unlike diversity of citizenship jurisdiction, discussed in Chapter 5, there is no controversy about whether the federal courts should have federal question jurisdiction. Everyone seems to agree that determining cases that arise under federal law is an appropriate task for the federal judiciary. Although there are many specialized federal statutes granting jurisdiction for cases arising thereunder, the focus is on the general federal question jurisdiction statute, 28 U.S.C. § 1331, which grants jurisdiction over cases arising under any federal law, without an amount in controversy requirement.

II. Constitutional and Policy Bases for Federal Question Jurisdiction

A. The Constitutional Grant of Judicial Power

1. Article III, § 2, clause 1 of the Constitution extends the federal judicial power of the federal courts to nine types of cases or controversies.

2. One of those categories includes cases "arising under this Constitution, the Laws of the United States, and treaties made, or which shall be made, under their authority."

3. In *Osborn v. Bank of the United States,* 22 U.S. 738 (1824), the Supreme Court gave this "arising under" clause an extremely broad construction.

    a. Chief Justice Marshall's opinion in *Osborn* held that when *any issue of federal law "might* form an ingredient" in the case, the case can be deemed to "arise under" federal law for purposes of Article III. This conclusion allows a federal court to decide all issues of *state* law involved, even if the federal issue never actually appears in the case—as long as a federal issue *might* be injected into the dispute.

    Example: P sues D, asserting that D has trespassed upon P's land. Although D does not raise the issue, the question of whether P actually owns the land could be injected into the case. Moreover, because the land was originally owned by the federal government and transferred to individual owners over a century ago, the chain of title questions could trace back to original federal ownership. Because a federal issue could conceivably be injected into the case (no matter how unlikely or farfetched), the case "arises under" federal law and falls within the constitutional definition of federal question jurisdiction.

b. Though *Osborn* has never been overruled, its broad language has been criticized in dicta by some justices in modern cases.

c. In *Verlinden B.V. v. Central Bank of Nigeria*, 461 U.S. 480 (1983), the Supreme Court indicated that the constitutional "arising under" provision continues to receive a broad construction. In that case, however, the Court declined to reconsider expressly the current status of *Osborn*.

4. Commentators suggest that the Court never intended to have *Osborn* read so broadly, despite its broad language. Rather, they argue, *Osborn* should be limited to cases involving a federal instrumentality (such as the Bank of the United States, involved in that case), because in such cases there is an especially strong federal interest, even if the dispute at hand only involves state law. Marshall's opinion, however, appears broader than this narrow construction.

5. A broad interpretation of the constitutional grant of federal question jurisdiction is appropriate. It permits Congress, in granting jurisdiction to the federal courts through jurisdictional statutes, to vest less than the full quantum of constitutional jurisdiction.

   a. If the constitutional grant were interpreted narrowly, it would be very difficult to overcome, because it is difficult to amend the Constitution. On the other hand, a narrow interpretation of a statutory grant is easier to amend; Congress simply has to redraft the statute.

   b. To provide arising-under jurisdiction, however, the virtually unlimited scope suggested in *Osborn* would effectively render Article III no limit at all on Congress's ability to usurp state judicial authority.

   c. As discussed below, the statutory grant of federal question jurisdiction is narrower than the constitutional grant. *See* § III, below. Thus, while the constitutional grant determines how far Congress *could* go in vesting federal question jurisdiction in the federal courts, its statutes determine how far Congress actually *has gone*.

B. "Protective Jurisdiction"

1. "Protective jurisdiction" is the term used to describe two distinct

theories to justify, under the "arising under" provision of Article III, the vesting of authority in the federal courts to hear cases involving solely issues of state law.

2. Since Congress has never attempted to vest such authority in the federal courts, the legal validity of these theories has never been determined. Justice Frankfurter severely criticized both theories, however, in his dissenting opinion in *Textile Workers Union v. Lincoln Mills*, 353 U.S. 448, 476 (1957).

3. In *Mesa v. California*, 489 U.S. 121 (1989), the Supreme Court declined to adopt a theory of protective jurisdiction in a case involving removal of a state prosecution of a federal officer when no substantive issue of federal law was involved.

4. The "Greater–Includes–the–Lesser" Theory.

   a. One version of protective jurisdiction, associated with Professor Herbert Wechsler, suggests that if Congress possesses constitutional authority to legislate substantively in an area, it can take the lesser step of choosing not to enact substantive law but simply vesting jurisdiction in the federal courts to apply relevant state law.

   b. The theory is subject to criticism because it is not necessarily true that the jurisdictional grant is somehow a "lesser" step than legislating substantively; rather, the two steps may be viewed as conceptually distinct.

   c. This theory also ignores the fact that one justification for federal question jurisdiction is the expertise of federal judges in matters of federal law. This policy is not furthered by vesting jurisdiction in the federal courts over cases involving only state law.

5. The "Articulated–and–Active–Federal–Policy" Theory.

   a. The other version of protective jurisdiction, developed by Professor Paul Mishkin, suggests that when Congress has a preexisting active and articulated policy in a substantive area, it may protect its program from being undermined by state court adjudication by allowing the federal courts to adjudicate even pure state law issues in areas related to the federal program.

   b. As an illustration, Professor Mishkin points to the cases upholding provisions of the bankruptcy law vesting jurisdiction in the federal courts to adjudicate non-diverse suits under state law when the bankrupt is a party. He also views *Osborn* as an illustration of his approach.

C. Policy Underpinnings for Federal Question Jurisdiction

1. The policy bases for the grant of federal question jurisdiction are clear and universally accepted.

2. Federal judges can be expected to develop expertise in interpreting federal law, and might be sympathetic to policies underlying federal law.

3. In addition, there seems to be no dispute, even in an era of overloaded dockets, that federal question jurisdiction is salutary. The adjudication and protection of federal rights is, arguably, the primary function of the federal courts.

4. It does not necessarily follow, however, that state court jurisdiction is automatically excluded each time Congress extends federal question jurisdiction to the federal courts. Usually, state and federal courts possess concurrent jurisdiction over cases arising under federal law.

III. The Statutory Grant of Federal Question Jurisdiction

A. Section 1331—The General Federal Question Statute

1. The general federal question statute is 28 U.S.C. § 1331, which provides that "[t]he district courts shall have original jurisdiction of all civil actions arising under the Constitution, laws, or treaties of the United States."

   a. The operative language of this statutory grant—"arising under [federal law]"—is identical to the constitutional grant of judicial power in Article III, § 2, clause 1. *See* II.A.2, above.

   b. However, the interpretation given to the statutory language has always been far narrower than that given to the constitutional language.

2. Despite the well-established policy underpinnings for federal question jurisdiction, *see* § II.C, above, Congress did not enact a permanent general federal question statute until 1875. Before then, there were

numerous specific grants of federal question jurisdiction over specified types of disputes, but there was no general statute such as § 1331.

3. Some historical evidence suggests that the drafters of the first general federal question statute intended that the statute have a scope identical to that given the constitutional provision for federal question jurisdiction.

4. Nonetheless, the statutory provision has received a construction much narrower than that given the constitutional provision. In part, courts assume, at least without stronger evidence, that Congress would not wish to burden the federal courts with so many cases having merely a tangential relation to federal interests that is required by the constitutional grant.

5. The concept of "arising under" includes not only claims that arise under the Constitution, federal statutes, and treaties, but federal common law as well.

6. Despite the presence of § 1331, many other jurisdictional statutes remain on the books, and constitute specific exercises of the "arising under" jurisdiction. One is 28 U.S.C. § 1338(a), which provides the federal courts with jurisdiction over cases arising under acts of Congress relating to patents, plant variety protection, copyrights, and trademarks.

7. Section 1338(a) expressly grants exclusive federal jurisdiction, which means that only federal courts may hear the cases falling within that grant. State courts have no jurisdiction over such cases. Although some argue that the grant of exclusive jurisdiction should counsel that § 1338 be interpreted especially narrowly, on the whole the statutes have been construed identically. *See, e.g., Holmes Group v. Vornado Air Circulation*, 535 U.S. 826 (2002)("arising under" in § 1338 means the same thing as it does in § 1331).

8. While other specific federal question statutes also provide for exclusive jurisdiction, it is important to remember that § 1331 does not. Thus, cases that arise under federal law and that do not fall within one of the narrow class of cases for which federal jurisdiction is exclusive may be brought either in federal or state court.

a. This fact recognizes the duty of state courts to follow federal law under the Supremacy Clause of the Constitution, and indicates faith in the state courts to do so.

b. Concurrent jurisdiction of the federal and state courts also serves a docket control function, and alleviates the federal courts of a greater caseload.

c. Just as federal courts determine cases arising under state law in diversity of citizenship jurisdiction, *see* Chapter 5, so concurrent jurisdiction of federal question cases allows state courts to gain expertise with federal law. These facts may keep both sets of courts from becoming overly specialized.

B. Scope of the Statutory Grant: The Well-Pleaded Complaint Rule

1. The well-pleaded complaint rule stands for the proposition that a federal court will consider only a plaintiff's "well-pleaded" complaint in assessing whether the case arises under federal law. In this sense, a "well-pleaded" complaint is one that sets forth only a claim, and does not add extraneous issues, such as anticipated defenses that the defendant might raise.

2. In applying the well-pleaded complaint rule, then, the court looks only to the plaintiff's *claim*, and ignores other things the plaintiff may allege. The question then becomes whether that claim itself arises under federal law.

3. The term "well-pleaded complaint" means that the plaintiff may not anticipate and respond to possible defenses that the defendant might raise.

Example: The Mottleys have lifetime passes on Railroad. Congress passes a law outlawing free passes. The Mottleys try to use their passes, and Railroad refuses to let them. They sue Railroad for specific performance of their lifetime pass agreements. They allege in their complaint that Railroad will rely on the new congressional statute, but assert that the statute does not apply to them and, if it does apply to them, it is unconstitutional. There is no federal question jurisdiction. The Mottleys' claim is for breach of contract—that Railroad is not living up to its agreement to give them free travel for life. There is nothing federal about that claim. The federal elements that do appear in the Mottleys' complaint are not part of the Mottleys' *claim*. Instead, they are part of an anticipated defense and their response thereto. These federal elements, not being part of the claim, are ignored in determining whether the case arises under federal law. Because there is nothing federal about the Mottleys' claim, the case does not invoke federal question jurisdiction. These facts are roughly equivalent to those in the leading case of *Louisville & Nashville Railroad v. Mottley*, 211 U.S. 149 (1908).

4. Some commentators defend the well-pleaded complaint rule as providing courts with a ready method of determining—on the face of the complaint—whether the case invokes federal question jurisdiction. Thus, it avoids having to await the defendant's response to see whether there really is a federal issue in the case.

5. Others attack the rule, however, as funneling out of the federal courts cases that actually will turn on the interpretation of federal law.

Example: In *Mottley* itself, as shown in the previous *Example*, the actual litigation will focus on two issues: (1) whether the federal statute applies to the Mottleys and (2) if so, whether it is constitutional. Both of these are federal issues. Yet the case cannot go to a federal trial court because the plaintiff's *claim itself* does not arise under federal law.

6. Obviously, because the well-pleaded complaint rule precludes a court from considering anything in the complaint but the plaintiff's claim, it also precludes a court from considering any defenses asserted by the defendant's answer. Again, it is the well-pleaded *complaint* that is assessed.

7. Accordingly, in 2002, the Supreme Court held that defendant's counterclaim cannot be considered to determine whether the case arises under federal law. "Admittedly, our prior cases have only required us to address whether a federal defense, rather than a federal counterclaim, can establish 'arising under' jurisdiction. Nonetheless, those cases were decided on the principle that federal jurisdiction generally exists 'only when a federal question is presented on the face of the plaintiff's properly pleaded complaint.' . . . It follows that a counterclaim—which appears as part of the defendant's answer . . . —cannot serve as a basis for 'arising under' jurisdiction." *Holmes Group v. Vornado Air Circulation*, 535 U.S. 826, 831 (2002).

a. The Court thus refused to draw any distinction between a defendant raising federal defenses and a defendant asserting a claim under federal law.

b. Arguably, the Court erred by not making such a distinction. After all, the defendant who asserts a counterclaim is acting as a plaintiff—it is asserting a claim for affirmative relief, which does indeed arise under federal law.

8. The existence of the well-pleaded complaint rule proves that the statutory phrase "arising under" is narrower that the constitutional phrase "arising under." The constitutional phrase is satisfied if any issue of federal law might conceivably be injected into the case at any time. *See* § II.A, above. Obviously, that standard would be satisfied in *Mottley*, since Railroad defended by arguing that the federal statute precluded them from honoring the Mottleys' lifetime pass and that the statute did not violate the Constitution.

9. Applying the well-pleaded complaint rule can be especially difficult when the plaintiff seeks declaratory relief.

    a. A declaratory judgment is a judicial decree of the respective rights and obligations of the parties. In federal court, this remedy may be available under the Declaratory Judgment Act. *See* 28 U.S.C. § 2201. The problems arise because the person bringing suit might not be the party who could have sued for damages or other "coercive" relief.

Example: A and B are parties to a contract. A claims that B has breached the contract and intends to sue B for damages. Before A sues, however, B sues A, seeking a declaratory judgment that she (B) did not breach the contract.

    b. It is now clear that the Declaratory Judgment Act was not intended to expand federal jurisdiction. So one cannot argue that the declaratory judgment action arises under federal law because it arises under the Declaratory Judgment Act. So, a plaintiff will not be permitted to circumvent the well-pleaded complaint rule by using the declaratory judgment device.

    c. If, without the declaratory judgment device, *either* party to the case could have brought an action for coercive relief that would satisfy the well-pleaded complaint rule, then the declaratory judgment action will invoke federal question jurisdiction. *See Skelly Oil Co. v. Phillips Petroleum Co.,* 339 U.S. 667 (1950).

Example: This *Example* refers to the facts above concerning the Mottleys in Note 3, above. Railroad sues the Mottleys, seeking a declaratory judgment that (1) the federal law prohibiting railroads from giving free passes applies to the Mottleys, and (2) the federal law is constitutional. The case does not invoke federal question jurisdiction because neither the Mottleys nor Railroad could have brought a case for damages or other coercive relief on these facts. The Mottleys could not do so because their well-pleaded complaint did not arise under federal law, as discussed in Note 3 above.

Example: Patent Holder claims that Manufacturer is infringing her patent. Manufacturer sues for a declaratory judgment that (1) she (Manufacturer) is not infringing the patent, and (2) that, at any rate, Patent Holder's patent is invalid. This case invokes federal question jurisdiction, because Patent Holder could have sued for coercive relief (probably damages), and the well-pleaded complaint for that claim would arise under federal law. Patent Holder's complaint would allege that her patent is valid and that Manufacturer is infringing it.

d. In *Franchise Tax Board v. Construction Laborers Vacation Trust for Southern California,* 463 U.S. 116 (1983), the Supreme Court held that these principles, developed for suits brought under the Declaratory Judgment Act, apply equally to suits brought under state declaratory judgment acts and removed to federal court. Thus, these principles, when applicable, bar not only original invocation of federal question jurisdiction, but bars removal to federal court as well.

10. Notwithstanding the well-pleaded complaint rule, there are substantive areas in which federal law is so all-encompassing that it takes over the subject matter of the entire field. In these situations, which are very rare, there is, effectively, no state law; state claims have been displaced by federal claims. Accordingly, when a plaintiff asserts what she thinks is a state law claim in state court, the defendant may be able to remove the case to federal court because the case, in reality, arises under federal law. For fuller discussion, *see* Chapter 7, § II.D. *See also Metropolitan Life Insurance Co. v. Taylor,* 481 U.S. 58 (1987)("[o]ne corollary of the well-

pleaded complaint rule . . . is that Congress may so clearly pre-empt a particular area, that any civil complaint raising this select group of claims is necessarily federal in character.").

C. Scope of the Statutory Grant

1. In addition to the well-pleaded complaint rule, courts impose another requirement under the federal question statute. It is more difficult to label than the well-pleaded complaint rule, but concerns whether the federal law is a sufficiently important ingredient to the case.

2. Through the years, the Supreme Court has adopted different tests for this aspect of federal question jurisdiction. The decisions have not always been consistent, and the present state of the law is not absolutely clear. The major cases are: (a) *American Well Works,* (b) *Smith,* (c) *Moore,* and (d) *Merrell Dow.*

3. *American Well Works Co. v. Layne and Bowler Co.,* 241 U.S. 257 (1916), sets forth the "cause of action" test for determining whether a claim arises under federal law. In that case, Justice Holmes adopted a narrow test, concluding that a case "arises under" the law that *creates* the cause of action. If state law creates the cause of action, the case does not fall within the statutory definition of "arising under" federal law. This is so even if the substance of the litigation will substantially concern issues of federal law.

    a. The test may be criticized as placing form over substance: if the bulk of the case will ultimately turn on matters of federal law, the need for the expertise of the federal courts is as great as when the cause of action is itself federal.

    b. Subsequent developments expanded the scope of statutory federal question jurisdiction.

    c. Nonetheless, at the very least, the *American Well Works* test remains accurate as a statement of cases that generally do arise under federal law: if federal law creates the cause of action, as a general rule, it will invoke federal question jurisdiction.

    d. On the other hand, even if Congress creates the cause of action, if Congress also directs that the substance of the law to be applied is state-created, cases under the cause of action may not be deemed to fall within the federal question statute. *See Shoshone Mining Co. v. Rutter,* 177 U.S. 505 (1900).

4. The Supreme Court expanded the statutory definition of "arising under" in *Smith v. Kansas City Title & Trust Co.*, 255 U.S. 180 (1921). In that case, the Supreme Court held that a case arises under federal law if the plaintiff's complaint establishes that her "right to relief depends upon the construction or application of the Constitution or laws of the United States." *Id.* at 199.

   a. This test looks not at the law that created the cause of action, but the reality of what issues will be presented in the litigation.

   b. In *Smith*, a stockholder of a corporation sued to stop the corporation from investing in bonds issued under a federal statute, which he thought was unconstitutional. Investing in illegal bonds would violate state law. Thus, the plaintiff's claim arose under state law, but the litigation would focus on the federal issue of whether the federal bonds were constitutional. The Court concluded that the case arose under federal law.

   c. In *Moore v. Chesapeake & Ohio Railway*, 291 U.S. 205 (1934), the plaintiff sued his employer under a state cause of action, claiming that the employer had violated the Federal Safety Appliance Act. If the plaintiff could show that the employer violated "any law enacted for the safety of employees," the employer could not assert the defense of contributory negligence. Although it seems that the litigation, like that in *Smith*, would focus on federal law—whether the employer violated the federal act—the Court held that the case did not arise under federal law.

   d. Only much later, in *Merrell Dow Pharmaceuticals Inc. v. Thompson*, 478 U.S. 804 (1986), did the Court try to reconcile *Smith* and *Moore*, as discussed below.

5. In *Merrell Dow*, the plaintiffs argued that the drug manufacturers had violated several state laws, including negligence *per se*. The latter claim was based upon the defendants' allegedly violating the Federal Food, Drug, and Cosmetic Act (FDCA) by misbranding pharmaceuticals. The parties agreed that the FDCA did not create a private right to sue for violations. If it had, jurisdiction would be clear under the *American Well Works* test.

Example: If the FDCA outlawed certain activity, such as misbranding drugs, and also provided that anyone harmed by a violation of the Act had the right to sue to recover for injuries, then federal law would create a cause of action. That being so, the claim would arise under the federal law. But, as noted, the FDCA did not create such a right to sue. The Court in *Merrell Dow* proceeded on the assumption that no implied federal private right of action exists.

a. The Court ruled, in a five-to-four decision, that the incorporation of the federal standard in the state-law private action did not render the action one arising under federal law for purposes of § 1331.

b. The majority opinion was influenced by the fact that Congress had not created a private right of action in the FDCA. Once Congress decided not to create a cause of action, the majority concluded, the courts are "not free to supplement that decision in a way that makes it meaningless." *Id.* at 814, n. 12.

c. Although this standard appears inconsistent with the *Smith* test, the Court in *Merrell Dow* did not purport to overrule *Smith*. Instead, it concluded that the two decisions were distinguishable, because of "the differences in the nature of the federal issues at stake. In *Smith* . . . the issue was the constitutionality of an important federal statute. . . . "

d. The Court in *Merrell Dow* thus appears to have adopted a nebulous "federal interest" standard which, in cases where the cause of action is itself not federal, reserves federal question jurisdiction for state claims presenting "important" issues of federal law.

e. The dissenting justices criticized the majority's reliance on the importance of the federal interest as indefinite, and subject to manipulation. Many commentators agree. The dissent argued that *Smith* and *Moore* simply cannot be reconciled, and that *Moore* should be overruled.

6. Finally, even if a claim arises under federal law, there is no jurisdiction if the claim is "frivolous" or "insubstantial." *Hagans v. Levine*, 415 U.S. 528, 536–37 (1974). This requirement does not refer to monetary value of the claim, but to its legal substance. Thus, this inquiry requires some assessment of the substantive merits of the claim. For example, a lawyer's claim that the federal law that authorizes the Patent and Trademark Office to regulate conduct of attorneys appearing before it

preempted discipline by a state bar association was so frivolous that it did not invoke federal question jurisdiction. *Kroll v. Finnerty*, 242 F.3d 1359 (Fed. Cir. 2001).

V

Diversity of Citizenship and Alienage Jurisdiction

■ ANALYSIS

I. Introduction
II. Constitutional, Statutory, and Policy Bases for Diversity of Citizenship and Alienage Jurisdiction
    A. The Constitutional Grants of Judicial Power
    B. The Statutory Grants of Diversity of Citizenship and Alienage Jurisdiction
    C. Policy Underpinnings for Diversity of Citizenship and Alienage Jurisdiction
III. Determining Whether the Case Involves Appropriate Litigants
    A. The Complete Diversity Rule
    B. Determining Citizenship of Human Beings
    C. Determining Citizenship of Corporations
    D. Determining Citizenship of Non–Incorporated Associations
    E. Determining Citizenship in Cases By or Against Representatives
IV. Determining Whether the Amount in Controversy Requirement is Satisfied

A. The Amount in Controversy Requirement and its Rationale
B. Assessing the Amount in Controversy
C. Aggregation of Claims
D. Claims for Equitable Relief

V. **Exceptions to Diversity of Citizenship and Alienage Jurisdiction**
A. Judge–Made Exceptions for Domestic Relations and Probate Cases
B. Statutory Prohibition of Collusive Joinder to Create Jurisdiction

I. Introduction

Diversity of citizenship and alienage cases are types of disputes that may be heard in the federal courts. They have been part of the congressional grants of jurisdiction since the first Judiciary Act of 1789. Diversity of citizenship cases are between citizens of different states of the United States. Alienage cases are between a citizen of a state of the United States and a citizen or subject of a foreign country. Either type of case must also satisfy the jurisdictional amount requirement by involving an amount in controversy exceeding $75,000. Alienage jurisdiction accounts for little of the federal docket, and has never been controversial. Diversity of citizenship jurisdiction accounts for about 20 percent of the federal trial court docket and has always been controversial. The debate about the wisdom of having federal courts decide cases governed by state law, as they do in diversity of citizenship cases, has never abated.

II. Constitutional, Statutory, and Policy Bases for Diversity of Citizenship and Alienage Jurisdiction

A. The Constitutional Grants of Judicial Power

1. Article III, § 2, clause 1, of the Constitution extends the judicial power of the federal courts to nine types of cases or controversies.

2. That constitutional basis of judicial power includes controversies "between Citizens of different States." That phrase is the constitutional authority for the grant of diversity of citizenship jurisdiction.

3. Another constitutional basis of judicial power includes controversies "between a State, or the Citizens thereof, and foreign States, Citizens or Subjects." Note the breadth of this phrase. It extends, for example, to cases between one of the states of the United States and a foreign country. Alienage jurisdiction, as commonly considered, involves disputes between a citizen of a state of the United States and a foreign citizen or subject.

    a. The words "citizen or subject" were employed to reflect the possibility that the foreigner might be deemed one or the other in her home country, depending upon the type of government that country has. Thus, people who reside in territories of a foreign country might not have all the rights of a citizen of the foreign country. Nonetheless, such a person would fall within the phrase "citizen or subject." The thrust is whether the person is a foreign national. *JPMorgan Chase v. Traffic Stream (BVI) Infrastructure*, 536 U.S. 88, 98–100 (2002)(British Virgin Island (BVI) corporation is a citizen or subject of the United Kingdom notwithstanding BVI's status as merely a territory of the United Kingdom).

    b. Instead of using the cumbersome phrase "foreign citizen or subject," courts routinely refer to such persons as "aliens."

    c. Note that alienage jurisdiction does not exist simply because an alien is a party to the case. The litigation must be between an alien, on one hand, and a citizen of one of the states of the United States, on the other.

    d. Congress once attempted to vest jurisdiction in the federal courts whenever an alien was a party to the case. The Supreme Court struck the provision as unconstitutional. *Hodgson v. Bowerbank*, 9 U.S. 303 (1809). The provision would have permitted jurisdiction over a case by an alien against an alien, and Article III simply does not include such a case within the judicial power of the federal courts.

4. Most of the constitutional bases of judicial power are not self-executing. In other words, the fact that a type of case is listed in Article III, § 2, clause 1, does not mean that federal courts can entertain such cases. The federal courts can hear such disputes *only* if Congress acts to grant jurisdiction over them. Thus, for the federal courts to exercise jurisdiction over a dispute, there must be (a) a constitutional grant of the judicial power and (b) a statutory grant of the subject matter jurisdiction over that dispute. In § B, below, we will see the current statutory grants of both diversity of citizenship and alienage jurisdiction.

5. Note that Article III does not impose an amount in controversy requirement. Such restrictions on jurisdiction, applicable in diversity of citizenship and alienage cases, are imposed by statute.

B. The Statutory Grants of Diversity of Citizenship and Alienage Jurisdiction

1. In 28 U.S.C. § 1332(a), Congress grants the federal courts subject matter jurisdiction over diversity of citizenship and alienage cases.

2. In both types of cases, the amount in controversy must "exceed[] the sum or value of $75,000, exclusive of interest and costs." We will discuss this amount in controversy requirement at § D, below.

3. Assuming the amount in controversy is met, § 1332(a)(1) grants jurisdiction over cases "between Citizens of different States." This is the grant of diversity of citizenship jurisdiction.

   a. In this provision, Congress employed precisely the same phrase as the constitutional grant of judicial power in Article III. *See* § A.2, above. As was seen with regard to federal question jurisdiction at Chapter 4, § III.A, however, the constitutional and statutory grants—identical in language—are interpreted to mean different things. *See* § III.A, below.

   b. Throughout the jurisdictional statutes, when "state" is capitalized, it refers to one of the United States.

4. Assuming the amount in controversy is met, § 1332(a)(2) grants jurisdiction over cases "between citizens of a State and citizens or subjects of a foreign state." This is the grant of alienage jurisdiction.

   a. In this provision, Congress carefully granted the alienage part of the constitutional grant of judicial power from Article III. *See* § A.3, above.

   b. As with the constitutional grant, most courts refer to "citizens or subjects of a foreign state" simply as "aliens." *See* § A.3, above.

   c. As with the statutory grant of diversity of citizenship jurisdiction, when "state" is capitalized, it refers to one of the United States. When it is not capitalized, it refers to a foreign country.

   d. The statutory grant is consistent with the constitutional provision in that it does not grant jurisdiction simply because an alien is a party to the case. The litigation must be between an alien, on one hand, and a citizen of one of the states of the United States, on the other.

5. The last sentence of § 1332(a), added to the statute in 1988, provides that "an alien admitted to the United States for permanent residence shall be deemed a citizen of the State in which such alien is domiciled."

   a. An alien, as noted above, is a citizen or subject of a foreign country.

This provision does not apply to all aliens, but only to those who are admitted to the United States for permanent residence.

    b. This provision gives a permanent resident alien the citizenship of the "State" in which she is domiciled. Because "State" is capitalized in this phrase, it refers to one of the United States. Thus, this part of the statute purports to ascribe to a permanent alien a citizenship of a state of the United States.

    c. There is a question about the validity of this provision. The Supreme Court has held that a human being is a citizen of a State *only* if she is (a) a citizen of the United States and (b) domiciled in a State. *Sun Printing & Publishing Association v. Edwards*, 194 U.S. 377, 383 (1904). By definition, the permanent resident alien cannot satisfy the first of these requirements. As discussed in § III.B.6, below, this statutory provision can result in litigation in a federal court by an alien against an alien. There is no constitutional authority for such jurisdiction. *See* § A.3, above

C. Policy Underpinnings for Diversity of Citizenship and Alienage Jurisdiction

1. The Founders apparently engaged in surprisingly little discussion of the justifications for diversity of citizenship jurisdiction.

2. The traditional justification of diversity jurisdiction is to provide a federal forum to avoid possible prejudice that an out-of-state litigant might suffer—or at least fear—in a state court.

3. A federal district court might be less inclined than a state court to engage in discrimination against an out-of-state litigant for two reasons.

    a. First, recall that federal judges are insulated from political influence because they serve lifetime appointments and their pay cannot be reduced. *See* Chapter 1, § II.A. Thus, they can rule against the local interest, and in favor of an out-of-state litigant, without fear of political reprisal. A state court judge, in contrast, may well be an elected official, whose job security may be threatened if she rules against local interests and in favor of an out-of-state litigant.

    b. The federal district court draws its jury from the entire federal district, which is defined by Congress. A state court draws its jury from a smaller geographic area, usually a county. Thus, the jury in federal court might harbor less pro-local bias than a group drawn from a more localized area.

4. In all likelihood, the Founders provided for diversity of citizenship jurisdiction to allay fears of commercial interests which might be investing in various states. Indeed, it seems clear that the existence of diversity jurisdiction fostered economic expansion to the Southern and Western United States. The availability of an impartial federal forum made it easier to invest in distant states by alleviating fears of bias in the local courts.

5. Many commentators argue, however, that diversity of citizenship jurisdiction is no longer needed. Specifically, in light of modern communication facilities and transportation systems, they argue, the fear of local bias is minimal. In an era of overcrowded courts, they assert, diversity jurisdiction is an unneeded drain of limited federal judicial resources.

6. Defenders of diversity of citizenship jurisdiction respond that fear of regional bias is still a problem in the United States. Moreover, they note that the existence of diversity jurisdiction gives the federal bench some opportunity to decide traditional common law disputes, including contracts and torts, and thus to avoid becoming specialized tribunals dealing exclusively with federal statutes and constitutional provisions. In addition, defenders praise the symbiosis that can evolve when federal courts must interpret state substantive law; federal input may prove beneficial to the development of state law.

7. If fear of local bias is the animating force behind diversity of citizenship jurisdiction, then it seems that the statutory grant of diversity jurisdiction should require that at least one litigant be a citizen of the home forum. But § 1332(a)(1) makes no such requirement. Thus, a citizen of Oklahoma can sue a citizen of Nevada in a federal court in Maine, where neither litigant would be the beneficiary of pro-local bias.

8. Unlike diversity of citizenship jurisdiction, alienage has never been controversial. It has widespread support as an appropriate investment of federal judicial resources. It is seen as serving two major purposes. *See JPMorgan Chase v. Traffic Stram (BVI) Infrastructure*, 536 U.S. 88, 93–97 (2002).

a. It provides aliens involved in litigation with American citizens a forum free from political influence, thereby fostering fair treatment of the aliens.

b. In so doing, the existence of alienage jurisdiction sends a signal to foreign countries that litigation involving their citizens or subjects is sufficiently important to demand determination by the national—as opposed to the local—judiciary.

III. Determining Whether the Case Involves Appropriate Litigants

Throughout this section, assume that the amount in controversy requirement (§ IV, below) is satisfied. Both it and the requirements discussed in this section must be satisfied to invoke diversity of citizenship or alienage jurisdiction.

A. The Complete Diversity Rule

1. In the famous decision of *Strawbridge v. Curtiss*, 7 U.S. 267 (1806), the Supreme Court held that diversity of citizenship jurisdiction extends only to cases of "complete" diversity. Complete diversity means that *every* plaintiff must be a citizen of a different state from *every* defendant.

    a. Thus, under *Strawbridge*, diversity of citizenship does not extend to cases involving mere "minimal diversity"—those in which at least one plaintiff is a citizen of a different state than at least one defendant.

    Example: A, a citizen of New York, and B, a citizen of Illinois, sue C, a citizen of Iowa, and D, a citizen of Oregon in federal district court. This case satisfies the complete diversity rule, because both plaintiffs are citizens of different states from both defendants.

    Example: A, a citizen of New York, and B, a citizen Illinois, sue E, a citizen of Illinois. This case demonstrates "minimal" diversity, because at least one plaintiff is of diverse citizenship from at least one defendant. But the case does not invoke diversity of citizenship jurisdiction, because it does not satisfy the complete diversity rule. Because one plaintiff (B) is a co-citizen with one defendant (E), the case does not satisfy *Strawbridge*. The case could proceed in federal court only if B (the non-diverse plaintiff) were dropped from the suit (or, obviously, if the case invoked some other basis of subject matter jurisdiction, such as federal question).

    b. The complete diversity rule does not require that every litigant be of diverse citizenship from every other litigant. It requires only that every *plaintiff* be of diverse citizenship from every *defendant*.

Example: A and B, both citizens of California, sue F and G, both citizens of Arizona. This case satisfies the complete diversity rule. Even though the plaintiffs are co-citizens and the defendants are co-citizens, no plaintiff is a citizen of the same state as any defendant.

2. Note that the basis of jurisdiction is diversity of *citizenship*, and not residence. Although some courts use the terms interchangeably, they should be kept distinct. Residence is relevant to venue, which you studied in Civil Procedure. Citizenship is relevant here. Although a litigant's residence and citizenship may be the same, the terms should not be mixed. Technically, if the plaintiff files a suit claiming to invoke diversity jurisdiction and alleges the residence (not citizenship) of the parties, the case should be dismissed.

3. For over a century and a half, it was not clear whether *Strawbridge* interpreted Article III or the statute granting diversity of citizenship jurisdiction. If the complete diversity rule is based upon the constitutional language "between citizens of different States," then the rule would be constitutionally mandated, and Congress could not permit jurisdiction based upon minimal diversity. On the other hand, if Chief Justice Marshall's opinion in *Strawbridge* simply interpreted the diversity *statute*, then the Constitution does not require complete diversity, and Congress may grant jurisdiction based upon minimal diversity.

4. The uncertainty on this score was put to rest in *State Farm Fire & Casualty Co. v. Tashire,* 386 U.S. 523 (1967). In that case, the Supreme Court held that the complete diversity requirement of *Strawbridge* is only a matter of statutory construction. The Court therefore upheld the Federal Interpleader Act, 28 U.S.C. § 1335, which extends diversity of citizenship jurisdiction to cases of minimal diversity in certain interpleader situations.

    a. Thus, the grant of general diversity of citizenship jurisdiction, § 1332(a)(1), includes the complete diversity rule. But the grant of diversity of citizenship jurisdiction in Article III does not have that requirement; it is satisfied by mere minimal diversity. This conclusion is interesting given that the two provisions—statutory and constitutional—use precisely the same operative language. *See* § B.3, above. We saw the same situation in federal question jurisdiction, in which the statutory and constitutional provisions, though using identical operative language, mean different things.

   b. Although Congress is clearly empowered to abolish the complete diversity requirement in § 1332(a)(1), it has not done so, and is not expected to do so.

5. There is some debate about the rationale for the complete diversity requirement. Some suggest that the presence of co-citizens on both sides of the litigation neutralizes the effect of local bias, and thus obviates the need for a neutral federal forum. But this will not always be true.

Example: A, a citizen of Alabama, and B, a citizen of Massachusetts, sue C, a citizen of Massachusetts in an Alabama state court. This case presents the possibility of pro-local bias. The fear is that the Massachusetts defendant will be "hometowned" in favor of the Alabama plaintiff (even though there is a Massachusetts co-plaintiff). Yet the Massachusetts defendant is stuck in the Alabama state court. This case does not invoke diversity of citizenship jurisdiction because it violates the complete diversity rule.

6. There is no question that the complete diversity rule has a docket control effect of minimizing the number of diversity cases brought in federal court. If jurisdiction could be based upon minimal diversity, the federal courts could be inundated with such cases.

7. Section 1332(d) provides that the District of Columbia, Puerto Rico, and American Territories are to be considered "States" for diversity of citizenship purposes. Many commentators questioned the constitutionality of this provision, for the simple reasons that those jurisdictions are not states. Indeed, the Supreme Court early held that a citizen of the District of Columbia was not a citizen of a "State" for purposes of diversity jurisdiction. *Hepburn & Dundas v. Ellzey*, 6 U.S. 445 (1804). Later, however, the Court upheld the constitutionality of the provision in *National Mutual Insurance Co. v. Tidewater Transfer Co.*, 337 U.S. 582 (1949). The case is curious because although its holding is clear, no single theory justifying it was adopted by a majority of the justices.

8. There is an argument that the supplemental jurisdiction statute, 28 U.S.C. § 1367, operates to overrule the complete diversity rule in some cases. *See* Chapter 6, § IV.F.

9. In alienage cases, courts apply a version of the complete diversity rule.

   Example: A, a citizen of France, sues B, a citizen of Florida, in federal court. This case invokes alienage jurisdiction, because it is between a citizen of a state of the United States and an alien. Note that it does not matter whether the alien is the plaintiff or the defendant. The case would also invoke alienage jurisdiction if B had sued A.

   Example: A, a citizen of Spain, sues B, a citizen of Australia. This case does not invoke alienage jurisdiction, because it is not (as required both by Article III and § 1332(a)(2)) between a citizen of a state of the United States and an alien.

   Example: A, a citizen of Italy, sues B, a citizen of Colorado, and C, a citizen of Venezuela. Most courts addressing this case hold that there is no alienage jurisdiction, because of the presence of aliens on both sides of the litigation. *See, e.g., Faysound, Ltd. v. United Coconut Chemicals, Inc.*, 878 F.2d 290 (9th Cir. 1989)(citizen of Hong Kong sued citizens of various states and a citizen of Switzerland). Thus, they adopt a complete diversity rule in alienage cases, despite the obvious fact that *Strawbridge* did not involve alienage.

B. Determining Citizenship of Human Beings

1. As noted in § A.2, above, diversity jurisdiction looks to the *citizenship* (not residence) of the litigants. In this section, we address the definition of the citizenship of human beings.

2. If the litigant is a citizen of the United States, she is deemed a citizen of the state in which she is domiciled.

3. One's domicile is usually referred to as her permanent home. There are several important points to consider in assessing domicile.

   a. An individual may have only one domicile at a time. It is impossible to have more than one domicile. Thus, it is impossible for a human being to be a citizen (for diversity of citizenship purposes) of more than one state at a time.

b. One's initial domicile is usually ascribed at birth, and is usually the citizenship of the person's parents. Later, one may change her domicile. She does so by establishing two things. Although courts differ sometimes in stating the requirements, they are often stated as: (1) presence in the "new" state and (2) the subjective intent to make that state her permanent home (or from which she has no intention to leave). Thus, there is a physical component and a mental component to changing one's domicile. Both must be established, or else the person retains her "old" domicile.

Example: Clara is born and raised in Oregon. After high school, she moves to Massachusetts to attend college for four years. After that, she moves directly to New York to attend law school for three years. After that, she moves directly to Virginia to attend medical school for four years. She has not set foot in Oregon in eleven years. She does not know where she wants to live permanently, although she is sure she will not go back to Oregon. Her domicile is still Oregon, because although she has been present in other states, she has never formed the subjective intent to make any of them her domicile. Thus, her citizenship for diversity jurisdiction is Oregon.

Example: Lars is a citizen of Minnesota. He forms the intent to make Florida his permanent home. On the drive to Florida, he is involved in an auto wreck in Tennessee. His domicile is still Minnesota. Even though he has left Minnesota and formed the intent to make Florida his domicile, he has not been present in Florida. Thus, his citizenship for diversity jurisdiction is Minnesota.

c. Obviously, from the foregoing, one's domicile is not necessarily the same as one's residence. Clara, in the above *Example*, was a resident of Massachusetts for four years, of New York for three years, and of Virginia for four years. The whole time, however, she was a domiciliary (and thus a citizen) of Oregon.

d. In contested cases, the court will determine one's domicile. In assessing intent, no single factor is determinative. The court will consider all relevant evidence, focusing on the person's conduct, and not just her statements of intent.

e. Never refer to "diversity of domicile." There is no such thing. It is always "diversity of citizenship." For an individual who is a citizen of the United States, her citizenship is her domicile.

4. Diversity of citizenship is assessed at the time the action is commenced, which means when it is filed. Thus, a subsequent change is irrelevant. If a citizen of Missouri files suit against a citizen of Ohio, and, after filing, becomes a citizen of Ohio, diversity of citizenship is unaffected. Similarly, a pre-suit change in citizenship is irrelevant. Assume that a citizen of Missouri has a claim against another citizen of Missouri in federal court. If she legitimately changes her domicile to Kansas before bringing suit, she can invoke diversity of citizenship jurisdiction.

5. A citizen of the United States who is domiciled in a foreign country has no State of citizenship and is also not an alien.

Example: Alice, a citizen of the United States domiciled in Spain, sues Gene, a citizen of Kentucky, in federal court. This case does not invoke diversity of citizenship jurisdiction because it is not "between citizens of different States." Alice is not a citizen of any State because she is not domiciled in any State.

Moreover, the case does not invoke alienage jurisdiction, because it is not "between a citizen of a State and a foreign citizen or subject." Alice is not a citizen or subject of Spain. The fact that she is domiciled in Spain does not make her a Spanish citizen. Only Spain can confer Spanish citizenship.

6. If a litigant is not a citizen of the United States, she is an alien. If an alien is admitted to the United States for permanent residence, however, § 1332(a) provides that she is to be deemed a citizen of the State in which she is domiciled. As noted in § B.5, above, this provision is problematic because it ascribes State citizenship to people who are not citizens of the United States. In addition, it arguably expands the jurisdiction of the federal courts beyond Article III.

Example: A, a citizen of Japan admitted to the United States for permanent residence and domiciled in North Carolina, sues B, a citizen of Canada. Based upon § 1332, A is deemed to be a citizen of North Carolina. If that is so, then this case invokes alienage jurisdiction, because it is between a citizen of a State (A) and an alien (B). In fact, however, this is a case by an alien against an alien. Article

III does not extend the judicial power to such a case. *See* § II.A.3, above. So far, courts have found ways to avoid confronting this issue meaningfully.

C. Determining Citizenship of Corporations

1. In *Bank of the United States v. Deveaux*, 9 U.S. 61 (1809), Chief Justice Marshall stated that a corporation is an "invisible, intangible, and artificial being" and therefore retains the citizenship of all of its stockholders. In light of the complete diversity requirement, this holding significantly reduced the number of potential diversity cases involving corporations. This resulted because if a corporation's stockholders were citizens of numerous states, it would be more difficult to satisfy the complete diversity rule.

2. The Court overruled *Deveaux*, however, in *Louisville, Cincinnati & Charleston Railroad Co. v. Letson*, 43 U.S. 497 (1844). There, the Court held that a corporation is a citizen for diversity purposes only in the state in which it is incorporated. The Court created an irrebuttable presumption that all of the stockholders were citizens of the state of incorporation.

3. In 1958, Congress finally undertook to define the citizenship of corporations by adding a provision now codified at 28 U.S.C. § 1332(c)(1). It provides that "a corporation shall be deemed a citizen of any State by which it has been incorporated and of the State where it has its principal place of business. . . . " Under this statute, the corporation is seen as an entity, not as an aggregate of the people who own or manage it.

    a. The language "any State by which it has been incorporated" implies that there may be more than one such State. While it is possible that a corporation will incorporate in more than one state, today, as a practical matter, multiple incorporation is virtually nonexistent. As a nearly universal rule, then, there will be only one State of incorporation.

    b. Just as clearly, the language "the State where it has its principal place of business" makes it clear that there is only one such State. Every corporation has one principal place of business. And no corporation can have more than one principal place of business.

    c. Thus, a corporation—unlike a human being—may be a citizen of more than one state. If a corporation is incorporated in Delaware and has its principal place of business in Kansas, it is a citizen of *both* Delaware *and* Kansas.

4. It is easy to determine the state in which a corporation is incorporated, or "chartered."

5. Determining a corporation's principal place of business, however, can be difficult. It is an ad hoc decision, based upon the facts of the case.

   a. Although the Supreme Court has never defined "principal place of business," the lower courts have addressed the issue many times, and have derived a relatively consistent set of principles for assessing the issue.

   b. Some courts have emphasized the corporation's decision-making activity. Under this "nerve center" approach, the place where corporate authority is exercised generally constitutes the principal place of business. Often, this place will be the corporate headquarters. A classic case discussing the nerve center approach is *Scot Typewriter Co. v. Underwood Corp.*, 170 F. Supp. 862 (S.D. N.Y. 1959).

   c. Other courts have emphasized the corporation's physical activity. Under this "muscle center," or "place of activities" approach, the place where the corporation does more of what it does—provide services, manufacture widgets, etc.—than anywhere else generally constitutes the principal place of business. A classic case discussing this approach is *Kelly v. United States Steel Corp.*, 284 F.2d 850 (3d Cir. 1960).

   d. The nerve center and muscle center approaches should not be seen as competing definitions of the principal place of business. Rather, they tend to be applied, respectively, to different fact patterns. They are reconciled in what many courts call the "total activities" approach. Under this view, most courts will adopt the nerve center approach when the corporation's physical activities are spread over several states. On the other hand, they will adopt the muscle center approach when the corporation's physical activities are focused in a single state. A leading discussion of this approach is found in *J.A. Olson Co. v. City of Winona*, 818 F.2d 401 (5th Cir. 1987).

   Example: Widget Corp. is incorporated in Delaware. It manufactures widgets in its plants in Kansas, Arizona, Maryland, and Texas. Corporate headquarters, where decisions tend to be made, are in Texas. Because the physical activities are spread over several states, most courts would find that the principal place of business is the nerve center, in Texas. Thus, this corporation is a citizen of both Delaware (state of incorporation) and Texas (principal place of business).

Example: Java Co. is incorporated in Louisiana, where it imports and grinds coffee. Its corporate headquarters are in Illinois. The principal place of business is probably Louisiana because the corporation only does what it does (import and grind coffee) there. Thus, most courts would likely find the muscle center to be the principal place of business. Note that Java Co. is a citizen only of Louisiana, because that is the state of its incorporation and its principal place of business.

D. **Determining Citizenship of Non–Incorporated Associations**

1. Many businesses are not incorporated. Partnerships, labor unions, and insurance associations are examples. Traditionally, the law has regarded such associations as aggregations of their members, and not as entities. This view contrasts with that of the corporation, which is seen as an entity, separate from its stockholders, directors, and officers. *See* § C.3, above.

2. Jurisdictional theory also adopts this "aggregate" approach for non-incorporated associations. In *Chapman v. Barney*, 129 U.S. 677 (1889), the Supreme Court held that a non-incorporated association's citizenship for purposes of diversity jurisdiction was to be determined by the citizenship of all of its members. The Court has consistently adhered to this view. Thus, although the view is judge-made (like the complete diversity rule), it is now seen as part of the definition of "citizen" in § 1332(a)(1).

3. This rule decreases the availability of diversity of citizenship jurisdiction, because it increases the likelihood that litigation will not satisfy the complete diversity rule.

Example: Big Law Firm is a partnership with partners who are citizens of California, Arizona, Texas, New York, New Jersey, Virginia, Maryland, and Illinois. It is deemed, for diversity purposes, to be a citizen of all eight of those states. Thus, no case involving it as a litigant can invoke diversity of citizenship jurisdiction if any party on the opposing side of the case is a citizen of any of those eight states.

4. There was long a question about how to treat limited partnerships—whether the court should assess only the citizenship of the general partners or include limited partners as well. The Supreme Court resolved the debate in *Carden v. Arkoma Associates*, 494 U.S. 185 (1990), when it held that the focus was the citizenship of all members—including both general and limited partners.

5. The "business trust," long a staple of Massachusetts law, has been treated differently from other non-incorporated businesses. In *Navarro Savings Association v. Lee*, 446 U.S. 458 (1980), the Supreme Court held that individual trustees of a business may invoke diversity of citizenship jurisdiction on the basis of their own citizenship, regardless of the citizenship of the trust beneficiaries. While such a business trust bears certain similarities to an association, the Court noted that in some ways it also resembled a corporation. So long as the trustees are active and the real parties in interest, their citizenship controls.

E. Determining Citizenship in Cases by or Against Representatives

1. Litigation by or against minors (sometimes referred to as "infants"), incompetents, and decedents usually is brought by or against a representative. Minors and incompetents lack legal capacity, and their interests in litigation should be represented by a fiduciary, such as a guardian, guardian ad litem, or conservator. The interests of decedents, obviously, must be represented in litigation by a fiduciary, such as an executor or administrator.

2. In suits involving decedents, minors, and incompetents, § 1332(c)(2) provides that "the legal representative of the estate of a decedent shall be deemed to be a citizen only of the same State as the decedent, and the legal representative of an infant or incompetent shall be deemed to be a citizen only of the same State as the infant or incompetent." Thus, the citizenship of the person *being represented* (and not the citizenship of the representative herself) is relevant in assessing whether there is diversity of citizenship.

Example: Executor, a citizen of Nevada, acting on behalf of the estate of Decedent, who was a citizen of Utah, sues Defendant, who is a citizen of Nevada. Diversity of citizenship jurisdiction is satisfied here, because Executor's citizenship is irrelevant. Section 1332(c)(2) requires that the citizenship of Decedent, and not

Executor, be "counted." Thus, the case is seen as brought by a citizen of Utah against a citizen of Nevada.

3. Section 1332(c)(2) does not apply to class action litigation. The Supreme Court laid down the applicable rule for class actions in *Supreme Tribe of Ben–Hur v. Cauble*, 255 U.S. 356 (1921), which holds that the citizenship of the class is deemed to be only the citizenship of the class representative. In other words, the citizenships of the class members (other than the representative) are irrelevant.

Example: P, suing as representative of a class, is a citizen of Florida. Class members are citizens of Georgia, Alabama, Mississippi, and South Carolina. The defendants are citizens of Georgia and South Carolina. The case invokes diversity of citizenship jurisdiction. The class's citizenship is deemed to be that of P, the representative; the other class members' citizenships are irrelevant. Thus, this case is seen as brought by a Florida citizen against citizens of Georgia and South Carolina.

IV. Determining Whether the Amount in Controversy Requirement is Satisfied

Throughout this section, assume that the requirement concerning the proper litigants for a diversity of citizenship or alienage case (§ III, above) is satisfied. Both it and the requirements discussed in this section must be satisfied to invoke diversity of citizenship or alienage jurisdiction.

A. The Amount in Controversy Requirement and its Rationale

1. For any case to invoke jurisdiction under § 1332—which includes diversity of citizenship and alienage jurisdiction—the amount in controversy must "exceed[] the sum or value of $75,000, exclusive of interest and costs." Note that the claim must "exceed" $75,000; thus, a claim for exactly $75,000 will not invoke diversity of citizenship or alienage jurisdiction.

2. The purpose of congressional imposition of a jurisdictional minimum is well accepted: the federal courts possess limited time and resources, and therefore Congress must employ some means of limiting what would otherwise be insurmountable judicial burdens. The imposition of a minimum amount requirement reflects the congressional judgment that cases not "worth" the specified amount simply do not justify the expenditure of federal judicial time and effort.

3. Congress amends the amount in controversy requirement periodically. The current requirement was set in 1997. From 1989 until that time, the requirement was an amount in excess of $50,000. Before that, for thirty years, the requirement was an amount in excess of $10,000.

B. Assessing the Amount in Controversy

1. In *St. Paul Mercury Indemnity Co. v. Red Cab Co.*, 303 U.S. 283 (1938), the Supreme Court held that "the sum claimed by the plaintiff controls if the claim is apparently made in good faith. It must appear to a legal certainty that the claim is really for less than the jurisdictional amount to justify dismissal."

    a. This decision gave rise to the "legal certainty" test for jurisdictional amount: before a case may be dismissed for failure to meet the amount in controversy requirement, it must appear to a legal certainty that the plaintiff cannot recover more than $75,000.

    b. This rule does *not* mean that the plaintiff has the burden to demonstrate that she will "certainly" recover more than $75,000. Rather, the burden is on the defendant to show that, to a legal certainty, the plaintiff cannot recover that much.

Example: Plaintiff brings a diversity suit for damages suffered allegedly due to defendant's negligence in an auto accident. At the outset of the case, it is impossible to know whether plaintiff's damages exceed $75,000. The plaintiff's claim will not be dismissed for lack of jurisdiction, despite this uncertainty, because it is not clear to a legal certainty that her damages do not exceed $75,000.

2. The clearest cases for dismissal, of course, are those rare instances in which the plaintiff demands $75,000 or less. Also clear are cases in which either the applicable substantive state law or a private arrangement between the parties imposes a ceiling on damages which does not exceed $75,000.

Example: Plaintiff sues Hotel for negligence in providing security; she alleges that $100,000 worth of valuables were stolen from her room. An applicable statute limits innkeepers' liability in such cases to $25,000. The case will be dismissed for failure to meet the amount in controversy requirement; it is clear to a legal certainty, given the statute, that Plaintiff cannot recover more than $75,000.

3. Absent a liquidated damage clause or a ceiling imposed by state law, courts only occasionally invoke the *St. Paul* test to deny jurisdiction. Doing so is proper only if the court concludes that a jury award in excess of $75,000 would be vacated as unreasonable on the basis of the available evidence. Thus, it is clear to a legal certainty that the jurisdictional requirement has not been met. Such cases are rare, however, and involve damages claims that seem shocking on their face.

Example: In a suit for negligence arising out of an auto accident, where plaintiff suffered a sprained wrist and her junker automobile was totaled, and where no other claim, such as loss of employment compensation or punitive damages, was made, the federal court would probably dismiss for lack of jurisdiction. Any jury award that exceeded $75,000, would have to be set aside as capricious. *See Nelson v. Keefer*, 451 F.2d 289 (3rd Cir. 1971).

4. In *St. Paul Mercury*, the Court also indicated that an amount in excess of the jurisdictional minimum must be claimed in good faith. This statement raises confusion over whether "good faith" and "legal certainty" impose distinct, necessary conditions for meeting the jurisdictional minimum, or whether they are simply different characterizations of the same test.

   a. While certain courts and commentators have expressed the view that "good faith" merely represents a means of finding "legal certainty," at least as an abstract matter the two might concern different questions.

Example: Plaintiff sues for injuries, including pain and suffering, caused by Defendant's negligence. The amount claimed far exceeds $75,000. Plaintiff and her lawyer say to friends that in reality they do not expect to recover anywhere near $75,000. Under a "good faith" test, Plaintiff's complaint might be dismissed. But if Plaintiff and her lawyer are actually undervaluing Plaintiff's claim, under the "legal certainty" test the claim should not be dismissed.

   b. Ultimately, it seems that the motivation for the jurisdictional amount requirement—keeping small claims cases out of federal court—dictates that an *objective* "legal certainty" test, rather than a *subjective* "good faith" test, should be employed.

   c. Of course, a demonstration that the plaintiff herself does not believe her claim to be worth more than $75,000 could be powerful evidence in making the objective "legal certainty" finding, and in this sense the two criteria may merge.

5. The plaintiff's actual recovery in the litigation is irrelevant to jurisdiction. Thus, if the plaintiff sues for $100,000 and ultimately recovers a judgment of $10,000, jurisdiction is not affected. Jurisdiction attached at the outset, with the good faith allegation that the claim exceeded $75,000, and because the court did not conclude that such an amount, to a legal certainty, could not be recovered.

6. Should the plaintiff ultimately recover less than $75,000, however, § 1332(b) provides that the court may deny her a recovery of her costs and may impose upon the plaintiff liability for the defendant's costs. Ordinarily, the prevailing party recovers her costs (which generally do not include attorney's fees) from the other side. In this instance, however, § 1332(b) permits the court to deviate from that rule.

C. Aggregation of Claims

1. Under long-accepted principles, *a single plaintiff* is allowed to aggregate the amounts of all of her separate claims against *a single defendant*, regardless of whether those claims arise out of the same transaction or occurrence.

Example: A sues B in federal court in a diversity of citizenship suit, joining a claim for $40,000 under a breach of contract claim and a wholly unrelated tort claim seeking $55,000. Although neither of these claims, alone, would satisfy the amount in controversy requirement, because this case involves one plaintiff suing one defendant, the claims are aggregated, or added. Thus, the amount in controversy is $95,000, and the case satisfies the amount in controversy requirement.

2. In contrast, multiple plaintiffs seeking to aggregate their claims against a single defendant, or a single plaintiff seeking to aggregate claims against multiple defendants, traditionally have not been allowed to do so. Courts indicated an exception, however, if their claims were deemed "joint," rather than "several." In such cases, the amount in controversy is the total value of the claims asserted. Although "joint" and "several" are abstract concepts which the courts have never adequately distinguished and which have caused substantial confusion, there are some clear cases.

Example: Plaintiff was injured by four joint tortfeasors. She sues all four in a single action, claiming damages of $80,000. The case satisfies the amount in controversy requirement. This is clearly a joint claim, so the court will look to the total value of the claim—$80,000—which, of course, exceeds $75,000.

3. There is an argument, adopted by some courts, that the supplemental jurisdiction statute, 28 U.S.C. § 1367, has overruled this principle in certain cases, to permit joinder of multiple plaintiffs, so long as one has a claim exceeding $75,000. *See* Chapter 6, § IV.E.

4. There have long been questions about how to determine the amount in controversy for a class action.

   a. In *Snyder v. Harris*, 394 U.S. 332 (1969), the Supreme Court held that plaintiff class members cannot aggregate their claims to meet the amount in controversy requirement. In *Snyder*, no class member's claim met the requirement, so the case could not invoke diversity of citizenship jurisdiction.

   b. In *Zahn v. International Paper Co.*, 414 U.S. 291 (1973), the Supreme Court held that the claim of *each* member of the plaintiff class—not just the named representative's claim—must meet the amount in controversy requirement (except in the rare situation in which the rights asserted are "joint"). Although the named representative's claim met the amount in controversy requirement, other class members' claims did not. Those other class members could not be included in the class.

   c. *Zahn* was an unfortunate decision, and many commentators have criticized it. There are two major objections to *Zahn*.

   d. First, the holding of the case is completely inconsistent with the manner in which citizenship is determined for a class action. For citizenship purposes, the Supreme Court held in 1921, in the *Ben-Hur* case, that only the named representative (not all class members) need be diverse from the opposing party. *See* § III.E.3, above.

   e. Second, the majority of the justices failed to consider the operation of supplemental (then called "ancillary") jurisdiction for the claims of class members.

f. *Zahn* undermines the class action device, which is designed in part to allow numerous relatively small claims to be joined in one suit when it would be inefficient or impractical for separate suits to be brought.

5. The supplemental jurisdiction statute, 28 U.S.C. § 1367, arguably overrules *Zahn* by permitting class members to invoke supplemental jurisdiction. Courts are badly split on the issue, with four Circuits having concluded that *Zahn* has been abrogated, and three having concluded that *Zahn* still applies. The issue is discussed in detail in Chapter 6, § IV.E.

D. Claims for Equitable Relief

1. In most cases, the plaintiff will be seeking damages, which are relatively easy to quantify. When the plaintiff seeks equitable relief—such as an injunction, declaratory judgment, rescission, or reformation—the court must determine whether the claim exceeds $75,000.

2. The courts have employed two tests to assess the value of equitable claims. One is the "plaintiff's viewpoint" test, which asks whether the defendant's act has caused harm to the plaintiff of more than $75,000. The other is the "defendant's viewpoint" test, which asks whether it would cost the defendant more than $75,000 to comply with the requested relief. The choice of test may yield quite different conclusions.

Example: Plaintiff sues to enjoin Defendant's operation of a power plant, alleging that it is a nuisance. The harm to Plaintiff is air pollution, which is largely immeasurable. If the injunction is entered, however, Defendant would be required to shut down its plant for a substantial time each day. Under the plaintiff's viewpoint test, the jurisdictional amount is not met. Under the defendant's viewpoint test, however, the amount in controversy requirement might well be met.

3. The defendant's viewpoint test is consistent with the main purpose of the amount in controversy requirement, which is to keep trivial cases out of the federal judicial system. If either party stands to be affected by more than $75,000, the case cannot be deemed trivial. Thus, some courts will invoke diversity of citizenship jurisdiction if the amount in controversy requirement is met under *either* the plaintiff's or defendant's viewpoint. *See, e.g., Smith v. Washington*, 593 F.2d 1097 (D.C. Cir. 1978).

4. An argument in favor of the plaintiff's viewpoint test is docket control. Using it results in fewer diversity of citizenship cases in the federal courts.

V. Exceptions to Diversity of Citizenship and Alienage Jurisdiction

A. Judge–Made Exceptions for Domestic Relations and Probate Cases

1. In two substantive areas, the federal courts will not exercise jurisdiction even if the requirements for diversity of citizenship jurisdiction are satisfied. They are: domestic relations and probate cases.

2. Although they are not spoken of in these terms, these judge-made exceptions are essentially forms of abstention. There is an interesting argument that courts should not be allowed simply to refuse to hear particular kinds of cases. Because it is Congress's responsibility to determine the jurisdiction of the federal courts (within Article III), the courts' refusal to adjudicate is, arguably, a violation of separation of powers principles. Nonetheless, these exceptions are well established.

3. The exception as to domestic relations cases derives from a dissenting opinion in *Barber v. Barber*, 62 U.S. 582, 603–05 (1859)(Daniel, J., dissenting). The Supreme Court answered questions about the scope of the exception in *Ankenbrandt v. Richards*, 504 U.S. 689 (1992). Although its statement was dictum (because, on the facts, the exception did not apply), *Ankenbrandt* contains the leading modern statement of the exception.

    a. According to *Ankenbrandt*, the federal courts will not hear cases "involving the issuance of a divorce, alimony, or child custody decree." *Id.* at 704.

    b. Thus, the exception is rather narrow. It does not apply, for example, to intra-family torts or other disputes between family members that do not constitute "issuance of a divorce, alimony, or child custody decree."

4. The domestic relations exception is rooted in history and policy.

    a. As a matter of history, the original Judiciary Act granted jurisdiction to federal courts over cases "at common law or in equity." Because domestic relations cases historically were heard by ecclesiastical courts, and not at law or equity, the statutory grant of federal jurisdiction did not include such disputes. The fact that more recent jurisdictional statutes do not use the phrase "at common law or in equity" is irrelevant. Any change to require federal courts to hear domestic relations cases will have to come from Congress. *Ankenbrandt v. Richards,* 504 U.S. at 700.

  b. As a matter of policy, state courts have developed expertise in domestic relations cases and there is a considerable local interest in how issues relating to marriage and child custody are handled.

5. The probate exception provides that a federal court will not probate a will or administer an estate. The scope of this exception is not clear, in part because the Supreme Court has not discussed it recently.

  a. The mere fact that an executor or administrator is a party to a diversity of citizenship case does not preclude jurisdiction.

  b. The court may, for example, decide a case brought against an executor to assert a claim, but not if the court is asked to take control over the estate or to interfere with probate proceedings in state court. *See Markham v. Allen*, 326 U.S. 490 (1946).

6. The probate exception undoubtedly is supported by similar policy bases as those supporting the domestic relations exception. Judge Richard Posner also notes that judicial economy is a relevant policy factor: "When a person dies, his will has to be admitted to probate somewhere, or if he dies intestate the control of his property has to be vested in some court initially, and it is hard to imagine in either case how the initial jurisdiction over the decedent's estate could be elsewhere than in a state court." *Dragan v. Miller,* 679 F.2d 712, 714 (7th Cir. 1982), *cert. denied,* 459 U.S. 1017 (1983).

B. Statutory Prohibition of Collusive Joinder to Create Jurisdiction

1. Section 1359, of Title 28 U.S.C., provides: "A district court shall not have jurisdiction of a civil action in which any party, by assignment or otherwise, has been improperly or collusively made or joined to invoke the jurisdiction of such court."

2. Today, this statute applies mostly with regard to assignments of claims to create diversity of citizenship jurisdiction. The leading case is *Kramer*

v. Caribbean Mills, Inc., 394 U.S. 823 (1969). In that case, a would-be plaintiff, realizing that there was no diversity between him and the would-be defendant, assigned his claim to someone who could invoke diversity jurisdiction against the defendant. The assignee agreed to return to the assignor 95 percent of any recovery. The Supreme Court held that § 1359 applied, because there was a collusive effort between assignor and assignee to create diversity.

a. The Court looked to all relevant facts in assessing whether the statute applied. Noting that the assignee had no previous connection with the business deal, the Court concluded that he was a mere collection agent for the assignor, and applied the statute.

b. Not all assignments of claims will run afoul of § 1359. Again, courts are to assess all relevant factors, including any legitimate business reason for the assignment, any interest retained by the assignor, and the subjective intent of the parties.

c. Section 1359 does not invalidate the assignment. Rather, if the statute applies, the court ignores the assignment, and assesses whether there is jurisdiction based upon the assignor's citizenship. The result in *Kramer*, of course, was to find that there was no federal subject matter jurisdiction, because the assignor was not of diverse citizenship from the defendant.

VI

Supplemental Jurisdiction

■ ANALYSIS

I. Introduction
II. Policy Issues
III. Historical Development of Supplemental Jurisdiction
   A. Definitional Issues: "Pendent," "Ancillary," and "Supplemental"
   B. Until 1990, the Doctrine Was Developed by Case Law, not Legislation
   C. The *Finley* Decision Led to Passage of the Supplemental Jurisdiction Statute in 1990
IV. The Supplemental Jurisdiction Statute
   A. Overview of the Statute
   B. The Grant of Supplemental Jurisdiction in § 1367(a)
   C. Restrictions on Supplemental Jurisdiction in § 1367(b)
   D. Discretionary Decline of Supplemental Jurisdiction Under § 1367(c)
   E. Tolling Provision of § 1367(d)
   F. Some Problems in Applying § 1367

I. Introduction

To be heard in federal court, the plaintiff must set forth at least one claim that invokes federal subject matter jurisdiction, such as diversity of citizenship or federal question. Thereafter, every claim asserted in the case must also have a basis of federal subject matter jurisdiction. If such a claim invokes diversity of citizenship or federal question jurisdiction, obviously, it can be heard by the federal court. But sometimes, claims are not supported by such an independent basis of subject matter jurisdiction. These claims may nonetheless be heard by the federal court if they invoke supplemental jurisdiction. Supplemental jurisdiction is appropriate only when the claim over which it is asserted bears a sufficiently close factual relationship with a claim that invoked an independent basis of federal subject matter jurisdiction (e.g., federal question or diversity of citizenship). The Supreme Court has long upheld the constitutionality of supplemental jurisdiction. Although the doctrine developed in the courts, it was codified in 1990 in 28 U.S.C. § 1367.

II. Policy Issues

1. Supplemental jurisdiction permits a federal court to hear claims over which it would have no independent basis of subject matter jurisdiction. In other words, it allows the court to hear non-federal, non-diverse claims.

   Example 1: P, a citizen of Arizona, asserts a $100,000 claim against D, a citizen of California, for damages suffered in an automobile crash between the two. The claim obviously invokes diversity of citizenship jurisdiction and can be filed in federal court. Assume D has a compulsory counterclaim against P (one that arises from the same wreck), but that D's claim is for $45,000. That claim is based upon state law, so it cannot invoke federal question jurisdiction. It also does not invoke diversity of citizenship jurisdiction because it does not meet the amount in controversy requirement for such a claim (it does not exceed $75,000). Because the claim is transactionally related to P's claim, which did invoke federal subject matter jurisdiction, however, the federal court can exercise supplemental jurisdiction over D's compulsory counterclaim.

   Example 2: P asserts a federal question claim against D. P also asserts in the same case a state-law claim against D that arises from the same transaction as the federal question claim. P and D are co-citizens. The federal question claim invokes federal question jurisdiction and is properly in federal court. The state-law claim, on the other hand, does not invoke federal question jurisdiction and, because P and D are co-citizens, cannot invoke diversity jurisdiction either. Because the state-law claim arises from the same operative facts as the federal question claim, however, a federal court may exercise supplemental jurisdiction over it.

2. Obviously, as both examples show, supplemental jurisdiction thus fosters efficiency, because it allows the federal court to determine all transactionally related claims in a single case. In *Example 1*, it would be wasteful if P's claim against D were in federal court but D's claim against P had to be litigated in state court. In *Example 2*, it would be wasteful if P's federal question claim were litigated in federal court but her state-law claim had to go to state court.

3. Note, however, that the plaintiff could ensure that both claims in both of the examples were litigated in a single forum by filing the case in *state* court. In *Example 2*, however, doing so would rob P of a federal forum for her federal claim. In part for this reason, there has always been broader acceptance of supplemental jurisdiction in federal question cases than in diversity of citizenship cases.

4. Moreover, untrammeled employment of supplemental jurisdiction in diversity of citizenship cases would threaten to eviscerate the complete diversity rule. *See* § IV.C, below. Thus courts struggled, as the Congress struggled with § 1367(b), to impose appropriate limitations on the use of supplemental jurisdiction in diversity cases.

5. Some commentators criticize supplemental jurisdiction because it relieves state courts from discharging their responsibility to adjudicate matters of state law, and prevents improvements of state court ability to interpret federal law by keeping federal claims out of the state courts. The opposite point, however, seems just as compelling: undue *limitation* of supplemental jurisdiction may preclude *federal* courts from exercising their primary responsibility of interpreting and developing federal law, and may limit federal court familiarity with state law issues, matters with which they must deal in the exercise of their diversity of citizenship jurisdiction.

III. Historical Development of Supplemental Jurisdiction

A. Definitional Issues: "Pendent", "Ancillary," and "Supplemental"

1. As noted, supplemental jurisdiction allows a federal court to entertain a claim that, by itself, could not be brought in federal court, because it fails independently to invoke diversity of citizenship or federal question or some other basis of federal subject matter jurisdiction. Supplemental jurisdiction is proper only if the claim has an appropriate relationship to the pending case that is properly in federal court. *See* § IV.B, below.

2. Historically, courts talked of two forms of supplemental jurisdiction—"pendent" and "ancillary" jurisdiction. Pendent jurisdiction generally operated over claims asserted by plaintiffs in a federal question case. Ancillary jurisdiction generally operated over claims asserted by a party other than the plaintiff, and usually in either diversity of citizenship or federal question cases.

3. Some scholars suggested that there was no principled difference between pendent and ancillary jurisdiction and thus that a generic term—"supplemental jurisdiction"—be used to refer to both.

4. Congress codified the general concept of supplemental jurisdiction for the first time in 1990, in 28 U.S.C. § 1367, and employed the unitary phrase "supplemental jurisdiction." Nonetheless, many courts still use the phrases "pendent" and "ancillary."

B. Until 1990, the Doctrine Was Developed by Case Law, Not Legislation

1. Supplemental jurisdiction is rooted in *Osborn v. Bank of the United States*, 22 U.S. 738, 822–23 (1824).

    a. In that case, Chief Justice John Marshall said "[t]here is scarcely any case, every part of which depends on the constitution, laws, or treaties of the United States." Thus, he concluded, "when a question to which the judicial power of the Union is extended by the constitution, forms an ingredient of the original cause, it is in the power of Congress to give the [federal] Circuit Courts jurisdiction of that cause, although other questions of fact or law may be involved in it."

    b. In other words, federal judicial power extends to "cases" as a whole under Article III, § 2, of the Constitution. A "case" includes all related facts and issues, not merely those falling independently within the federal judicial power.

2. In *Freeman v. Howe*, 65 U.S. 450 (1860), the Supreme Court held that a federal court had authority in a diversity of citizenship case to adjudicate the rights of non-diverse parties whose interests are affected by the disposition of property within the control of the federal court. The doctrine was not subsequently limited to *in rem* or *quasi in rem* cases.

3. In *Moore v. New York Cotton Exchange*, 270 U.S. 593 (1926), the Supreme Court allowed a defendant in a federal antitrust suit to assert a counterclaim under state law, even though the adverse parties were not of diverse citizenship. The counterclaim came within the federal court's "ancillary" jurisdiction because the defendant's state-law counterclaim arose from the same transaction or occurrence as plaintiff's federal question (antitrust) claim.

4. In *Hurn v. Oursler*, 289 U.S. 238 (1933), the Supreme Court indicated that "pendent" jurisdiction could apply only where the federal and state claims are part of the same "cause of action."

   a. The term, "cause of action" is by no means self-defining. The *Hurn* Court found a state claim arising out of the very same work of art that had given rise to plaintiff's federal copyright claim to be part of the same cause of action, because "[plaintiff] alleges the violation of a single right, namely, the right to protection of the copyrighted play" and because "the claims of infringement and unfair competition so precisely rest upon identical facts as to be little more than the equivalent of different epithets to characterize the same groups of circumstances."

   b. The Court found different "causes of action," however, when the plaintiff sought to append an additional state claim for the copying of a somewhat modified, uncopyrighted version of the work of art.

   c. Though the decision was ambiguous, courts generally interpreted *Hurn* to require a total factual identity between state and federal claims for a federal court to have power over the state claim.

5. The Supreme Court's leading discussion of the propriety of what is today called supplemental jurisdiction is *United Mine Workers v. Gibbs*, 383 U.S. 715 (1966). There, a Tennessee plaintiff asserted a federal

question claim against a Tennessee defendant and also appended a state-law claim that arose from the same dispute that gave rise to the federal question. Although the federal claim invoked federal question jurisdiction, the state-law claim did not invoke federal question or diversity of citizenship jurisdiction. The Court permitted federal courts to hear such claims, however, if they satisfy the test laid out in *Gibbs*.

   a. *Gibbs* replaced the difficult "cause of action" concept of *Hurn* with a pragmatic, fact-based inquiry. A federal court has *power* to hear a supplemental claim in these circumstances: "The state and federal claims must derive from a common nucleus of operative fact. But if, considered without regard to their federal or state character, a plaintiff's claims are such that he would ordinarily be expected to try them all in one judicial proceeding, then, assuming substantiality of the federal issues, there is *power* in federal courts to hear the whole." *Gibbs*, 383 U.S. at 725.

   b. There is no doubt that *Gibbs* extends supplemental jurisdiction beyond the narrow factual identity required by *Hurn*. Courts have interpreted *Gibbs* to permit supplemental jurisdiction to claims arising from the same transaction or occurrence as the claim that invoked federal subject matter jurisdiction. In such situations, parties generally would expect the claims to be tried in a single proceeding.

   c. The Court has not explicated its language about whether a plaintiff would ordinarily expect to try the jurisdiction-invoking claim and the supplemental claim together. And the fact that the Court began the sentence discussing the point with "But if" seems odd. Nonetheless, as noted, courts subsequently have read *Gibbs* pragmatically, to permit supplemental jurisdiction over claims that involve a common nucleus of operative fact, or arise from the same transaction or occurrence as, a claim that invoked federal subject matter jurisdiction.

   d. In *Gibbs*, the Court recognized discretionary factors that may counsel a court in a given case to decline the exercise of supplemental jurisdiction.

   e. The *Gibbs* Court recognized that the plaintiff's federal question claim had to be "substantial." In this regard, the Court was merely reiterating a requirement for invoking federal question jurisdiction in any case. *See* Chapter 4, § III.A.

6. Supplemental jurisdiction may allow a federal court to decide an issue that does not fall within the federal "judicial power" in Article III, § 2, of the Constitution. For example, it can permit federal courts to determine state-law issues despite the lack of diversity of citizenship between adverse parties. Accordingly, there was long a suspicion that supplemental jurisdiction might be unconstitutional.

7. The line of cases discussed immediately above, however, clearly establishes the constitutionality of supplemental jurisdiction. As noted, they recognize that while a single claim may invoke federal subject matter jurisdiction (for instance, either federal question or diversity of citizenship), other claims may be decided by the federal court because they are part of the same "case or controversy" as the claim that invoked subject matter jurisdiction. Federal courts take jurisdiction over the entire case, even those non-federal, non-diverse aspects that fall within the *Gibbs* test.

8. There remains a serious question, however, of whether the exercise of supplemental jurisdiction requires a statutory grant by Congress.

    a. In *Hurn* and *Gibbs*, the Supreme Court seemed simply to assume that federal courts have the authority to exercise supplemental jurisdiction in appropriate cases, notwithstanding the failure of Congress to grant supplemental jurisdiction statutorily. There was at that time no general statutory grant of supplemental jurisdiction.

    b. Some scholars opined that the federal courts' creation of supplemental jurisdiction violated separation of powers principles. Because the bases of federal judicial power in Article III, § 2 of the Constitution generally are not self-enacting, but require a statutory grant. Critics argued that the federal courts' creation of supplemental jurisdiction usurped a legislative function.

    c. The Supreme Court questioned the legitimacy of supplemental jurisdiction without a statutory foundation in *Finley v. United States*, 490 U.S. 545 (1989).

C. The *Finley* Decision Led to Passage of the Supplemental Jurisdiction Statute in 1990

1. *Finley v. United States*, 490 U.S. 545 (1989), involved the "pendent parties" type of supplemental jurisdiction, in which the non-federal, non-diversity

claim is asserted against (or by) a party other than the one involved in the claim invoking federal subject matter jurisdiction.

Example: P, a citizen of California, asserts a Federal Tort Claims Act claim against D–1, which is the United States. P also asserts a state-law claim against D–2, which is a citizen of California. The two claims arise from a single airplane crash, and thus share a common nucleus of operative fact. The claim against D–2 does not invoke federal question or diversity of citizenship jurisdiction. In addition, that claim is against a different defendant than the one against whom the jurisdiction-invoking claim is asserted.

2. On these facts, the Supreme Court in *Finley* rejected supplemental jurisdiction. The Court recognized that the state-law claim against D–2 satisfied the constitutional test for supplemental jurisdiction, because it arose from the same transaction as the federal question claim; thus, the claim satisfied the *Gibbs* test for supplemental jurisdiction. *See* § III.B.5, above.

3. In his majority opinion for himself and four others, Justice Scalia based the Court's holding on the fact that Congress had failed to grant supplemental jurisdiction. Because there was no statute permitting supplemental jurisdiction, the power to exercise it "lies dormant." *Finley*, 490 U.S. at 548.

4. The result in *Finley* was consistent with an earlier pendent parties case, *Aldinger v. Howard*, 427 U.S. 1 (1976). There, P asserted a federal civil rights claim under 42 U.S.C. § 1983 against a state officer. She appended a state-law claim against a second defendant, which was a non-diverse municipality. Though the claim against the second defendant satisfied *Gibbs*, the Court rejected supplemental jurisdiction.

   a. The holding was based upon the then-existing law that municipalities were not "persons" and thus could not be sued under § 1983. *See* Chapter 14, § III.D.5. That being so, permitting a municipality to be sued under a state-law tort claim under the circumstances would violate that understanding. Thus, the Court concluded that there was a statutory impediment, from § 1983, to the exercise of supplemental jurisdiction.

   b. Twelve years later, the Court changed its understanding on whether municipalities were "persons" under § 1983. *Monell v. Department of Social Services of the City of New York*, 436 U.S. 658 (1978). *See* Chapter 14, § III.D.5.

    c. In *Aldinger*, the Court expressly left open the possibility that the pendent parties form of supplemental jurisdiction would be upheld in cases involving exclusive federal question jurisdiction. *Aldinger*, 427 U.S. at 18. Of course, in *Finley*, the Court rejected supplemental jurisdiction in such a situation.

    d. The reasoning of *Aldinger* was different from that of *Finley*. In the former, the Court seemed to assume that supplemental jurisdiction was appropriate unless Congress precluded it by statute. In the latter, the Court indulged the opposite presumption—supplemental jurisdiction was inappropriate unless permitted by Congress in a statute.

5. Commentators have criticized the reasoning and the result in *Finley*.

    a. The reasoning—that there is no supplemental jurisdiction without a congressional grant for it—is inconsistent with the Court's approach in every other supplemental jurisdiction case. In those cases, the Court seemed to assume that the federal courts had authority to exercise supplemental jurisdiction when the appropriate test, such as *Gibbs*, was satisfied.

    b. The result was most unfortunate for the plaintiff and inefficient for the judicial system. Because the Federal Tort Claims Act claim invokes exclusive federal jurisdiction, it can only be asserted in federal court. Without supplemental jurisdiction over the state-law claim, the plaintiff was forced to pursue litigation in two courts systems concerning potential liability for a single airplane crash.

    c. The Court's broad language about the need for a statutory basis of supplemental jurisdiction created uncertainty about whether *all* forms of supplemental jurisdiction—even, for example, the simple fact pattern of *Gibbs*—might be suspect.

6. In response to *Finley*, Congress passed the supplemental jurisdiction statute, 28 U.S.C. § 1367, which became effective for actions filed on or after December 1, 1990. The stated purposes of the statute were to overrule the result in *Finley* and thus to permit pendent parties jurisdic-

tion in federal question cases, and to codify pre-*Finley* practice. While the statute has succeeded in some respects, it has also caused considerable confusion and controversy.

IV. The Supplemental Jurisdiction Statute

A. Overview of the Statute

1. The supplemental jurisdiction statute is divided into five subsections: § 1367(a) grants supplemental jurisdiction, § 1367(b) cuts back upon that grant, but only in diversity of citizenship cases; § 1367(c) lists discretionary factors that justify a court's refusing to exercise supplemental jurisdiction; § 1367(d) provides for tolling the statute of limitations for a supplemental claim that is dismissed in federal court; and § 1367(e) merely provides that the word "State," as used in the statute, includes the District of Columbia, Puerto Rico, and "any territory or possession of the United States."

2. The statute was drafted and passed in haste, and has been the target of considerable criticism. The statute overruled the result in *Finley*, but has created enormous uncertainty in other areas, particularly in the operation of § 1367(b).

3. Under the statute, as in this Chapter, the concept of allowing federal courts to hear non-federal, non-diversity claims is referred to by the generic phrase "supplemental jurisdiction." Previously, under case law, there were two closely related concepts—"pendent" and "ancillary" jurisdiction. They are subsumed under the single phrase in § 1367. As noted above, however, many courts continue to use the terms pendent and ancillary.

B. The Grant of Supplemental Jurisdiction in § 1367(a)

1. Section 1367(a) grants supplemental jurisdiction to the full extent of Article III. It provides that in a civil case invoking the original jurisdiction of the federal courts, the "courts shall have supplemental jurisdiction over all other claims that are so related to claims in the action . . . that they form part of the same case or controversy under Article III. . . . " This grant clearly codifies the *Gibbs* test and includes all claims that share a "common nucleus of operative fact" with a jurisdiction-invoking claim. *See* § III.B.5, above.

2. In addition, the last sentence of § 1367(a) provides that the grant "shall include claims that involve the joinder or intervention of additional parties." This sentence effectively overrules the result in *Finley* (and *Aldinger*). *See* § III.C, above.

3. Nothing in the grant of supplemental jurisdiction in § 1367(a) limits it to federal question cases involving the exclusive jurisdiction of the federal courts.

Example: P, a citizen of California, files a federal question claim against D–1 and a transactionally related state-law claim against D–2. P and D–2 are co-citizens. The claim against D–2 does not invoke federal question jurisdiction (because it is based upon state law) and does not invoke diversity jurisdiction (because P and D–2 are not diverse). Section 1367(a) grants supplemental jurisdiction over the claim, however, because it satisfies the *Gibbs* relatedness test. The fact that the claim involves a different defendant from that sued in the federal question claim is irrelevant. Likewise, the fact that the basis of federal question jurisdiction is not exclusive to the federal court is irrelevant.

4. Nothing in the grant of supplemental jurisdiction in § 1367(a) limits it to cases in which the original jurisdiction is based upon federal question jurisdiction. Thus, the grant in § 1367(a) applies in diversity of citizenship cases as well. Unless that grant is fettered in diversity cases, however, it risks overruling the complete diversity rule of *Strawbridge v. Curtiss*. *See* § IV.C, below.

Example: P, a citizen of California, files a state-law claim of $500,000 against D–1, a citizen of Arizona, and a transactionally related state-law claim against D–2, who is a citizen of California. The case violates the complete diversity rule because P and D–2 are co-citizens. Nonetheless, § 1367(a) grants supplemental jurisdiction over the claim against D–2 because the claim satisfies the *Gibbs* relatedness test. Nothing in § 1367(a) limits that subsection's application to federal question cases, so the grant of supplemental jurisdiction applies. However, § 1367(b) will operate to restrict that grant in this fact pattern and to preserve the complete diversity rule.

5. The grant of supplemental jurisdiction in § 1367(a) does not override the Eleventh Amendment. Thus, if a state has not waived its immunity

under that Amendment from suit in the federal courts, § 1367(a) cannot force it to defend a claim asserted under supplemental jurisdiction. *Raygor v. Regents of the University of Minnesota*, 534 U.S. 533 (2002).

C. Restrictions on Supplemental Jurisdiction in § 1367(b)

1. Because the unrestricted use of supplemental jurisdiction in diversity of citizenship cases would eviscerate the complete diversity rule and vastly increase the case load of the federal courts, Congress had to restrict the grant in diversity cases.

2. Section 1367(b) restricts the grant of supplemental jurisdiction from § 1367(a), but applies *only* in cases in which original jurisdiction is "founded solely" on § 1332. Thus, the restrictions in § 1367(b) apply in diversity of citizenship cases, and do not apply in federal question cases.

3. The restrictions in § 1367(b) apply to specific claims:

    a. claims asserted "by plaintiffs against persons made parties under Rule 14, 19, 20, or 24 of the Federal Rules of Civil Procedure";

    b. claims asserted "by persons proposed to be joined as plaintiffs under Rule 19 of such rules"; and

    c. claims by persons "seeking to intervene as plaintiffs under Rule 24 of such rules."

4. Note that these claims over which supplemental jurisdiction is not permitted in diversity cases are asserted by plaintiffs, not defendants.

Example 1: P, a citizen of New York, asserts a $100,000 state-law claim against D, a citizen of Pennsylvania. The claim obviously invokes diversity of citizenship jurisdiction. D asserts a compulsory counterclaim (one that arises from the same transaction or occurrence as P's claim) against P. The claim is for $45,000. The counterclaim does not invoke federal question jurisdiction (because it is based upon state law) and does not invoke diversity jurisdiction (because it does not satisfy the amount in controversy requirement therefor). The counterclaim invokes supplemental jurisdiction, however, under § 1367(a), because it arises from the same transaction or occurrence as the underlying claim. Section 1367(b) applies, because this is a diversity case, but does not remove the grant of supplemental jurisdiction. Section 1367(b) removes supplemental jurisdiction only from claims by plaintiffs; this claim is by a defendant. So it invokes supplemental jurisdiction and can be heard in the pending case.

Example 2: Same facts as the preceding *Example*, except that D's claim against P is a permissive counterclaim, one that does not arise from the same transaction or occurrence as P's claim. This claim will not invoke supplemental jurisdiction because it does not arise from the same transaction or occurrence as the jurisdiction-invoking claim. Thus, § 1367(a) does not grant supplemental jurisdiction at all, and there is no need to assess § 1367(b).

5. The prohibition of supplemental jurisdiction in a diversity of citizenship case over a claim by a plaintiff against a person made a party under Rule 14 is based upon *Owen Equipment & Erection Co. v. Kroger*, 437 U.S. 365 (1978). In that case, the Supreme Court held that recognizing supplemental jurisdiction over a claim by the plaintiff against a third-party defendant impleaded by the defendant would eviscerate the complete diversity rule.

Example 1: P, a citizen of Illinois, asserts a $100,000 state-law claim against D, a citizen of New Jersey. The claim invokes diversity of citizenship jurisdiction. Now D impleads a third-party defendant (TPD) who allegedly owes D indemnity on the underlying claim (Rule 14 permits such joinder of a new party). But TPD is a citizen of New Jersey. Thus, the claim by D against TPD does not invoke diversity; we will stipulate that it also does not invoke federal question jurisdiction, because the indemnity claim arises under state (not federal) law. Nonetheless, the court can exercise supplemental jurisdiction over that claim by D against TPD. Why? First, it invokes supplemental jurisdiction under § 1367(a) because it involves the same nucleus of operative facts as the underlying claim by P against D. Second, although § 1367(b) applies (because this is a diversity case), it does not remove the grant of supplemental jurisdiction. Why not? Because this not a claim by a plaintiff, and thus does not fall within the list of prohibited claims in § 1367(b).

Example 2: P, a citizen of Illinois, asserts a $100,000 state-law claim against D, a citizen of New Jersey. The claim invokes diversity of citizenship jurisdiction. Now D impleads TPD, a citizen of Illinois, for indemnity on the underlying claim. This claim invokes diversity of citizenship jurisdiction, because it is by a citizen of New Jersey against a citizen of Illinois, and exceeds $75,000 (it is for $100,000). Now assume that P asserts a claim in the same case against TPD (Rule 14(a) permits her to do so). There is no diversity over that claim, because P and TPD are co-citizens. (And we will agree there is no federal question because these are state-law claims.) Section 1367(a) grants supplemental jurisdiction because the claim is transactionally related to the underlying dispute (Rule 14(a) requires that). But § 1367(b) removes that grant, because this is a claim, asserted in a diversity case, by a plaintiff "against a person[] made a party under Rule 14. . . . "

6. The prohibition of supplemental jurisdiction in a diversity of citizenship case over claims involving necessary parties under Rule 19 comports with pre-*Finley* practice.

7. The prohibition of supplemental jurisdiction in a diversity of citizenship case over claims involving intervenors is inconsistent with pre-*Finley* practice. Federal courts had long recognized supplemental jurisdiction over claims by or against intervenors of right before § 1367 was passed.

8. The prohibition of supplemental jurisdiction in a diversity of citizenship case over claims by a plaintiff against "persons made a party under Rule . . . 20. . . . " was necessary to avoid evisceration of the complete diversity rule. Rule 20 permits joinder of multiple initial parties to a civil case. Without this part of § 1367(b), there would be supplemental jurisdiction over a transactionally related claim by the plaintiff against a non-diverse defendant.

D. Discretionary Decline of Supplemental Jurisdiction Under § 1367(c)

1. In *Gibbs*, the Supreme Court distinguished between a court's *power* to exercise supplemental jurisdiction and its *discretion* to refuse to exercise it. The power aspect of that case is codified in § 1367(a) and extends to claims sharing a common nucleus of operative fact with a claim that invokes federal subject matter jurisdiction. *See* § IV.B, above.

a. The *Gibbs* Court recognized that supplemental jurisdiction need not be exercised in every situation in which it is available.

   b. The Court suggested that a court may decline supplemental jurisdiction when (i) the federal question claim (if any) is dismissed before trial; (ii) if state-law issues "predominate" in the case; or (iii) if the exercise of supplemental jurisdiction is likely to confuse the jury.

2. In § 1367(c), Congress purported to codify the *Gibbs* discretionary factors. Some commentators criticized the statute for not adhering faithfully to the *Gibbs* statement. Nonetheless, the statute provides that a court "may decline to exercise supplemental jurisdiction" under any of these circumstances:

   a. if the supplemental claim raises "a novel or complex issue" of state law;

   b. if the supplemental claim "predominates over the claim or claims over which the district court has original jurisdiction";

   c. if the district court "has dismissed all claims over which it has original jurisdiction"; or

   d. if, "in exceptional circumstances, there are other compelling reasons for declining jurisdiction."

E. Tolling Provision of § 1367(d)

1. Section 1367(d) provides that the statute of limitations for any claim invoking supplemental jurisdiction under § 1367(a) "and for any other claim in the same action that is voluntarily dismissed at the same time as or after the dismissal" of a claim invoking supplemental jurisdiction "shall be tolled while the claim is pending and for a period of 30 days after it is dismissed. . . . " The subsection also provides that state law might permit a longer tolling of the limitations period.

2. The Supreme Court upheld the provision in the face of a constitutional challenge in *Jinks v. Richland County, S.C.*, 538 U.S. 456 (2003).

   a. There, the plaintiff sued a county in federal court, asserting a claim under 42 U.S.C. § 1983. He also asserted state-law claims against the county under supplemental jurisdiction. The district court dismissed the § 1983 claim on the merits and then exercised its discretion under § 1367(c)(3) to decline supplemental jurisdiction over the state-law claim. Plaintiff then sued the county on the state-law claims in state court.

    b.   The South Carolina Supreme Court held that § 1367(d) was unconstitutional because it interfered with state "sovereign authority to establish the extent to which its political subdivisions are subject to suit."

    c.   The Supreme Court unanimously reversed and upheld the tolling provision as "necessary and proper for carrying into execution Congress's power" to establish the lower federal courts and assure that they fairly exercise the judicial power of the United States. 123 S.Ct. at 1671.

3.   The Supreme Court has held, however, that the tolling provision cannot extend the period in which a nonconsenting state may be sued in state court for claims dismissed on Eleventh Amendment grounds. *Raygor v. Regents of the University of Minnesota*, 534 U.S. 533 (2002).

F.   Some Problems in Applying § 1367

1.   Section 1367 was drafted in haste and without sufficient consultation. As a result, it has created confusion in some areas and some unfortunate changes from pre-*Finley* practice in others.

2.   The most contentious issue is whether § 1367 changed prior practice concerning the amount in controversy requirement for a diversity of citizenship class action.

    a.   Before § 1367 became law, the Supreme Court ruled that each member of a diversity class action must meet the amount in controversy requirement. *Zahn v. International Paper Co.*, 414 U.S. 291 (1974).

    b.   Under § 1367(a), however, a court would have supplemental jurisdiction over claims by all class members, assuming their claims met the *Gibbs* test (*see* § D, above). So long as the class representative's claim exceeded $75,000, and she was of diverse citizenship from the defendant, § 1367(a) would permit the court to hear the claims of class members that did not exceed $75,000.

c. Nothing in § 1367(b) refers to class actions. Thus, nothing in that subsection appears to remove the grant of supplemental jurisdiction in the class action context.

d. One sentence in the legislative history of § 1367 purports to indicate that Congress did not intend to overrule the requirement in *Zahn* that each member of the class assert a claim in excess of $75,000.

e. To date, five courts of appeals (the Fourth, Fifth, Seventh, Ninth, and Eleventh Circuits) have concluded that § 1367 overrules the result in *Zahn*. Three other courts of appeals (the Third, Eighth, and Tenth Circuits) hold that *Zahn* survived the statute.

3. Pre-*Finley* practice permitted diversity class actions to proceed so long as the class representative's citizenship was diverse from that of each defendant. In other words, the citizenships of the individual class members were irrelevant. *Supreme Tribe of Ben–Hur v. Cauble*, 255 U.S. 356 (1921).

    a. The *Ben-Hur* rule recognizes supplemental jurisdiction over the claims by the non-diverse class members.

    b. Nothing in § 1367 purports to change the *Ben-Hur* rule.

4. As noted above, the statute changed the practice concerning supplemental jurisdiction over claims involving intervenors of right, thereby making efficient joinder in diversity cases more difficult than it had been.

5. Section 1367(b), read literally, does not allow supplemental jurisdiction in diversity cases over claims by plaintiffs asserted in a defensive capacity. For example, an impleader claim by a plaintiff against whom a counterclaim has been asserted would seem to run afoul of the provision that there be no supplemental jurisdiction over claims by plaintiffs against persons made parties under Rule 14.

*

VII

Removal Jurisdiction

■ **ANALYSIS**

I. Introduction
II. General Principles of Removal Jurisdiction
    A. Removal Contrasted with Remand
    B. Removal Is Available Only to Defendants
    C. General Venue Provisions Do Not Apply in Removal Cases
    D. Generally, A Case is Removable Only if Federal Court Would Have Subject Matter Jurisdiction Over It
    E. Case Is Removable Even If State Court Lacked Subject Matter Jurisdiction
III. Grants of Removal Jurisdiction
    A. Removal Is Governed By Statute
    B. The "General" Provision for Removal of Diversity and Federal Question Cases
    C. Special Considerations Regarding Removal of Federal Question Cases
    D. Special Considerations Regarding Removal of Diversity Cases
    E. Specialized Grants of Removal Jurisdiction
IV. Procedures for Removal and Remand
    A. Defendant Files Notice of Removal in Federal Court
    B. Timing of Removal
    C. Remand to State Court

I. Introduction

When there is a choice of proper courts, the plaintiff has the initial choice of where the litigation will go forward. In certain instances, however, the defendant may be permitted to override the plaintiff's choice of forum. Removal, for instance, allows the defendant to have a case initially filed in state court removed to the federal court "embracing" the state court in which it was filed. Removal is not an appeal of a case from state to federal court. Rather, it is a transfer from a state trial court to a federal district court. Obviously, as a general rule subject to limited exceptions, a case can be removed only if it would invoke federal subject matter jurisdiction.

II. General Principles of Removal Jurisdiction

A. Removal Contrasted With Remand

1. Removal operates in one direction only: it permits a case filed in state court to be transferred to a federal court. It does not operate in the opposite direction; there is no such thing as "removing" a case from federal court to a state court.

2. If a case is improperly removed, either procedurally or because the federal court lacks subject matter jurisdiction, the federal court will "remand" the case to state court.

3. Thus, the combination of original jurisdiction statutes and removal statutes provides both the plaintiff and the defendant with a right to have an appropriate case decided in a federal court.

    a. If the plaintiff selects the federal forum and the requirements of subject matter jurisdiction are met, the defendant has no power to veto plaintiff's choice and have the case sent to the state court.

    b. On the other hand, if the plaintiff sues in state court and the requirements of removal jurisdiction are met, the defendant may remove the case to federal court, and the plaintiff has no authority to have the case returned to state court.

B. Removal is Available Only to Defendants

1. The general removal statute, 28 U.S.C. § 1441(a), provides for removal by "the defendant or the defendants." Similarly, the statute addressing procedure for removal, 28 U.S.C. § 1446, refers to "[a] defendant or defendants desiring to remove."

2. Courts have concluded that all defendants served in the case in state court must join in the notice of removal. *Chicago, R.I. & P. Ry. Co. v. Martin*, 178 U.S. 245 (1900). If any defendant refuses to join, the case cannot be removed, unless the case satisfies the requirements of 28 U.S.C. § 1441(c), discussed at § III.D, below.

3. Courts also have concluded that a plaintiff may not remove a case, even if the defendant asserts a counterclaim against the plaintiff which would invoke federal subject matter jurisdiction. The ruling is based upon the fact that the removal statutes refer to removal by "defendant or defendants." *Shamrock Oil & Gas Corp. v. Sheets*, 313 U.S. 100 (1941).

4. If the case is removable at the outset and the defendant fails to remove it, a later-added defendant cannot then remove the case. *Noble v. Bradford Marine, Inc.*, 789 F.Supp. 395 (S.D. Fla. 1992). This rule is consistent with the notion, in paragraph 2 above, that all defendants must agree to the removal. If the original defendant did not remove, then she is seen as not agreeing to removal. Moreover, as a practical matter, it would be cumbersome to allow removal after the later addition of a defendant, because the state court's efforts in the meantime would be rendered meaningless.

C. General Venue Provisions Do Not Apply in Removal Cases

1. The general venue statute for federal civil actions, 28 U.S.C. § 1391, allows the plaintiff to lay venue in any district in which all defendants reside or in which a substantial part of the events forming the basis of the claim arose. But this statute applies only to cases in which the plaintiff files the case in federal court; thus, it does not apply in cases removed from state court.

2. Venue is proper in only one district in all removed cases: in the federal district "embracing" the place in which the state action was filed. 28 U.S.C. § 1441(a). That means the defendant(s) can remove only to the federal district in which the state court (in which the case was filed) is located.

D. Generally, a Case is Removable Only if the Federal Court Would Have Subject Matter Jurisdiction Over it

1. 28 U.S.C. § 1441(a) provides for removal of a civil action "of which the district courts of the United States have original jurisdiction." Thus, as a

starting point, the defendant may remove the case only if the case would invoke some basis of federal subject matter jurisdiction, such as diversity of citizenship or federal question jurisdiction.

2. This general rule is subject to substantial revision, however, because of other provisions in the removal statutes. We will see these revisions in § III.C, below.

3. Ordinarily, the federal court will determine whether it has subject matter jurisdiction before addressing any other issue. In *Ruhrgas AG v. Marathon Oil Co.*, 526 U.S. 574 (1999), the Supreme Court rejected an "unyielding jurisdictional hierarchy." It held that where the subject matter jurisdiction issue was difficult but the court clearly lacked personal jurisdiction, the federal court did not abuse its discretion by dismissing on the basis of lack of personal jurisdiction without addressing the subject matter jurisdiction issue.

E. Case is Removable Even if State Court Lacked Subject Matter Jurisdiction

1. For many years, it was thought that a federal court's removal jurisdiction was "derivative" of the state court's subject matter jurisdiction. Thus, if the case filed in state court fell within the exclusive subject matter jurisdiction of the federal courts, the defendant could not remove it. Rather, the state court would have to dismiss and the plaintiff would have to refile the case in federal court.

2. This problem no longer arises, however, because of 28 U.S.C. § 1441(f), which provides that removal jurisdiction is not defeated by the fact that the state court lacked subject matter jurisdiction over the claim.

III. Grants of Removal Jurisdiction

A. Removal is Governed by Statute

1. The right to remove a case from state to federal court is statutory only. There is no constitutional provision for removal.

2. The Supreme Court has consistently upheld removal from constitutional attacks. *See, e.g., Ames v. Kansas ex rel. Johnston*, 111 U.S. 449 (1884).

3. Removal statutes are strictly construed, however, to avoid untoward deprivation of state court jurisdiction. *See, e.g., Shamrock Oil & Gas Corp.*

v. Sheets, 313 U.S. 100, 108–09. Thus, any doubts about removability should be resolved by remanding the case to state court.

B. The "General" Provision for Removal of Diversity and Federal Question Cases

1. Most removal is authorized by 28 U.S.C. § 1441(a), which permits the defendant to remove a civil action of which the federal district court would have original jurisdiction. This grant clearly encompasses cases that would invoke diversity of citizenship or federal question jurisdiction.

2. The requirements for invoking diversity of citizenship and federal question jurisdiction as an original matter apply in removed cases as well.

    a. Thus, to remove a case under diversity of citizenship, the complete diversity rule and amount-in-controversy requirement must be satisfied. *See* Chapter 5, § III. & IV.

    b. In federal question cases, the well-pleaded complaint rule and "centrality" requirements must be met. *See* Chapter 4, § III.

    c. As a result, defendant cannot remove a case in which the plaintiff sues under state law simply by asserting a federal defense. Under the well-pleaded complaint rule, the case invokes federal question jurisdiction only if the plaintiff's claim itself (not a defense or counterclaim) arises under federal law.

    d. Resolving a split among courts of appeals, the Supreme Court held that the All Writs Act, 28 U.S.C. § 1651, does not support removal, because it does not confer a basis of federal subject matter jurisdiction. *Syngenta Crop Protection, Inc. v. Henson*, 537 U.S. 28 (2002).

3. There are important statutory limitations, however, on the defendant's ability to remove a case on the basis of diversity of citizenship or federal question jurisdiction.

C. Special Considerations Regarding Removal of Federal Question Cases

1. 28 U.S.C. § 1441(a) provides for removal of appropriate civil actions "[e]xcept as otherwise expressly provided by Act of Congress."

2. Thus, Congress can obviate removal even of cases that would otherwise arise under federal law and invoke federal question jurisdiction under 28 U.S.C. § 1331. It has done so in several particulars in 28 U.S.C. § 1445.

3. In addition, statutes in other parts of the United States Code may prohibit removal.

Example: For example, a case brought under the Federal Employers' Liability Act (FELA), which authorizes railroad employee negligence suits against employers, cannot be removed. *See* 28 U.S.C. § 1445(a). In these cases, Congress has chosen to provide the plaintiff with an unchallengeable option to proceed in either state or federal court.

4. As noted in the preceding subsection, the well-pleaded complaint rule, which is a general limitation on the ability to invoke federal question jurisdiction, precludes removal based upon the assertion of a federal defense. Thus, many courts conclude that the plaintiff is the "master of her claim" and can avoid removal by asserting only state law causes of action and eschewing any applicable federal question claims.

5. In *Federated Department Stores, Inc. v. Moitie,* 452 U.S. 394 (1981), however, the Supreme Court held that a state plaintiff cannot employ "artful pleading" to avoid removal.

   a. In that case, the plaintiff's state court complaint purported to raise only state law claims, though they tracked closely the federal government's action under the federal antitrust laws.

   b. In a footnote, the Supreme Court indicated that the court of appeals had correctly affirmed the district court's conclusion that removal was proper because the claims presented were "federal in nature." It hinted that the existence of a defense of federal preclusion could be a basis for removal.

6. The Supreme Court rejected this interpretation of *Moitie* in *Rivet v. Regions Bank of Louisiana,* 522 U.S. 470 (1998). There, the Court upheld the "fundamental" rule "that a defendant cannot remove on the basis of a federal defense." *Id.* at 478.

7. There are situations, however, in which federal law so completely occupies a substantive area of law that there is no state law claim to

assert. In such cases, the defendant can remove even though the plaintiff purports to assert only a state law claim. The Supreme Court has endorsed this principle under § 301 of the Taft–Hartley Act, 29 U.S.C. § 185, *see Avco Corp. v. Aero Lodge No. 735*, 390 U.S. 557 (1968), and ERISA, 29 U.S.C. § 1132(a)(1)(B), *see Metropolitan Life Ins. Co. v. Taylor*, 481 U.S. 58 (1987).

Example: Plaintiff sues in state court to enforce rights under a labor collective bargaining agreement. Federal law so dominates the area in such labor cases that state law essentially has been supplanted by federal law. Thus, federal law does not simply provide a defense to a state law contract action, but forms the basis for all rights under the labor contract. The defendant can remove the case.

D. Special Considerations Regarding Removal of Diversity Cases

1. Congress has imposed restrictions on the defendant's ability to remove a case on the basis of diversity of citizenship jurisdiction.

2. Under 28 U.S.C. § 1441(b), the defendant can remove a case based upon diversity of citizenship jurisdiction "only if none of the parties in interest properly joined and served as defendants is a citizen of the State in which such action is brought." Because of this restriction, cases in which the plaintiff could invoke diversity of citizenship jurisdiction if she sued in federal court cannot be removed to federal court.

Example: Plaintiff, a citizen of Arizona, sues Defendant, who is a citizen of Colorado, in a state court in Colorado. Assume that the claim would satisfy the amount-in-controversy requirement for diversity of citizenship jurisdiction. Although Plaintiff could have brought this case in federal court under diversity of citizenship jurisdiction (because the amount-in-controversy and complete diversity requirements are met, *see* Chapter 5 §§ III. & IV.). Defendant cannot remove the case to federal court, because she is a citizen of the forum.

3. This rule is consistent with the accepted purpose of the diversity of citizenship jurisdiction, which is to avoid state court prejudice against out-of-state citizens. Because the defendant is a citizen of the forum state, the theory goes, she need not fear local bias in the state courts.

4. The result is equally clear, but more difficult to justify, in the case of two defendants, only one of whom is a citizen of the forum.

Example: Same facts as in the preceding *Example*, except there are two defendants, D–1, a citizen of Colorado, and D–2, a citizen of Texas. Again, plaintiff sues in state court in Colorado. The defendants cannot remove, because § 1441(b) precludes removal of a diversity case if *any* defendant is a citizen of the forum, as D–1 is here. The result here seems inconsistent with the underlying rationale for diversity, however, because D–2, as a non-local defendant, might fear local bias in the Colorado courts. She would worry that the state court in Colorado would be more likely to impose liability on her than on her Colorado co-defendant.

5. Ordinarily, there must be federal subject matter jurisdiction both at the time the case was filed in state court and at the time of removal. Nonetheless, courts have permitted removal of a case that *becomes* removable through the plaintiff's voluntary dismissal of a party that thwarted removal of the case when it was initially filed in state court.

Example: Plaintiff, a citizen of New York, sues D–1, a citizen of Georgia, and D–2, a citizen of New York, in a state court. Assume that the claim would satisfy the amount-in-controversy requirement for diversity of citizenship jurisdiction. The defendants cannot remove the case, however, because the complete diversity rule is not satisfied. *See* Chapter 5 § III. Now assume Plaintiff voluntarily dismisses her claim against D–1. Now the case has become removable, because now the complete diversity rule is satisfied (a citizen of New York is suing a citizen of Georgia) and the amount-in-controversy requirement is met. In this instance (where plaintiff voluntarily dismisses her claim against the defendant who defeats removal), courts will allow the remaining defendant to remove.

6. Unfortunately, 28 U.S.C. § 1446(b) provides that no one may remove a case on the basis of diversity "more than one year after commencement of the action." This provision opens the door to unfair gamesmanship by plaintiffs.

Example: Same facts as the preceding *Example*, but plaintiff waits one year and one day after filing the case in state court before dismissing the claim against D–1. Even though all the requirements of diversity of citizenship jurisdiction now exist, the remaining defendant cannot remove.

7. Neither the one-year limitation discussed in paragraph 5 nor the in-state defendant rule discussed in paragraph 2 above applies in federal question cases. They apply only in cases in which the defendant attempts to remove based upon diversity of citizenship jurisdiction.

E. Specialized Grants of Removal Jurisdiction

1. 28 U.S.C. § 1442 provides for removal of either civil actions or criminal prosecutions commenced in a state court against the United States or any agency thereof or against an officer of the United States or of any agency thereof for an act taken under color of his office. This provision is often referred to as "federal officer removal."

    a. Until 1948, the federal officer removal provision was limited to actions against revenue officers. In that year, Congress expanded the provision to include all federal officers.

    b. The Supreme Court upheld the constitutionality of federal officer removal jurisdiction in *Tennessee v. Davis,* 100 U.S. 257 (1879). Even though the state court proceeding was based entirely upon state law, the case could be removed. Because this branch of removal does not rely upon federal question jurisdiction under 28 U.S.C. § 1331, the well-pleaded complaint rule does not apply. The possible assertion of a federal defense, combined with the interest of the federal government in insulating its programs from attack in state court, support federal officer removal jurisdiction under Article III, § 2, of the Constitution.

    c. In *Mesa v. California,* 489 U.S. 121 (1989), the Court indicated that eliminating the requirement that a federal defense be present for federal officer removal would raise "serious doubt whether, in enacting § 1442(a), Congress would not have 'expand[ed] the jurisdiction of the federal courts beyond the bounds established by the Constitution.'"

2. 28 U.S.C. § 1443 provides for so-called civil rights removal. We discuss this provision with the materials on civil rights cases generally. *See* Chapter 14, § VI.

3. 28 U.S.C. § 1441(c) is a difficult provision of limited utility. It provides that when a claim that would invoke subject matter jurisdiction under 28 U.S.C. § 1331 (the general federal question statute) is joined with a "separate and independent" claim that cannot be removed, the defendant can remove the entire case. The federal court may then determine all issues in the case or, in its discretion, keep the federal question and remand claims on which state law predominates.

   a. Courts have had enormous difficulty determining what constitutes a "separate and independent" federal question claim. Historically, they have read it very narrowly, meaning that the statute is rarely invoked.

   b. The best-know Supreme Court case applying a narrow interpretation is *American Fire & Cas. Ins. Co. v. Finn*, 341 U.S. 6 (1951), which involved an earlier version of the statute, which allowed removal of separate and independent diversity of citizenship claims. The narrow interpretation may be less appropriate in federal question cases, but there is very little authority applying the statute as now drafted.

IV. Procedures for Removal and Remand

A. Defendant Files Notice of Removal in Federal Court

1. Pursuant to 28 U.S.C. § 1446(a), a defendant desiring to remove a case files in the federal court a "notice of removal," which is signed under Federal Rule 11. The notice contains "a short and plain statement of the grounds for removal, together with a copy of all process, pleadings, and orders served upon [the defendant] in such action."

2. Promptly after filing the notice of removal in federal court, the defendant must give written notice to all adverse parties. She must file a copy of the notice with the clerk of the state court. Such filing of the copy of notice "shall effect removal and the State court shall proceed no further unless and until the case is remanded." 28 U.S.C. § 1446(d).

3. Notice that the defendant does not make a motion or request permission to remove. She simply effects removal as indicated in the statute. If removal is improper, the federal court may remand the case to state court.

B. Timing of Removal

1. In a civil case, the defendant must file the notice of removal in federal court within 30 days after her receipt, "through service or otherwise," of a copy of the initial pleading or within 30 days "after the service of summons upon the defendant if such initial pleading has then been filed in court and is not required to be served on the defendant, whichever period is shorter."

   a. This provision recognizes that states may adopt different methods for notifying a defendant that she has been sued. In most states, the defendant is served with a summons and a copy of the complaint. In some, however, the complaint is filed and the defendant is then served with a summons, without a copy of the complaint. The statute intends to give the defendant at least 30 days from formal service in which to file her notice of removal.

   b. The Supreme Court has interpreted the phrase "through service or otherwise" in this sense in *Murphy Bros. v. Michetti Pipe Stringing, Inc.*, 526 U.S. 344 (1999). In that case, plaintiff faxed to the defendant a "courtesy copy" of the complaint but did not serve a summons on the defendant until two weeks later. The Court held that the 30 days ran from the service of summons, not from the receipt of the fax.

2. If a civil case is not removable at the outset, the defendant must file her notice of removal within 30 days of receipt of the document that made the case removable.

3. The notice of removal in a criminal case must be filed within thirty days after arraignment in state court, or at any time prior to trial, whichever is earlier. However, for good cause shown, the federal court may grant permission to file the notice later.

C. Remand to State Court

1. If the plaintiff feels that the case was improperly removed, she can move to remand it to state court. She might do so either because the federal court lacks subject matter jurisdiction or because of a procedural defect in the defendant's removal.

2. If the motion to remand is based upon "any defect other than lack of subject matter jurisdiction," the plaintiff must move to remand the case

no later than 30 days after the defendant filed her notice of removal. 28 U.S.C. § 1447(c). In other words, defects in removal other than lack of subject matter jurisdiction are waivable.

Example: Defendant files a notice of removal in federal court but fails to attach all documents served upon her in the state court proceeding. This is a defect in removal unrelated to subject matter jurisdiction. Plaintiff must raise the defect in a motion to remand within 30 days of Defendant's filing. If Plaintiff fails to do so, she has waived the procedural defect in removal.

3. Obviously, however, lack of federal subject matter jurisdiction is not waivable, and the plaintiff or the court on its own motion may raise the issue at any time. If there is no federal subject matter jurisdiction, the federal court must remand the case to the state court from which it was removed. 28 U.S.C. § 1447(c).

4. If, after removal, the plaintiff seeks to join additional defendants whose joinder will destroy diversity of citizenship jurisdiction, the federal court may either deny the joinder, or permit joinder and remand the case to state court. 28 U.S.C. § 1447(e).

5. An order remanding the case to state court cannot be reviewed by appeal or otherwise. 28 U.S.C. § 1447(d). There is an exception for remand of a "civil rights" case removed under 28 U.S.C. § 1443. *See* § III.E.2, above.

VIII

Supreme Court Jurisdiction

■ ANALYSIS

I. Introduction
II. Constitutional and Statutory Structure
    A. Article III Draws Distinction Between Original and Appellate Jurisdiction of the Supreme Court
    B. Relationship Between the Supreme Court's Original and Appellate Jurisdiction
III. Original Jurisdiction of the Supreme Court
    A. Cases Between Two or More States
    B. Other Cases in Which a State is a Party
    C. Cases Involving Ambassadors, Public Ministers, Etc.
IV. Appellate Jurisdiction of the Supreme Court
    A. Statutory Provisions for the Supreme Court's Appellate Jurisdiction
    B. Review of State Court Decisions: Background
    C. Review of State Court Decisions: Highest State Court
    D. Review of State Court Decisions: The Final Judgment Rule
    E. Review of State Court Decisions: The "Independent and Adequate State Ground" Doctrine
    F. Review of State Court Decisions: Findings of Fact

G. Review of Decisions of the Courts of Appeals

I. Introduction

To the general public, the Supreme Court is the most visible part of the federal judiciary. Few citizens know of the district courts and the courts of appeals, but every citizen has some sense of the work and importance of the Supreme Court. In this Chapter, we review the types of cases that the Supreme Court entertains, and how those cases get to the high court. It is no surprise, of course, that the Supreme Court has appellate jurisdiction over cases decided by the federal courts of appeals; after all, it is the ultimate tribunal in the federal system. It is more surprising that the Supreme Court has appellate power to review decisions of state courts; this fact obviously implicates federalism concerns. As we will see, though, such review is only available on questions of federal law, in keeping with the Supreme Court's role as the ultimate arbiter of the meaning of federal law and enforcer of the Supremacy Clause. Most surprising, perhaps, are the provisions for Supreme Court original jurisdiction, a narrow class of cases in which the Supreme Court can serve as the trial court. With regard to each of these types of jurisdiction, there are important (and sometimes arcane) rules and restrictions.

II. Constitutional and Statutory Structure

A. Article III Draws Distinction Between Original and Appellate Jurisdiction of the Supreme Court

1. As discussed in Chapter 2, § II.B, Article III, § 2, clause 1 of the Constitution lists all cases to which the "judicial power" of federal courts reaches. It lists nine types of cases that, as a constitutional matter, can be heard by federal courts. The Supreme Court cannot hear any case— either as a matter of original or appellate jurisdiction—that does not fall within this enumeration.

2. Article III, § 2, clause 2 of the Constitution then provides that the United States Supreme Court "shall have original Jurisdiction" over two types of cases: those "[1] affecting Ambassadors, other public Ministers and Consuls, and [2] those in which a State shall be Party." The clause continues to say that "in all other cases before mentioned," meaning all other cases falling within the judicial power of the federal courts, the Supreme Court "shall have appellate Jurisdiction. . . . "

3. Original jurisdiction means trial jurisdiction. Thus, in cases "affecting Ambassadors, other public Ministers and Consuls" and in cases "in

which a State shall be a Party" the Supreme Court has jurisdiction actually to try the case. Such cases are rare. We address such cases in § III.C, below.

4. Appellate jurisdiction means that the Supreme Court reviews the decisions of another court. The other court may be a lower federal court or the supreme court of a state. Such cases constitute the overwhelming bulk of the Supreme Court docket. We address this appellate jurisdiction in § IV, below.

B. Relationship Between the Supreme Court's Original and Appellate Jurisdiction

1. In *Marbury v. Madison*, 5 U.S. 137 (1803), Chief Justice Marshall opined that the divisions between the Supreme Court's original and appellate jurisdictions are rigid. That is, he treated the original jurisdiction of the Supreme Court as exclusive. To Marshall, no court other than the Supreme Court could have original jurisdiction over cases affecting ambassadors and cases in which a state is a party, and the Supreme Court thus could not have appellate jurisdiction over such cases.

2. The Supreme Court has since rejected Marshall's view. Today, these rules are clear:

   a. The Supreme Court's original jurisdiction extends only to the two types of cases listed in the exclusive jurisdiction clause—cases affecting ambassadors and cases in which a state is a party.

   b. The Supreme Court's original jurisdiction over those cases is not exclusive. Thus, Congress may vest original jurisdiction over those two types of cases in a lower federal court, such as the federal district court.

   c. When such a case is decided initially in a lower federal court, the Supreme Court has appellate jurisdiction over it.

Example: The state of Illinois sues the city of Milwaukee to stop pollution of Lake Michigan. The case falls within the Supreme Court's original jurisdiction, because a state is a party. Nonetheless, by statute, Congress has also vested original jurisdiction in the federal district courts. The Supreme Court chooses to allow the district court take original jurisdiction under general federal question jurisdiction, and the Supreme Court can exercise appellate jurisdiction. *Illinois v. City of Milwaukee*, 406 U.S. 91 (1972).

3. The Supreme Court's original jurisdiction is assumed to be self-executing. Thus, no congressional grant of such jurisdiction is required. *Kentucky v. Dennison*, 65 U.S. 66 (1860).

4. Nonetheless, Congress has enacted a jurisdictional statute, 28 U.S.C. § 1251, dealing with those types of cases falling within the Supreme Court's original jurisdiction. Interestingly, the statute does not treat all cases in which a state is a party in the same way. It specifies one class of such cases—those between two or more states—for different treatment from other cases in which a state is a party. Specifically, § 1251 does the following:

    a. Section 1251(a) grants to the Supreme Court *exclusive* original jurisdiction, but only over controversies "between two or more states." Such cases, then, cannot be tried in a lower federal court.

    b. Section 1251(b) grants to the Supreme Court *nonexclusive* original jurisdiction over: (1) actions or proceedings to which ambassadors, other public ministers, consuls, or vice consuls of foreign states are parties; (2) controversies between the United States and a State; and (3) actions or proceedings by a State against the citizens of another State or against aliens. Such cases *may* be tried in the Supreme Court or *may* be tried in a federal district court.

5. It is crucial to remember, however, that neither the constitutional provision nor these statutory provisions for original Supreme Court jurisdiction extends the judicial power to such cases. That is, there is no federal subject matter jurisdiction simply because a case involves a state or an ambassador as a party. Rather, the case must fall within one of the grants of judicial power contained in Article III, such as federal question jurisdiction. *Duhne v. New Jersey*, 251 U.S. 311 (1920).

6. One major difference between the Supreme Court's original jurisdiction and its appellate jurisdiction is the ability of Congress to regulate and limit the latter.

    a. Article III, § 2, clause 2 of the Constitution expressly provides that the Court's appellate jurisdiction is given "with such exceptions, and under such regulations as the Congress shall make." We discussed this "exceptions clause" in Chapter 2, at § V.A.

b. The Constitution gives Congress no such power regarding the Court's original jurisdiction.

III. Original Jurisdiction of the Supreme Court

A. Cases Between Two or More States

1. As discussed in § II.A.2, above, one of two classes of cases in which the Constitution grants original jurisdiction to the Supreme Court is "those in which a State shall be a Party." As seen in § II.B.4, above, Congress has subdivided such cases, declaring that the Court's original jurisdiction is exclusive when the "between two or more States." 28 U.S.C. § 1251(a).

2. For purposes of this statute, political subdivisions, such as cities and counties, are not considered to be states. Thus, a case brought by a state against a city in another state is not "between two or more States" and does not fall within the exclusive original jurisdiction of the Supreme Court. *Illinois v. City of Milwaukee*, 406 U.S. 91 (1972).

3. Jurisdiction over cases between two or more states has been important in interstate disputes over boundaries, water rights, and in those rare cases in which more than one state claims a right to tax an estate or fund. *See, e.g., California v. Texas*, 457 U.S. 164 (1982)(concerning estate of Howard Hughes).

4. In such cases, the remedy sought is usually equitable, such as a declaration of the border or an injunction stopping one state from doing something. *See, e.g., Pennsylvania v. West Virginia*, 262 U.S. 553 (1923)(Pennsylvania sought to enjoin West Virginia from distributing natural gas that would diminish the supply available for Pennsylvania residents).

5. Often, the Supreme Court refers matters in such cases to special masters, so that the Court is not often tied up with lengthy trial proceedings. *See Maryland v. Louisiana*, 451 U.S. 725, 734 (1981)("as is usual, we appointed a Special Master to facilitate handling of the suit.").

6. Rarely, a state will sue to recover money from another state. *See Virginia v. West Virginia*, 246 U.S. 565 (1918)(awarding Virginia a judgment of $12 million).

7. Occasionally, the Supreme Court refuses to grant leave to file an original proceeding before it. *See* § III.B, below. Such refusal to hear a case creates

no great problem in other areas of original jurisdiction, because there the Court's original jurisdiction is not exclusive and thus the case can be filed in a federal district court.

a. For cases involving a dispute between two or more states, however, the Court's refusal to allow the parties to proceed is quite troublesome, because the Court's original jurisdiction is exclusive. Thus, there is no other court that can entertain the case.

b. Despite this, the Court has refused to hear some such cases. *See, e.g., Wyoming v.* Oklahoma, 502 U.S. 437 (1992)(Justice Thomas filed a dissenting opinion, joined by Chief Justice Rehnquist and Justice Scalia); *Arizona v. New Mexico*, 425 U.S. 794 (1976)(Justice Stevens dissented).

B. Other Cases in Which a State is a Party

1. As noted in § II.B.4, above, § 1251(b) lists various types of cases in which a state is a party but as to which the Supreme Court's original jurisdiction is not exclusive. There are two types of cases under this part of the statute:

    a. "between the United States and a State," and

    b. "by a State against the citizens of another State or against aliens."

2. Because the Supreme Court's original jurisdiction over these cases is not exclusive, they may be brought in federal district court. Such a case would, of course, have to invoke a basis of federal subject matter jurisdiction, such as arising under federal law. The fact that such cases may be tried in a district court will usually lead the Supreme Court to decline its original jurisdiction over such matters. After all, district courts are far better suited to exercise original jurisdiction, and the press of the appellate docket keeps the Supreme Court plenty busy.

3. The Supreme Court may refuse to exercise its original jurisdiction on other grounds as well. In *Ohio v. Wyandotte Chemicals Corp.*, 401 U.S. 493 (1971), a state sued citizens of another state and aliens, seeking abatement of a nuisance created by the defendants' allegedly dumping mercury into rivers that empty into Lake Erie. The Court recognized that the case fell within its original jurisdiction and that there was federal subject matter jurisdiction (the claim arose under federal law). Nonethe-

less, the Court exercised its discretion to refuse to exercise original jurisdiction. It noted that the case presented complex scientific issues more readily tried to a district court.

4. The Court has indicated that it exercises "original jurisdiction sparingly and [is] particularly reluctant to take jurisdiction of a suit where the plaintiff has another adequate forum in which to settle his claim." *United States v. Nevada*, 412 U.S. 534 (1973)(per curiam).

5. The Eleventh Amendment, discussed in detail in Chapter 10, removes the judicial power over cases against a state by a citizen of another state.

C. Cases Involving Ambassadors, Public Ministers, etc.

1. As noted in § II.A.2, above, the Constitution provides for original jurisdiction over cases falling within the judicial power "in all Cases affecting Ambassadors, other public Ministers and Consuls." As noted in § III.A.7, above, Congress provides that the Supreme Court's original jurisdiction in such cases is not exclusive.

2. The Supreme Court has exercised original jurisdiction in such cases very rarely. One reason may be that ambassadors and public ministers (but not consuls) have diplomatic immunity from suit in the United States. Another, of course, is the fact that its original jurisdiction is not exclusive in such cases, so denying attempts to invoke its original jurisdiction routes the plaintiff to federal district court.

3. In one case, a Paraguayan national was convicted of murder in a state court. Paraguay attempted to invoke the Supreme Court's original jurisdiction and argued, *inter alia*, that its national had been denied the opportunity to consult with Paraguayan consular officials regarding the criminal prosecution. The Court denied permission to file the case under its original jurisdiction, and concluded that there was no right of private action in the case. *Breard v. Greene*, 523 U.S. 371 (1998).

IV. Appellate Jurisdiction of the Supreme Court

A. Statutory Provisions For The Supreme Court's Appellate Jurisdiction

1. 28 U.S.C. § 1257 provides that the Supreme Court may exercise appellate jurisdiction by writ of certiorari over final decisions of a state's highest court in any of the following situations: (1) where the validity of a federal

law or treaty is challenged on constitutional grounds, (2) where a state statute is challenged as repugnant to federal law, and (3) where any title, right, privilege, or immunity is claimed under the Constitution, treaties, or laws of the United States.

2. Under 28 U.S.C. § 1254(1), the Supreme Court may, by use of the writ of certiorari, exercise appellate jurisdiction to review any decision of a federal court of appeals.

3. The Supreme Court can grant a writ of certiorari only if at least four justices agree that the writ should be granted. Of course, the writ is denied in the overwhelming majority of cases in which Supreme Court review is sought.

4. Until 1988, the Court's appellate jurisdiction was divided between appeal and certiorari. Theoretically, the Supreme Court's appellate jurisdiction was mandatory, while its certiorari jurisdiction was discretionary.

    a. In other words, the Court was required to adjudicate cases falling within its appellate jurisdiction, but retained total discretion to decide whether it would hear cases falling within its certiorari jurisdiction. The requirement that it hear cases on appeal created significant caseload burdens for the Court.

    b. The Court found ways in which to get around the supposed mandatory nature of its appellate jurisdiction. In response to this practice, and in recognition of the caseload burden faced by the Supreme Court, Congress amended the statutes to their present form in 1988. As noted, the statutes abolish the mandatory appellate jurisdiction, and leave the question of whether to hear almost all cases to the discretion of the Court.

5. Note, however, that the Supreme Court still retains "appeal" jurisdiction under 28 U.S.C. § 1253 in the review of decisions of special three-judge courts. Such cases are quite rare, and force the Court to rule without the guidance of an opinion from the court of appeals. The trend in the past generation has been to reduce the number of cases reviewed in this way. Occasionally, though, Congress will pass a law and provide for a special three-judge district court to hear a challenge to the law. (Of course, the dispute must be justiciable and invoke subject matter jurisdiction.) The law then may expressly provide that the case will be appealed directly to

Supreme Court review, bypassing the court of appeals. The recent campaign finance reform legislation follows this model.

B. Review Of State Court Decisions: Background

1. The Constitution does not specifically provide that the Supreme Court shall have appellate jurisdiction over state court decisions. On the other hand, after laying out those cases in which the Supreme Court has original jurisdiction, the Constitution provides that the Supreme Court shall have appellate jurisdiction in all other cases falling within the judicial power of the federal courts. We discussed this point at § II.A.2, above.

2. Thus, so long as the case being reviewed falls within the subject matter jurisdiction of the federal courts, as delineated in Article III, § 2, clause 1 of the Constitution, the Supreme Court has the constitutional power to exercise appellate jurisdiction.

3. Congress has always provided legislation allowing the Supreme Court to review state court decisions, but with restrictions. Today, those restrictions are contained in 28 U.S.C. § 1257, which we saw at § IV.A, above.

4. First, the decision must be "rendered by the highest court of a State in which a decision could be had." We discuss this point in § IV.C, below.

5. Second, the decision of the state court must be a "final judgment[] or decree[]." We discuss this point in § IV.D, below.

6. Third, the decision of the state court must either (1) "draw[] in question" the validity of a treaty or federal statute, (2) "draw[] in question" the validity of a state statute as being contrary to federal law, or (3) set up any title, right, privilege, or immunity claimed under federal law or of any commission held under federal law.

    a. A case falling within any of the three enumerated areas will fall within the constitutional grant of federal question jurisdiction, assuming the federal question is sufficiently substantial. *See Zucht v. King* 260 U.S. 174 (1922). Thus, the Supreme Court will have subject matter jurisdiction of any such case without regard to amount in controversy or citizenship of the parties.

    b. Until 1914, the list of state court cases over which the Court could exercise appellate jurisdiction was narrower. Specifically, it did not permit review of cases in which the state court upheld an argument that a state statute was invalid as repugnant to federal law. In such a case, there seems less need for Supreme Court review because the federal law has been vindicated by the state court.

c. Nonetheless, Congress extended the appellate jurisdiction in 1914 to permit the Supreme Court to hear any case in which the validity of a state statute is "drawn in question" as being contrary to federal law. Accordingly, the Court now may review even state court opinions striking a state law as contrary to federal law.

7. In addition, the Supreme Court has established an important limitation on its power to review state court decisions. We discuss this "adequate and independent state ground" limitation at § IV.E, below.

8. It is a hallmark of American federalism that the supreme court of one sovereign has the power to review decisions of the judiciary of another sovereign.

C. Review Of State Court Decisions: Highest State Court

1. Section 1257 permits appellate review only of decisions by the highest state court in which review could be had.

2. In many (probably most) cases, the highest state court in which review could be had will be the state's supreme court. This is not always true, however. In *Thompson v. City of Louisville*, 362 U.S. 199 (1960), the Supreme Court took appellate jurisdiction over a case decided by a state police court. The case involved such a small amount of money that the state supreme court lacked jurisdiction. Thus, the police court was the highest state court in which review could be had.

3. In many states, the fact that review "could" be had does not mean that review "will" be had by a higher court. In other words, review by the highest state court will be discretionary. In such situations, the case cannot be taken to the Supreme Court unless a litigant seeks that discretionary review in the higher state court. *Costarelli v. Massachusetts*, 421 U.S. 193 (1975).

D. Review Of State Court Decisions: The Final Judgment Rule

1. Section 1257 allows the Supreme Court to review only "final" judgments or decrees from the state court.

2. The final judgment rule in this context serves two purposes:

   a. *Efficiency,* because it avoids piecemeal appeals and may moot numerous potential grounds for appeal because the would-be appellant receives a favorable decision on the merits in the state court.

   b. *Protection of federalism,* by possibly avoiding Supreme Court friction with state courts, which might result from Supreme Court review of state court decisions.

3. The concept of a final judgment is more ambiguous than one might suspect. The Supreme Court has often looked to the practicalities of the situation. If, as a practical matter, nothing further remains to be done in the state courts, the Court will deem the case final, even though technically a final judgment has not been entered in the state court.

4. In addition, the Supreme Court has developed doctrines of appealability under § 1257 that amount to *exceptions* to the statutory requirement of finality.

   a. In *Radio Station WOW, Inc. v. Johnson*, 326 U.S. 120 (1945), the Court recognized an exception for cases in which property has been ordered transferred and all that remained to be done in the state court was an accounting of profits. The Court reasoned that the two orders were distinct, and therefore in effect constituted multiple litigation. It also stressed that the bulk of the case was completed in state court and that delay of appellate review might cause irreparable harm.

   b. In *Cohen v. Beneficial Industrial Loan Corp.*, 337 U.S. 541 (1949), the Supreme Court recognized an exception to the finality requirement in appeals from federal district courts to federal courts of appeals "in that small class [of cases] which finally determine claims of right separable from, and collateral to, rights asserted in the action, too important to be denied review and too independent of the cause itself to require that appellate consideration be deferred until the whole case is adjudicated." The Court applied an analogy to this doctrine in allowing appellate review of a state court order under § 1257 in *Local No. 438, Construction & General Laborers' Union v. Curry*, 371 U.S. 542 (1963), and *Mercantile National Bank v. Langdeau*, 371 U.S. 555 (1963).

5. Moreover, in *Cox Broadcasting Corp. v. Cohn*, 420 U.S. 469 (1975), the Supreme Court significantly altered the traditional approach to finality and in so doing appeared to expand the concept to the breaking point. It described four categories of cases in which appeal might be allowed, despite the absence of technical finality:

   a. Cases of "practical finality," where, though there exists no technically final judgment, as a practical matter nothing remains to be done in the state court.

   b. Cases, such as *Radio Station WOW*, "in which the federal issue, finally decided by the highest court in the State, will survive and require decision regardless of the outcome of future state-court proceedings." In its discussion, the Court in *Cox* appeared to abandon the earlier prerequisites in such cases that the bulk of the case have been completed in state court and that there was a danger of irreparable injury if appeal were to be denied.

   c. Cases in which, "if the party seeking interim review ultimately prevails on the merits, the federal issue will be mooted; if he were to lose on the merits, however, the governing state law would not permit him again to present his federal claim for review."

   d. Cases in which the state courts have finally decided the federal issue and in which reversal of the state court on the federal issue would preclude any further litigation and a refusal to provide immediate review "might seriously erode federal policy."

6. The last two categories listed by the Court in *Cox* represent considerably more than a construction of the concept of finality. In each, it is simply undeniable that the case has not been completed in the state court. By so expanding the meaning of "final," some commentators note that the Court may be undermining the purposes behind the final judgment rule and promoting the possibility that the Supreme Court will engage in an unnecessary clash with a state court.

7. In its holding in *Cox* itself, the Court applied the fourth category to justify Supreme Court review.

   a. The case involved a claim for invasion of privacy brought in a Georgia state court by the father of a rape victim. He sought damages from a local television station that had broadcast his daughter's name in connection with the trial of the accused rapists. Defendants contended that the First Amendment right of free press precluded the suit.

    b. The state trial court, rejected the defendants' arguments and entered summary judgment for the plaintiff on the merits. The question of damages remained, however, and was to be determined at trial.

    c. The state supreme court also held that the First Amendment defense should be rejected. But it reversed the grant of summary judgment and remanded the case for a trial on the merits to determine whether an invasion of privacy had actually occurred.

    d. The Supreme Court took appellate jurisdiction under § 1257, even though the state supreme court had remanded the case for plenary trial. The Court noted that the state supreme court's decision "is plainly final on the federal issue and is not subject to further review in the state courts." The Court recognized that the defendants might prevail at trial on the merits, but found it significant that if the defendants were correct on the First Amendment issue, there should be no trial at all. The Court was concerned that if defendants won on non-federal grounds the state court's determination on the first amendment issue would stand unreviewed.

8. In *Pennsylvania v. Ritchie*, 480 U.S. 39 (1987), the Supreme Court applied *Cox*'s fourth category to review a state supreme court decision that remanded a case for further proceedings. The state supreme court held that the criminal defendant's Fifth and Sixth Amendment rights had been violated and ordered that defense counsel be permitted to review a relevant juvenile file.

    a. The Supreme Court reasoned that "the Sixth Amendment issue will not survive for the Court to review, regardless of the outcome of the proceedings on remand."

    b. Justice Stevens, dissenting, correctly pointed out that the Court's reasoning was "wholly contrary to our long tradition of avoiding, not reaching out to decide, constitutional decisions when a case may be disposed of on other grounds for legitimate reasons."

9. The Supreme Court has great discretion in determining whether the judgment for which its appellate jurisdiction is sought is final. Because

one ordinarily expects the Court to avoid constitutional questions and disputes with state courts that might ultimately be avoided, the liberality of *Cox, Ritchie,* and similar cases is surprising. On the other hand, there are cases in which the Court has refused to strain to invoke any of the four *Cox* factors. *See, e.g., Florida v. Thomas,* 532 U.S. 774 (2001).

E. Review Of State Court Decisions: The "Independent And Adequate State Ground" Doctrine

1. The Supreme Court has long held that it lacks the authority to review state court decisions that interpret state law. See *Murdock v. City of Memphis,* 87 U.S. 590 (1875). It is not clear that this rule is required by the Constitution. It is, however, well established as a matter of Supreme Court doctrine and practice.

2. The Supreme Court established a corollary to this principle in *Murdock,* which provides that the Court lacks authority to review federal issues contained in state court decisions when those decisions are premised on "adequate and independent" state law grounds. This doctrine can be divided into two sub-categories:

    a. Substantive state law grounds: when the state court decision rests upon both federal and non-federal grounds, the Supreme Court will not review if the non-federal ground, standing alone, would support the judgment.

    b. Procedural state law grounds: when the state court refuses to adjudicate a federal issue because the litigant has failed to comply with a legitimate state procedural rule, the Supreme Court will not review the federal claim.

3. The *substantive* branch of the doctrine is often justified on the basis of the "advisory opinion" rationale; no federal court is permitted to issue an advisory opinion, one that does not resolve actual cases or controversies. *Herb v. Pitcairn,* 324 U.S. 117 (1945). We discussed this issue in Chapter 1, § III. If an adequate state ground would support the state court judgment, no matter how the federal issue is resolved, then a Supreme Court resolution of the federal issue will have no effect on the outcome of the case. This branch of the doctrine, however, could just as easily be rationalized by the prudential principle that the Supreme Court should avoid unnecessary pronouncements of federal law, particularly when doing so might result in friction with state courts or state substantive policies.

4. The *procedural* branch of the doctrine, on the other hand, is not justified by the "advisory opinion" rationale. Instead, it is generally justified by the Supreme Court's desire to avoid undermining the maintenance of uniform and predictable state procedures. This aim would be harmed if the Supreme Court were to encourage litigants to circumvent state procedures by allowing them to raise their federal issue before the Court, even though they had not complied with valid state procedural rules.

5. The Supreme Court will not deem itself bound, however, by a state substantive or procedural rule law that it finds to be inadequate. It has stated that it is less likely to find inadequate a state substantive finding than a state procedural rule.

6. Thus, over the years, the Court has established certain categories of procedural rules which it deems inadequate to bar its appellate review.

   a. *Arbitrary state rules.* If a state rule "lacks fair or substantial support" or can be characterized as arbitrary, the Supreme Court will deem it to be nothing more than an attempt to insulate the state court holding from federal review and will therefore disregard it.

   Example: Defendant moved to quash a murder indictment on the ground that blacks had been systematically excluded from the grand jury. The state supreme court refused to consider the motion because it was "prolix," even though the motion took up only two pages in the printed record. The Supreme Court found the state ground to be inadequate, and proceeded to consider the federal issue. *Rogers v. Alabama,* 192 U.S. 226 (1904).

   b. *Novel state rules.* When the state court has applied a state rule that is inconsistent with prior state practice, the Supreme Court may find the rule inadequate to bar its appellate review.

   c. *Discretionary rules.* The Supreme Court has closely scrutinized state procedural rules that are invoked solely at the discretion of the state court, suggesting that it unduly interferes with state prerogatives. The Court's rationale is that such discretionary rules may be employed expressly to insulate the state decision from federal review.

   Example: Plaintiff asserted a federal right against racial discrimination, but the state appellate court denied the appeal because opposing counsel had not received reasonable notice and a copy of the transcript, as required by state court rules. Because the state court had not consistently applied this notice requirement to amount to a denial of its power to adjudicate the federal issue, the Court found the state rule "discretionary [rather] than jurisdictional" and adjudicated the federal issue. *Sullivan v. Little Hunting Park, Inc.*, 396 U.S. 229 (1969).

7. The Supreme Court's decision in *Henry v. Mississippi*, 379 U.S. 443 (1965), appeared to expand significantly the scope of the exceptions to the adequate state ground doctrine, and, thus, to expand the opportunity for the Court to review state decisions. It is unclear, however, what impact *Henry* ultimately has had.

8. In *Henry*, the state supreme court upheld the defendant's conviction; it held that the defendant waived his objection to the introduction of illegally seized evidence by failing to raise a contemporaneous objection to the introduction of the evidence. The Supreme Court exercised appellate jurisdiction and remanded the case for a hearing on whether defense counsel consciously waived the Fourth Amendment objection.

   a. Regarding an adequate state ground, the Court said: "[A] litigant's procedural defaults in state proceedings do not prevent vindication of his federal rights unless the State's insistence on compliance with its procedural rule serves a legitimate state interest." 379 U.S. at 447.

   b. This language is expansive, and seems to require that the state offer a justification of its rule before it can be deemed an adequate state ground for decision.

   c. The Court's implication that the "contemporaneous objection" rule—which requires that before a litigant may challenge the admissibility of evidence on appeal it must object at the time the evidence is introduced at trial—is not an adequate state ground was controversial.

   d. While the Court acknowledged that the rule served a legitimate state interest by giving the trial court the opportunity to conduct the trial without the tainted evidence, it also noted that this purpose could be served as well by a defense motion for directed verdict at the close of the state's evidence. Commentators criticize this position as unduly interfering in the state's choice of procedural rules and for improperly equating the value of the two procedural practices.

    e. The Court's remand to determine whether the failure to object was as a result of defense counsel's negligence or conscious choice demonstrated that the Court's potentially broad exception to the adequate state ground doctrine was to be tempered by a waiver doctrine: even if the state rule fails to serve a legitimate state interest, if the defendant consciously chose not to comply with it, the rule would still be deemed valid.

9. The Supreme Court has not relied upon *Henry* often in the intervening years. The Court's decisions in the area have not been entirely consistent, and most observers conclude that *Henry* ultimately has not diluted the adequate and independent state grounds doctrine considerably.

    a. In *Camp v. Arkansas*, 404 U.S. 69 (1971), the Court relied upon *Henry* to hear a case in which the state court had refused to consider an issue because the defense counsel had made no contemporaneous objection. The Court concluded that the "alleged procedural default does not bar consideration of his constitutional claim in the circumstances of this case." *Id.* at 69.

    b. In *Wainwright v. Sykes*, 433 U.S. 72 (1977), however, the Court, in a habeas corpus case, expressed significant doubt about the assertion, made in *Henry*, that a directed verdict motion could adequately serve as a substitute for the contemporaneous objection rule, pointing out what it considered the unique values of the contemporaneous objection rule. The decision did not overrule *Henry*, though, and did not deal directly with the adequate state ground doctrine as it applies to Supreme Court review of state court decisions.

10. The Supreme Court has occasionally encountered difficulty in determining whether a state court decision is based upon state, versus federal, law. If the decision is based on federal law, then the adequate and independent state ground doctrine becomes irrelevant, and the Supreme Court may hear the case.

11. In cases of ambiguity, the Supreme Court may vacate the judgment and remand the case to the state court for clarification of the basis for the holding.

12. In *Michigan v. Long*, 463 U.S. 1032 (1983), the Supreme Court held that when the basis for a state court's opinion is ambiguous, "when the adequacy and independence of any possible state law ground is not clear from the face of the opinion," it will presume that the state court intended to decide the case on the basis of federal law. This presumption permits the Supreme Court to take the case, and applies whether the state law basis for decision would be substantive or procedural.

    a. *Long* does not preclude a state court from choosing to rely on state, rather than federal law. Rather, it establishes a plain statement rule; if the state court wishes to rule on the basis of state law, it must make that basis explicit.

    b. Even with this rule, there are occasionally cases in which the Court vacates a judgment and remands for further proceedings to clarify the ground of the decision. The Court vacated the decision of the Florida Supreme Court, which had directed manual recounts of the votes in the 2000 presidential election in specified counties. The Court indicated that there was "considerable uncertainty as to the precise grounds for decision" by the Florida court. *Bush v. Palm Beach County Canvassing Bd.*, 531 U.S. 70, 78 (2000).

    c. The Supreme Court has never prescribed the exact verbal formula by which a state court might indicate its reliance on state law. Some state courts have stated that the "holding and the opinion which follows are based entirely on state constitutional grounds; federal authority is cited only for the purpose of guidance and not because it compels the result." *Kenyon v. Hammer*, 688 P.2d 961, 963 (1984) (Arizona).

    d. Although the Supreme Court has indicated that an adequate state ground may be found even in the absence of such express language when the state court opinion contained a detailed analysis of state law, generally the Court will review a case in the absence of explicit reliance on state law. *See, e.g., Ohio v. Johnson*, 467 U.S. 493 (1984).

13. Occasionally, state court decisions will indicate that the state court construes state constitutional provisions as identical with federal constitutional provisions. In such circumstances, the Supreme Court will consider the decision to rest on federal grounds; the Court can thus decide to hear the case. *Pennsylvania v. Muniz*, 496 U.S. 582 (1990)(there is no adequate and independent state basis for decision when the state and federal constitutional rules are "identical").

Example: State law taxes proceeds from slot machine gambling at 20 percent if the machines are on riverboats, but at 36 percent if the machines are at race tracks. Plaintiffs challenge the provision as violating the equal protection provisions of the United States Constitution and of the state constitution. State supreme court holds that the law violates equal protection and states that it applies "the same analysis in considering the state equal protection claims as . . . in considering the federal equal protection claims." The Supreme Court rejects the assertion that the state court holding rests on an adequate and independent state ground. The Court treats the decision as resting on federal constitutional grounds, and thus has appellate jurisdiction. *Fitzgerald v. Racing Assn. of Central Iowa*, 539 U.S. 103, 106 (2003).

F. Review of State Court Decisions: Findings of Fact

1. Traditionally, the Supreme Court has denied itself any authority to review state court factual findings.

2. On the other hand, the Court has recognized its duty to make an independent examination of the record when constitutional deprivations are alleged.

3. If the Court concludes that the findings of the state court in such cases lack supporting evidence in the record or if factual findings are so intermingled with the state court's conclusion of law about the federal right, it will make its own independent judgment about the facts.

Example: The state court held that the state Syndicalism Act did not violate the federal Constitution as applied to a specific case in which it found that the defendant was a member of an organization that taught and advocated violent overthrow of the government. The Supreme Court found that there was no evidence to support the state court's conclusion about the organization's aims. *Fiske v. Kansas*, 274 U.S. 380 (1927).

G. Review Of Decisions Of The Courts Of Appeals

1. It is not surprising, of course, that the Supreme Court should have appellate jurisdiction over cases decided by the federal courts of appeals. The Constitution, after all, expressly granted appellate jurisdiction to the Supreme Court in all cases invoking federal subject matter jurisdiction

and over which the Court does not have original jurisdiction. In addition, Congress has granted appellate review here in very broad terms. 28 U.S.C. § 1254(1) provides for Supreme Court review by writ of certiorari "upon the petition of any party to any civil or criminal case, before or after rendition of judgment or decree."

2. This statutory grant is appropriately broad. First, Supreme Court review of decisions by the courts of appeals does not implicate federalism concerns; the Court is reviewing another federal tribunal. Second, cases decided in the courts of appeals, by definition, involve at least a colorable claim of federal subject matter jurisdiction.

3. As the statute makes clear, there is no final judgment requirement. The Supreme Court may review even an interlocutory ruling of a court of appeals. Ordinarily, however, the Court waits until the court of appeals has entered a final judgment, but it is not required to do so. *See American Construction Co. v. Jacksonville, T. & K.W.R. Co.*, 148 U.S. 372 (1893).

4. Indeed, the Court may grant a writ of certiorari at any point after a case has been docketed in the courts of appeals. In essence, this practice permits the Supreme Court to bypass the court of appeals. The practice is quite rare and is followed only when there is a question of great importance and time is of the essence.

5. Under 28 U.S.C. § 1254(2), the court of appeals may certify to the Supreme Court "any question of law in any civil or criminal case as to which instructions are desired, and upon such certification the Supreme Court may give binding instructions or require the entire record to be sent up for decision of the entire matter in controversy." This provision, rarely invoked, permits the court of appeals to request a ruling from the Supreme Court on difficult and discrete questions of law. Although the statute does not appear to make it so, the Supreme Court's jurisdiction over such questions is discretionary. *See, e.g., National Labor Relations Bd. v. White Swan Co.*, 313 U.S. 23 (1941).

REVIEW QUESTIONS (PART II; CHAPTERS 4–8)

True or False Questions

1. **T or F** The scope of the current federal question statute, 28 U.S.C. § 1331, is co-extensive with the scope of the "arising under" jurisdiction provision of Article III, § 2, of the Constitution.

2. **T or F** P sues two defendants, D–1 and D–2, in a single case. P's claim against D–1 arises under federal law. P's claim against D–2 arises under state law. The claims against D–1 and D–2 arise from the same transaction. P and D–2 are citizens of the same state. A federal court can adjudicate P's claim against D–2 only if the claim against D–1 invokes *exclusive* federal question jurisdiction.

3. **T or F** The supplemental jurisdiction statute, § 1367(a), permits supplemental jurisdiction to the same extent in diversity of citizenship cases as it does in federal question cases.

4. **T or F** The "complete diversity rule"—which requires that all plaintiffs be of diverse citizenship from all defendants for a diversity of citizenship case—is mandated by the Constitution.

5. **T or F** For purposes of diversity of citizenship jurisdiction, a corporation generally has at most the citizenship of two states, while an unincorporated association may have the citizenship of an unlimited number of states.

6. **T or F** Any case that falls within the Supreme Court's original (trial) jurisdiction may not be heard by a lower federal court.

7. **T or F** The "independent and adequate state ground" doctrine concerning the appellate jurisdiction of the Supreme Court is based entirely on the doctrine that federal courts may not issue advisory opinions.

8. **T or F** In interpreting the final judgment requirement for appellate jurisdiction under 28 U.S.C. § 1257, the Supreme Court has allowed appeals of orders which could not in any rational sense be classified as "final."

9. **T or F** To meet the amount-in-controversy requirement for a diversity of citizenship case, a plaintiff must establish to a legal certainty that

her claim is worth $75,000 or more.

10. **T or F** For a class action to invoke diversity of citizenship jurisdiction, each member of the class must assert a claim meeting the amount-in-controversy requirement for a diversity of citizenship case.

11. **T or F** P, a citizen of State A, sues D, also a citizen of State A, in state court, alleging that D breached a contract between them by failing to build an incinerator for P at P's lake home. P alleges that D will defend by saying that federal law prohibits incinerators within 20 miles of a National Park, and alleges further that this federal law does not apply because P's lake home is more than 20 miles from a National Park. D removes the case to federal court. The federal court will remand the case to state court.

12. **T or F** P, a citizen of State A, sues D, a citizen of State B, in a state court in State B, alleging breach of contract under state law and damages of $80,000. D removes the case to federal court. P makes a motion in federal court to remand the case to state court. Assume that the removal and the motion to remand were timely. The federal court denies the motion to remand and retains the case. The federal court ruled correctly.

13. **T or F** P, a citizen of the Netherlands, sues D, a citizen of the United States domiciled in France, in federal claim. P asserts a claim of $80,000 arising under state law. The case invokes alienage jurisdiction, but not diversity of citizenship jurisdiction.

14. **T or F** P, a citizen of State A, sues D, a citizen of State B, in federal court, alleging diversity of citizenship jurisdiction. In the suit P asserts five separate and completely unrelated claims against D. No individual claim exceeds $20,000. In total, the claims add up to $76,000. The federal court cannot exercise diversity of citizenship jurisdiction because the claims are not transactionally related and therefore cannot be aggregated.

15. **T or F** Under the "well-pleaded complaint" rule, a federal court may exercise subject matter jurisdiction under § 1331 if the plaintiff's claim or the defendant's counterclaim arise under federal law.

Essay Question

The legislature of State A enacted the following statute: "Any conduct that would be found to violate federal Antitrust Laws if conducted in interstate commerce is hereby deemed to constitute a violation of this law when engaged in solely within the borders of this state."

Paul, a citizen of State A, brings an action under this state statute in federal district court, seeking recover of $58,000. In Claim 1, Paul sues two defendants: Monster Corporation and Goliath Corporation, both of which are incorporated in State A and have their principal place of business in State A. He alleges that the defendants conspired to interfere with Paul's business. None of the parties conducts any business outside State A. In Claim 2 in the same case, Paul joins a claim against Monster for an unrelated act of fraud, in violation of state common law.

You are a law clerk to the federal district judge hearing the case. She wants to know whether the federal court has subject matter jurisdiction over Claim (1) or Claim (2). Explain fully.

PART THREE

Federal Courts, Federalism and the States

■ ANALYSIS

9. State Courts and Federal Power
10. State Sovereign Immunity and the Eleventh Amendment
11. Abstention
12. The Anti–Injunction Statute
13. "Our Federalism": The Doctrine of *Younger v. Harris*
14. Actions to Vindicate Federal Civil Rights
15. Habeas Corpus
16. Federal Common Law
17. Claim and Issue Preclusion in the Federal System

IX

State Courts and Federal Power

■ ANALYSIS

I. Introduction
II. The Role of the State Courts in the Federal System
    A. Constitutional Presumptions About State Courts
    B. Statutory Scheme and the Concepts of Concurrent and Exclusive Subject Matter Jurisdiction
III. State Court Power to Adjudicate Federal Matters
    A. The Presumption of Concurrent Jurisdiction and the Doctrine of Implied Exclusivity
    B. State Court Adjudication of Issues Seeming to Fall Within Exclusive Federal Jurisdiction
IV. State Court Obligation to Adjudicate Federal Claims
    A. The Traditional Rule
    B. The "Valid Excuse" Doctrine
    C. State Court Obligation to Employ Federal Procedures in Adjudicating Federal Claims
V. State Court Power to Control Federal Officers
    A. Writs of Habeas Corpus
    B. Mandamus and Injunctions

C. Relevance of Federal Officer Removal

I. Introduction

In this chapter, we examine the relationship between state courts and the enforcement of federal policy. First, we discuss the role of the state courts in the federal system; it is clear that the Founders envisioned the state courts as an important resource for enforcing federal law. Second, we address when the state courts have the authority to adjudicate claims arising under federal law. This issue requires the assessment of whether Congress provides for exclusive or concurrent jurisdiction (and what rule applies when Congress is silent on that point). Having seen when state courts *may* enforce federal rights, we then address whether state courts *must* do so. This issue implicates the Supremacy Clause of the Constitution. Finally, we review whether a state court can issue an order, such as a writ of habeas corpus, compelling a federal officer to do (or refrain from doing) something. Throughout the chapter, we will see the delicate theme of federalism—the proper functioning of the state judicial systems in enforcing federal law.

II. The Role of the State Courts in the Federal System

A. Constitutional Presumptions About State Courts

1. As described in Chapter 2, § III.A, the Framers of the Constitution assumed that the state courts would play an important role in the adjudication and enforcement of federal law.

2. First, the Constitution did not mandate the creation of lower federal courts. Only the existence of the Supreme Court is constitutionally mandated. The Constitution provides that the Supreme Court will have original jurisdiction in certain cases and appellate jurisdiction in all other cases falling within the judicial power of the federal courts. *See* Chapter 8, §§ III. & IV.

3. Second, the Supremacy Clause of the Constitution, Article VI, clause 2, expressly binds state courts to enforce federal law ("the Constitution, laws and treaties of the United States") as "the supreme law of the land . . . anything in the Constitution or laws of any state to the contrary notwithstanding."

4. Thus, it is beyond dispute that state courts were expected to entertain cases arising under federal law, subject to the Supremacy Clause and subject ultimately to the appellate review of the Supreme Court.

B. Statutory Scheme and the Concepts of Concurrent and Exclusive Subject Matter Jurisdiction

1. Although Congress created lower federal courts in 1789. it did not vest them with general authority to try cases arising under federal law until 1875. *See* Chapter 4, § III.A. Thus, for over 80 years, the state courts were indeed the only trial courts for general federal question cases.

2. Congress has broad power to allocate jurisdiction over federal question cases between state and federal courts. Even when Congress vested the lower federal courts with general federal question jurisdiction, it did not make such jurisdiction exclusive to the federal courts. Thus, Congress consistently has assumed that cases arising under federal law might be brought either in a state or federal trial court, *i.e.*, that the two systems would have concurrent subject matter jurisdiction.

    a. *Concurrent* jurisdiction means that both state and federal courts may entertain the case. The plaintiff has the initial choice of whether to sue in state or federal court. Usually, as discussed in Chapter 7, however, the defendant has the option of removing a suit filed in state court to federal court.

    b. Congress occasionally chooses to give the plaintiff an irrebuttable option, as it has in the Federal Employers' Liability Act (FELA), which provides a negligence cause of action to railroad workers, which can be enforced in state or federal court. If the plaintiff sues in state court, the FELA precludes the defendant from removing the case to federal court.

    c. *Exclusive* jurisdiction means that only the federal courts are allowed to adjudicate the case. In those cases, a finding that a federal court has jurisdiction automatically excludes state court jurisdiction in the case.

3. The congressional authority to vest concurrent jurisdiction in state courts derives from its enumerated powers under Article I of the Constitution, combined with its power under the "Necessary and Proper" clause, read in conjunction with the dictates of the Supremacy Clause.

4. The congressional authority to *exclude* state courts from the adjudication of suits arising under federal law also derives from its Article I, § 8 powers and the "Necessary and Proper" Clause.

Example: Congress may enact a statute allowing patent holders to sue for patent infringement. It derives this authority from its enumerated power in Article I to provide for patents. It derives its authority to exclude state court jurisdiction (as it has in fact done in such cases in 28 U.S.C. § 1338(a)) from its power to do anything "necessary and proper" to the execution of its enumerated power.

III. State Court Power to Adjudicate Federal Matters

A. The Presumption of Concurrent Jurisdiction and the Doctrine of Implied Exclusivity

1. Obviously, when Congress creates a claim and provides that federal jurisdiction is exclusive, the courts are bound by that statement. There are several instances, including bankruptcy proceedings, patent and copyright cases, and cases brought under the Securities Exchange Act, that can only be brought in federal courts.

2. Likewise, if Congress were to provide expressly for concurrent jurisdiction, the courts would be bound by that statement as well.

3. A difficult question arises, however, when Congress is silent on the issue of whether federal jurisdiction is to be exclusive. Often, Congress creates a right and provides that the federal courts shall have jurisdiction to enforce the right, but says nothing about whether the jurisdiction is exclusive.

4. The Supreme Court created a presumption for such situations in *Claflin v. Houseman*, 93 U.S. 130, 136 (1876). There, the Court held that a "state court has jurisdiction where it is not excluded by express provision, or by incompatability in its exercise arising from the nature of the particular case." Thus, there is a presumption that when federal law creates a claim, the claim can be enforced either in state or federal court.

5. After *Claflin*, however, the Supreme Court has occasionally been inconsistent in applying the presumption the case purported to create. For example, the Court discussed claims under the National Bank Act and seemed to assume that congressional silence meant that federal jurisdiction was exclusive. *Mercantile National Bank v. Langedeau*, 371 U.S. 555 (1961).

6. More recently, however, the Supreme Court has seemed more consis-

tently to adhere to the presumption of concurrent jurisdiction. *See Tafflin v. Levitt*, 493 U.S 455 (1990); *Gulf Offshore Co. v. Mobil Oil Corp.*, 453 U.S. 473 (1981). For instance, in 1990 the Court restated the presumption, and indicated that exclusive federal jurisdiction can be found through: "an explicit statutory directive, by unmistakable implication from the legislative history, or by a clear incompatibility between state-court jurisdiction and federal interests." *Tafflin v. Levitt*, 493 U.S. at 460.

7. Another problem was the statement in *Claflin* that the presumption of concurrent jurisdiction can be overcome even without express congressional statement or from legislative history.

   a. Specifically, the Court there suggested that exclusive federal jurisdiction could be dictated by "incompatibility" between federal interests and concurrent jurisdiction "from the nature of the particular case."

   b. As restated in *Tafflin*, the standard is "incompatibility between state-court jurisdiction and federal interests."

   c. The federal courts have inferred, for example, that federal jurisdiction is exclusive over antitrust claims arising under the Sherman and Clayton Acts.

8. The Supreme Court has not been precise in indicating what factors are relevant to the inquiry of an implied finding of exclusivity.

   a. In *Charles Dowd Box Co. v. Courtney*, 368 U.S. 502 (1962), the Supreme Court found concurrent jurisdiction for suits under § 301(a) of the Labor Management Relations Act. It rejected arguments that the statute's ambiguous scope and the need for uniform interpretation dictated exclusive federal jurisdiction because of the absence in the legislative history of references to concern over the need for exclusive federal jurisdiction. The Court thus seemed to limit its assessment to the language of the statute and the legislative history.

   b. More often, however, the Court has expressly countenanced the consideration of pragmatic factors. In one case, it explained that "[t]he factors generally recommending exclusive federal-court jurisdiction over an area of federal law include the desirability of uniform interpretation, the expertise of federal judges in federal law, and the assumed greater hospitality of federal courts to peculiarly federal claims." *Gulf Offshore Co. v. Mobil Oil Corp.*, 453 U.S. at 483–84.

9. Commentators have criticized the use of pragmatic factors on separation-of-powers principles, noting that it is the legislature's job to determine when jurisdiction should be exclusive; thus, they argue, the assessment should be limited to legislative language and history.

10. Nonetheless, the Court continues to look to pragmatic factors. Usually, such factors have buttressed the presumption of concurrent jurisdiction.

    a. In *Tafflin v. Levitt*, the Court found concurrent jurisdiction for suits under the Racketeer Influenced and Corrupt Organizations (RICO) Act. It rejected arguments that a supposed need for uniform federal interpretation overcame the presumption of concurrent jurisdiction; indeed, the Court expressed "full faith in the ability of state courts to handle the complexities of civil RICO actions." 493 U.S. at 465.

    b. In *Yellow Freight System, Inc. v. Donnelly*, 494 U.S. 820, 826 (1990), the Court found concurrent jurisdiction for suits alleging discrimination under Title VII. The Court recognized that the majority of legislators engaged in drafting the law "expected" that there would be exclusive federal court jurisdiction. It concluded, though, "that such anticipation does not overcome the presumption of concurrent jurisdiction that lies at the core of our federal system."

B. State Court Adjudication of Issues Falling Within Exclusive Federal Jurisdiction

1. On occasion, state courts are faced with issues of federal law that may form the basis for a suit arising under a law within the exclusive jurisdiction of the federal courts. For example, federal courts have exclusive jurisdiction over a case "arising under any Act of Congress relating to patents, plant variety protection, copyrights and trademark. . . ." 28 U.S.C. § 1338(a). Nonetheless, patent issues may arise in contract cases in state court.

Example: Patent holder (P) gives a license to A to manufacture the patented product. A manufactures and sells the product but fails to pay required royalties to P. P sues A in state court for breach of contract. As a defense, A claims that P's patent is invalid. The state court has jurisdiction over the issue of the patent validity.

Example: The same situation occurs when plaintiff sues in state court for breach of contract and the defendant claims that the contract violated federal antitrust law.

2. The fact that state courts determine such issues in these cases raises a dilemma.

   a. On the one hand, if the state courts are allowed to decide these questions, they will effectively be adjudicating issues of federal law which Congress has deemed to be beyond their competence.

   b. On the other hand, if the state courts are prohibited from deciding these matters, the federal courts will be inundated. In essence, the well-pleaded complaint rule, discussed at Chapter 4, § III.B, will be overruled; the mere presence of federal law as a defense would have to be enough to have the case heard in federal court. Such a rule could swamp the federal courts.

3. The Supreme Court has resolved this dilemma by authorizing the state courts to decide such questions. *See, e.g., Lear, Inc. v. Adkins*, 395 U.S. 653 (1969)(contract case raising patent issues).

IV. State Court Obligation to Adjudicate Federal Claims

A. The Traditional Rule

1. In the famous case of *Martin v. Hunter's Lessee*, 14 U.S. 304 (1816), the Supreme Court made it clear to any recalcitrant state courts that it does indeed have appellate jurisdiction to review the decisions of state courts as to matters of federal law. *See* Chapter 8, (The Virginia Supreme Court essentially refused to accept that the Supreme Court had this power, and Justice Story's opinion for the Court enlightened Virginia on the subject.) Thus, it has long been clear that a state court must apply federal law that becomes applicable in the course of adjudicating state claims.

2. That left the question, however, of whether a state court was under an obligation to open its doors to permit the enforcement of a federal claim. That is: when federal law created a claim and did not provide for exclusive federal court jurisdiction, was the state court required to entertain the claim?

3. The answer is plainly yes. In *Mondou v. New York, N.H. & H.R.R.*, 223 U.S. 1 (1912), the Supreme Court held that claims arising under the Federal Employers' Liability Act (FELA) can be enforced in state courts.

   a. The Court relied on the Supremacy Clause of the Constitution, which is noted at § II.A, above.

b. The Court rejected the argument that the state court could decline to enforce a federal right if that right was found to be inconsistent with state policy. The Supremacy Clause operated to ensure that the federal policy was to be treated as state policy. As said in a more recent case: "Federal law is enforceable in state courts . . . because the Constitution and laws passed pursuant to it are as much laws in the States as laws passed by the state legislature." *Howlett by Howlett v. Rose*, 496 U.S. 356 (1990).

4. On the other hand, the Supreme Court has held that a state might refuse to enforce a federal claim in some circumstances. We discuss these circumstances, enumerated "valid excuses," in § IV.B, immediately below.

5. Many observers thought that a state court would have a valid excuse to refuse to enforce a federal *penal* law. Specifically, there has long been a school of thought that one jurisdiction is under no obligation to enforce the penal laws of another jurisdiction.

   a. The Rhode Island Supreme Court took this position in a case arising under the Emergency Price Control Act (EPCA). This federal law authorized suits for treble damages for violations of the Act (which fixed prices that could be charged during World War II). The Rhode Island Supreme Court concluded that the treble-damages provision made the statute "penal" and held that it was under no obligation to enforce such a law from a "foreign" government (the United States).

   b. The Supreme Court reversed unanimously. Rather than simply holding that the EPCA was a remedial (and thus not penal) statute, the Court chose to drive home the point that the United States is not a foreign government. Again, the Supremacy Clause requires Rhode Island to apply federal law, regardless of whether it considers the law "penal." *Testa v. Katt*, 330 U.S. 386 (1947).

   c. Because Rhode Island courts would enforce the same kind of claim that arose under state law, the Supremacy Clause required it to apply the federal law.

B. The "Valid Excuse" Doctrine

1. As we saw in the subsection immediately above, the Supremacy Clause requires state courts to enforce federal claims. The Supreme Court has

moderated this view, however, by recognizing that state courts might have a "valid excuse" not to apply federal law.

2. The Court has never given a full justification for the "valid excuse" doctrine. Commentators have suggested two possibilities.

   a. First, some argued that it is rooted in the Constitution. In *National League of Cities v. Usery*, 426 U.S. 833 (1976), the Supreme Court recognized a Tenth Amendment protection against disruption of important state functions. This protection could justify the "valid excuse" doctrine.

   b. But the Supreme Court overruled *National League of Cities* in *Garcia v. San Antonio Metropolitan Transit Authority*, 469 U.S. 528 (1985).

   c. Second, some commentators assert that the "valid excuse" doctrine might be based on congressional intent. Specifically, when Congress has made no statement as to whether state courts should be obligated to enforce a particular federal cause of action, had Congress foreseen a particular situation it would not have intended to burden the state courts with jurisdiction.

   d. As a legal matter, the justification for the "valid excuse" doctrine will be important only in the unlikely event that Congress attempts to overturn judicial recognition of a particular valid excuse. If the rationale were solely an inference of congressional intent, Congress could reverse a particular valid excuse. On the other hand, if the rationale is constitutional, Congress would lack any power to overturn the decision.

3. To date, the Supreme Court has recognized two "valid excuses" which will permit a state court to refuse enforcement of a federal claim. We also note a third situation in which a state court has refused to enforce a federal claim in circumstances which the Supreme Court seems likely to approve.

   a. If the state court has limited subject matter jurisdiction under state law, and that jurisdiction does not extend to the federal suit, wholly apart from its federal nature.

Example: In *Herb v. Pitcairn*, 324 U.S. 117 (1945), a city court in Illinois was allowed to decline jurisdiction over a claim under the Federal

Employers' Liability Act (FELA). Under the Illinois Constitution, the city court lacked competence to adjudicate a claim (state or federal) that arose outside its city limits. Because the FELA claim in this case arose outside the city, it did not have to entertain it. A contrary ruling would allow the federal law to interfere with the state court system's allocation of subject matter jurisdiction.

    b.   The doctrine of *forum non conveniens*, if the doctrine would be applied in a similar situation for a state law claim.

Example: Plaintiff brings a FELA case in state court. State law provides for dismissal of any claim (state or federal) in which no party is a resident of the state. Because no party to the FELA case was a resident of the state, dismissal was appropriate. *Missouri ex rel. Southern Ry. v. Mayfield*, 340 U.S. 1 (1950). *See also Douglas v. New York, N.H. & H.R.*, 279 U.S. 377 (1929).

    c.   Where a parallel suit between the same parties is pending in federal court. *Barnett v. Baltimore & Ohio Ry.*, 200 N.E.2d 473 (Ohio Ct.App. 1963).

4.   Some commentators have argued for recognition of a "valid excuse" when the state does not recognize a state law right "analogous" to the federal right being asserted.

    a.   The concept finds some support in several Supreme Court opinions. Notably, in *Testa v. Katt*, 330 U.S. at 394 (discussed at § IV.A, above), the Court required Rhode Island courts to enforce a federal "penal" law. In the opinion, the Court said: "It is conceded that this same type of claim arising under Rhode Island law would be enforced by that State's courts. . . . Under these circumstances the State courts are not free to refuse enforcement of the petitioners' claims."

    b.   The Supreme Court first used the phrase "analogous right" in *FERC v. Mississippi*, 456 U.S. 742, 760 (1982), in which it required Mississippi courts to enforce a federal claim. It noted that a state administrative commission "has jurisdiction to entertain claims analogous to those granted by [the federal act] and it can satisfy [that act's] requirements simply by opening its doors to claimants."

    c.   The Supreme Court has never expressly adopted an "analogous right" form of the "valid excuse" doctrine.

d. Some commentators conclude that there should be no such recognition. First, requiring a state court to enforce a federal claim for which there is no analogous right in state law does not seem unduly burdensome. Second, allowing a state to invoke such an excuse gives undue weight to the Supremacy Clause. As we saw in § IV.A, above, federal law becomes, in essence, the law of the state.

5. A state may not claim a right simply to reject federal law.

   a. In *McKnett v. St. Louis & San Francisco Ry.*, 292 U.S. 230 (1934), Alabama courts refused to entertain a FELA claim because a state statute permitted claims against foreign corporations only based upon state law, and not federal law.

   b. The Supreme Court noted: "The denial of jurisdiction by the Alabama court is based solely upon the source of the law sought to be enforced. The plaintiff is cast out because he is suing to enforce a Federal Act. A state may not discriminate against rights arising under Federal laws." 292 U.S. at 294.

   c. Thus, *McKnett* did not involve a "valid excuse." Instead, it involved naked discrimination against federal law, which violated the Supremacy Clause.

C. State Court Obligation to Employ Federal Procedures in Adjudicating Federal Claims

1. In the preceding subsections, we have seen that state courts have a general obligation to enforce federal claims. The question here is whether, in the course of such cases, the state courts must also adopt federal procedures related to those claims.

2. This question raises the need to balance two important principles. First, the state courts, as independent systems, obviously have a right to adopt their own procedures. But second, adequate protection of federal interests may require that a state adhere to federal dictates on the procedures for enforcing federal claims.

3. In *Dice v. Akron, Canton & Youngstown R.R. Co.*, 342 U.S. 359 (1952), the Supreme Court held that a state court adjudicating a suit under the Federal Employers' Liability Act (FELA) was required to allocate decision-making authority between judge and jury in the same manner as a

federal court would. Specifically, state law would have allowed the judge to determine whether a release was invalid because of fraud. The Supreme Court held that the issue must be decided by the jury.

   a. Though the Court's reasoning is not entirely clear, it seems that the Court relied on the following factors: (a) ensuring an important role for the jury was essential to the achievement of Congress' substantive goal in enacting the FELA, and (b) requiring state courts to follow the federal allocation of responsibility in the FELA suits would not unduly burden the state judicial system.

   b. The Court distinguished the case from *Minneapolis & St. Louis R. Co. v. Bombolis*, 241 U.S. 211 (1916), in which it held that a state court is not required to employ a unanimous verdict requirement in adjudicating FELA cases, even though federal courts would require jury unanimity. Presumably, the Court was saying that a requirement of unanimity might significantly burden and delay the functioning of the state courts and was not essential for vindicating the substantive federal right.

4. Similarly, in adjudicating a FELA case, the state court may not adhere to its general pleading rule of construing a pleading strictly against the pleading party. Instead, it must construe pleadings liberally in favor of the pleading party. *Brown v. Western Ry. of Alabama*, 338 U.S. 294 (1949).

5. Some commentators suggest that the holdings in such cases are limited to FELA cases. Most seem to agree, however, that they are not, and that Congress may create other claims which, when enforced in state court, will require adoption of federal procedure.

V. State Court Power to Control Federal Officers

A. Writs of Habeas Corpus

1. In *Ableman v. Booth*, 62 U.S. 506, 516 (1859), a state court issued a writ of habeas corpus to compel the release of a person in federal custody, who was later prosecuted criminally in federal court. The Supreme Court held that the state court had no power to issue the writ. Chief Justice Taney wrote that the courts of a state simply could not be allowed to interfere with the workings of the federal government, which he characterized as "another and independent Government."

2. The Supreme Court reiterated and extended this holding in *Tarble's Case* (*In re Tarble*), 80 U.S. 397 (1871). There, a state court issued a writ of habeas corpus to compel the release from the United States Army of an enlisted man who allegedly was under the required age for service. The Supreme Court reversed and held that the state court lacked any judicial power to issue the writ.

   a. The Court relied heavily on its opinion in *Ableman*, and stressed that a state court cannot be permitted to interfere with the operation of the federal government.

   b. The Court feared the possibility that a contrary ruling would permit state courts to inhibit the functioning of the federal government. "In many exigencies the measures of the National government might . . . be entirely bereft of their efficacy and value." *Tarble*, 80 U.S. at 409.

   c. Conceivably, the Court could have limited *Ableman* to cases of judicial comity—in which a state writ of habeas corpus interfered with federal litigation. The holding in *Tarble's Case* rejects such limitation, however, and seems to embrace a broad principle that state courts lack judicial power to interfere with the activities of federal officers.

   d. Some have suggested that these holdings should be limited to situations involving national emergency or some vital federal interest, such as the functioning of the military, as in *Tarble*. Any such limitation would seem too nebulous to be meaningful; moreover, courts have not adhered to any such limitation.

3. Some commentators criticize *Tarble's Case* as inconsistent with the traditional view, discussed in § IV.A, above, that state courts are expected to enforce federal law to the same extent as a federal court would. Simply stated, some criticize *Tarble's Case* as evincing insufficient faith in the state courts to apply federal law.

4. On the other hand, other commentators argue that the traditional view substantially disregards the fundamental changes in the relation between state courts and the federal government and in the general philosophy of federalism growing out of the Civil War and post-Civil War constitutional amendments.

   a. The availability of federal officer removal, discussed in § C, below, bolsters the notion that state courts are not seen as equal to federal courts in applying and enforcing federal law.

    b. *Tarble* might be viewed as recognizing a type of implied exclusivity under *Claflin*, subject to express congressional reversal.

5. Whatever its merits, the rule of *Tarble's Case* is still good law. It provides a clear rule: the state courts lack judicial power to issue writs of habeas corpus to a federal officer.

6. It is important to note, however, that the petitioner in *Tarble* was free to seek a writ of habeas corpus from a *federal* court. The Supreme Court expressly noted this fact in its opinion. *Tarble's Case*, 80 U.S. at 411. Because the Constitution, art. I, § 9, clause 2, guarantees the right of habeas corpus, there must be some avenue—either in federal or state court—to seek it.

    a. The Court in *Tarble* did not expressly hold that federal availability of habeas corpus was a prerequisite to its limitation on state court authority.

    b. It is conceivable, however, that the *Tarble* bar on state court power might be unconstitutional in situations in which Congress has removed a *federal* judicial avenue for habeas corpus. In such a situation, there would be no judicial recourse for one seeking the writ, which clearly would violate the constitutional guaranty of habeas corpus.

    c. On the other hand, perhaps the constitutional guaranty of habeas corpus should be seen as invalidating any congressional effort to remove federal court jurisdiction over claims for the writ.

B. Mandamus and Injunctions

1. As we saw in the preceding subsection, *Ableman* and *Tarble* held that state courts may not issue a writ of habeas corpus to a federal officer. The question is whether that ban applies to state court authority to issue mandamus or an injunction to a federal officer.

2. The answer as to mandamus is clear. Even before deciding the habeas corpus cases, the Supreme Court in *McClung v. Silliman*, 19 U.S. 598 (1821), held that state courts lacked authority to issue writs of mandamus to federal officers.

3. The Supreme Court has never definitively decided whether the principle of *Tarble* extends to bar state court *injunctions* against federal officers as well.

   a. The lower federal courts have split on this question, though the majority of these decisions have concluded that such writs are also barred.

   b. Commentators have taken contradictory positions on the issue, mostly depending upon their view of whether *Tarble* was properly decided.

   c. It is difficult to reconcile the continued viability of *Tarble* with a conclusion that a state court may issue an injunction against a federal officer. After all, such an injunction would interfere with federal sovereignty as much as issuing a writ of habeas corpus.

C. **Relevance of Federal Officer Removal**

   1. 28 U.S.C. § 1442(a)(1) provides for "federal officer removal." A federal officer sued in her personal or official capacity "for any act under color of such office" may remove the case to the federal district court embracing the state court in which she has been sued.

      a. The statute allows removal of civil and criminal cases in which the federal officer is a defendant.

      b. Other defendants in the case need not participate in the removal.

      c. The federal officer must raise a federal defense in the action.

   2. Some commentators argue that the availability of federal officer removal renders irrelevant the *Tarble* prohibition of state court jurisdiction to issue habeas corpus.

      a. Once the federal officer is sued for habeas, according to this argument, she can simply remove the case to federal court.

      b. On the other hand, without the *Tarble* rule, a state court might work some restraint on the operation of a federal program before the federal officer removed the case. Thus, *Tarble* removes any danger of even a limited state judicial interference with federal sovereignty.

   3. Moreover, the provision for federal officer removal traces back to early in the history of the United States. Even at an early date, there was concern

that state courts might be hostile to federal programs and federal officers. This fact contradicts the argument of commentators that *Tarble* is inconsistent with a traditional view that state and federal courts are fungible for the enforcement of federal rights. *See* § IV.A, above. Early in the nation's history, Congress entertained doubts about state courts' willingness to enforce federal law.

*

X

State Sovereign Immunity and the Eleventh Amendment

■ ANALYSIS

I. Introduction
II. Background and History of the Eleventh Amendment
   A. The Evolving Concept of Sovereign Immunity
   B. The *Chisholm* Decision and Ratification of the Amendment
III. Interpretation of the Eleventh Amendment
   A. Narrow Literal Terms Have Not Limited Application of the Amendment
   B. The Amendment Does Not Bar All Suits Against States
   C. The Amendment Bars Specified Suits in Federal Court Regardless of Jurisdictional Basis
   D. Nature of the Eleventh Amendment Defense
   E. What Constitutes the State

    F.   Summary of Methods for Avoiding the Bar of the Amendment
- IV. **Avoiding the Bar of the Eleventh Amendment: The *Ex Parte Young* Doctrine**
    - A. The *Ex Parte Young* Case
    - B. Development of Current Doctrine on Specific Issues
    - C. Development of Current Doctrine Concerning Remedies
- V. **Avoiding the Bar of the Eleventh Amendment: Waiver by the State**
    - A. The Traditional Waiver Rule
    - B. Actions by the State Constituting Waiver
- VI. **Avoiding the Bar of the Eleventh Amendment: Congressional Abrogation**
    - A. Background on the Concept of Congressional Abrogation
    - B. Direct Abrogation by Congress
    - C. Determining Whether Congress Intended Direct Abrogation Under § 5 of the Fourteenth Amendment
    - D. Indirect Abrogation by Congress (Or "Constructive Waiver")

I. Introduction

The Eleventh Amendment, ratified in reaction to a case that upheld federal jurisdiction over a case against a state, removes federal judicial power over cases by a citizen of a state against another state; the Supreme Court has interpreted the amendment to bar cases by a citizen against the state in which she is a citizen as well. The amendment embodies the concept of sovereign immunity, and has come to stand for the proposition that a state cannot be sued (by certain plaintiffs) in federal court. Many people criticize the principle that a state should not have to answer in federal court when it commits an actionable wrong. Despite narrow literal terms, the Supreme Court has interpreted the amendment broadly in some ways. It is clear, for instance, that immunity may be invoked in cases in which the state is not a named party. When the amendment applies, it bars suit against a state in federal court. Plaintiffs may be able to avoid the operation of the amendment, however, by invoking one of three well-established but narrow exceptions. The existence of the amendment and of the exceptions raise important questions of federalism—whether a citizen ought to be able to seek justice from a state in a federal court.

II. Background and History of the Eleventh Amendment

A. The Evolving Concept of Sovereign Immunity

1. The concept of sovereign immunity is generally thought to mean that the sovereign—in this case the state—cannot be held liable. It is said to derive from the medieval English dictate that "the king can do no wrong," which in turn was said to derive from the precept that no man can be sued in his own court.

2. Some commentators have suggested that the precept that "the king can do no wrong" has been grossly misinterpreted, and that all it meant originally was that the king was not *allowed* to do any wrong.

3. Certainly, one may question the logic of applying such a principle, developed in a monarchy, to a democratic society.

4. Nevertheless, there is no doubt that the framers of the Constitution contemplated the existence of some form of sovereign immunity.

5. For generations, the Supreme Court treated the immunity principle of the Eleventh Amendment as one that ensured that a state could not be

held liable in a federal court. The Court saw the primary goal of the Eleventh Amendment as protecting the state treasury from imposition of liability. *See, e.g., Hess v. Port Authority Trans–Hudson Corp.*, 513 U.S. 30 (1994)(protection of state treasury from judgments in federal court was "impetus" for the Eleventh Amendment and is the most "salient" factor in determining when an action is against a state).

6. More recently, the Court has emphasized a broader concept of immunity. Specifically, it now sees the principle of the Eleventh Amendment as freeing the states from being subjected to litigation at all. *Alden v. Maine*, 527 U.S. 706 (1998).

B. The *Chisholm* Decision and Ratification of the Amendment

1. Article III, § 2 of the Constitution, which lists the classes of cases falling within the federal juridical power, originally provided for jurisdiction over cases "between a State and Citizens of another State."

    a. The provision, as structured, was a special form of diversity jurisdiction.

    b. At the Constitutional Convention, some people were troubled that the clause might permit suits against a state, and thus that it might abrogate sovereign immunity.

    c. Various framers responded to this concern by stating that the provision was not intended to apply to suits in which a state was the defendant. Rather, these framers thought that the clause would allow a case by a state *against* a citizen of another state.

2. Despite this sentiment, the Supreme Court upheld jurisdiction under this clause in a case against Georgia in *Chisholm v. Georgia*, 2 U.S. 419 (1793). There, a citizen of South Carolina sued Georgia to recover for items sold to the state to prosecute the Revolutionary War. The Court exercised original (trial) jurisdiction even though Georgia had not waived its immunity.

3. The *Chisholm* decision led to public uproar and to the rapid passage and ratification of the Eleventh Amendment, which provides: "The judicial power of the United States shall not be construed to extend to any suit in law or equity, commenced or prosecuted against one of the United States by citizens of another state, or by citizens or subjects of any foreign state."

III. Interpretation of the Eleventh Amendment

A. Narrow Literal Terms Have Not Limited Application of the Amendment

1. The language of the Eleventh Amendment is quite narrow, and purports to remove federal judicial power only over cases "commenced or prosecuted against one of the United States by Citizens of another State, or by Citizens or Subjects of any Foreign State."

2. Of course, the amendment bars suits by a citizen of one state against another state, and by a foreign citizen or government against a state. *See, e.g., Principality of Monaco v. Mississippi*, 292 U.S. 313 (1934).

2. On its face, the amendment appears not to bar a suit in federal court by a citizen of a state against her own state. Nonetheless, the Court held in *Hans v. Louisiana*, 134 U.S. 1 (1890), that the amendment bars suits in such a situation.

3. In addition, the Court has held that the amendment bars suits by Indian tribes against a state, by a municipality against a state, and by another state against a state.

4. The amendment also bars suits against Puerto Rico and other territories, notwithstanding that such entities are not states. *See, e.g., Puerto Rico Aqueduct Auth. v. Metcalf & Eddy, Inc.*, 506 U.S. 139 (1993).

5. The Court's refusal to abide by the narrow literal terms of the amendment reflects a political philosophy premised on notions of federalism and state power.

B. The Amendment Does Not Bar All Suits Against States

1. Of course, the Eleventh Amendment, even broadly construed, does not bar all suits against a state.

2. For instance, it does not bar the United States from suing a state in federal court. *See United States v. Mississippi*, 380 U.S. 128 (1965). There is no way to interpret the Amendment in a way that would preclude such suits.

3. Also, because the amendment affects only the federal judicial power, it does not apply to suits brought against a state in state court.

4. The amendment also does not bar the Supreme Court from exercising appellate jurisdiction over a case brought against a state in state court. *Nevada v. Hall*, 440 U.S. 410 (1979).

C. The Amendment Bars Specified Suits in Federal Court Regardless of Jurisdictional Basis

1. For many generations, it was unclear whether the Eleventh Amendment operated to bar federal court suits against a state only if that suit invoked a particular type of federal subject matter jurisdiction.

2. From time to time, judges and commentators opined that the amendment should bar only cases brought against a state pursuant to the diversity of citizenship clause of Article III, § 2. After all, this was the provision construed in *Chisholm v. Georgia*, which led to adoption of the amendment.

   a. The logical consequence of the "diversity" theory is that the Eleventh Amendment does not bar suit against a state premised on federal question jurisdiction, regardless of the citizenship of the plaintiff.

   b. In support of the theory, some argued that to extend state immunity to suits brought to enforce federal statutes would be inconsistent with the plan of the constitutional convention, which embraced the notion that states ceded their sovereignty to the extent that they ratified Article I's vesting of legislative authority in the federal government.

   c. The greatest problem with the "diversity" theory of the amendment is that the language does not suggest that it is so limited. The amendment bars "any suit" against a state by a citizen of another state. Thus, it draws no distinction on the basis of federal subject matter jurisdiction.

3. In *Hans v. Louisiana*, 134 U.S. 1 (1890), the Supreme Court held that the amendment barred a suit brought under federal question jurisdiction by a citizen of the defendant state. Thus, the Court implicitly rejected the idea that the amendment applied only to bar diversity-type suits against a state.

4. Since then, the Court has clearly established that the jurisdictional basis is not important.

a. The amendment bars suits against a state under diversity jurisdiction,

b. Likewise for federal question jurisdiction,

c. And for a claim asserted under supplemental jurisdiction,

d. And for claims asserted under admiralty jurisdiction.

e. In *Cory v. White*, 457 U.S. 85 (1982), the Court held that an interpleader claim against a state was barred by the amendment.

D. Nature of the Eleventh Amendment Defense

1. If the amendment applies, a claim brought originally in federal court will be dismissed. If the case was removed from state court, it will be remanded to state court.

2. Thus, the defense that the amendment bars suit appears to be like a defense that a court lacks subject matter jurisdiction over a case. But if the defense is jurisdictional, two facts would follow: (1) the court would have to raise the issue sua sponte, and (2) the state would not be able to waive the defense, because doing so would be tantamount to "creating" subject matter jurisdiction.

3. The Supreme Court has sent conflicting signals as to whether the defense is jurisdictional in this sense.

   a. The Court has said that the defense can be raised at any time during proceedings, which is consistent with raising a defense of subject matter jurisdiction. *Edelman v. Jordan*, 415 U.S. 651, 679 (1974).

   b. On the other hand, the Court also has said that an appellate court is not required to raise the issue, *see, e.g., Patsy v. Board of Regents of Florida*, 457 U.S. 496, 515 n.19 (1982), which is inconsistent with the way courts treat subject matter jurisdiction.

4. Further, there is no doubt that the state can waive the Eleventh Amendment defense and thereby consent to suit in federal court. We will discuss such methods of waiver in § V, below. This fact is contrary to the treatment of subject matter jurisdiction.

5. Some courts treat the Eleventh Amendment defense as a "personal privilege" of the state, which is waived if not asserted as an affirmative

defense in a timely fashion. *See, e.g., Agua Caliente Band of Cahuilla Indians v. Hardin*, 223 F.3d 1041 (9th Cir. 2000), *cert. denied* 532 U.S. 958 (2001).

6. The fact that a state may be immune from suit in state court does not necessarily mean that it has Eleventh Amendment immunity in federal court.

E. What Constitutes the State?

1. The amendment bars suits in federal court against a "state." Clearly, then, it bars claims which actually name the state as a defendant party of record.

2. Most cases, then, do not name the state as a defendant, but involve some political subdivision, agency, or individual. The question of whether such a defendant should be considered an "arm of the state" and entitled to immunity under the amendment is often difficult.

3. The Supreme Court has made it clear that the case will be considered against a state, and therefore barred, even if the state is not a named party, if the state is the real party in interest. The court must look to the "essential nature and effect of the proceeding" to determine whether the case is in fact against the state. *Ford Motor Co. v. Dept. of Treasury of State of Indiana*, 323 U.S. 459 (1945). (In *Lapides v. Board of Regents of Univ. Sys.*, 535 U.S. 613 (2002), the Supreme Court overruled that of *Ford Motor Co.* that permitted a state to assert Eleventh Amendment immunity after having litigated and lost.)

4. The burden is on a political entity to establish that it is an arm of the state and thus entitled to immunity under the amendment.

5. The question of whether a political entity is considered part of the state for purposes of the amendment is determined by federal law. Though the federal court will consider whether the state considers the entity to be an arm of the state, it is not bound by state law on the question.

6. The state is usually considered the real party in interest if the action seeks recovery from the state treasury. *Quern v. Jordan*, 440 U.S. 332 (1979).

7. That test is rough, however, and the courts look to other factors as well in determining whether the defendant is entitled to immunity. For

instance, courts look at the autonomy enjoyed by the defendant, whether it is enforcing statewide (as opposed to merely local) rules, and state funding. Cases are often difficult to reconcile, but there are some general rules.

   a. Municipalities and municipal agencies usually are not considered arms of the state, and thus are not entitled to Eleventh Amendment immunity. *See, e.g., Owen v. City of Independence, Missouri*, 445 U.S. 622 (1980).

   b. School districts usually are not considered to be arms of the state.

   c. Cases are split on whether state universities, correctional facilities, highway departments, and bar associations are arms of the state.

8. More recently, the Court has emphasized the concept of legal liability, rather than whether the plaintiff seeks to collect from the state treasury. In *Regents of the University of California v. Doe*, 519 U.S. 425 (1997), any judgment against the state university would be indemnified by the federal government. Thus, the case could not have had a negative impact on the state treasury. Nonetheless, the Court held that the case was barred by the Eleventh Amendment because the case sought to impose legal liability on the state university.

9. The state cannot create immunity by agreeing to indemnify a political entity that is not an arm of the state. Thus, if the defendant is not an arm of the state, the case is not barred by the amendment. The fact that the state may agree to indemnify the defendant does not convert the case into one against the state.

10. Even a suit against an individual may be barred because it is in fact against the state. If the plaintiff seeks a money judgment that would be paid from the state treasury, the Eleventh Amendment may bar the action. *Ford Motor Co. v. Dept. of Treasury of State of Indiana*, 323 U.S. 459 (1945)(suit by state taxpayer against state officers to recover refund of taxes allegedly illegally imposed deemed to be against the state). (In *Lapides v. Board of Regents of Univ. Sys.*, 535 U.S. 613 (2002), the Supreme Court overruled the holding of *Ford Motor Co.* that permitted a state to assert Eleventh Amendment immunity after having litigated and lost.)

   a. Suits against a state officer in his individual capacity, to impose personal liability upon her, are not barred. *Scheuer v. Rhodes*, 416 U.S. 232 (1974).

b. Suits against a state officer might be pursued under 42 U.S.C. § 1983, which is discussed in Chapter 14.

c. Suits against a state officer might implicate the doctrine of *Ex Parte Young*, discussed in § IV, below.

F. **Summary of Methods for Avoiding the Bar of the Amendment**

1. The amendment bars a case in federal court against a state, as defined above. But the Supreme Court has recognized three ways in which a plaintiff might avoid the amendment and sue a state (or an arm of the state) in federal court. We address them in the remainder of this Chapter.

2. One is through the common law doctrine of *Ex Parte Young*, which we discuss in § IV.

3. Another is by waiver of the immunity by some conduct by the state, which we discuss in § V.

4. The third is by congressional act to abrogate the immunity, which we discuss in § VI.

IV. Avoiding the Bar of the Eleventh Amendment: The *Ex Parte Young* Doctrine

A. **The *Ex Parte Young* Case**

1. The holding of *Ex Parte Young*, 209 U.S. 123 (1908), provides an important way to avoid the bar of the Eleventh Amendment. Through it, a plaintiff can sue a state actor for certain equitable relief and, if successful, stop the state from doing something allegedly illegal.

2. In *Ex Parte Young*, the plaintiff sued the attorney general of Minnesota, seeking an injunction against his enforcing state law that required railroads to reduce their rates. The plaintiff contended that the state law was confiscatory in violation of due process. If the court issued the injunction, it would have the effect of stopping the state from enforcing its statute. Thus, the case would seem to be against the state and thus barred by the Eleventh Amendment.

a. The Supreme Court nonetheless permitted the case to proceed in federal court, based upon the following reasoning: because the officer acted in an illegal way, he was stripped of the immunity provided to the state by the Eleventh Amendment. After all, said the Court, the state could not instruct an officer to behave in an illegal way.

    b. Thus, the maverick state official did not act for the state, and the case would be seen as simply against a private individual, and not against the state. As such, it was not barred by the Eleventh Amendment.

3. *Ex Parte Young* is analytically flawed.

    a. On the one hand, the Court held that the illegal acts of a state officer do not constitute state action for purposes of the Eleventh Amendment.

    b. On the other hand, the Court held that the very same acts could be challenged under the Fourteenth Amendment because they did constitute "state action."

    c. Many commentators have criticized the result-oriented inconsistency of *Ex Parte Young* as logically indefensible and unprincipled.

4. Despite its fictive quality and considerable criticism, *Ex Parte Young* remains vital and has provided an important vehicle for federal court challenges of the constitutionality of state statutes under which state officers act.

B. Development of Current Doctrine on Specific Issues

1. First, the state officer sued must have a *duty* to enforce the challenged state law. Though the duty need not be found in the challenged statute itself, it must be more than a mere general duty to enforce the law. Thus, *Ex Parte Young* is not available to challenge discretionary acts or tasks of the state officer.

2. Second, the state action must constitute a violation of federal law. Often, the federal law will be the Constitution, but a federal statute is sufficient. The point is that *Ex Parte Young* is not a vehicle for challenging violations of state law. *Pennhurst State School & Hospital v. Halderman*, 465 U.S. 89 (1984)(Eleventh Amendment barred federal court from ordering state officials to conform their conduct to state law).

3. Third, the federal law vindicated must be the "supreme law of the land."

Example: State adopts a federal program, such as Medicaid. If the program requires the state to adhere to federal guidelines, then those federal guidelines are the supreme law. In contrast, if the federal program permits the state to set its own standards, such law, though federal in origin, is not enforceable under *Ex Parte Young*.

4. Fourth, the Supreme Court has recently narrowed the availability of *Ex Parte Young* by holding that the theory is not available if federal law provides such intricate remedies that it is clear that Congress did not intend for *Ex Parte Young* cases. In other words, if federal law sets up its own remedial scheme for violation of the federal law, the court might conclude that Congress intended to foreclose *Ex Parte Young* suits. *Seminole Tribe of Florida v. Florida*, 517 U.S. 44, 75 (1996)(because Indian Gaming Regulatory Act contained a "carefully crafted and intricate remedial scheme," Congress did not intend *Ex Parte Young* to apply).

5. Fifth, in *Idaho v. Coeur d'Alene Tribe of Idaho*, 521 U.S. 261 (1997), the Court held that the *Ex Parte Young* theory is not available if it would interfere with special state sovereignty interests, such as those implicated by quiet title actions to real property.

C. Development of Current Doctrine Concerning Remedies

1. The question of what remedies are available under the *Ex Parte Young* theory has generated more discussion and confusion than the requirements discussed in § B, above.

2. In *Ex Parte Young* itself, the plaintiff sought an injunction against the future enforcement of the challenged state law. On the other hand, it is clear that a recovery of damages from the state treasury is barred by the Eleventh Amendment. Some suggested, then, that the dividing line for the propriety of *Ex Parte Young* was whether the plaintiff sought damages (which are barred) or equitable relief (which is not). This distinction, however, is too facile.

3. The Supreme Court altered the focus in the important case of *Edelman v. Jordan*, 415 U.S. 651 (1974). There, plaintiffs sought a mandatory injunction to force state officials to comply with a federal program concerning aid to disabled persons by paying back benefits wrongfully withheld.

    a. The Court rejected the argument that payment of back benefits was permissible because deemed "equitable restitution" rather than damages. "We do not read *Ex Parte Young* . . . to indicate that any form of relief may be awarded against a state officer, . . . out of the state treasury, so long as the relief may be labeled 'equitable' in nature." *Id.* at 665–66.

    b.   The Court recognized, however, that proper relief, such as the injunction in *Ex Parte Young* itself, may have an ancillary effect on the state treasury. Such an effect is acceptable if it is caused by a prospective remedy, such as an injunction or declaratory judgment.

    c.   On the other hand, a retroactive award from the state treasury—even if not labeled "damages"—is not permitted.

4. Some commentators have criticized the prospective-versus-retrospective approach of *Edelman*, but the case retains vitality.

5. Thus, federal courts may grant prospective injunctive and declaratory relief in cases brought under *Ex Parte Young*. In addition, they can enter injunctions requiring expenditure of state funds to comply with federal law, so long as the order is prospective.

Example: An order requiring state officials to desegregate schools in Detroit was proper, notwithstanding that it would cost the state about $6,000,000, because the order was prospective. Thus, the effect on the state treasury was considered ancillary and acceptable. *Milliken v. Bradley*, 433 U.S. 267 (1977).

6. Because prospective relief is permitted, obviously the suit must concern an ongoing violation of federal law. If the violation has ceased, the only remedy available would be compensatory damages, which are barred by the Eleventh Amendment.

7. The Court has permitted recovery of money directly from the state in limited circumstances when such an order was ancillary to prospective relief.

    a.   In *Hutto v. Finney*, 437 U.S. 678 (1978), the Court upheld an award of attorney's fees against the state for bad faith failure to comply with a court order.

    b.   In *Quern v. Jordan*, 440 U.S. 332 (1979), the Court permitted the issuance of a court order notifying class members of their right to pursue retroactive relief in a state forum.

c. In *Green v. Mansour*, 474 U.S. 64 (1985), the Court restricted the availability of such notice relief as was allowed in *Quern*. Plaintiffs in *Green* sought prospective relief that became inapposite when Congress changed relevant statutes during the pendency of the case. They sought an order giving notice to class members of the possibility of pursuing retroactive relief in a state forum. The Court affirmed dismissal of the case, and held that "notice relief" was appropriate only when other prospective relief was granted, to which the notice relief could be ancillary.

V. Avoiding the Bar of the Eleventh Amendment: Waiver by the State

A. The Traditional Waiver Rule

1. It has long been understood that a state may waive its sovereign immunity, and allow itself to be sued.

2. This concept applies to the protection of the Eleventh Amendment, which a state may waive in a variety of ways, discussed in § B, below.

3. Because the amendment accords constitutional protection, however, waiver is not to be inferred easily. It must be unequivocal either by act or language. *Port Authority Trans–Hudson Corp. v. Feeney*, 495 U.S. 299 (1990).

4. In this section, we address a state's waiver by its conduct, which may include state constitutional provisions, state legislation, or actions taken in litigation. This is to be contrasted with a doctrine of implied abrogation of Eleventh Amendment immunity by Congress, a doctrine now repudiated, which is discussed in § VI.D, below.

B. Actions by the State Constituting Waiver

1. A state may waive its Eleventh Amendment immunity by statute. For example, in *Port Authority Trans–Hudson Corp. v. Feeney*, the Supreme Court held that a state venue statute waived the state's immunity. The statute "expressly indicat[ed]" the state's consent to suit in federal court. Such waiver must be express.

2. A state may waive its immunity expressly by constitutional provision.

3. A state may waive its immunity by giving express consent to a suit in federal court.

4. A state may waive its immunity by litigation conduct. For instance, in *Lapides v. Board of Regents of Univ. Sys.*, 535 U.S. 613 (2002), the Supreme Court held that joining in a removal to federal court waives the immunity by voluntarily invoking federal jurisdiction. Though the Court emphasized that its holding involved only questions of state law, removed on the basis of diversity, the reasoning seems clearly to apply to any case in which a state removes from state court.

5. There may be a question about who is empowered to waive the state's immunity. In *Lapides*, the Supreme Court held that the state attorney general's office waived the immunity by removing the case to federal court. The state argued that the attorney general's office could not waive the immunity unless a statute gave it authority to do so. The Court rejected the argument.

6. The fact that a state consents to suit in state courts does not compel the conclusion that it has waived its Eleventh Amendment immunity from suit in federal court. *Florida Department of Health and Rehabilitation Services v. Florida Nursing Home Association*, 450 U.S. 147 (1981)(per curiam).

VI. Avoiding the Bar of the Eleventh Amendment: Congressional Abrogation

A. Background on the Concept of Congressional Abrogation

1. The issues in this are whether Congress may abrogate the states' Eleventh Amendment immunity and, if so, how.

2. The concept of "direct abrogation" involves Congress' passing a statute which provides that states may be sued in federal court for violating it. In recent years, the Supreme Court has narrowed the circumstances in which Congress can do this, but has also brought increased clarity to the area. *See* §§ B & C, below.

3. The concept of "indirect abrogation" involves congressional legislation that provides that a state will lose its Eleventh Amendment immunity by participating in a federal program. Some judges and commentators refer to this process as "constructive waiver." This wing of abrogation theory is now moribund. *See* § D, below.

B. Direct Abrogation by Congress

1. There is substantial scholarly opinion that Congress may abrogate states'

Eleventh Amendment immunity by proper legislation rendering the states amenable to suit in federal court.

2. There has been serious question, however, about what parts of the Constitution permit Congress to abrogate immunity. Only if Congress acts under a proper constitutional provision will the abrogation be effective.

3. Some commentators argued that the Fourteenth Amendment automatically overrode Eleventh Amendment immunity because the Fourteenth Amendment was ratified after the eleventh. As a result, they argued, any claim against a state for deprivation of a right protected by the Fourteenth Amendment could be brought in state court.

4. It is now clear that the Fourteenth Amendment does not automatically cause abrogation of the Eleventh Amendment immunity. Rather, Congress can override the immunity by passing a statute pursuant to § 5 of the Fourteenth Amendment.

5. Section 5 is the "enforcement" provision of the Fourteenth Amendment, and allows Congress to enforce the protection of the Fourteenth Amendment through appropriate legislation. The Supreme Court has insisted upon a clear statement of congressional intent, as discussed in § C, below.

6. Lower courts had found congressional abrogation under other constitutional provisions. Though the Supreme Court once embraced this theory, it has since rejected it.

   a. In *Pennsylvania v. Union Gas*, 491 U.S. 1 (1989), the Court held that Congress can abrogate immunity by legislation passed pursuant to the Interstate Commerce Clause.

   b. The Court overruled *Union Gas*, however, in *Seminole Tribe of Florida v. Florida*, 517 U.S. 44 (1996), in which it held that neither the Interstate Commerce Clause nor the Indian Commerce Clause may be the basis of direct abrogation.

   c. Indeed, the Court seems clearly to have established in *Seminole Tribe* that Congress may abrogate Eleventh Amendment immunity *only* through legislation under § 5 of the Fourteenth Amendment. In other words, abrogation cannot be based upon Article I powers. *See also Alden v. Maine*, 527 U.S. 706 (1999)(Congress cannot abrogate state immunity in state court pursuant to its Article I powers).

7. After wrestling with the issue in a series of cases, the Court finally held that Congress did not intend that 42 U.S.C. § 1983 abrogate state immunity under the Eleventh Amendment. *Will v. Dept. of State Police*, 491 U.S. 58 (1989). We discuss § 1983 in Chapter 14.

C. Determining Whether Congress Intended Direct Abrogation Under § 5 of the Fourteenth Amendment

1. Merely enacting a statute under § 5 of the Fourteenth Amendment does not cause abrogation of Eleventh Amendment immunity. Congress must also make an express statement in the statute itself of its intent to allow states to be sued.

    a. Title VII of the Civil Rights Act of 1964 properly authorized suit against states for damages. *Fitzpatrick v. Bitzer*, 427 U.S. 445 (1976).

    b. On the other hand, the Education of the Handicapped Act did not abrogate immunity because Congress made no clear statement of its intent to make states amenable to suit in the statutory language. Abrogation cannot be found in the legislative history. *Dellmuth v. Muth*, 491 U.S. 223 (1989). *See also Blatchford v. Native Village of Noatak & Circle Village*, 501 U.S. 775, 785 (1991)(Congress must speak with "unmistakable clarity").

2. The Court clarified the issue of determining congressional intent in *City of Boerne v. Flores*, 521 U.S. 507 (1997), which upheld the right to sue a state for violation of the Voting Rights Act. The Court established two inquiries.

    a. First, § 5 is remedial, so it can only be used to enforce provisions of the Fourteenth Amendment and cannot be employed to pass substantive legislation. In a later case, the Court struck Title I of the Age Discrimination in Employment Act in part because Congress improperly used § 5 to pass substantive legislation. *Kimel v. Florida Bd. of Regents*, 528 U.S. 62 (2000).

    b. Second, there must be "congruence and proportionality," which means that the legislation must be tailored to remedy a particular constitutional violation; it must not be overly broad. In situations of widespread and pervasive violation by states, broader measures such as the Voting Rights Act are appropriate.

3. In *Board of Trustees of the University of Alabama v. Garrett*, 531 U.S. 356 (2001), the Court applied *City of Boerne* to strike Title I of the Americans With Disabilities Act. The Court held that Congress failed to demonstrate the existence of a pattern of irrational state discrimination against the disabled. Thus, the legislation did not validly abrogate states' immunity.

4. Similarly, in *Florida Prepaid Postsecondary Education Expense Board v. College Savings Bank*, 527 U.S. 627 (1999), the Court applied *City of Boerne* and held that the Patent Remedy Act exceeded congressional authority under § 5 of the Fourteenth Amendment. Nothing in the legislative record showed that Congress considered whether states were depriving patent holders of property without due process.

5. In *Kimel v. Florida Board of Regents*, 528 U.S. 62 (2000), the Court again applied *City of Boerne* and held that Title I of the Age Discrimination in Employment Act did not validly strip states of Eleventh Amendment immunity. Because states may discriminate on the basis of age if doing so is rationally related to a legitimate state interest, the legislation restricted state behavior unduly. Congress failed to show that such discrimination by states was a widespread problem which would justify the need for abrogation. Moreover, as noted in paragraph 1(a), above, Congress improperly used § 5 of the Fourteenth Amendment to pass substantive legislation.

6. In *Nevada Department of Human Resources v. Hibbs*, 538 U.S. 721 (2003), the Court again applied the *City of Boerne* approach, this time upholding provisions of the Family Medical Leave Act as validly abrogating Eleventh Amendment immunity. In passing the Act, Congress addressed gender discrimination by states, which triggers heightened scrutiny and thus made it "easier for Congress to show a pattern of state constitutional violations" justifying the legislation. In addition, the remedy chosen by Congress—the family-care leave provision—was congruent and proportional to the targeted violation.

D. **Indirect Abrogation by Congress (or "Constructive Waiver")**

1. Occasionally, the Supreme Court has held that states waived Eleventh Amendment immunity by participating in federal programs after Con-

gress conditioned such participation upon the states' waiving immunity. In other words, Congress provided that a state's decision to participate in a federal program constituted its constructive waiver of immunity.

2. The best example is *Parden v. Terminal Railway*, 377 U.S. 184 (1964), in which the Court held that Alabama waived its immunity by operating an interstate railroad after passage of the Federal Employers Liability Act. That Act made railroad employers amenable to suit for negligence in federal court.

   a. The Court reasoned that when the state chose to operate the interstate railroad, it was presumed to be aware of the condition set by Congress for the operation of such a railroad—amenability to suit in federal court.

   b. The opinion was criticized for conflicting with the "unconstitutional conditions" doctrine, which provides that the government may not condition the loss of a constitutional right on the receipt of a benefit. Others, however, questioned whether the logic of the "unconstitutional conditions" doctrine (which was developed to protect individuals against the state) had any place in defining the relationship between federal and state governments.

   c. At any rate, *Parden* was not to last long. The Court eroded the impact of its holding and finally overturned it.

3. In *Edelman v. Jordan*, 415 U.S. 651 (1974), the Court held that such indirect abrogation or constructive waiver cannot be inferred. It is appropriate only if Congress expressly conditions a state's participation in a federally-funded program upon consent to suit in federal court.

4. Other cases cut back further on the *Parden* doctrine. In *Welch v. State Dept. of Highways and Public Transportation*, 483 U.S. 468 (1987), the Court rejected indirect abrogation under the Jones Act because the statute did not have express language conditioning participation in a federal program upon consenting to suit in federal court. It overruled *Parden* to the extent that it was inconsistent with the clear-statement principle enunciated in *Edelman*.

5. Finally, the Court overruled what was left of *Parden* in *College Savings* (1999). There, the Court held that constructive waiver has no place regarding constitutional rights such as Eleventh Amendment immunity.

a. The majority rejected an argument that there should be a difference between state conduct that it can choose to abandon, such as a business venture, and conduct that it cannot choose to abandon, such as its police power.

b. The majority concluded that no such distinction was warranted concerning indirect abrogation or waiver of immunity under the Eleventh Amendment.

XI

Abstention

■ ANALYSIS

I. Introduction
II. **Sources of the Abstention Doctrines**
    A. The Concept of Judge–Made Abstention
    B. Comparative Aspects of the Different Forms of Abstention
III. *Pullman* **Abstention**
    A. The *Pullman* Case
    B. Rationale and Requirements of *Pullman* Abstention
    C. Costs of *Pullman* Abstention
IV. *Burford* **Abstention**
    A. The *Burford* Decision
    B. Rationale and Requirements of *Burford* Abstention
V. *Thibodaux* **Abstention**
    A. The *Thibodaux* and *Frank Mashuda* Cases
    B. Rationale and Requirements of *Thibodaux* Abstention
VI. *Colorado River* **Abstention**
    A. The *Colorado River* Case and Progeny
    B. Rationale and Requirements of *Colorado River* Abstention
VII. **Procedural Aspects of Abstention**
    A. The *England* Doctrine–Procedure in *Pullman* Abstention
    B. Certification to State Court

I. Introduction

This Chapter concerns judge-made doctrines by which a federal court refuses to exercise its subject matter jurisdiction. Despite a strong argument that federal courts should have no authority to abstain to exercise their decision-making power when their subject matter jurisdiction is properly invoked, these abstention doctrines are well established, though invoked only in extraordinary circumstances. Mainly, abstention is justified by considerations of federalism and display great deference to state decision-making bodies and courts in circumstances in which federal court involvement might be disruptive or disrespectful of state efforts. Each abstention doctrine has different requirements, however, and slightly different justifications. Procedures may vary for the different types as well. The abstention doctrines are similar to that explored in Chapter 13, which also counsels federal courts to decline to exercise their jurisdiction. All abstention doctrines are controversial, and overzealous employment of them could be seen as abdication of their constitutional function.

II. Sources of the Abstention Doctrines

A. The Concept of Judge–Made Abstention

1. "Abstention" is a generic label for several distinct but related doctrines under which a federal court will either decline to exercise jurisdiction or postpone decision in a case that validly invokes federal subject matter jurisdiction.

2. Congress can order the federal courts to abstain, and has done so in the Anti–Injunction Act and the Tax Injunction Act, which are considered in Chapter 12. The abstention doctrines discussed in this Chapter, however, are judge-made.

3. Some scholars criticize abstention doctrines as a violation of separation of powers. They note that it is Congress that is to vest the federal courts with subject matter jurisdiction. The Constitution does not give the federal courts power to determine which cases they will hear and which they will not. Chief Justice John Marshall, speaking of the federal bench, said: "We have no more right to decline the exercise of jurisdiction which is given, than to usurp that which is not given. The one of the other would be treason to the Constitution." *Cohens v. Virginia*, 19 U.S. 264, 404 (1821).

4. Nonetheless, abstention is an accepted practice.

a. It bears emphasis at the outset that the invocation of abstention is exceptional.

b. Moreover, mere difficulty in ascertaining the meaning of state law does not itself "afford a sufficient ground for a federal court to decline to exercise its jurisdiction to decide a case which is properly brought to it for decision." *Meredith v. City of Winter Haven*, 320 U.S. 228, 235 (1943).

c. After all, federal courts routinely must apply state substantive law in diversity of citizenship cases. Allowing them to abstain simply because of difficult questions of state law would eviscerate the grant of diversity jurisdiction.

B. Comparative Aspects of The Different Forms of Abstention

1. There are four major abstention doctrines. Each is known by the name of the case that introduced it. Thus, courts and lawyers speak of *Pullman* abstention, *Thibodaux* abstention, *Burford* abstention, and *Colorado River* abstention.

2. It is a mistake to think that the four types of abstention are hermetically sealed from one another. It is possible for a given case to fall within more than one type of abstention. Moreover, courts have not always been clear which abstention doctrine they have invoked.

3. With each type of abstention, it is important to note the Supreme Court's justification for permitting a federal court to refuse to exercise its jurisdiction. Abstention may be justified by the desire to avoid a constitutional pronouncement, by respect for the need to have state courts determine difficult questions of state law, by a desire to avoid overlapping litigation, by respect for state regulatory mechanisms, or by a combination of such justifications.

4. With each type of abstention, it is also important to note whether the federal court will dismiss the pending case or simply stay that case, with the possibility that the parties may return to the federal forum after decision-making by state courts.

5. Also, with each type of abstention, it is important to note whether it applies in federal question cases or diversity of citizenship cases, or both.

III. *Pullman* Abstention

A. The *Pullman* Case

1. *Railroad Commission of Texas v. Pullman*, 312 U.S. 496 (1941), concerned an order entered by the Texas Railroad Commission (TRC), an important state administrative agency in Texas, which oversees the operation of railroads and, as we will see below, the oil and gas industry as well. The TRC ordered that "no sleeping car shall be operated on any line of railroad in the State of Texas . . . unless such cars are continuously in the charge of an employee . . . having the rank and position of Pullman Conductor."

    a. Only trains on relatively heavily-traveled routes had Pullman Conductors. On trains serving lesser-traveled routes, because there were no conductors aboard, trains had permitted porters to be in charge of sleeping cars.

    b. Conductors were white. Porters were black. Thus the result of the TRC order (and its presumed intent) was to prohibit blacks from being in charge of sleeping cars. This order thus kept black persons from having the responsibility (and, presumably, receiving the pay) of being in charge of sleeping cars.

2. The Pullman Company sued in federal court, invoking federal question jurisdiction, and challenged the order as violating equal protection and due process. Porters also challenged the order on grounds of racial discrimination. There was, however, a serious issue as to whether the TRC had the statutory authority to enter the order.

3. The Supreme Court, noting that the meaning of the Texas statute permitting the TRC to enter such orders was "far from clear," ordered the federal court to abstain. Doing so would allow the parties to go to the state courts to obtain a definitive interpretation of the meaning of the Texas statute.

    a. If the Texas courts determined that the TRC lacked authority to enter the order, the order would be stricken without having to reach the federal constitutional issues raised by the parties.

    b. If, on the other hand, the Texas courts determined that the TRC had authority to enter the order, the federal court could then address the federal constitutional issues raised by the parties, because those issues would then be ripe.

c. Thus, *Pullman* abstention counsels the federal court to *stay* proceedings pending determination by the state courts. It does not counsel the federal court to *dismiss* the pending case. The procedure by which this is done is discussed in § VI, below.

B. Rationale and Requirements of *Pullman* Abstention

1. *Pullman* abstention is supported by two major justifications: (1) avoidance of needless constitutional adjudication, and (2) avoidance of federal court interference with important state functions.

2. In addition, all abstention doctrines are occasionally said to be justified by a desire to lessen the federal court docket. It is doubtful that this rationale should be ascribed much force when important federal issues are involved.

3. Thus, *Pullman* abstention is appropriate only when (1) there is a federal constitutional challenge (2) to an ambiguous or uncertain state law that involves (3) an important state function.

4. By "ambiguous" or "uncertain," courts mean that the state law is subject to at least two interpretations, one of which would obviate the need to address the federal constitutional challenge. State law must be "fairly subject to an interpretation which will render unnecessary or substantially modify the federal constitutional question." *Harman v. Forssenius*, 380 U.S. 528, 534 (1965).

Example 1: In *Pullman* itself, if state law did *not* permit the TRC to enter the challenged order, there would be no need to address the federal constitutional issues raised; the order could be stricken under state law.

Example 2: Chiropractors sue a state medical licensing board which refused to license them to practice in the state. Plaintiffs claim that the application of the licensing statute violated federal constitutional rights. Abstention was proper, however, because it was not apparent that the state licensing statute applied to chiropractors at all. If it did not, then their federal constitutional challenge would be moot.

5. The mere fact that a state law has not yet been interpreted by state courts does not render it "ambiguous" or "uncertain." While it is always

theoretically possible that a state court might construe state law to avoid a federal constitutional problem, "the relevant inquiry is not whether there is a bare, though unlikely, possibility that state courts *might* render adjudication of the federal question unnecessary." *Hawaii Housing Authority v. Midkiff*, 467 U.S. 229, 237 (1984)(refusing to apply *Pullman* abstention; statutory language, though not yet interpreted by state courts, unambiguously raised federal constitutional issues).

6. Similarly, the fact that a state law is challenged as unconstitutionally vague does not automatically justify invoking *Pullman* abstention.

7. There is some difficulty if a state law is clear, and implicates a federal constitutional problem, but might be stricken under a *state constitutional* provision.

    a. Generally, if the state constitutional provision merely mirrors the federal constitution (e.g., with a clause substantially similar to the federal due process clause), abstention is not appropriate. *Wisconsin v. Constantineau*, 400 U.S. 433 (1971)(refusing abstention even though state constitution, which mirrored federal Constitution on the relevant issue, might provide a basis for striking the state statute).

    b. On the other hand, if there is a specialized state constitutional provision, the application of which may fairly obviate the federal constitutional challenge, abstention might be appropriate. *Reetz v. Bozanich*, 397 U.S. 82 (1970)(upholding abstention to permit state court consideration of whether state law should be stricken under specialized state constitutional provisions relating specifically to fishing).

8. Of course, in any case, the federal court could simply interpret the unclear state law. Any such interpretation of state law would not be definitive, however, which is why *Pullman* abstention requires that the ambiguous state law concern an important state function or interest. In such a situation, the federal courts consider it wise to defer to a state-court interpretation of state law.

    a. Doing so avoids federal interference with important state functions. *Harman v. Forssenius*, 380 U.S. 528, 534 (1965).

    b. On the other hand, if the state law clearly implicates federal constitutional issues, the federal court cannot avoid its responsibility to determine those issues. Thus, in *Hawaii Housing Authority v. Midkiff*, 467 U.S. 229 (1984), the state law, though involving an important state interest, was not ambiguous and unavoidably raised federal constitutional concerns, which the federal courts were not free to avoid by abstaining.

9. In *Pullman* abstention, the federal court stays the case, and does not dismiss it. The rather complex procedure by which both federal and state courts are involved is discussed in § VII, below.

C. Costs of *Pullman* Abstention

1. *Pullman* abstention imposes high costs on the administration of justice.

    a. Use of the doctrine usually results in significant delays in resolving a litigant's federal constitutional claims.

    b. As discussed in detail in § VI, below, *Pullman* abstention requires the participation of both federal and state court systems, with much of the waste of resources normally involved in the conduct of duplicative proceedings.

2. To avoid such harms, the Supreme Court has held that abstention is less appropriate when the need for resolution of federal constitutional claims is great. This is especially true in cases challenging state statutes which may chill the exercise of the first amendment right of free expression.

IV. *Burford* Abstention

A. The *Burford* Decision

1. *Burford v. Sun Oil Co.*, 319 U.S. 315 (1943), gave rise to a second type of abstention. Like *Pullman*, *Burford* also involved a challenge to an order made by the Texas Railroad Commission (TRC). In addition to regulating the operation of trains, the TRC has considerable authority over allocation of oil and gas drilling rights. The TRC entered an order granting Burford the right to drill for oil in specific areas.

    a. Sun Oil Company challenged the TRC order by filing suit in federal district court. The suit invoked diversity of citizenship jurisdiction and also invoked federal question jurisdiction by raising a federal constitutional challenge to the TRC order. Sun Oil contended that the order granting Burford the right to drill violated its rights in various particulars.

b. Texas had established a complex regulatory scheme for such orders and the judicial review of them. The TRC was given jurisdiction to make initial determinations of this type, and specific state courts were permitted to review them. The Texas legislature was clear in stating the need for such a system, to avoid having various state courts become involved in review of TRC orders.

2. The Supreme Court held that the federal district court should have abstained by dismissing Sun Oil Company's case. Federal judicial review of TRC orders would threaten the regulatory scheme devised by Texas and cause the very confusion the Texas system was designed to avoid. In other words, federal courts would honor the state decision to channel judicial review of TRC orders into particular state courts.

3. *Burford* abstention is sometimes called "administrative abstention" because it defers to state administrative regulation of specific topics.

Example: State regulatory commission refused to permit Railroad to discontinue certain train routes. Railroad was permitted, under the state regulatory scheme, to appeal the commission order to a particular state court. Instead, Railroad sued in federal court to challenge the commission order. The Supreme Court held that the federal court should have dismissed: "As adequate state court review of an administrative order based upon predominantly local factors is available to appellee, intervention of a federal court is not necessary for protection of federal rights." *Alabama Public Service Commission v. Southern R. Co.*, 341 U.S. 341, 349 (1951).

B. Rationale and Requirements of *Burford* Abstention

1. *Burford* abstention is appropriate only when a federal court decision might "disrupt[] . . . state efforts to establish a coherent policy with respect to a matter of substantial public concern." *Colorado River Water Conservation District v. United States*, 424 U.S. 800, 814 (1976).

2. Thus, it is imperative that the state have established some mechanism for handling an important issue, such as allocation of oil drilling rights in Texas, and that federal court involvement risks interfering with that mechanism. The state system features expertise in the relevant substantive area and state decision-makers can be expected to display appropriate sympathy with the underlying state policy.

3. *Burford* abstention is not appropriate simply because a federal judgment might overturn state policy. Constitutional challenges to state law routinely do this. It is only when a federal proceeding would disrupt a scheme the state has established for dealing with an important local issue that *Burford* is invoked.

Example: State statute provides that anyone under a legal obligation to support his children of whom he does not have custody may not remarry without court permission. Plaintiff challenges the statute in federal court on equal protection grounds. *Burford* abstention is *not* proper. The case did not involve complex issues of state law in which federal resolution might disrupt coherent state policy. *Zablocki v. Redhail*, 434 U.S. 374 (1978).

4. Although the majority opinion in *Burford* mentioned the difficulty of a federal court's interpreting state law, this form of abstention, unlike *Pullman* does not require uncertain state law. Again, the point of *Burford* is that a federal court decision will involve the federal courts in an area in which the state has established a complex mechanism for resolution of disputes.

5. *Burford* itself involved, at least in part, a federal constitutional challenge to a state administrative decision.

   a. By relegating decision-making to the state system, *Burford* abstention funnels resolution of the federal constitutional issue to the state courts. Their decision on the federal constitutional issue can be reviewed in the federal system only by appeal to the Supreme Court of the United States. Because that Court's review is discretionary, there is little chance, then, that the federal issues will be addressed by a federal court.

   b. Noting this fact, some scholars have argued that abstention is less appropriate in cases involving federal constitutional challenges. While it may be appropriate to have state courts deal with the intricacies of complex state administrative schemes, these scholars argue that the federal courts should not abdicate their responsibility to determine federal constitutional issues.

   c. For whatever reason, the Supreme Court's more recent efforts in the *Burford* area have made little of the fact that that case involved a federal constitutional issue. Indeed, it has discussed *Burford* abstention (while not necessarily applying it) as applicable in cases not involving constitutional challenges to state law.

6. The mere existence of a state mechanism for dealing with important local issues does not guaranty the application of *Burford* abstention. The court must look carefully at the claim asserted and determine whether federal resolution of that claim will enmesh it in a complex area for which the state has established dispute resolution and review mechanisms. Thus, the Supreme Court rejected *Burford* abstention in *New Orleans Public Service, Inc. v. Council of New Orleans*, 491 U.S. 350 (1989), despite the existence of a state regulatory body.

   a. In that case, an electric utility company had incurred costs in participating in nuclear power plant venture. It sought reimbursement of those costs. A state rate-making authority determined that the utility company should not be reimbursed in full, because the utility had been negligent in some respects.

   b. The utility company sued in federal court, seeking an injunction and a declaration that the state rate-making authority had no power to make the determination on costs because the issue was pre-empted by federal law.

   c. In rejecting *Burford* abstention, the Supreme Court noted that "[t]he present case does not involve a state law claim, nor even an assertion that the federal claims are 'in any way entangled in a skein of state law that must be untangled before the federal case can proceed.'"

   d. The Court added that "[w]hile *Burford* is concerned with protecting complex state administrative processes from undue federal interference, it does not require abstention whenever there exists such a process, or even in all cases where there is a 'potential for conflict' with state regulatory law or policy."

   e. Applying these principles to the case before it, the Court found that "[u]nlike a claim that a state agency has misapplied its lawful authority or has failed to take into consideration or properly weigh relevant state-law factors, federal adjudication of this sort of pre-emption claim would not disrupt the State's attempt to ensure uniformity in the treatment of an 'essentially local problem.'"

   f. *New Orleans Public Service, Inc.* is thus helpful in defining *Burford* as appropriate (1) when there are "difficult questions of state law bearing on policy problems of substantial public import whose importance transcends the result of the case at bar" or (2) when "the exercise of federal review of the question . . . would be disruptive of state efforts to establish a coherent policy with respect to a matter of substantial public concern." 491 U.S. at 361.

7. *Burford* counseled that the federal court invoking this form of abstention would dismiss the case before it, rather than merely staying the case (as is done in *Pullman* abstention).

   a. Dismissal of the federal case seems appropriate because the parties do not anticipate returning to federal court for litigation of federal issues, as they do in *Pullman* abstention. Rather, the dispute is to be resolved entirely in the state system.

   b. Nonetheless, more recently, the Supreme Court indicated that a court invoking *Burford* abstention should stay the action, rather than dismiss. *Quackenbush v. Allstate Ins. Co.*, 517 U.S. 706 (1996).

V. *Thibodaux* Abstention

A. The *Thibodaux* and *Frank Mashuda* Cases

1. *Thibodaux* abstention is named for *Louisiana Power & Light Co. v. City of Thibodaux*, 360 U.S. 25 (1959). The basis and scope of this form of abstention has always been confused, in part because of inconsistencies between *Thibodaux* and another case decided the same day, *County of Allegheny v. Frank Mashuda Co.*, 360 U.S. 185 (1959). Both cases involved condemnation of land through the power of eminent domain.

2. In *Thibodaux*, a city brought a condemnation action in state court to seize Owner's land. Owner removed the case to federal court on the basis of diversity of citizenship jurisdiction. The state condemnation law under which the city proceeded was old and had not been construed by state courts; there was some question as to whether the statute allowed condemnation on the facts of the case.

   a. The trial judge abstained by staying proceedings to permit the state courts to construe the statute.

   b. The Supreme Court upheld abstention, in a six-to-three opinion. It emphasized the "special nature of eminent domain" proceedings, which are "intimately involved with sovereign prerogative." 360 U.S. at 28.

3. In *Frank Mashuda*, the owner whose land was being condemned sued in federal court, properly invoking diversity of citizenship jurisdiction. The claim was for ouster, which was permitted by state law, and thus challenged the validity of the taking. In this case, unlike *Thibodaux*, the state law on condemnation was apparently clear.

   a. The trial judge abstained on the basis that hearing the case would interfere with the administration of local affairs.

   b. The Supreme Court held that abstention was improper, in a five-to-four opinion. It ordered the trial court to entertain the case.

   c. In language inconsistent with that in *Thibodaux*, the Court in *Frank Mashuda* said that eminent domain "is no more mystically involved with 'sovereign prerogative' than [a series of other matters in which abstention is improper]." And "the fact that a case concerns a State's powers of eminent domain no more justifies abstention than the fact that it involves any other issue related to sovereignty." 360 U.S. at 192.

4. The Court's position on whether eminent domain embodies a "sovereign prerogative" in the two cases simply cannot be reconciled. Moreover, the dissent in *Thibodaux* is largely indistinguishable from the majority opinion in *Frank Mashuda*. Portions of the two opinions are verbatim.

5. Some commentators have argued that the two cases can be reconciled by the fact that state law was unclear in *Thibodaux* while it was clear in *Frank Mashuda*. Thus, in the latter case, the federal trial court merely had to resolve disputes of fact at trial, and did not have to engage in a difficult exercise of divining the meaning of the state statutes.

B. Rationale and Requirements of *Thibodaux* Abstention

1. Unlike *Pullman* abstention, *Thibodaux* abstention was not designed to avoid determination of a federal constitutional question. The basis of federal jurisdiction in *Thibodaux* was diversity of citizenship, rather than federal question. Thus, the case did not involve a constitutional challenge to the condemnation of property.

2. The rationale of *Thibodaux* abstention appears to be the special nature of eminent domain, and the fact that it involves an important sovereign prerogative. The problem with this interpretation, of course, is that the

Court seemed to shoot down that notion of eminent domain as involving a special prerogative in *Frank Mashuda*.

3. Given the factual differences in *Thibodaux* and *Frank Mashuda*, perhaps *Thibodaux* abstention is appropriate when the case involves the exercise of eminent domain *and* the state law on condemnation is unclear. In such an instance, abstention will permit the state court to determine the difficult state law issue, rather than have the federal court make a guess at that law's meaning.

   a. If this is the rationale of *Thibodaux* abstention, we might expect the federal court to stay proceedings while the litigants go to state court for the determination of state law. In *Thibodaux*, the Court upheld such a stay.

   b. It is not clear that a stay makes sense, however, given that there is no federal challenge to the condemnation law. If there were, *Pullman* abstention would be appropriate, and the parties would return to federal court for resolution of the federal constitutional matters after the state court interpretation of state law. In *Thibodaux*, however, there is no federal issue for decision, and, seemingly, no need for the litigants to return to federal court.

   c. If *Thibodaux* abstention is appropriate in part because state law is unclear, it comes dangerously close to permitting abstention on that basis. The Court has routinely rejected the idea, however, that a federal court can abstain in a diversity of citizenship case to avoid having to determine difficult issues of state law. *See* § II.A.4, above.

   d. Thus, *Thibodaux* abstention must also be based upon some notion that eminent domain indeed involves a special prerogative of local sovereignty.

VI. *Colorado River* Abstention

A. The *Colorado River* Case and Progeny

1. The most controversial and potentially the most far-reaching abstention doctrine takes its name from *Colorado River Water Conservation District v. United States*, 424 U.S. 800 (1976). In that case, the United States sued in federal court in Colorado, seeking a declaration of its rights and the rights of Indian reservations to water in a certain area of Colorado; it also

sought appointment of a special master to administer waters decreed to the United States. The suit named as defendants about 1,000 water users in the geographic area concerned.

- a. Colorado had established a complex system of water allocation and adjudication of water claims. It had divided the state into water divisions and appointed referees and judges for these purposes.

- b. The water at issue in the *Colorado River* case was subject to allocation in a state proceeding, to which the United States had been joined as a party. That proceeding was ongoing in southeastern Colorado, about 300 miles from the federal court in which the United States sued.

- c. The Supreme Court held that the federal district court was correct in *dismissing* the federal proceeding.

2. The Court in *Colorado River* noted that none of the other bases of abstention—*Pullman, Burford,* or *Thibodaux* applied. (Some scholars have argued that the case did fall within *Burford* abstention, however.) Nonetheless, federal dismissal was justified by considerations of "wise judicial administration."

3. The Court emphasized that abstention on this basis is truly "exceptional." Ordinarily, there is "a virtually unflagging obligation of the federal courts to exercise the jurisdiction given them."

4. The Court set out four factors for determining whether "wise judicial administration" justified abstention. No factor is necessarily determinative. Rather, the trial court is to address each to determine whether there is the "clearest of justification" for dismissal.

- a. The factors identified were: (1) whether either court first assumed jurisdiction over property; if so, it is well established that that court should proceed free from interference from other courts; (2) inconvenience of the federal forum; (3) desirability of avoiding piecemeal litigation; and (4) the order in which jurisdiction was obtained.

- b. Applying the factors, the Court noted: (1) neither court had attached property; (2) the federal court was inconvenient; it was 300 miles from the site of the water being allocated; the state litigation was proceeding at that site; (3) federal legislation allowing the United

States to be joined as a party in the state water proceedings evinced a desire to avoid piecemeal litigation of water rights in a river system; and (4) the state litigation was filed first, involved the same parties, and had progressed farther than the federal litigation; indeed, the federal court had not invested much time or effort in litigation; aside from the filing of pleadings, the federal court had done nothing, which meant that dismissal of the federal case would not result in wasted effort by that court.

5. In *Will v. Calvert Fire Insurance Co.*, 437 U.S. 655 (1978), the Supreme Court upheld abstention on *Colorado River* grounds in a very confusing context. There, a district judge had stayed a federal antitrust action in deference to a state court case in which the federal antitrust issues had been raised as a defense. The Seventh Circuit issued mandamus to the district judge, requiring him to proceed in a federal antitrust action. The Supreme Court reversed.

   a. Some commentators saw *Will* as an expansion of the use of *Colorado River* abstention.

   b. Others read *Will* narrowly because it involved complicating factors such as the issuance of mandamus and antitrust claims, in which federal subject matter jurisdiction is exclusive.

   c. Moreover, the Court was sharply divided, and the holding—that mandamus should not have issued—was not supported by a majority opinion.

6. The Court emphasized the extraordinary nature of abstention in *Moses H. Cone Memorial Hospital v. Mercury Construction Corp.*, 460 U.S. 1 (1983). There, Hospital sued Construction Company in state court, seeking a declaration that (1) it owed the company nothing under a contract and (2) that the company had waived its right to arbitrate the dispute. Just 19 days later, Construction Company sued Hospital in federal court, invoking diversity of citizenship jurisdiction, seeking an order compelling the parties to arbitrate the dispute.

   a. The federal trial court stayed proceedings under *Colorado River*, in deference to the previously-filed state case. The Supreme Court held that abstention was not justified under any of the *Colorado River* factors. It also added some factors to the *Colorado River* test.

b. The Court noted: (1) neither court had obtained jurisdiction over property; (2) the federal forum was not less convenient to the parties, because it and the state court were in the same city; (3) a stay was not required to avoid piecemeal litigation; and (4) although the state court action was filed first, it was only by 19 days, and the state court had not invested significant effort in the case.

c. In addition, the *Moses Cone* Court noted that the federal case, although invoking diversity of citizenship jurisdiction, did involve a federal issue—whether arbitration was compelled under the Federal Arbitration Act—which counseled against abstention. Finally, it noted that the state court proceeding might not protect the Construction Company's rights, because it was not clear that the Federal Arbitration Act would require a state court to compel arbitration.

7. A district court has greater discretion to abstain when the federal litigant seeks declaratory judgment. In such a case, abstention does not require a showing of the exceptional circumstances required by *Colorado River*. The Declaratory Judgment Act gives the district court greater discretion to determine whether to declare the rights of the parties. *Wilton v. Seven Falls Co.*, 515 U.S. 277 (1995). Thus, *Colorado River* and its progeny did not affect the holding of *Brillhart v. Excess Insurance Co.*, 316 U.S. 491 (1942)(district court has great discretion to refuse to declare rights of litigants under Declaratory Judgment Act).

B. Rationale and Requirements of *Colorado River* Abstention

1. Unlike the other bases of abstention discussed above, *Colorado River* abstention is not clearly rooted in federalism. Instead, it is justified by a desire to avoid duplicative litigation.

2. The doctrine flies in the face of the well-established doctrine that parallel *in personam* proceedings generally are permitted to proceed independently. The mere pendency of an overlapping case generally does not justify abstention or, as we will see in Chapter 12, an injunction to avoid the wasteful duplicative litigation. Instead, both proceed, though the first judgment entered may have a claim or issue preclusive effect against the other.

3. Thus, the Supreme Court went to great lengths to emphasize the extraordinary nature of its holding in *Colorado River*.

a. Many commentators questioned whether the case was as "extraordinary" as Justice Brennan's majority opinion said it was.

b. Some commentators felt that abstention in *Colorado River* might have been appropriate on *Burford* grounds, because the state had set up a complex regulatory scheme for adjudication of water disputes; involvement of the federal courts might disrupt that system. Nonetheless, the Court rejected *Burford* abstention.

4. Though *Moses Cone* did not change the factors to be assessed in *Colorado River* abstention, it did establish that the presence of a federal question in the federal case will make abstention less appropriate.

5. Moreover, the "message" from the *Moses Cone* Court seems to be that *Colorado River* abstention is truly extraordinary. Though duplicative litigation is wasteful, federal abstention is not the usual tool for avoiding such waste.

VII. Procedural Aspects of Abstention

A. The *England* Doctrine—Procedure in *Pullman* Abstention

1. As discussed in § III, above, *Pullman* abstention involves litigation in both state and federal courts; the federal court stays the proceeding before it to allow litigation of state issues in state courts. The leading discussion of procedure in such cases is *England v. Louisiana State Board of Medical Examiners*, 375 U.S. 411 (1964).

2. In *England*, graduates of chiropractic schools sued a state medical licensing board which refused to license the plaintiffs because they failed to comply with state law for medical licensure. The plaintiffs sued in federal court, arguing that application of the state law to them was unconstitutional. The trial court invoked *Pullman* abstention because it was unclear whether the state law on licensing requirements applied to chiropractors. It stayed the federal action pending litigation in state court on the meaning of the state law.

3. The Supreme Court made clear that once the state law issue is resolved in state court, the plaintiff has the option to return the case to federal court for the adjudication of the federal constitutional issues, if any remain.

4. The Court held that when the state issue is presented to the state court,

however, the federal issue also must be presented, even though the plaintiff has retained the option to return to federal court.

    a. The reason for this requirement is that the state court should be given the opportunity to narrow the construction of the ambiguous state statute to avoid constitutional problems.

    b. The difficulty with this requirement is that if the plaintiff raises the federal constitutional issue in the state court, as required, it will often be unclear whether the plaintiff has waived his right to return to federal court.

    c. To avoid this problem, the Supreme Court has required that waiver of the option to return to federal court be made explicitly.

    d. Of course, the litigation in state court may be protracted by appeal in the state court system. Once that litigation is exhausted, and the state law issues determined definitively, the federal matters may be litigated.

5. The *England* doctrine is widely criticized for causing enormous delay in the resolution of disputes. Nevertheless, the Court has reaffirmed its commitment to the doctrine in *Pullman* abstention cases.

6. Occasionally, restrictions on state court jurisdiction may mandate that the federal court dismiss the federal action, although such dismissal should be without prejudice, so the plaintiff can refile it after the state litigation is complete. *See, e.g., Harris County Commissioners Court v. Moore*, 420 U.S. 77 (1975)(dismissal without prejudice appropriate because Texas courts would not permit litigation on the state-law issues if federal action was pending).

B. Certification to State Court

1. One method for avoiding the waste and delay of abstention is resort to the process of "certification," which may be employed by a federal court *only* if the state has chosen to adopt the procedure. About three-fourths of the states have adopted certification procedures. In the other states, obviously, it is not available.

2. Under this procedure (sometimes adopted by state statute and sometimes by state court rule), the federal court may refer unsettled state law

questions directly to the state's highest court, thereby avoiding the necessity of proceeding through the entire state judicial system.

3. The Supreme Court has indicated that if a state certification procedure is available, it is highly advisable for a federal court to resort to it in the presence of an unclear issue of state law. *See Lehman Brothers v. Schein*, 416 U.S. 386 (1974).

4. On the other hand, the Court has also indicated that the mere availability of a certification procedure will not automatically trigger resort to that process. It is inappropriate, for example, to certify a question in a case where there is no uncertain question of state law whose resolution might affect the pending federal claim; the state law must by truly unclear. "A federal court may not properly ask a state court if it would care in effect to rewrite a statute." *City of Houston v. Hill*, 482 U.S. 451, 471 (1987).

5. The relationship between abstention and certification may be confusing. In *Arizonans for Official English v. Arizona*, 520 U.S. 43 (1997), two lower federal courts held an Arizona ballot initiative unconstitutional; the initiative would have made English the state's official language. The Supreme Court held that the decisions were premature, noting that the state law was unclear and had not been interpreted by the state courts. The Court suggested that the lower courts should have certified the novel or unsettled question of state law to the Arizona Supreme Court. Some language in the Court's opinion, however, may suggest that *Pullman* abstention may be more difficult to obtain than certification, because abstention requires "unique circumstances" while certification does not.

*

XII

The Anti–Injunction Statute

■ ANALYSIS

I. Introduction
II. The Statute and Background
    A. The Statutory Provision
    B. History and Background
III. The Scope of the Statutory Exceptions
    A. The "Expressly Authorized" Exception
    B. The "In Aid of Jurisdiction" Exception
    C. The "Relitigation" Exception
IV. Other Statutory Restrictions on Federal Injunctions Against State Activities
    A. The Tax Injunction Act of 1937
    B. The Johnson Act of 1934
V. Injunctions of Federal Judicial Proceedings
    A. Injunction by a Federal Court
    B. Injunction by a State Court

I. Introduction

In this Chapter, we consider whether a court may enjoin parties from litigating in another court. The central focus is the Anti–Injunction Statute, 22 U.S.C. § 2283, which limits the power of a federal court to enjoin state court proceedings. The statute reflects an important point of federalism and respect by the federal judiciary of the state judiciary. The statute contains three exceptions, which we will address in detail. In addition, we consider other statutory limitations on federal injunctive power against state actions and the question of when a federal court might enjoin proceedings in another federal court. The latter situation does not implicate federalism concerns, because no state court is involved.

II. The Statute and Background

A. The Statutory Provision

1. The Anti–Injunction Statute (also called the Anti–Injunction Act), 28 U.S.C. § 2283, provides that "A court of the United States may not grant an injunction to stay proceedings in a State court except as expressly authorized by Act of Congress, or where necessary in aid of its jurisdiction, or to protect or effectuate its judgments."

2. Obviously, the starting point of the statute is that a federal court may not enjoin state-court proceedings. Although not numbered, the statute expresses three exceptions to this starting point. The exceptions are generally referred to as:

    a. The "expressly authorized" exception;

    b. The "in aid of jurisdiction" exception; and

    c. The "relitigation" exception.

3. The prohibition of the Anti–Injunction Statute must be considered in conjunction with non-statutory comity restrictions that the Supreme Court has imposed on federal court injunctive power, which we discuss in Chapter 13.

B. History and Background

1. The original version of the Anti–Injunction Statute appeared in section 5 of the Judiciary Act of 1793.

a. For most of its history, the Act was largely absolute in its prohibition on federal court authority to enjoin state proceedings. However, over the years various common law exceptions were recognized.

b. The most significant common law exception concerned jurisdiction over property, or a "res." It has long been understood that in *in rem* and *quasi-in-rem* cases, as well as in cases such as interpleader, in which a court attaches property which is either a basis of the dispute or a basis of jurisdiction, the court in possession of the property may enjoin parties from litigating in another forum. Thus, federal courts that had seized property recognized an exception to the Anti–Injunction Statute to permit them to enjoin subsequently filed state cases.

c. Congress enacted the current version of the Act, with its three stated exceptions, in 1948. The primary motivation for the current version was to overrule the Supreme Court's decision in *Toucey v. New York Life Insurance Co.*, 314 U.S. 118 (1941), which held that there was no common law exception for cases in which a party sought to relitigate in state court a case or factual question that had previously been litigated in a completed federal court proceeding.

2. The motivations for the 1793 Act have long been debated. It may be that the Act was intended to curb equity jurisdiction of the federal courts and reflected a bias against equity powers. Over time, however, the Act has come to be seen as an important centerpiece in federalism, "to prevent needless friction between federal and state courts." *Oklahoma Packing Co. v. Oklahoma Gas & Electric Co.*, 309 U.S. 4, 9 (1940).

    a. The Statute certainly reflects the Framers' original understanding that the state courts were fully competent to interpret and enforce federal law. *See* Chapter 2, § III.A.

    b. The federal judiciary's review of state court interpretations of federal law may come on direct review in the United States Supreme Court, rather than through the disruptive device of a federal court injunction against state proceedings.

    c. Because the assumed fungibility of state and federal courts for determining federal questions is a matter for congressional judgment, it has provided for the specified exceptions to the otherwise absolute bar on federal court power to enjoin state court actions.

3. Though the statute seems clearly to allow three exceptions to the general rule that federal courts may not enjoin state court proceedings, the Supreme Court appeared to "invent" another exception to the Anti–Injunction Statute in *Leiter Minerals, Inc. v. United States*, 352 U.S. 220 (1957).

   a. There, the Court held that the Act's prohibition did not apply to a case brought by the United States (even though the Act makes no such provision). The Court expanded this "exception" in *NLRB v. Nash–Finch Co.*, 404 U.S. 138 (1971), to include suits by federal agencies.

   b. The Court concluded that the language of what it called "an ambiguous statute" could not be considered to have limited the federal government's ability to seek an injunction of state court proceedings.

   c. Thus, when the United States seeks an injunction against state court proceedings, the Anti–Injunction Statute does not create a barrier.

   d. The *Leiter* decision led some courts to conclude that they could "find" other exceptions to the operation of the statute.

4. The Supreme Court ended such speculation, however, in *Atlantic Coast Line R.R. v. Brotherhood of Locomotive Engineers*, 398 U.S. 281 (1970). There, the Court made it clear that adding exceptions to the basic operation of the statute is a legislative, not a judicial, function. Thus, while Congress may create new exceptions, the federal courts cannot.

4. Note that when an exception applies, the party seeking an injunction is not automatically entitled to it. The party must satisfy the equitable requirements of the injunction, including, usually, a showing that irreparable harm is likely if the injunction is not issued.

5. Note also that when an exception applies, and an injunction is appropriate to stay state-court proceedings, the injunction issues against the litigants, and not directly against the state court. If a litigant is enjoined from proceeding in state court, and violates the injunction, the federal court enforces the injunction through contempt proceedings, which can include incarceration until the litigant agrees to abide by the injunction.

6. It is important to note also that the Anti–Injunction Statute generally

prohibits federal injunctions of state court "proceedings." This means that the statute applies if the state "proceeding" has commenced.

    a.   Thus, the statute does not apply if no state case has been commenced; in such a situation, there is no "proceeding" to be enjoined.

    b.   Accordingly, a federal court injunction stopping persons from filing a state court case in the first instance does not implicate the Anti–Injunction Statute. *Dombrowski v. Pfister*, 380 U.S. 479 (1965).

III. The Scope of the Statutory Exceptions

A. The "Expressly Authorized" Exception

1. The Anti–Injunction Statute prohibits federal injunctions of state court proceedings "except as expressly authorized by Act of Congress." Thus, obviously, Congress may withdraw the bar of the statute whenever it deems it appropriate.

2. The term "expressly" does not require that Congress refer to § 2283. Statutory language allowing for a federal court injunction against state court proceedings is sufficient. Indeed, statutory language allowing for a federal court injunction against "any proceeding," without mentioning state courts, is probably sufficient.

3. Indeed, the Supreme Court has found an "express" authorization by Congress in the absence of *any* statutory reference to federal court authority to issue an injunction. In *Mitchum v. Foster*, 407 U.S. 225 (1972), the Supreme Court held that the Civil Rights Act of 1871, 42 U.S.C. § 1983, constitutes an "expressly authorized" exception to the operation of the Anti–Injunction Statute, even though § 1983 is silent about whether a federal court can issue an injunction against state court proceedings.

    a.   In *Mitchum*, the Court set forth this test to determine whether a federal statute is an "expressly authorized" exception: "whether an Act of Congress, clearly creating a federal right or remedy enforceable in a federal court of equity, could be given its intended scope only by the stay of a state court proceeding."

    b.   The Court found the test to be met by § 1983, because (1) the Act specifically provides for equitable relief, and (2) legislative history established that the Act was passed largely because of congressional mistrust of state court ability or willingness to protect federal constitutional rights. *See* Chapter 14, § II.

    c.   In effect, the *Mitchum* Court developed an implied version of the "expressly authorized" exception.

4.   The Supreme Court had difficulty applying the *Mitchum* test in *Vendo Co. v. Lektro–Vend Corp.*, 433 U.S. 623 (1977). There, the defendant in a state court fiduciary duty case, against which a substantial judgment was entered, sought a federal court injunction against collection of the judgment. It argued that the judgment violated a provision of the federal antitrust laws, § 16 of the Clayton Act, by having an anti-competitive purpose. The federal district court entered the injunction.

    a.   The Supreme Court, five-to-four, concluded that the court should not have issued the injunction, but Justices were so badly split on the reason that the case may not be helpful in applying the *Mitchum* test.

    b.   Three Justices concluded that the *Mitchum* test was not met, because while the particular antitrust law did provide for equitable relief, the legislative history did not indicate that Congress believed the laws could be given their intended scope only by means of a stay of state court proceedings.

    c.   Two other Justices comprising the majority concluded that the particular antitrust law constituted an exception to the Anti–Injunction Statute only in very narrow circumstances, such as when state proceedings are used to assert baseless claims for an anticompetitive effect; they concluded that this narrow circumstance was not present in *Vendo*.

    d.   Four Justices, in dissent, concluded that the particular antitrust law was an exception to the Anti–Injunction Statute, and that the injunction was proper.

B. The "In Aid of Jurisdiction" Exception

1.   The Anti–Injunction Statute prohibits federal injunctions of state court proceedings "except . . . where necessary in aid of its jurisdiction."

2.   The most clearly established case in which the "in aid of jurisdiction" exception applies is when the federal court has taken possession of

property which is either the subject of the litigation or a basis for jurisdiction. This exception was recognized by case law before passage of the 1948 version of § 2283, and continues to apply.

    a. When an action is in rem and the federal court is in possession of property, "the exercise by the state court of jurisdiction over the same res necessarily impairs and may defeat, the jurisdiction of the federal court already attached." *Kline v. Burke Construction Co.*, 260 U.S. 226, 230 (1922).

    b. Thus, an injunction against the state court proceedings is appropriate to allow the federal court to maintain authority over the property.

    c. The converse is also true: if a state court "has first attached, the federal court is precluded from exercising its jurisdiction over the same res to defeat or impair the state court's jurisdiction." *Kline*, 260 U.S. at 230.

3. According to the Reviser's Note to the 1948 revision, this exception was also intended to authorize federal injunction of state proceedings following removal of a case to federal court.

4. Scholars have argued that the "in aid of jurisdiction" exception should be read more broadly, to permit a federal court to enjoin state court proceedings outside the attachment-of-property situation. The general rule, however, is that parallel in personam proceedings may proceed without injunctive interference, notwithstanding the waste such duplicative litigation causes. *See* Chapter 11, § VI.B (noting that abstention generally is not available to avoid duplicative litigation).

5. Some courts have expanded the use of the "in aid of jurisdiction" exception to in personam cases, at least in limited circumstances.

    a. When an insurance company seeks a federal declaratory judgment that a policy is invalid because of fraud, some federal courts have enjoined the insured from pursuing litigation in state court to recover under the policy. Such injunctions may be considered to be in aid of the federal court's jurisdiction.

    b. Some federal courts overseeing desegregation of a school system have issued injunctions to stop state court litigation that would interfere with their efforts. Such injunctions may be considered to be in aid of the federal court's jurisdiction.

    c. Some federal courts overseeing complex litigation, such as class actions or multidistrict litigation, have issued injunctions to stop state court litigation that would interfere with their efforts. Again, such injunctions may be considered to be in aid of the federal court's jurisdiction.

C. The "Relitigation" Exception

1. The Anti–Injunction Statute prohibits federal injunctions of state court proceedings "except . . . to protect or effectuate its judgments."

2. As noted in § II.B, above, the present version of the Anti–Injunction Statute was passed in part to overrule the holding in *Toucey* that allowed relitigation in state court of matters already determined in a federal judgment. The third exception to the statute accomplished the overturning of the holding in *Toucey*.

3. Thus, the Supreme Court in *Chick Kam Choo v. Exxon Corp.*, 486 U.S. 140, 147 (1988), explained that the relitigation exception is "founded in the well-recognized concepts of res judicata and collateral estoppel."

    a. Res judicata and collateral estoppel (also known, respectively, as claim and issue preclusion) flow only from valid final judgments, which generally requires that the federal court have entered an appealable order. Thus, final judgments and interlocutory rulings that are appealable as of right may generally be protected by the federal court's issuing an injunction against relitigation in state court.

    b. Curiously, the Court in *Chick Kam Choo* also said that "an essential prerequisite for applying the relitigation exception is that the claims or issues which the federal injunction insulates from litigation in state proceedings actually have been decided by the federal court." 486 U.S. at 148. This phrase seems to indicate that issue preclusion and not claim preclusion fall within this exception to the statute (because a requirement of issue preclusion (but not claim preclusion) is that the issue on which preclusion is sought actually be litigated and determined).

    c. Some courts have adopted this overly narrow interpretation of the third exception to the Anti–Injunction Statute.

4. The Supreme Court has indicated that a litigant may not raise a defense of claim preclusion in a state proceeding before seeking injunctive relief in the federal court under the relitigation exception. In *Parsons Steel, Inc. v. First Alabama Bank*, 474 U.S. 518 (1986), the Court held that a litigant who has unsuccessfully argued claim preclusion in a state court proceeding may thereby be precluded from seeking federal relief under the relitigation exception.

IV. Other Statutory Restrictions on Federal Injunctions Against State Activities

A. The Tax Injunction Act of 1937

1. This Act, now codified at 28 U.S.C. § 1341, provides that "[t]he district courts shall not enjoin, suspend or restrain the assessment, levy or collection of any tax under State law where a plain, speedy and efficient remedy may be had in the courts of such State."

2. This Act "reflects a congressional concern to confine federal intervention in state government. . . . " *Arkansas v. Farm Credit Services of Central Arkansas*, 520 U.S. 821, 826–27 (1997). While states always have an interest in the integrity of their own processes, the interest is particularly great concerning state taxation.

3. Thus, there can be no federal interference with state tax collection if state law provides the taxpayer with a "plain, speedy and efficient remedy. . . . "

    a. The phrase, "plain, speedy and efficient" addresses only *procedural* criteria, and not to concern a state's unwillingness to pay interest. *Rosewell v. LaSalle National Bank*, 450 U.S. 503 (1981).

    b. Allowing the taxpayer to raise a defense in an action to collect the tax constitutes a "plain, speedy and efficient remedy" under the Act. *Kohn v. Central Distributing Co.*, 306 U.S. 531 (1939).

    c. Requiring the taxpayer to pay the tax and then sue for a refund also constitutes a "plain, speedy and efficient remedy" under the Act.

    d. On the other hand, if state procedure requires multiple suits involving the taxpayer, there is no "plain, speedy and efficient remedy" and federal courts may issue relief to the taxpayer. *Georgia R.R. & Banking Co. v. Redwine*, 342 U.S. 299 (1952).

4. Although the Act limits the authority of federal courts to "enjoin, suspend, or restrain" the assessment or collection of state taxes, the Supreme Court held that it "also prohibits a district court from issuing a declaratory judgment holding state tax laws unconstitutional." *California v. Grace Brethren Church*, 457 U.S. 393, 408 (1982).

5. In addition to the statutory bar, the Court has recognized non-statutory limits of comity on the power of federal courts to interfere with state taxing systems. Thus, comity precludes a taxpayer from suing in federal court under 42 U.S.C. § 1983 for damages for allegedly unconstitutional administration of a state tax system. *Fair Assessment in Real Estate Association, Inc. v. McNary*, 454 U.S. 100 (1981).

B. The Johnson Act of 1934

1. This statute, now codified at 28 U.S.C. § 1342, prohibits a district court in diversity cases from enjoining, suspending, or restraining the operation of or compliance with a public utility rate which was set by a state or local administrative agency, so long as the order does not interfere with interstate commerce, reasonable notice and hearing have been given, and a "plain, speedy and efficient remedy" is available in the state courts.

2. The "plain, speedy and efficient" requirement is interpreted in the same manner as it is in the Tax Injunction Act.

V. Injunctions of Federal Judicial Proceedings

A. Injunction by a Federal Court

1. The Anti–Injunction Statute fetters the power of federal courts to enjoin state court proceedings. It does not apply to cases involving a federal court injunction of other federal court proceedings.

2. In addition, obviously, a federal injunction of another federal action does not implicate considerations of federalism. Such an injunction does not involve an affront to the state courts.

3. Thus, a federal district court has great discretion to determine whether to enjoin litigants from proceeding in a parallel *in personam* federal case. As an alternative, a federal court may stay proceedings before it to allow parallel litigation in another federal district to proceed. Either type of order may be entered to avoid duplicative litigation in the federal system.

4. Although the Supreme Court has not definitively addressed the power of a federal court to enjoin proceedings in another federal court, *Kerotest Manufacturing Co. v. C–O–Two Fire Equipment Co.*, 342 U.S. 180 (1952), the lower federal courts generally recognize equitable considerations of wise judicial administration to determine whether to enjoin parties from engaging in parallel federal litigation or to stay litigation in favor of a parallel case in another federal court.

   a. In general, the federal courts follow the "first-filed rule," which provides that the court in which the first of related cases was filed should proceed.

   b. Generally, then, the court in which the first related case was filed may enjoin the parties for proceeding in parallel federal litigation.

   c. And, generally, courts in which subsequent related cases are filed may stay the proceedings in those cases, to allow the first-filed action to proceed to judgment.

   d. The "first-filed rule" is merely a rule of thumb, however, and circumstances of a given dispute may render it appropriate that a later-filed case be the one that proceeds, with that court enjoining parties from litigating in other federal cases. *See, e.g., Semmes Motors, Inc. v. Ford Motor Co.*, 429 F.2d 1197 (2d Cir. 1970).

5. And, of course, a federal court that has attached property that is the subject of litigation or as a basis of jurisdiction *in rem* or *quasi-in-rem* may enjoin litigants from proceeding in another federal court concerning that property.

B. Injunction by a State Court

1. As a general rule, state courts cannot enjoin *in personam* proceedings in a federal court. *Donovan v. City of Dallas*, 377 U.S. 408 (1964).

2. As noted above, however, a state court may enjoin a federal proceeding when the state court initially obtained jurisdiction over property and the federal case would interfere with the exercise of that jurisdiction. *See* § II.B, above.

XIII

"Our Federalism": The Doctrine of *Younger v. Harris*

■ ANALYSIS

I. Introduction
II. Background
    A. The Concept and Contours of "Our Federalism"
    B. Relationship to the Anti–Injunction Statute
III. Historical Development
    A. Early Cases
    B. The *Dombrowski* Case
    C. *Younger v. Harris* and the Modern Concept of "Our Federalism"
    D. Exceptions to the Operation of *Younger*
IV. The Timing of Federal Intervention
    A. The Distinction Between Future and Ongoing Prosecutions
    B. Post–Trial Intervention
V. Applicability of *Younger* to Civil Proceedings
    A. Background
    B. Developments After *Younger*

VI. Applicability of *Younger* to Non-Judicial State Action
   A.   State Executive Actions
   B.   State Administrative Actions
   C.   State Legislative Actions

I. Introduction

"Our Federalism" is a judicially-created doctrine that serves a function similar to that of the Anti–Injunction Statute, which we discussed in Chapter 12. It counsels federal courts to abstain from issuing equitable relief to interfere with a state proceeding. In its original form, the doctrine prohibited federal courts from enjoining ongoing state criminal proceedings, unless some extraordinary circumstance (such as bad faith or harassment) was present. Through the years, the Supreme Court has had to determine whether this doctrine of deference should apply as well to claims for federal declaratory relief, to claims concerning future state proceedings, and to claims involving non-judicial state actions. The doctrine is controversial. Some hail it as an appropriate accommodation and sign of deference to the states. Others decry it as an abdication of the federal judiciary's power to enforce federal constitutional law.

II. Background

A. The Concept and Contours of "Our Federalism"

1. "Our Federalism," espoused most famously in *Younger v. Harris*, 401 U.S. 37 (1971), is a judge-made doctrine developed by the Supreme Court. It imposes significant restrictions on the power of federal courts to interfere with state proceedings. In its classic form, the doctrine prohibits federal courts from enjoining ongoing state criminal proceedings.

    Example: D operates an adult book store. Local authorities prosecute D for violating state law concerning obscenity. D asks a federal court to enjoin the local authorities from prosecuting in state court because, D argues, the state law violates the First Amendment. "Our Federalism" counsels the federal court to refuse to entertain the case. Instead, D can raise the question of whether state law is unconstitutional as a defense in the criminal prosecution in state court.

2. Some commentators and judges refer to "Our Federalism" as an abstention doctrine, akin to those discussed in Chapter 11. Indeed, the Supreme Court has referred to it as an abstention doctrine. *Colorado River Water Conservation District v. United States*, 424 U.S. 800, 816 (1976).

3. Some commentators argue that "Our Federalism" simply embodies a well-known rule of equity jurisprudence: that equity will not act if there

is an adequate remedy at law. Seen this way, "Our Federalism" counsels the federal court not to issue an injunction (which is, of course, equitable relief) because the party seeking it has an adequate remedy at law; that remedy is the right to raise his federal constitutional defense in the state criminal proceedings.

4. Although the doctrine was born in cases in which federal *injunctive* power was sought to stop state prosecutions, the Supreme Court has also applied it to bar most *declaratory relief* against ongoing state criminal judicial proceedings. *Samuels v. Mackell*, 401 U.S. 66 (1971).

   a. The Court in *Samuels* reasoned that the level of interference caused by a declaratory judgment was generally as high as that caused by an injunction, because the federal court's conclusion would have to be given issue preclusive effect in the state proceedings, and, pursuant to the terms of the Declaratory Judgment Act, the declaratory judgment could form the basis for a subsequent injunction.

   b. The Court did leave open the possibility that exceptions might be recognized, but gave no indication what they might be.

5. Traditionally, "Our Federalism" has limited federal judicial interference with *pending* state judicial proceedings. One important question is whether the doctrine applies to fetter federal involvement even when no state proceeding is yet pending. *See* § V, below.

6. Traditionally, the doctrine applied to limit federal judicial interference with state criminal or quasi-criminal matters. More recently, however, the doctrine has been applied in limited civil contexts and regarding state administrative and executive action. *See* §§ VI and VII, below.

7. The doctrine is subject to important exceptions. *See* § IV.C, below.

B. Relationship to the Anti–Injunction Statute

1. Usually, federal court authority to interfere with ongoing state judicial proceedings is prohibited by the Anti–Injunction Statute, 28 U.S.C. § 2283, which we discussed in Chapter 12.

2. In *Mitchum v. Foster*, 407 U.S. 225 (1972), however, the Supreme Court held that federal civil rights suits under 42 U.S.C. § 1983 constituted an "expressly authorized" exception to the Anti–Injunction Statute. *See* Chapter 12, § III.A. Thus, if the federal judiciary's power to protect

federal rights by interfering with state court actions is to be limited, the limitation must come from judge-made doctrines such as "Our Federalism."

3. A year before deciding *Mitchum*, the Supreme Court held in *Younger v. Harris*, 401 U.S. 37 (1971), the seminal case in the development of "Our Federalism," that even if the Anti–Injunction Statute did not apply in § 1983 suits seeking to enjoin state judicial proceedings, the federal courts would generally not be allowed to take such action.

III. Historical Development

A. Early Cases

1. In a series of decisions from the 1920s through the 1940s, the Supreme Court developed the principle that a federal court could not enjoin the bringing of a state prosecution except in the most extraordinary circumstances. *See, e.g., Douglas v. City of Jeannette*, 319 U.S. 157 (1943); *Fenner v. Boykin*, 271 U.S. 240 (1926).

2. Several modern commentators contend that these cases were aberrational, and that better established Supreme Court doctrine permitted federal interference with state proceedings far more readily than the typical cases from the 1920s through 1940s. It is worth noting, however, that these commentators analyze mostly situations in which no state case is yet pending, and not a federal injunction against an ongoing state prosecution.

B. The *Dombrowski* Case

1. In *Dombrowski v. Pfister*, 380 U.S. 479 (1965), the Supreme Court authorized a federal injunction of a *threatened* state prosecution of civil rights workers in Louisiana. The plaintiffs alleged that the threatened prosecution was not intended to gain a valid conviction, but was part of systematic harassment against the exercise of the federal constitutional right of free expression.

2. The Court recognized that usually the right to raise a constitutional defense during the state prosecution provides adequate protection of federal constitutional rights.

    a. On the facts alleged, however, such was not the case, because the threat of prosecution had a chilling effect on the right of free speech;

the persons seeking the injunction from federal court would be cowed by the threat of prosecution.

    b. Moreover, the threat of prosecution, allegedly, was made in bad faith.

3. *Dombrowski* was widely perceived as opening the doors of the federal courts to exercise a significant role in protecting federal constitutional rights, at least with regard to threatened, as opposed to pending, state criminal prosecutions. Hopes that it would be interpreted broadly were dashed, however, in *Younger v. Harris*.

C. *Younger v. Harris* and the Modern Concept of "Our Federalism"

1. As noted above, *Younger v. Harris*, 401 U.S. 37 (1971), is the cornerstone of the modern concept of "Our Federalism." In that case, Harris, a member of the Progressive Labor Party, was indicted by state authorities for distributing leaflets allegedly in violation of the California Criminal Syndicalism Act. He sued in federal court, and sought an injunction of the prosecution; he alleged that the law under which he was being prosecuted violated his federal constitutional rights.

2. The Supreme Court, in an opinion by Justice Black, refused to allow the injunction.

    a. The Court relied heavily on the earlier Supreme Court decisions of the 1920s through 1940s.

    b. It distinguished *Dombrowski* on the grounds that no bad faith or harassment was alleged in the present prosecution.

    c. It concluded that "the possible unconstitutionality of a statute 'on its face' [as alleged by Harris] does not in itself justify an injunction against good-faith attempts to enforce it. . . . " 401 U.S. at 54.

    c. The Court described its deference to the state court prosecution in terms of "equity," "comity," and "federalism."

3. The Court's reliance on "equity" refers to the traditional equitable principle that an equity court will not enjoin a criminal prosecution and that equity will not act when there is an adequate remedy at law. *See* § II.A.3, above.

a. Because a defendant in a state criminal prosecution may always raise his constitutional argument as a defense in the course of that prosecution, the Court concluded that Harris had available an adequate remedy at law.

b. In so holding, however, the Court disregarded the long-established principle that adequacy of remedy for purposes of equitable federal jurisdiction was to be determined exclusively on the basis of available remedies within the *federal* court system.

c. The Court also rejected the argument that the possible chilling effect caused by the delay in adjudication of first amendment rights renders the availability of a criminal defense an inadequate remedy.

4. The "comity" and "federalism" justifications reflect what the Court called "a proper respect for state functions."

    a. More particularly, as the *Younger* doctrine has developed, the deference is to both state courts and to state substantive policies, such as those reflected in the state criminal law.

    b. Allowing a federal court to enjoin a state prosecution, according to the theory of *Younger*, would reflect negatively on the abilities of state judges to interpret and enforce federal constitutional rights; it would constitute an affront to the state judiciary.

    c. It is also thought that allowing state, rather than federal, courts to adjudicate the constitutionality of state laws will provide a more appropriate, presumably more substantial deference to state policies, whether manifested in state legislation or in the discretionary activities of state executive officers.

    d. Finally, *Younger* reflects the fear that wide exercise of the federal court injunctive authority could seriously disrupt the smooth operation of the state judicial process.

5. If *Younger* applies, the federal case is dismissed, unless the person seeking federal equitable relief can satisfy an exception to the operation of *Younger*.

D. Exceptions to the Operation of *Younger*

1. In *Younger*, the Court recognized that there might be exceptions to the otherwise absolute bar to federal court injunctive power which it

erected. After noting possible examples, the Court said that other "unusual situations calling for federal intervention might also arise, but there is no point in our attempting now to specify what they might be." 401 U.S. at 54.

2. First, if the state prosecution is brought in bad faith, or is part of a series of harassing prosecutions, federal courts should be able to enjoin an ongoing state prosecution.

3. Second, in the absence of bad faith and harassment, there may be "extraordinary circumstances" that would justify federal injunctive relief. The example given by the Court indicates the narrowness of this exception: when state law is "flagrantly and patently violative of express constitutional prohibitions in every clause, sentence and paragraph, and in whatever manner and against whomever an effort might be made to apply it." 401 U.S. at 53–54, *quoting Watson v. Buck*, 313 U.S. 387, 402 (1941).

4. A third exception, not mentioned in *Younger*, but established in *Gerstein v. Pugh*, 420 U.S. 103 (1975), is when the federal issue, such as the argument that the state law is unconstitutional, simply cannot be raised in the state action.

5. In sum, even when *Younger* applies to a fact pattern, the federal court may grant relief if there is bad faith, harassment, or some other extraordinary circumstance that justifies an exception to the standard deference. Such cases are rare, but do occasionally arise.

Example: In *Gibson v. Berryhill*, 411 U.S. 564, 578 (1973), the Court found that the State Board of Optometry, which was to adjudicate the matter, was "so biased by prejudgment and pecuniary interest that it could not constitutionally conduct hearings looking toward the revocation of [plaintiff's] license to practice optometry." Thus, it was incompetent to adjudicate the issue presented by the person seeking federal relief.

IV. The Timing of Federal Intervention

A. The Distinction Between Future and Ongoing Prosecutions

1. *Younger* itself dealt with an injunction of an *ongoing* state criminal prosecution.

a. Many observers feel that a federal court injunction against an ongoing state proceeding is a greater invasion of state prerogative, and a greater affront to the state court system, than an injunction against *future* state court proceedings.

b. After all, an injunction against an ongoing proceeding stops state court litigation that is underway. An injunction against a future proceeding stops parties from initiating a state court proceeding.

c. On the other hand, it might be more difficult for a person subject only to possible state prosecution to have standing to invoke the federal judicial power.

2. The cases relied upon in *Younger* had prohibited federal injunctive relief against *future* prosecutions. Nonetheless, the Court in *Younger* left unresolved whether the equity power of the federal courts should be limited in those circumstances.

3. In *Steffel v. Thompson*, 415 U.S. 452 (1974), the Supreme Court held that the *Younger* doctrine does *not* apply to the issuance of declaratory relief against *future* state prosecutions. Thus, federal courts may, where appropriate, issue declaratory judgment against future state proceedings.

   a. The decision did not explicitly deal with the question of whether *injunctive* relief could also be obtained against future prosecutions.

   b. The decision emphasized that declaratory relief is less invasive than injunctive relief. In doing so, the Court contradicted its analysis in *Samuels v. Mackell*, 401 U.S. 66 (1971), which generally equated the invasiveness of declaratory and injunctive relief.

   c. Other portions of the *Steffel* opinion implied the *Younger* doctrine might not apply to limit federal power to issue any form of federal equitable relief (including declaratory and injunctive) against *future* state court litigation.

   d. Such an interpretation would be consistent with Anti-Injunction Statute precedent, which provides that that statute's restriction on federal injunctive power applies only when a state "proceeding" is pending. In other words, the Anti-Injunction Statute does not limit federal injunctive power to stop *future* state court proceedings. *See* Chapter 12, § II.B.

e. The result in *Steffel* comports with common sense. If there is no state court proceeding pending, there is no opportunity for the person threatened with prosecution to raise his federal constitutional defenses in state court. Thus, assuming that person can present a justiciable case, the federal court should be available.

4. In *Hicks v. Miranda*, 422 U.S. 332 (1975), the Supreme Court dealt with the difficult issue of delay in the issuance of a federal injunction. In *Hicks*, a theater owner sought a federal injunction before he was named as a defendant in a state criminal prosecution for obscenity. Some of the theater's employees had been charged. But by the time the federal court actually issued the injunction in favor of the theater owner, however, the state prosecution had been amended to name him as a criminal defendant. Thus, when the theater owner sued in federal court, there was no state case pending against him; when the federal court issued the injunction, however, there was.

   a. The Court concluded that the federal court could not issue an injunction after the state court proceeding was commenced, even in these circumstances, unless the federal court had already had "proceedings of substance on the merits" before the state case was filed.

   b. The Court gave no real indication as to the meaning of the quoted phrase, and its interpretation remains ambiguous.

   c. In dissent, Justice Stewart noted that after *Hicks*, when notified of a pending federal court action for an injunction, a state prosecutor could simply file a state prosecution instead of responding in the federal proceeding, thereby significantly reducing any benefit to the private litigant deriving from the *Steffel* doctrine.

5. In *Doran v. Salem Inn, Inc.*, 422 U.S. 922 (1975), the Supreme Court held that at least *preliminary* injunctive relief, where appropriate, could be obtained against a future state prosecution. Some of the opinion's language, however, hinted that the Court might draw a distinction between *preliminary* and *permanent* injunctive relief.

6. In *Wooley v. Maynard*, 430 U.S. 705 (1977), the Supreme Court authorized permanent injunctive relief against a future state prosecution. The decision was somewhat ambiguous, however, as to whether it represented a full extension of *Steffel* and *Doran* to permanent injunctive relief,

or whether it merely fell within one of the exceptions recognized in *Younger*. Most commentators view the decision as a full extension of *Steffel* to the injunctive arena. *See also Zablocki v. Redhail*, 434 U.S. 374 (1978).

B. Post–Trial Intervention

1. Again, *Younger* held that a federal court could not enjoin an ongoing state criminal proceeding.

2. The Court has also held, however, that even after the state proceeding has been completed in the state trial court, "a necessary concomitant of *Younger* is that a party . . . must exhaust his state appellate remedies before seeking relief in the District Court." *Huffman v. Pursue, Ltd.*, 420 U.S. 592, 608 (1975). In that case, a theater owner lost in state court, and judgment was entered closing the theater as a nuisance. The theater owner then sought federal injunctive relief from enforcement of the state judgment. He argued that *Younger* did not apply, because no state case was then pending.

    a. The Court held that the federal courts could not issue relief. If a losing litigant in state court fails to appeal the state judgment, he can gain equitable relief from a federal court only by showing that the case fits one of the exceptions to the operation of *Younger*. See § III.D, above.

    b. The Court reasoned that "[v]irtually all of the evils at which *Younger* is directed would inhere in federal intervention prior to completion of state appellate proceedings, just as surely as they would if such intervention occurred at or before trial." 420 U.S. at 608.

3. The Court distinguished *Huffman* in *Wooley v. Maynard*, 430 U.S. 705 (1977). There, the person seeking federal relief was convicted three times for violating a state statute by covering up the state motto on his license plates. He failed to appeal the convictions, but sought a federal injunction against future prosecution. The Court allowed him to proceed in federal court. Unlike the plaintiff in *Huffman*, the plaintiff in *Maynard* did not seek an injunction against the enforcement of the state judgment. Rather, he sought an injunction against future prosecutions.

V. Applicability of *Younger* to Civil Proceedings

A. Background

1. *Younger* itself applied only to a *criminal* proceeding, leaving unresolved the doctrine's applicability to purely civil proceedings.

2. Some observers argued that "Our Federalism" should apply to state civil proceedings as well. They asserted that federal equitable relief against a state proceeding is as intrusive and insulting to the state judiciary in a civil case as in a criminal case.

3. On the other hand, it is arguable that the substantive state legislative policies are not as compelling in civil proceedings as they are in criminal matters.

B. Developments After *Younger*

1. In *Huffman v. Pursue, Ltd.*, discussed in § IV.B, above, the plaintiff sought a federal injunction against state judicial enforcement of a state public nuisance statute. Though the state proceeding was not technically a criminal matter, the Court applied *Younger*.

    a. It explained that "we deal with a state proceeding which in important respects is more akin to a criminal prosecution than are most civil cases," and noted that the federal injunction "has disrupted [the] State's efforts to protect the very interests which underlie its criminal laws. . . . " 420 U.S. at 604–05.

    b. Though *Huffman* extended *Younger* to quasi-criminal civil proceedings, it left unresolved the doctrine's applicability to purely civil proceedings.

2. In *Trainor v. Hernandez*, 431 U.S. 434 (1977), the Court extended *Younger* to a state civil proceeding brought by the Illinois Department of Public Aid to recoup welfare payments allegedly obtained through fraud. The defendant in the state action sought federal equitable relief against the state's use of the Illinois Attachment Act to attach his funds, arguing that the Attachment Act was unconstitutional.

    a. *Younger* applied because the state was a party to the suit in its role of administering its public-assistance programs. Moreover, suit and the accompanying writ of attachment were seen as vindicating important state policies, including safeguarding the fiscal integrity of the programs.

    b. The Court thus explained the extension of *Younger* to civil cases as limited to suits brought by the State in its sovereign capacity.

    c. In dissent, Justice Brennan argued that the case was simply another step on the road toward extending *Younger* to all state civil proceedings.

3. In *Juidice v. Vail*, 430 U.S. 327 (1977), the Supreme Court applied *Younger* to a federal suit against state statutory contempt procedures; in *Moore v. Sims*, 442 U.S. 415 (1979), the Court applied *Younger* to a federal suit to enjoin the operation of the Texas rule of judicial protection of minors.

4. In *Pennzoil Co. v. Texaco, Inc.* 481 U.S. 1 (1987), the Supreme Court applied *Younger* to a civil suit in Texas state court between two private parties.

    a. The case involved a federal court challenge to an allegedly prohibitive bond requirement employed in Texas state courts to prevent execution of a judgment prior to appeal.

    b. The Court reasoned that the federalism concerns underlying *Younger* "mandate[ ] application of *Younger* abstention not only when the pending proceedings are criminal, but also when certain civil proceedings are pending, if the State's interests in the proceeding are so important that the exercise of the federal judicial power would disregard the comity between the States and the National Government." 481 U.S. at 11.

    c. It is not entirely clear whether this decision was intended to extend *Younger* to all civil proceedings.

    d. Four Justices, while concurring in the judgment because of their rejection of the claim on the merits, rejected the majority's application of *Younger*.

VI. Applicability of *Younger* to Non–Judicial State Action

A. State Executive Actions

1. In *Rizzo v. Goode*, 423 U.S. 362 (1976), the Supreme Court relied on *Younger*, at least in part, in holding that a federal trial court erred by

issuing an injunction to restructure the Philadelphia police disciplinary system. No state judicial proceeding was pending, or even contemplated.

2. Thus, principles of "Our Federalism" can apply to counsel federal abstention in cases seeking review of state executive decisions.

3. Many lower courts have construed *Rizzo* merely to dictate significant concern on the part of the federal court for state executive officer discretion, but not to require the rigid and total federal judicial abstention of *Younger*.

B. State Administrative Actions

1. Though the Supreme Court has held that a litigant need not exhaust state administrative remedies prior to seeking relief in federal court under § 1983, the Court has indicated that *Younger* may play at least some role in certain types of state administrative proceedings.

2. In *Middlesex County Ethics Committee v. Garden State Bar Association*, 457 U.S. 423 (1982), an attorney claimed that a state disciplinary proceeding against him violated the First Amendment. He sought an injunction from a federal court. The Supreme Court applied *Younger* and held that federal injunctive relief could not be issued.

    a. The Court noted that the proceedings "bear a close relationship to proceedings criminal in nature, as in *Huffman*," and emphasized "the unique relationship" between the state supreme court and the local ethics committee. 457 U.S. at 432.

    b. The Court also noted that before the attorney had filed his petition for certiorari in the case, the Supreme Court of New Jersey had, on its own, entertained the federal constitutional issues. Thus, the *Middlesex* decision might be limited to cases in which the administrative action is closely intertwined with the state judicial process.

3. In *Hawaii Housing Authority v. Midkiff*, 467 U.S. 229, 238 (1984), the Court rejected an extension of *Middlesex* to administrative proceedings which "are not part of, and are not themselves, a judicial proceeding. . . . " Thus, *Younger* did not apply in that case.

4. In *Patsy v. Board of Regents*, 457 U.S. 496 (1982), the Court held that

exhaustion of state administrative remedies was not required in suits brought pursuant to 42 U.S.C. § 1983. *See* Chapter 14, § III.

5. On the other hand, in *Ohio Civil Rights Commission v. Dayton Christian Schools, Inc.*, 477 U.S. 619 (1986), the Court held that *Younger* applied and barred federal injunctive relief. There, a religious school sought the federal relief to prevent the state civil rights commission from exercising jurisdiction over a sex discrimination complaint filed by a teacher who had been fired. The school contended that the federal relief was required to protect its First Amendment right of religious freedom.

C. State Legislative Actions

1. In *New Orleans Public Service, Inc. v. Council of City of New Orleans*, 491 U.S. 350 (1989), the Supreme Court held that *Younger* did not apply to a federal court challenge brought by an electric utility to the results of a city council rate-making proceeding on preemption grounds. Thus, the federal court could proceed.

2. The Court stated that "it has never been suggested that *Younger* requires abstention in deference to a state judicial proceeding reviewing legislative or executive action." 491 U.S. at 268.

*

XIV

Actions to Vindicate Federal Civil Rights

■ ANALYSIS

I. Introduction
II. Principal Civil Rights Statutes
    A. Section 1983
    B. Contrast With Habeas Corpus
    C. Other Reconstruction–Era Civil Rights Statutes
    D. Modern Civil Rights Statutes
III. Litigation Under § 1983
    A. Section 1983 Was Little–Used Until 1961
    B. *Monroe v. Pape* Invigorated the Statute
    C. Plaintiff Must be a Citizen or Person Within U.S. Jurisdiction
    D. Defendant Must be a "Person"
    E. Defendant Must Have Acted "Under Color" of "State Law"
    F. Defendant Must Have Deprived Plaintiff of a Federal Right
    G. Remedies, Including Attorney's Fees
    H. Miscellaneous Litigation Issues
IV. Immunity from § 1983 Cases
    A. Background and Definitions
    B. Absolute Immunity

- C. Qualified ("Good Faith") Immunity
- **V. Deprivations Under Color of Federal Law: *Bivens* Claims**
  - A. Section 1983 Does Not Apply to Federal Actors
  - B. *Bivens* Recognizes a Right to Sue a Federal Actor for Damages for Deprivation of a Constitutional Right
  - C. Limitations on the Scope of the *Bivens* Claim
  - D. Procedural Issues in Cases Asserting a *Bivens* Claim
- **VI. Civil Rights Removal Jurisdiction**
  - A. Background and the Provision for Civil Rights Removal
  - B. "Equal Rights" Interpreted Narrowly
  - C. The Distinction Between State Statutes and State Practices
  - D. The Modern Era

I. Introduction

Following the ratification of the Thirteenth, Fourteenth, and Fifteenth Amendments, Congress enacted a series of statutes designed to permit persons to sue to enforce federal rights. Some of these Reconstruction-era statutes are quite specific. The most important of the statutes, the major focus of this chapter, however, is fairly broad: 42 U.S.C. § 1983 allows a civil suit by one whose federal rights have been deprived under color of *state* law. Section 1983 remains an important and widely studied tool for the vindication of civil rights, and we focus on it in §§ II through VI of this Chapter. In § VII we discuss the important common law right to sue for deprivation of constitutional rights under color of *federal* law. In § VIII we return to another Reconstruction-era statute, one that allows removal of civil and criminal cases from state to federal court if, *inter alia*, the state court will not protect a litigant's rights of racial equality.

II. Principal Civil Rights Statutes

A. Section 1983

1. Section 1983 of Title 42, U.S.C., provides:
Every person who, under color of any statute, ordinance, regulation, custom, or usage, of any State or Territory or the District of Columbia, subjects, or causes to be subjected, any citizen of the United States or any other person within the jurisdiction thereof to the deprivation of any rights, privileges, or immunities secured by the Constitution and laws, shall be liable to that party injured in an action at law, suit in equity, or other proper proceeding. . . . *

2. The section clearly establishes a right to sue any "person" who, under "color of" state law, deprives the plaintiff of some federal "rights, privileges, or immunities." Each of these quoted phrases, and others, have caused uncertainty, and their meanings continue to develop.

3. The statute does not create any rights. Rather, it provides a vehicle for the vindication of "rights, privileges, or immunities" secured by federal law. Thus the plaintiff must allege and prove a deprivation of some cognizable federal right. *See* § III.F, below.

4. Before the 1960s, the number of § 1983 cases in the federal courts were counted in the dozens each year. Now, they are counted in the tens of

---

* The statute was amended in 1996 to add a phrase at the end, which will be discussed in § V, below, and a sentence in 1979, which will be discussed in § IV.C, below.

thousands. The increased use of the statute reflects modern expanded recognition of constitutional and other federal rights and liberalized interpretations of § 1983 itself.

5. Cases under § 1983 may be brought in federal court under the general federal question statute, § 1331. Because § 1983 became effective in 1871, before there was a general federal question statute, Congress also provided a jurisdictional statute for its invocation. That statute, now codified at 28 U.S.C. § 1343(a)(3), also creates subject-matter jurisdiction for § 1983 claims.

   a. Now that § 1331 carries no amount-in-controversy requirement, the existence of § 1343(a)(3) is largely redundant.

   b. It was long thought that § 1343(a)(3) would grant jurisdiction only over claims for personal rights that could not be readily valued monetarily; for others, only § 1331 could be used. The Court rejected this distinction in 1972 in *Lynch v. Household Finance Corp.*, 405 U.S. 538 (1972). So § 1343(a)(3) and § 1331 have the same jurisdictional reach.

6. Federal jurisdiction over § 1983 cases is not exclusive. Thus, § 1983 claims may be brought in state court. *Maine v. Thiboutot*, 448 U.S. 1, 3 n.1 (1980). Indeed, state courts *must* entertain § 1983 claims if they would hear analogous claims under state law. *Howlett v. Rose*, 496 U.S. 356 (1990).

B. Contrast With Habeas Corpus

1. Habeas corpus, which we discuss in Chapter 15, allows state prisoners to go to federal court to challenge the legality of their incarceration in a state institution. Unlike the § 1983 plaintiff, a habeas petitioner is not suing for damages or other relief against officers who violated his federal rights. Rather, he is arguing that he should be released from custody because of some constitutional infirmity with the fact or duration of his imprisonment.

2. Habeas petitioners, unlike most plaintiffs in § 1983 cases, must exhaust state remedies before seeking the writ from the federal court. (There is a requirement of exhaustion of remedies in § 1983 cases brought by prisoners under the Prison Litigation Reform Act, which we discuss at § V.D, below.)

3. Moreover, while the general rules of claim and issue preclusion apply in § 1983 litigation (*see* § III.H.7, below), they apply less stringently in habeas proceedings. Thus, the fact that something has been decided adversely to the habeas petitioner in a previous state court proceeding will not generally bar him from raising the issue again in the habeas proceeding. The § 1983 plaintiff, on the other hand, generally will be barred from relitigating an issue decided against him in a previous state case (*see* § III.H below).

C. **Other Reconstruction–Era Civil Rights Statutes**

1. 42 U.S.C. § 1981 provides that "[a]ll persons within the jurisdiction of the United States shall have the same right in every State and Territory to make and enforce contracts, . . . and to the full and equal benefit of all laws and proceedings for the security of persons and property as is enjoyed by white citizens . . . "

    a. This statute prohibits racial discrimination in making and enforcing private contracts. *Runyon v. McCrary*, 427 U.S. 160 (1976).

    b. A contract for educational purposes is a "contract" under this statute. A state university's freshman admissions policy violated § 1981 because its use of race was not narrowly tailored to achieve the university's purported interest in diversity. *Gratz v. Bollinger*, 539 U.S. 244, 276 n.23 (2003)("purposeful discrimination that violates the Equal Protection Clause of the Fourteenth Amendment will also violate § 1981.").

2. 42 U.S.C. § 1982 provides that "[a]ll citizens of the United States shall have the same right, in every State and Territory, as is enjoyed by the white citizens thereof to inherit, purchase, lease, sell, hold, and convey real and personal property." This statute is a valid exercise of legislative power under the Thirteenth Amendment and bars private and public racial discrimination in the sale or rental of real property. *Jones v. Alfred H. Mayer Co.*, 392 U.S. 409 (1968).

3. 42 U.S.C. § 1985(3) permits recovery for private conspiracies to deny one of equal protection of the laws or to interfere with civil rights.

4. 42 U.S.C. § 1988(a) provides that when a civil rights statute is "deficient in the provisions necessary to furnish suitable remedies," the federal courts are to apply "the common law, as modified and changed by the

constitution and statutes of the State wherein the court having jurisdiction . . . is held," at least so long as such law is not "inconsistent" with federal law. As we will see in § III.H.2, below, the Supreme Court has found § 1983 "deficient" in several particulars, as to which federal courts will apply state law.

D. Modern Civil Rights Statutes

1. Congress has passed many civil rights statutes in recent times, including the Civil Rights Act of 1964, the Voting Rights Act of 1965, the Americans with Disabilities Act, the Violence Against Women Act of 1994, and Title IX of the 1972 Education Amendments to the Civil Rights Act. A detailed listing, let alone consideration, of such legislation is beyond the scope of this book.

2. As important as these statutes are, most courses on Federal Courts focus on § 1983, which is a vehicle for enforcing a panoply of federal rights, as we will see in § III.F, below.

3. One modern statute worthy of especial focus is 28 U.S.C. § 1988(b), which was added by the Attorney's Fees Award Act in 1976. As amended today, it permits a court, in its discretion, to allow "the prevailing party" to recover a reasonable attorney's fee from another party. The statute expressly provides that it applies to cases brought "to enforce a provision" of specific statutes, including § 1983.

    a. The general rule is that each party bears its own attorney's fees. A court ordinarily cannot order one party to pay another's attorney's fees without statutory authorization, such as that in § 1988(b).

    b. The questions of when one is a "prevailing party" who may qualify for an attorney's fee award and what fee is "reasonable," have generated considerable litigation, especially in the § 1983 context, as we will see in § III.G, below.

III. Litigation Under § 1983

A. Section 1983 Was Little–Used Until 1961

1. As discussed in § II.A, above, Congress passed § 1983 during Reconstruction. Although on its face it clearly provides a remedy for one whose federal rights have been deprived under color of state law, the

statute sat in disuse for generations. One study showed that only 19 reported cases construed or applied the statute in its first 65 years of existence.

2. In contrast, for fiscal 2000, over 55,000 civil rights cases were filed in the federal courts. This constituted about 21 percent of the civil cases filed that year. The stunning increase in the use of § 1983 can be traced, at least in some measure, to the impact of a single case decided in 1961.

B. *Monroe v. Pape* Invigorated the Statute

1. *Monroe v. Pape*, 365 U.S. 167 (1961), involved these facts:
Officers of the Chicago Police Department burst into Monroe's house in the early morning, forced him and his family out of bed, and made Monroe stand naked in the living room while they searched the house. They arrested Monroe and took him to the police station, where he was held for ten hours without being allowed to call his lawyer. He was not arraigned promptly. The city never prosecuted Monroe.

2. Monroe sued the individual police officers, seeking damages for the violation of constitutional rights. Specifically, he asserted that the warrantless search was unreasonable and violated the Fourth Amendment, which applied to the states through the due process clause of the Fourteenth Amendment.

3. The Supreme Court upheld Monroe's right to sue under § 1983. Although one aspect of the opinion was later overruled (as we will see in § D, below), the Court established two critical points in *Monroe* that continue to apply in § 1983 litigation.

   a. First, a § 1983 plaintiff need not exhaust state remedies (such as tort suits or administrative claims with the police department) before filing under § 1983. The Court made clear that the § 1983 claim supplements any such remedy the plaintiff has under state law. Thus, it is no defense to a § 1983 case to say that the plaintiff could have sued in state court. Similarly, it is no defense to say that the plaintiff could have sought administrative review under state law. *Patsy v. Florida Bd. of Regents*, 457 U.S. 496 (1982)(plaintiff under § 1983 need not exhaust administrative remedy before commencing suit). (Congress has abrogated this no-exhaustion rule in the certain types of cases in the Prison Litigation Reform Act, which we will see at § V.D, below.)

    b. Second, the police officers' actions in *Monroe* were "under color" of state law, as required by § 1983, even though their actions constituted violations of state law. As we discuss in detail in § III.E, below, the "under color" requirement looks to whether the defendant had some badge of authority to enforce state law, not to whether his actions were authorized by state law.

C. Plaintiff Must be a Citizen or Person Within U.S. Jurisdiction

1. Section 1983 permits suit by "any citizen of the United States or other person within the jurisdiction thereof."

2. Thus, aliens may sue for deprivation, under color of state law, of federal rights to which they are entitled. In addition, because corporations are considered "persons" for purposes of the due process and equal protection clauses, they may sue under § 1983 to vindicate rights under those provisions.

3. Of course, the plaintiff must have standing to assert the claim that she has been deprived of a federal right.

D. Defendant Must be a "Person"

1. Section 1983 permits suit only against (1) a "person" who (2) acts under color of state law. Here, we address only the first of these requirements; we will discuss the second in the succeeding subsection.

2. A state is not a person under § 1983, and thus cannot be sued, either in state court or federal court, under the statute. *Will v. Michigan Dept. of State Police*, 491 U.S. 58, 66 (1989). *See also Lapides v. Board of Regents of State Univ. System*, 535 U.S. 613, 617 (2002). This construction of the statute avoids the question of whether it would constitute sufficient abrogation of a state's immunity from suit in federal court under the Eleventh Amendment.

3. Officers sued in their official capacities are also not "persons" under § 1983 and cannot be sued under the statute. *Will*, 491 U.S. at 71.

4. On the other hand, officers sued in their personal capacities are "persons" under § 1983 in actions for acts they took in their official capacity. *Hafer v. Melo*, 502 U.S. 21, 26 (1991)("State officers sued for damages in their official capacity are not 'persons' for purposes of the

suit because they assume the identity of the government that employs them. . . . By contrast, officers sued in their personal capacity come to court as individuals.").

Example: Plaintiff has a claim that Officer Friday, of the Los Angeles Police Department, violated his constitutional rights while the officer was on duty. Plaintiff may not file a § 1983 case naming "Joe Friday, in his capacity as an Officer of the Los Angeles Police Department." But he may file a § 1983 case against "Joe Friday, in his personal capacity" and sue for the deprivation of rights caused by Officer Friday's on-duty behavior.

5. Many § 1983 cases assert claims against municipalities, such as cities and counties. The Supreme Court has taken different positions on whether municipalities can be sued under the statute, but the law now seems relatively clear.

   a. In *Monroe v. Pape*, 365 U.S. 167 (1961), the Supreme Court interpreted the legislative history of § 1983 as dictating that a municipal corporation is not a "person" under the statute, at least not for damages claims. Later, it extended the holding to claims for equitable relief as well. *City of Kenosha v. Bruno*, 412 U.S. 507 (1973). It also held that a county is not a "person" that can be sued under the statute. *Moor v. County of Alameda*, 411 U.S. 693 (1973).

   b. Shortly after these cases however, the Court revisited the issue and decided that the same legislative history required a different answer, at least in part. In *Monell v. Department of Social Servs.*, 436 U.S. 658 (1978), the Court held that a municipality can be sued under § 1983, but only for "a policy statement, ordinance, regulation, or decision officially adopted and promulgated by that body's officers" or for a "governmental 'custom' even though such a custom has not received formal approval through the body's official decision-making channels." *Id.* at 690–91.

   c. Under *Monell*, then, municipalities cannot be held liable on the basis of *respondeat superior*. The body can be liable only if the deprivation was caused by some policy or custom of the municipality.

Example: Assume that Officer Friday, of the Los Angeles Police Department, violated Plaintiff's federal rights by using excessive force while on duty. As we saw above, Plaintiff can sue Officer Friday in his private capacity. The City of Los Angeles is not liable under § 1983 simply because its officer committed a tort, even a constitutional tort. To proceed against the City, Plaintiff would have to show that the City had some policy or custom of hiring police officers with conscious disregard for a high risk that the officer would use excessive force. *Board of County Commissioners v. Brown*, 520 U.S. 397 (1997).

    d.   Regardless of the existence of a policy or custom, a municipality cannot be held liable under § 1983 for punitive damages. *City of Newport v. Fact Concerts, Inc.*, 453 U.S. 247 (1981).

6. A private corporation can be sued as a "person" under § 1983, basically along the same lines as a municipality.

7. It is important to keep in mind that a proper defendant might be entitled to immunity—either absolute or qualified—from suit under § 1983. We address that issue in § IV, below.

E. Defendant Must Have Acted "Under Color" of "State Law"

1. In addition to being a "person," as discussed immediately above, the defendant in a § 1983 case must have deprived the plaintiff of a federal right (discussed immediately below) and must have done so "under color" of state law.

2. *Monroe v. Pape* established that a defendant may satisfy this requirement even though he acts contrary to state law or if his action is not authorized by state law. Thus, in *Monroe*, the police officers acted under color of state law because they committed the violations while wielding governmental power, while undertaking a task ordinarily rendered by police officers.

    a.   The acts were "under color" of state law even though they were (1) unconstitutional and (2) not authorized by their superiors or by the City.

    b.   Thus, § 1983 is not limited to cases involving official regulations, policies, or customs that violate constitutional norms. It also addresses abuse of power by one "who is a repository of state power." The action reaches those "who carry a badge of authority of a State and represent it in some capacity, whether they act in accordance with their authority or misuse it." *Monroe*, 365 U.S. at 172.

3. Of course, a Fourteenth Amendment violation requires a showing of state action.

   a. As a general rule, if the constitutional requirement for state action is present, the statutory requirement that the defendant act "under color" of state law will also be satisfied. *See Lugar v. Edmondson Oil Co.*, 457 U.S. 922, 929 (1982)("in a § 1983 action brought against a state official, the statutory requirement of action 'under color of state law' and the 'state action' requirement of the Fourteenth Amendment are identical").

   b. Moreover, § 1983 may be used to vindicate other constitutional and even statutory rights that do not require a showing of state action; in such cases, the plaintiff still must show that the defendant acted under color of state law.

4. The "under color" of state law requirement is rarely problematic, then, when the acts are taken by state or local officers exercising their authority or appearing to exercise their authority.

Example: Barney Fife, a deputy sheriff, moonlights off-duty as a security guard. While doing so, he wears his uniform. He accosts a suspected shoplifter in an unconstitutional way. His acts may be "under color" of state law, rendering him susceptible to a § 1983 case. *See, e.g., Lusby v. T.G. & Y Stores, Inc.*, 749 F.2d 1423 (10th Cir. 1984).

5. On the other hand, not every act of a state officer is taken "under color" of state law.

Example: Barney Fife, while on duty as a deputy sheriff, accosts his cousin Virgil over a debt Virgil owes to Barney. Barney probably did not act "under color" of state law because the fact that he is an officer had nothing to do with the altercation.

6. Private actors—those who do not "carry a badge of authority of a State"—may be sued under § 1983 if they nonetheless act "under color" of state law.

Example: Private individuals employ a state attachment statute to attach P's property. P sues the private individuals, alleging that the attachment statute is unconstitutional because it denies P due process. The private individuals acted "under color" of state law, because they engaged in joint activity with the state in seizing the property. *Lugar*, 457 U.S. at 1423.

Example: Private individuals conspire with a state judge to have them win pending litigation. The private individuals acted "under color" of state law, because they engaged in joint activity with a state actor in depriving the other party of a constitutional right. The private individuals may be sued even though the judge is immune from suit (as we will see in § IV, below). *Dennis v. Sparks*, 449 U.S. 24 (1980).

7. On the other hand, not all private actors having some relationship with a state will be found to act "under color" of state law.

Example: State University imposes discipline against Coach pursuant to regulations and recommendations by the National Collegiate Athletic Association (NCAA). NCAA did not act "under color" of state law, since the University's acceptance of the NCAA regulations did not transform them into state rules. *NCAA v. Tarkanian*, 488 U.S. 179 (1988).

8. The defendant in a § 1983 case must have acted "under color," as we have just seen, of "state law." Specifically, he must act under color of "any statute, ordinance, regulation, custom, or usage, of any State or Territory, or the District of Columbia."

    a. On its face, the statute includes the law not only of any State, but also of the Territories and the District of Columbia.

    b. In 1979, Congress added a sentence to § 1983 to provide that any congressional act "applicable exclusively to the District of Columbia shall be considered to be a statute of the District of Columbia."

    c. Section 1983 does not apply if the defendant acts under color of federal law. Such actions may be vindicated by a *Bivens* case, as discussed in § V.A, below.

F. Defendant Must Have Deprived Plaintiff of a Federal Right

1. The gravamen of a § 1983 case is that the defendant has deprived the plaintiff of any "rights, privileges, or immunities secured by the Constitution and laws."

2. The section does not create any substantive rights, but creates only a remedy for enforcing some substantive right granted by federal law. Not all rights are federal, obviously, and suit for deprivation of purely state rights cannot be vindicated through § 1983.

3. Not all provisions of the Constitution confer rights that can be enforced through § 1983. The Supreme Court has held, for instance, that the Supremacy Clause does not confer such right. *Chapman v. Houston Welfare Rights Organization*, 441 U.S. 600 (1979). Neither is there a First Amendment right to provide legal assistance to fellow inmates. *Shaw v. Murphy*, 532 U.S. 223 (2001).

4. Clearly, however, the Reconstruction-era Amendments, including the equal protection and due process provisions of the Fourteenth Amendment and those portions of the Bill of Rights applicable to the states, can be enforced in a § 1983 case. The Supreme Court has also held that the Commerce Clause also creates a right enforceable under § 1983. *Dennis v. Higgins*, 498 U.S. 439 (1991)(claim that local regulation unduly burdens interstate commerce or discriminates against it).

Example: Prisoner claims that prison officers took intentional acts with deliberate indifference to his rights. He states a claim for violation of his Eighth Amendment right (applied to the states through the Fourteenth Amendment) to be free from cruel and unusual punishment. *Estelle v. Gamble*, 429 U.S. 97 (1976).

Example: The plaintiff in *Monroe v. Pape*, the facts of which were discussed at § III.B, above, claims that the police officers made a search and seizure that was objectively unreasonable. He states a claim under the Fourth Amendment, as incorporated for the states through the Fourteenth Amendment. *Graham v. Connor*, 490 U.S. 386 (1989).

5. The Supreme Court has drawn a distinction between what some commentators call "fundamental rights" and "non-fundamental rights," and the distinction is important under § 1983. Fundamental rights include those guaranteed by the Bill of Rights and *substantive* due process rights, including those related to reproductive choice. Non-fundamental rights include those deprivations of property and perhaps even liberty in violation of some less important, perhaps state-created, right.

a. Plaintiff asserting a fundamental right may proceed in a § 1983 case and, generally, need not exhaust any available state court remedies. We discussed this point at § III.B.3.a, above.

b. There is not a right to proceed under § 1983 in non-fundamental rights cases, if the state has provided an appropriate opportunity for hearing.

Example: Prison officials lose Prisoner's hobby kit, worth $23.50. Prisoner sues under § 1983, asserting that the officials deprived him of his property without due process of law. State law provides a mechanism by which Prisoner can recover the value of the hobby kit from the state. The Supreme Court held that Prisoner could not proceed under § 1983 because the state provided a meaningful post-deprivation remedy. *Parratt v. Taylor*, 451 U.S. 527 (1981).

Some observers conclude that *Parratt* imposes a rule, contrary to *Monroe v. Pape*, that the plaintiff exhaust state remedies. The better way to interpret the case, however, is that state law did not deprive Prisoner of a constitutional right, since the availability of the post-deprivation remedy meant that there was no deprivation of property without due process.

Example: Student was paddled by the principal of the public school he attended; the corporal punishment was meted out without a hearing in advance. Student sued the principal under § 1983, seeking damages for a denial of his liberty without due process. The Supreme Court held that Student could not proceed under § 1983. As in *Parratt*, the Court noted that Student could proceed against the principal in tort in state court. *Ingraham v. Wright*, 430 U.S. 651 (1977).

Again, the Court seems to be saying there is no cognizable deprivation, even of a liberty interest, if the state makes available a post-deprivation remedy. A pre-deprivation hearing may be required when the risk of an erroneous deprivation outweighs the government's interest in expedition. *Mathews v. Eldridge*, 424 U.S. 319 (1976). In such a case, denial of a pre-deprivation hearing could be the basis of a damages claim under § 1983. Neither *Parratt* nor *Ingraham* involved such a situation.

c. Mere negligence by state actors cannot cause a deprivation of due process.

Example: Prisoner was injured when he was beaten by a fellow prisoner. The beating was made possible by the negligence of prison guards. The Supreme Court held that mere negligence does not implicate due process. Thus, Prisoner could not proceed under § 1983 even though it seemed clear that state law afforded him no remedy. *Davidson v. Cannon*, 474 U.S. 344 (1986).

6. Section 1983 is not limited to deprivations of federal constitutional rights, but applies also to rights, privileges, and immunities secured by "the laws" of the United States. Thus, it is clear, for example, that deprivation of federal statutory rights may be the basis of a § 1983 claim. *Maine v. Thiboutot*, 448 U.S. 1 (1980)(permitting § 1983 case to enforce claim for violation of Social Security Act).

7. In relatively early cases, the Supreme Court seemed more willing than in recent times to permit enforcement of federal statutory rights through § 1983. *Compare, e.g., Wright v. Roanoke Redevelopment & Housing Auth.*, 479 U.S. 418 (1987)(allowing suit by tenants to recover overcharges under a rent-ceiling provision of the Public Housing Act) *with Suter v. Artist M.*, 503 U.S. 347 (1992)(rejecting § 1983 suit to enforce provision of Adoption Assistance and Child Welfare Act of 1980 requiring states receiving funds for adoption assistance to have a plan to make reasonable efforts to keep children out of foster homes).

8. Most recently, the Court revisited the issue and clarified the standard. In *Gonzaga University v. Doe*, 536 U.S. 273 (2002), the Court likened the inquiry, at least in one respect, to the question of whether a statute creates a private right of action. The Court concluded that a statute can be enforced under § 1983 only if Congress indicates "an unambiguously conferred right." Thus, even if a statute does not create a private right to sue, it can be enforced through § 1983 if Congress clearly indicated that the statute created a *right*, and not just a general interest, for the plaintiff to enforce. Applying the test, the Court held that provisions of the Family Educational Rights and Private Act prohibiting federal funding of educational institutions that release educational records to unauthorized persons did not create a personal right and could not be enforced under § 1983.

G. Remedies, Including Attorney's Fees

1. Section 1983 expressly provides that the defendant "shall be liable to the party injured in an action at law, suit in equity, or other proper proceeding for redress."

2. Obviously, the statute permits recovery of damages, and most § 1983 cases involve such claims. Because the § 1983 claim is in the nature of tort, the damages should be aimed at compensating the plaintiff for the harm done. Compensatory damages do not include abstract "value" or "importance" of the constitutional right. *Memphis Community Sch. Dist. v. Stachura*, 477 U.S. 299, 310 (1986).

    a. Punitive damages are available in appropriate circumstances, but, as noted in § III.D, above, may not be recovered from municipalities.

    b. The Supreme Court held that a showing that the defendant acted with subjective ill will or malice is sufficient for the imposition of punitive damages, but is not a prerequisite. Punitive damages can be awarded as well for callous or reckless indifference to the denial of one's rights. *Smith v. Wade*, 461 U.S. 30 (1983).

3. Equitable remedies, including declaratory judgments and injunctions, are available in appropriate circumstances.

    a. Under the Prison Litigation Reform Act, the entry of injunctive relief in prison reform litigation must include the court's finding that the relief is narrowly drawn, extends no further than necessary to correct the subject violation, and constitutes the least intrusive means needed to correct the violation. 18 U.S.C. § 3626(a).

    b. The defendants can move to terminate an order of prospective relief if the court did not make such express findings in its order. 18 U.S.C. § 3626(b).

4. 42 U.S.C. § 1988(b), noted at § II.D.3, above, permits the court to award a reasonable attorney's fee to the "prevailing party" in § 1983 litigation.

    a. A party prevails under this statute if he obtains relief on the merits of the claim that "materially alters the legal relationship between the parties by modifying the defendant's behavior in a way that directly benefits the [party]." *Farrar v. Hobby*, 506 U.S. 103, 111–12 (1992).

b. Attorney's fees may be awarded even if the plaintiff won only nominal damages, so long as the amount recovered is not outrageously less than what he sought, the case raised significant legal issues, and the public goal of the suit was served. *Murray v. City of Onawa, Iowa*, 323 F.3d 616, 619–20 (8th Cir. 2003)(upholding award of $7,428 in attorney's fees for plaintiff who won $1 in damages).

H. Miscellaneous Litigation Issues

1. 42 U.S.C. § 1988(a), noted at § II.C.4, above, applies to § 1983 suits in federal court. It directs the court to apply "the common law, as modified and changed by the constitution and statutes of the State wherein the court is held" whenever § 1983 is "deficient."

2. Section 1983 may be "deficient" when it fails to address a particular issue.

   a. The statute says nothing about whether a claim survives the death of the plaintiff. The Supreme Court has held that this "deficiency" requires the federal court to apply § 1988(a) and apply a state statute on the point. *Robertson v. Wegmann*, 436 U.S. 584 (1978).

   b. Section 1988(a) contains a further clause allowing the court to ignore state law if it would be inconsistent with policies underlying § 1983. On the facts of the case in *Robertson*, the Court concluded that the state law—which directed that the case be dismissed because the plaintiff left no relatives—was not inconsistent with such policies. Only few cases would involve a plaintiff with no relatives and would thus be abated by death of the plaintiff.

3. Congress has never prescribed a statute of limitations, nor a rule for tolling the statute of limitations, for § 1983 cases.

   a. The Supreme Court has held that these "deficiencies" also require that the federal courts apply state statutes of limitations. *Board of Regents v. Tomanio*, 446 U.S. 478 (1980).

   b. Specifically, the court looks to the state statute "governing an analogous cause of action under state law." *Wilson v. Garcia*, 471 U.S. 261, 271 (1985). The problem, of course, is that § 1983 claims might have different state-law analogs. For instance, a claim that police officers beat the plaintiff may implicate a different statute of limitations than a claim that the plaintiff was fired on the basis of his race. In *Wilson*, however, the Court indicated that there should be a single statute of limitations for cases arising in a particular state. It counseled that a § 1983 case will generally be considered analogous to a personal injury claim.

    c. If state law has more than one statute of limitations for personal injury cases, the federal court should look to "the general or residual statute for personal injury actions" from state law. *Owens v. Okure*, 488 U.S. 235, 250 (1989).

4. Although § 1983 does not create a right to jury trial, parties to a § 1983 case in federal court have the same Seventh Amendment right to jury trial as litigants in other federal civil cases. *City of Monterey v. Del Monte Dunes at Monterey, Ltd.*, 526 U.S. 687 (1999).

5. Some lower courts have imposed heightened requirements for specificity on § 1983 plaintiffs. The Supreme Court rejected the practice, noting that nothing in the Federal Rules of Civil Procedure permitted the courts to impose anything more than the typical "notice" requirements for pleadings in § 1983 cases. *Leatherman v. Tarrant County*, 507 U.S. 163 (1993).

    a. The opinion in *Leatherman* left open the question of whether a court might impose more rigorous pleading requirements on defendants raising a defense of qualified immunity (which we discuss in § IV. C, below). *Id*. at 168.

    b. Some lower courts appear to be flaunting the *Leatherman* ruling by continuing to require the plaintiff to adhere to more detailed pleading norms. *See, e.g., Schultea v. Wood*, 47 F.3d 1427 (5th Cir. 1995); *Kimberlin v. Quinlan*, 6 F.3d 789 (D.C. Cir. 1993).

6. Reacting to a large number of frivolous § 1983 and Federal Tort Claims Act claims by prisoners, Congress passed the 1996 Prison Litigation Reform Act (PLRA). As one court has explained: "This statute is intended to reduce the number of frivolous cases filed by imprisoned plaintiffs, who have little to lose and excessive amounts of free time with which to pursue their complaints." *Napier v. Preslicka*, 314 F.3d 528, 531 (11th Cir. 2002). To that end, it imposes various restrictions, including:

    a. A prisoner cannot file a proceeding concerning prison conditions until he has exhausted administrative remedies. Thus, unlike other

§ 1983 plaintiffs, the prisoner raising such issues is required to exhaust alternative remedies before suing. This exhaustion requirement "applies to all inmate suits about prison life, whether they involve general circumstances or particular episodes, and whether they allege excessive force or some other wrong." *Porter v. Nussle*, 534 U.S. 516, 532 (2002).

    b.   Prisoners are prohibited from bringing more than three frivolous suits or appeals in a lifetime.

    c.   A convicted felon may not sue for mental or emotional injury suffered while in custody without showing physical injury.

7. As a general rule, the principles of issue preclusion (collateral estoppel) apply in § 1983 litigation. *Allen v. McCurry*, 449 U.S. 90 (1980)(federal court in § 1983 case must apply issue preclusion to issue litigated and determined in state proceedings against § 1983 plaintiff, if the state court system would apply preclusion). The same is true for application of claim preclusion (res judicata). *Migra v. Warren City School District*, 465 U.S. 75 (1984)(discharged public school teacher's state court suit for damages would bar subsequent § 1983 case against the same defendants if state court system would apply preclusion).

8. In addition, the *Rooker-Feldman* doctrine may operate to preclude a federal court from litigating some issues that have already been determined by the state court. This doctrine stands for the proposition that a federal district court cannot review judicial proceedings of a state court. *Rooker v. Fidelity Trust Co.*, 263 U.S. 413 (1923)(federal district courts may not review judicial proceedings of state courts).

Example: Graduates of non-accredited law schools sought admission to the District of Columbia bar, and a waiver of that bar's rule that members must be graduates of accredited law schools. The case is litigated and the graduates lost in a judgment entered by the District of Columbia Court of Appeals (the highest court of the District of Columbia's analog to a state court system). They then sued in federal district court, asserting that their exclusion from the bar violated the United States Constitution. The federal court has no jurisdiction to review the decision of the District of Columbia court. The graduates should have sought appellate review by the Supreme Court of the District of Columbia court's ruling. *District of Columbia Court of Appeals v. Feldman*, 460 U.S. 462 (1983).

IV. Immunity From § 1983 Cases

A. Background and Definitions

1. Section 1983 says nothing about any defendant's being immune from suit. Nonetheless, the courts have consistently recognized that certain defendants may be immune from § 1983 litigation. There is a long history of immunity for certain official acts, and the Supreme Court refused to believe that Congress intended to override it by passing § 1983 without some clear statement to that effect. *Tenney v. Brandhove*, 341 U.S. 367 (1951).

2. Generally, this common law immunity constitutes the right not to be sued at all. In other words, it is not merely an immunity from *liability*. It is immunity from *suit*. Consequently, the courts have endeavored to mold immunity rules that can be applied at the outset of litigation, so if an immunity exists, the case can be dismissed. In other words, the immunity factors should be applicable without having to get deeply involved in the litigation of the underlying suit. If a defendant can only determine whether she is immune by litigating the underlying suit, the immunity would not spare the person what it is supposed to spare her—the necessity of going through trial.

3. Generally, immunity is from a suit for *damages*. Ordinarily, a person who has an immunity from a suit for damages will *not* be immune from suit for equitable relief, such as an injunction or declaratory judgment.

4. Immunity is usually available only to state actors. As noted in § III.E.6, above, a private individual may be found to have acted under color of state law when he acted in concert with a state official in depriving the plaintiff of a federal right.

    a. Although the state official may be entitled to immunity, generally the immunity is "not transferable to private parties." *Wyatt v. Cole*, 504 U.S. 158, 168 (1992). *See also Dennis v. Sparks*, 449 U.S. 24 (1980)(judge entitled to immunity while private party with whom he acted to deny plaintiff of federal rights could be sued under § 1983).

    b. There are situations in which private parties act in lieu of a local government. For example, an increasing number of localities contract with private corporations to run prison facilities. Arguably, employees of such facilities ought to be able to claim the same sort of immunity as an officer in a public prison.

5. There are two types of immunity.

   a. "Absolute" immunity, as the name implies, protects the defendant from suit without exception. As we will see in § IV.B, below, only certain officers are entitled to absolute immunity, and only while performing certain types of tasks.

   b. "Qualified," or "good faith" immunity (the terms are interchangeable) protects a state actor from suit only if she acted in good faith. As we will see in § C, below, the question of good faith is intimately connected with whether the right allegedly violated was well established at the time the claim arose.

B. Absolute Immunity

1. Judges are absolutely immune from suit for damages for acts taken in their judicial capacity. This immunity attaches even if the judge was wrong or unreasonable or even corrupt—just so the judge was performing a judicial function. Courts tend to find that an act is judicial unless taken with a "clear absence of all jurisdiction." *Stump v. Sparkman*, 435 U.S. 349, 356 (1978). Even an act taken with no legal basis can be protected.

Example: State court judge of general jurisdiction grants petition by Mother to have minor Daughter sterilized. He grants the order without a hearing and without notice to Daughter. Pursuant to the order, Daughter is subjected to surgery rendering her incapable of having children. Later, after Daughter is married and finds she cannot have children, she sues several persons, including the judge who issued the order. Although no state law permitted a parent to consent to sterilization or provided for such an order, the Supreme Court held that the judge was absolutely immune from suit. Although acting in excess of his legal authority, the judge was performing a judicial function.

Example: State court judge for County A enters an order affecting persons in County B. Under state law, the judge has no authority in County B. "For a judge to assume authority outside the geographic bounds of his office is the kind of clear judicial usurpation which cannot be condoned by any grant of immunity." *Maestri v. Jutkofsky*, 860 F.2d 50, 53 (2d Cir. 1988).

2. Absolute judicial immunity is justified by (1) the need to keep judges free from suits by disappointed litigants and (2) to ensure that they act without fear of adverse personal consequences.

3. Judges are not absolutely immune from claims for equitable relief, even for judicial acts. *Pulliam v. Allen*, 466 U.S. 522 (1984). Although the Court in *Pulliam* held that a judge could be held liable for attorney's fees by the prevailing party in such a case, Congress overruled that portion of the holding and prohibited fee awards against judges.

4. Moreover, judges are not absolutely immune for acts taken in a non-judicial capacity. For such acts, the judge would be entitled only to qualified immunity (*see* § C, below).

Example: Judge allegedly engaged in gender discrimination in demoting and firing a probation officer. Because this was an administrative, and not a judicial, act, the judge was not absolutely immune from a damages claim. He could argue only for qualified immunity. *Forrester v. White*, 484 U.S. 219 (1988).

5. Jurors and witnesses in litigation are absolutely immune from damages claims. This rule clearly is necessary to enable them to act without fear of reprisal. *See Briscoe v. LaHue*, 460 U.S. 325 (1983)(witnesses).

6. Prosecutors are absolutely immune from damages claims while performing the traditional functions performed by advocates. In performing administrative functions, however, prosecutors are entitled only to qualified immunity. *See Kalina v. Fletcher*, 522 U.S. 118 (1997)(prosecutor's preparing and filing documents charging a crime protected by absolute immunity, but executing certificate for determination of probable cause was not a traditional function of an advocate, and therefore is not protected by absolute immunity); *Buckley v. Fitzsimmons*, 509 U.S. 259 (1993)(alleged misconduct in course of investigation was administrative, subject only to qualified immunity).

7. Legislators are absolutely immune for actions taken "within the sphere of the legitimate legislative activity." *Supreme Court of Virginia v. Consumers Union of United States*, 446 U.S. 719, 732 (1980).

a. This immunity applies not only to claims for damages but to claims for equitable relief as well.

b. Legislative immunity is based upon the Speech and Debate Clause of the Constitution. U.S. Const., Article I, § 6, cl. 1.

c. Thus a legislator cannot be sued for legislation that turns out to be unconstitutional or for anything said in the debate concerning the legislation.

d. This immunity applies as well to officials who, while not legislators, are engaged in a legislative function. For example, a state supreme court that promulgates attorney discipline rules is acting in a legislative function. *Supreme Court of Virginia*, 446 U.S. at 734.

e. The immunity does not apply, however, to employees of the legislative body.

C. Qualified ("Good Faith") Immunity

1. Most § 1983 cases are brought against state or local officials, such as governors, mayors, or police officers, who do not enjoy absolute immunity. In addition, as we saw in § B, some state actors are entitled to absolute immunity only when performing particular functions; when acting outside those functions, they do not enjoy absolute immunity.

2. In such circumstances, the defendant may be able to claim "qualified" immunity, which is also known by the more descriptive term "good faith" immunity. The basic notion, obvious from the name, is that the defendant should not be liable for damages if he acted with good faith. *Harlow v. Fitzgerald*, 457 U.S. 800 (1982). *Harlow* was not a § 1983 case; it was a *Bivens* action against a federal official (*see* § V, below). But the Supreme Court has embraced the *Harlow* approach in § 1983 cases. *See Davis v. Scherer*, 468 U.S. 183 (1984)).

3. It is now absolutely clear that the defendant's good faith is to be measured *objectively*.

   a. The question is not whether this particular defendant actually knew whether what he did constituted a violation of the plaintiff's constitutional rights. Rather, the question is whether a "reasonable official would have known" that his activity violated a constitutional right of the plaintiff. *Harlow v. Fitzgerald*, 457 U.S. at 800.

b. The crux of whether one "would have known" of a constitutional violation is whether the violation was "clearly established." More specifically, the law must have been clearly established *at the time of the alleged misconduct*. Hope v. Pelzer, 536 U.S. 730 (2002).

c. This does not mean that there must be case law specifically holding that the very conduct at issue in the case is unconstitutional.

Example: Notwithstanding lack of case law specifically addressing a claim that sexual harassment in the classroom constituted a deprivation of equal protection, clear authority concerning sexual harassment in the workplace as a denial of equal protection would place a reasonable teacher on notice at the time of the events that the alleged sexual harassment gave rise to a denial of equal protection. *Sh.A. ex rel. J.A. v. Tucumcari Mun. Schools*, 321 F.3d 1285 (10th Cir. 2003).

d. Qualified immunity is thought necessary to permit state actors to exercise their discretion boldly. If they were liable every time their act caused a constitutional deprivation, officers would be hesitant to do anything close to the line of constitutionality. With good faith immunity, the officers can approach that line more readily. In fact, they can even cross over the line and commit an unconstitutional act without liability for damages if a reasonable official would not have known that the act constituted a violation.

Example: Police Officer arrested Plaintiff, who was heckling the governor at a speech. Plaintiff sues Police Officer under § 1983, seeking damages for using excessive force in effecting the arrest. Even if the use of force was unconstitutional, a court might determine that Police Office is entitled to good faith immunity because a reasonable officer at the time might have thought such force was necessary to protect the governor. *See Saucier v. Katz*, 533 U.S. 194 (2001).

4. The Supreme Court recently clarified the order in which a court should assess issues in cases involving a claim of qualified immunity. *Saucier v. Katz*, 533 U.S. 730 (2001)(although *Saucier* was a *Bivens* case, there is no reason to believe that the Court would not apply it in § 1983 cases; *see* § c.2, above). As noted at § A.2, above, because qualified immunity is immunity from *suit itself*, courts endeavor to determine the issue before trial, often on summary judgment.

a. First, the court asks: "[t]aken in the light most favorable to the [plaintiff], do the facts alleged show the officer's conduct violated a constitutional right?" *Id.* at 201.

b. If the answer to that question is no, "there is no necessity for further inquiries concerning qualified immunity" because the plaintiff has not stated an actionable wrong. *Id.*

c. If the answer to that question is yes, however, then the court proceeds to the second inquiry: whether the right was clearly established at the time the claim arose. If so, qualified immunity is rejected and the case proceeds to trial. If not, qualified immunity protects the defendant and the case is dismissed.

V. Deprivations Under Color of Federal Law: *Bivens* Claims

A. Section 1983 Does Not Apply to Federal Actors

1. As seen in the express language of the statute and discussed in detail in § II.A, above, § 1983 applies only to deprivations of federal rights caused by persons acting under color of state law. Thus, a person acting under color of federal law cannot be sued under that statute. *See, e.g., Rockefeller v. Court of Appeals, Tenth Circuit Judges*, 248 F.Supp.2d 17, 24 (D. D.C. 2003)(federal judges not amenable to suit under § 1983 because they act under color of federal law).

2. There is no general statute analogous to § 1983 that allows suit against federal actors.

3. Other statutes, however, provide remedies for the acts of federal actors under certain circumstances. For example, a provision of the Federal Tort Claims Act, 28 U.S.C. § 2680(h), allows suit against the United States for many torts committed by federal officers. As amended in 1974, it now permits recovery for intentional torts of officers, but the suit is against the United States, not against the officers.

4. Nonetheless, the Supreme Court has recognized a right of action directly against a federal actor, routinely referred to as a "*Bivens* claim."

B. *Bivens* Recognizes a Right to Sue a Federal Actor for Damages for Deprivation of a Constitutional Right

1. In *Bivens v. Six Unknown Federal Agents*, 403 U.S. 388 (1971), the Supreme

Court held that a plaintiff may sue federal officers on an implied right of action under the Fourth Amendment to recover damages for an unconstitutional search and seizure.

Example: Narcotics officers enter Plaintiff's apartment, handcuff him and threaten members of his family with arrest. The officers strip search Plaintiff and tear up the apartment ostensibly searching for illegal drugs. Although the officers arrest Plaintiff and charge him with narcotics violations, he is never prosecuted. Plaintiff claims that the warrantless search was made without probable cause and with excessive force and therefore violated the Fourth Amendment. (These are the basic facts of the *Bivens* case.)

Variation One: If the officers were from the local police department, acting under color of state law, Plaintiff could sue them for damages under § 1983.

Variation Two: If, however, the officers were agents of a federal agency (as was the case in *Bivens*), Plaintiff cannot sue under § 1983. Moreover, at the time, the Federal Tort Claims Act provided no remedy, because it then exempted intentional torts such as those alleged here.

2. In *Bivens* (Variation Two immediately above), the Supreme Court held that Plaintiff could sue for damages under the Fourth Amendment. Although (1) the Fourth Amendment does not expressly provide a cause of action or any other remedy for persons whose rights are violated, and (2) Congress had not provided a statutory remedy, the Court held that the federal courts have the power to recognize such a remedy.

   a. The Court concluded that the lack of congressional remedy was no bar to recognizing the damages claim when the judiciary concludes such a remedy to be an appropriate means of enforcing a constitutional right.

   b. It seems likely the Court was influenced in part by the fact that Plaintiff would have no recourse at all if it did not recognize a damages claim. An injunction would do no good, because the unconstitutional behavior was unlikely to recur.

3. *Bivens* raises a serious separation-of-powers issue, which Justice Harlan addressed in his concurring opinion in the case. Specifically, it might be suggested that it is the role of Congress, not the courts, to provide for a

right of action to enforce constitutional guarantees. Even Justice Harlan concluded, however, that the judiciary had the authority to recognize a remedy in the case. Harlan noted that the judiciary had long recognized injunctive remedies against an officer who acted unconstitutionally, permitting an order that the officer cease the unconstitutional behavior or else face contempt.

4. The suit is brought against the individual actors and seeks imposition of liability for damages on them in their personal capacity. Because suit is not against the United States, it does not implicate the sovereign immunity of the federal government.

5. The *Bivens* claim is for violation of *constitutional* protections. As we will see below, the Court expanded the claim beyond the Fourth Amendment context in subsequent cases.

6. Federal courts have subject-matter jurisdiction over *Bivens* claims under the general federal-question statute, § 1331. Thus, there is no amount in controversy requirement.

C. Limitations on the Scope of the *Bivens* Claim

1. *Bivens* itself involved a violation of the Fourth Amendment. Some observers concluded that the Court might recognize a common law claim for damages for violation of any constitutional deprivation under color of federal law. This possibility raised the questions of whether Congress might repeal or limit the *Bivens* right and whether the Court might refuse to recognize a *Bivens* claim in any circumstances.

2. The *Bivens* opinion indicated two potential factors that could defeat a *Bivens* claim:

   a. The Court cautioned that "special factors counseling hesitation in the absence of affirmative action by Congress" might obviate a *Bivens*-type action. *Bivens*, 403 U.S. at 396.

   b. The Court was influenced in *Bivens* by the fact that there was "no explicit congressional declaration that persons injured by a federal officer's violation of the Fourth Amendment may not recover money damages from the agents, but must instead be remitted to another remedy, equally effective in the view of Congress." *Bivens*,

403 U.S. at 397. This language suggests that Congress might repeal or modify a *Bivens* claim, but seems to require a clear statement of congressional intent to do so.

3. In *Davis v. Passman*, 442 U.S. 228 (1979), the Court recognized a *Bivens* claim against a Congressman who failed to consider the plaintiff for an administrative post because she was a woman. The allegations stated a violation of the equal protection clause of the Fifth Amendment.

   a. The Court recognized the claim even though Congress had established remedies for employment discrimination in Title VII of the Civil Rights Act of 1964. Although the statute was amended in 1972 to permit federal employees to sue, it exempted congressional employees.

   b. Although the statutory scheme arguably demonstrated that Congress had decided that a person in the plaintiff's situation should not have a claim, the Court was undeterred, and seemed, according to some commentators, to imply that *Bivens* claims should be recognized to vindicate all constitutional rights.

4. Similarly, in *Carlson v. Green*, 446 U.S. 14 (1980), the Court permitted a federal prisoner to sue a federal prison official for his alleged infliction of cruel and unusual punishment, in violation of the Eighth Amendment. The Court reiterated the two factors that could defeat a *Bivens* claim, discussed in *Bivens* itself, but concluded that they did not preclude suit on the facts of *Carlson*.

   a. Although Congress had recently amended the Federal Tort Claims Act (FTCA) to permit persons in the plaintiff's position to sue the United States, the Court rejected the notion that Congress had enacted a remedy as effective as a *Bivens* claim.

   b. Specifically, the Court noted that the *Bivens* claim gave the plaintiff several advantages he would not enjoy under the FTCA: he could sue the officer directly, rather than the United States; he could recover punitive damages; he would have a right to jury trial; and he would not have to exhaust administrative remedies before suing. Thus, the Court concluded, a *Bivens* claim was a superior deterrent to unconstitutional behavior than the FTCA claim.

5. On other occasions, however, the Court has been willing to forego a

Bivens claim in light of congressional action. These cases recognize a broader legislative power to preclude the *Bivens* remedy.

a. In *Bush v. Lucas*, 462 U.S. 367 (1983), plaintiff, a federal employee, sued for violation of the First Amendment, alleging that he was demoted for making critical comments, alleged by his superior to be false, to the press about the facility at which he worked. Congress had established an elaborate set of remedies under civil service statutes. Although those remedies did not afford a jury trial or a chance to recover for emotional distress, the Court noted that the claim arose from a government relationship controlled by comprehensive remedial provisions against the United States.

b. Similarly, in *Schweiker v. Chilicky*, 487 U.S. 412 (1988), the Court refused to permit suit for unconstitutional denial of welfare disability benefits. Plaintiffs had succeeded in administrative review proceedings to have payments reinstated and to recover for interim benefits. Under those proceedings, however, they were not permitted to seek recovery for harm suffered as a result of the denial of benefits. The Court concluded that "Congress has provided what it considers adequate remedial mechanisms for constitutional violations," which ended the matter. *Id.* at 423.

c. These cases implicitly expand the situations in which Congress can replace the *Bivens* claim, and thus reduce the availability of that claim.

6. The Court has found "special factors counseling hesitation" to preclude *Bivens* suits in the military context. *See United States v. Stanley*, 483 U.S. 669 (1987)(denying a right to sue on a claim that plaintiff had been given LSD unknowingly, as part of an Army experiment concerning the hallucinogenic drug); *Chappell v. Wallace*, 462 U.S. 296 (1983)(denying a right to sue on a claim of racial discrimination by enlisted personnel against officers). Without excessive elaboration, the Court found that the claims involving military service, coupled with an absence of congressional remedy, counseled hesitation in recognizing a damages claim.

D. Procedural Issues in Cases Asserting a *Bivens* Claim

1. As in § 1983 cases, a *Bivens* plaintiff generally need not exhaust administrative remedies before filing suit. On the other hand, the Prison Litigation Reform Act, discussed in § II.B.2, above, does apply in *Bivens*

cases, so a federal prisoner filing a case falling within that Act must exhaust administrative remedies in accord with the Act.

2. As we saw in § III.H.1, above, 42 U.S.C. § 1988(a) directs federal courts in specific types of cases, including § 1983 to look to state law when the federal law is "deficient." The statute does not apply to *Bivens* claims. Thus, federal common law, and not state law, fills most of the gaps in the law.

   a. Statutes of limitations are governed by federal common law, although that law may direct the adoption of state law.

   b. Issues such as survival of the claim after death of a litigant are governed by federal common law.

3. There appears to be no provision permitting a court to award attorney's fees to the prevailing party in a *Bivens* case. As we saw in § III.6.4, above, 42 U.S.C. § 1988(b) permits recovery of a reasonable attorney's fee by the "prevailing party" in § 1983 cases. The statute does not apply in a *Bivens* case.

4. Immunities from suit are basically the same as in § 1983 litigation, which we discussed at § IV, above. *See Harlow v. Fitzgerald*, 457 U.S. 800 (1982)(discussing qualified immunity of executive official in a *Bivens* case).

   a. The President of the United States has absolute immunity, at least from suits for damages, for actions taken in his official capacity. *Nixon v. Fitzgerald*, 457 U.S. 731 (1982).

   b. The President is not immune, however, from damages suits for acts taken before becoming President, even if the suit is filed during his presidency. *Clinton v. Jones*, 520 U.S. 681 (1997).

VI. Civil Rights Removal Jurisdiction

A. Background and the Provision for Civil Rights Removal

1. The civil rights removal statute, 28 U.S.C. § 1443, like removal that was the subject of discussion in Chapter 7, allows a party to state trial court litigation to have a case moved to a federal trial court.

   a. The statute has its roots in the Reconstruction era. The original version of the statute was part of the Civil Rights Act of 1865. It implemented the Thirteenth Amendment, and seemed clearly intended to permit relatively blacks to have access to the federal courts, which, presumably, would be more sympathetic than state courts to their newly enfranchised status.

    b. Civil rights removal is broader than removal discussed in Chapter 7 in that it permits removal of criminal as well as civil cases.

    c. Civil rights removal is narrower than removal discussed in Chapter 7, however, because it permits removal only under circumstances that raise some question about whether the state court will protect a party from discrimination on the basis of race.

2. The current version of the statute provides:

Any of the following civil actions or criminal prosecutions, commenced in a state court, may be removed by the defendant to the district court of the United States for the district and division embracing the place wherein it is pending:

(1) Against any person who is denied or cannot enforce in the courts of such state a right under any law providing for the equal civil rights of citizens of the United States, or of all persons within the jurisdiction thereof;

(2) For any act under color of authority derived from any law providing for equal rights, or for refusing to do any act on the ground that it would be inconsistent with such law.

3. Note that the statute contains three main clauses, each of which describes a situation in which removal will be allowed:

    a. The "denial" clause in subsection (1), which allows removal when a person is denied or cannot enforce in state court some right under a law that provides for equal rights;

    b. The "authority" clause in subsection (2), where a defendant is sued or prosecuted for performing an act under a law that provides for equal rights; and

    c. The "refusal" clause in subsection (3), where a defendant is sued or prosecuted for failing to perform an act that would be inconsistent with a law that provides for equal rights.

4. Although most reported cases have involved the "denial" clause, in practice today all three are relatively moribund.

5. Congress revised the original 1865 statute significantly in 1875 in a way that continues to affect its availability.

   a. Under the original version, removal was authorized either before or after trial in the state court. The availability of post-trial removal would have permitted a federal court to review the entire record of a case in determining whether the state court in fact denied a party some civil right dealing with equality.

   b. The 1875 legislation made post-trial removal unavailable, even though it was apparently Congress' original understanding that post-trial removal would function as the primary means of enforcing the Act.

   c. As a result of the revision, which remains in effect today, removal decisions under the denial clause must be based on a *prediction* as to whether the state court would deny the defendant a civil right of equality, since the case could only be removed before trial.

   d. Because removal is thus based upon a prediction of unconstitutional behavior by a state court, the statute creates great potential for friction between the federal and state court systems.

6. To avoid the unseemliness of predicting that a state court will behave in an unconstitutional way, the Supreme Court has interpreted § 1443, especially the denial clause, narrowly. Very few cases have been removed under the statute.

B. "Equal Rights" Interpreted Narrowly

1. As seen above, clause (1) of the civil rights removal statute permits removal when a party cannot enforce a law providing for the "equal civil rights" of citizens of the United States. Clause (2) refers to cases involving an act under, or refused to be taken under, a law providing for "equal rights."

2. The Supreme Court has concluded that § 1443 applies to allow vindication of laws concerning equality not only to civil rights in existence in 1875 (when the current version of the statute was enacted), but to civil rights recognized later. On the other hand, however, the Court has concluded that the "equal rights" implicated by the statute refers only to laws involving *racial* equality. *Georgia v. Rachel*, 384 U.S. 780 (1966).

a. Thus, First Amendment rights to free speech and Fourteenth Amendment rights to due process cannot provide a basis for removal under § 1443.

b. Moreover, even constitutional rights concerning equality of treatment based upon factors other than race cannot provide a basis for removal under § 1443. It is only racial equality that is implicated.

c. Commentators have criticized the Court's limitation of the statute to provisions concerning racial equality as inconsistent with the text and the purpose of the statute, but the Court reaffirmed the point in *Johnson v. Mississippi,* 421 U.S. 213 (1975), and has not reviewed it more recently.

C. The Distinction Between State Statutes and State Practices

1. In *Strauder v. West Virginia,* 100 U.S. 303 (1879), a black man was indicted in state court for murder. He attempted to remove the prosecution from state court to federal court, arguing that his equal rights would be denied in state court, since state law permitted only white men to serve on a grand or petit (trial) jury.

2. The Supreme Court held that pretrial removal was required. The defendant demonstrated that he would be unable to enforce his equal civil rights in state court because of the state's juror selection statute, which, the Court held, violated the Fourteenth Amendment.

3. On the same day, however, the Supreme Court also decided *Virginia v. Rives,* 100 U.S. 313 (1879). In that case, the state court criminal defendants, who were black, had argued that their equal rights would be denied in state court because Virginia had never permitted blacks to serve on county juries in trials involving a black defendant. The difference from *Strauder* was simply this: in Virginia, the "rule" excluding blacks from jury service was not embodied in a statute; it was, instead, simply a practice followed by the state.

4. The Supreme Court denied removal in *Rives*. It relied upon the fact that the Virginia practice was not embodied in a statute. In *Strauder*, because there was a statute outlawing black participation, the state trial courts had no option but to exclude blacks from the jury. In *Rives*, the absence of a statute meant that the state courts were not bound, but could allow black participation.

5. The Court's distinction, known generally as the "*Strauder-Rives* doctrine," is questionable at best, and commentators have criticized it.

   a. State courts are bound by the Supremacy Clause of the Constitution to enforce federal law, including all constitutional provisions. Thus, there should have been no reason in *Strauder* to assume the state courts would fail to enforce the Fourteenth Amendment by holding contrary state statutes unconstitutional.

   b. Moreover, if state courts cannot be trusted to invalidate state statutes that clearly violate the Fourteenth Amendment, one may wonder whether they can be trusted to invalidate unconstitutional non-statutory state practice.

   c. It is also doubtful that a holding that exposes inherent mistrust of a state court's ability or willingness to invalidate a plainly unconstitutional state statute does much to reduce friction between the two judicial systems.

   d. The dichotomy created by the two cases shows that it was unfortunate that Congress decided, in 1875, to make post-trial removal unavailable. *See* § VIII.A.5, above. Had post-trial removal been available, as it was under the original civil rights removal statute of 1865, the defendant in *Rives* could have removed the case after he was tried in state court by a jury that in fact included no blacks.

D. The "Modern" Era

1. Because of statutory limitations on the right to appeal cases denying removal to federal court, the Supreme Court had few opportunities to review denials of removal under § 1443.

2. Congress liberalized the Supreme Court's ability to review such cases in 1964 by expressly providing that denials of removal under § 1443 could be reviewed on appeal. 28 U.S.C. § 1447(d). Two years later the Court decided two cases in which it reexamined, and in some ways changed, longstanding principles.

3. In *Georgia v. Rachel*, 384 U.S. 780 (1966), blacks who had sought service at certain hotels and restaurants were indicted under a local trespass statute for refusing to leave when so requested. The Supreme Court allowed removal under the denial clause of § 1443(1), and emphasized

that the defendants asserted a right to equal service at public accommodations, which was expressly guaranteed by the recently-enacted 1964 Civil Rights Act.

    a.   The Court held that the defendants had a right not just to avoid conviction, but to avoid the very act of being prosecuted in state court. "It is no answer in these circumstances that the defendants might eventually prevail in the state court. The burden of having to defend the prosecutions is itself the denial of a right explicitly conferred by the Civil Rights Act of 1964." *Rachel*, 384 U.S. at 805.

    b.   Because the prosecution itself was a denial of a federal right, the Court had no problem predicting that the federal right would be denied in state court; it was denied when the case was filed.

    c.   *Rachel* is significant because the Court found a denial of equal rights in state court even in the absence of a state statute embodying discrimination.

4.   The *Rachel* Court's lack of respect for the state courts is inconsistent with *Rives*.

    a.   The prosecutions violated the Civil Rights Act only if the defendants had been asked to leave the premises, and therefore charged with trespass because of their race. It is possible, however, that the defendants were asked to leave the premises for other reasons—for example, they were being rowdy or the store was closing—in which case the state court prosecution would not violate a law concerning equal rights.

    b.   Thus, a court would have to hold a hearing concerning the complaining witness's motivation before determining whether the Civil Rights Act was implicated. A state court could hold that hearing just as readily as a federal court.

    c.   By endorsing removal before such a hearing, the Supreme Court seems to be signaling that the state court could not be trusted to engage in a meaningful factual hearing on the complaining witness' motivation.

    d.   This conclusion, however, is contrary to the message implicit in *Rives*—that the state courts are to be trusted to do the right thing under the Constitution and laws of equal rights.

5. In *City of Greenwood v. Peacock,* 384 U.S. 808 (1966), decided the same day as *Rachel,* civil rights workers in Mississippi were charged with obstructing the public streets, assault, disturbing the peace, creating a public disturbance, and inciting a riot. They sought removal to federal court, asserting that they were being prosecuted because of their efforts to register black voters. The Supreme Court held that removal was not proper under § 1443.

   a. According to the Court, the civil rights statute in *Peacock* contained no protection from a state's attempt to prosecute. In contrast, the defendants in *Rachel* relied upon the public accommodations provision of the Civil Rights Act, which included protection even from attempted prosecution in violation of equal rights.

   b. The Court also distinguished *Rachel* by noting that "no federal law confers an absolute right on private citizens . . . to obstruct a public street" or commit any other of the violations with which the defendants were charged.

6. Thus, after *Rachel* and *Peacock,* civil rights removal continues to receive an extremely narrow construction.

   a. The *Strauder-Rives* dichotomy has remained in force, so only in the extremely rare instance in which a state *statute,* rather than a state *practice,* denies equal rights in state judicial procedures will civil rights removal be authorized.

   b. There is a very limited exception to this rule when the state prosecution is for conduct protected by a federal right against the very initiation of a prosecution, such as in the public accommodations provision of the Civil Rights Act.

XV

Habeas Corpus

■ ANALYSIS

I. Introduction
II. Background, Origins of the Writ, and Overview of Current Statutory Provisions
    A. The Concept of Habeas Corpus
    B. History of the Writ
    C. Overview of Current Statutory Provisions, as Amended by the Antiterrorism and Effective Death Penalty Act of 1996 (AEDPA)
III. Habeas Corpus for State Prisoners
    A. Basic Statutory Provisions
    B. Statutory Requirement of Exhaustion of State Remedies
    C. Waiver by the State of the Exhaustion Requirement
    D. Review of State Court Findings
    E. Deprivations Cognizable in Federal Habeas Corpus Proceedings
    F. Statute of Limitations and Limits on Successive Applications for Federal Habeas Relief
    G. Appellate Review of Federal Habeas Decisions
    H. Special Provisions for Capital Cases
IV. "Abortive State Proceedings"—The Problem of Independent and Adequate State Grounds
    A. Background: Case Law Through *Wainwright v. Sykes*
    B. Subsequent Developments

V. **Habeas Corpus for Persons In the Custody of the United States**
   A. Statutory Provisions
   B. Some Specific Issues Concerning Habeas Corpus by Persons in Federal Custody

I. Introduction

The writ of habeas corpus permits a federal court to order the release of someone being held in custody of the government. The release is justified only if the person is being held in violation of federal law, usually constitutional law. Though habeas corpus will lie to challenge detention by the federal government, the overwhelming use of the writ is to challenge detention by a state. Usually, the writ is sought by a state prisoner. This person (the "applicant") usually alleges that her conviction and incarceration violated some constitutional right. The possibility that a federal court might issue an order mandating the release of someone from state custody obviously raises significant concerns of federalism and comity. In recent years, in some areas, the Supreme Court has restricted the availability of habeas corpus relief. More significantly, in 1996, Congress imposed notable restrictions on its availability. That legislation is controversial, and some argue that it went too far. Others contend, however, that further restrictions on habeas are needed in the interests of federalism and finality of state court judgments. The Constitution guarantees only that the writ cannot be suspended entirely.

II. Background, Origins of the Writ, and Overview of Current Statutory Provisions

A. The Concept of Habeas Corpus

1. "Habeas corpus" is the traditional name of a writ technically known as the writ of "habeas corpus ad subjiciendum." Frequently, it is referred to simply as "the Great Writ." By whatever name, it provides a means by which the judiciary can test the legality of a person's detention by government authority.

2. The writ thus provides an important vehicle for preventing lawlessness by the government and of protecting the individual from secret and unjustified restraint.

3. Though habeas corpus applies to any government detention, it is usually used to seek the release of prisoners incarcerated pursuant to state criminal convictions.

4. Issuance of the writ commands the government authority to release the person being restrained.

    a. The release may be complete, such as when it is used to give a prisoner his freedom from incarceration.

b. Or the release might be for a limited purpose, such as commanding that a prisoner be brought to a court to testify in a particular matter.

5. Issuance of the writ by a federal court concerning a person in state custody obviously raises serious federalism considerations. Some commentators consider it the greatest source of friction between the federal courts and the states.

B. History of the Writ

1. The writ developed in England, and was firmly codified by the Habeas Corpus Act of 1679.

2. The Framers inserted the protection of the writ into Article I, § 9 of the Constitution, which provides: "The privilege of the writ of habeas corpus shall not be suspended, unless when in cases of rebellion or invasion the public safety may require it."

3. Congress first provided for federal court jurisdiction to issue the writ in § 14 of the Judiciary Act of 1789.

4. Congress expanded the availability of habeas corpus in federal courts in 1867 by authorizing issuance "in all cases where any person may be restrained of his or her liberty in violation of the constitution, or of any treaty or law of the United States."

   a. This provision plainly made federal habeas relief available for persons restrained illegally by state authorities.

   b. Though Congress has amended the statutory grants of federal habeas authority several times since 1867, the scope of the writ still permits a federal court to issue the writ to order the release of someone held under state authority.

C. Overview of Current Statutory Provisions, as Amended by the Antiterrorism and Effective Death Penalty Act of 1996 (AEDPA)

1. Several provisions relate to habeas corpus in the federal courts. They are found at 28 U.S.C. §§ 2241 through 2255. In this section, we provide an overview of these statutes, followed in separate sections by detailed discussions of the most important provisions.

2. The Antiterrorism and Effective Death Penalty Act of 1996 ("AEDPA") contains the most sweeping changes to the habeas provisions in over a

generation. The Act, which we will address throughout the Chapter, restricts federal habeas relief significantly.

3. Section 2241 contains important basic provisions about who may issue a writ of habeas corpus and the circumstances under which the writ may be granted.

   a. Section 2241(a) provides that "[w]rits of habeas corpus may be granted by the Supreme Court, any justice thereof, the district courts and any circuit judge within their respective jurisdictions." Section 2241(b) permits the Supreme Court, any justice thereof, and circuit judges to decline habeas relief and transfer the application to the federal district court having jurisdiction over the matter.

   b. Section 2241(c) lists five circumstances in which the writ may be issued concerning "a prisoner." The writ may issue only if one of the five conditions is satisfied:

      1. the prisoner "is in custody under or by color of the authority of the United States or is committed for trial before some court thereof," or

      2. the prisoner "is in custody for an act done or omitted in pursuance of an Act of Congress, or an order, process, judgment or decree of a court or judge of the United States," or

      3. the prisoner "is in custody in violation of the Constitution or laws or treaties of the United States;" or

      4. the prisoner is a citizen of a foreign state and is domiciled there, but is in custody for an act done under her government's authority, which act is to be judged by international law, or

      5. "It is necessary to bring [the person] into court to testify or for trial."

   c. Of these five provisions, the third has caused most difficulty and will be the focus of discussion. It applies to cases in which state prisoners challenge the legality of their confinement.

4. Sections 2242, 2243, and 2245 through 2252 concern procedural matters for a federal court's hearing of the application for the writ. For example,

§ 2242 provides that the application for habeas corpus must be in writing, signed, and verified, and §§ 2245 through 2249 address evidentiary matters for the habeas hearing.

5. Section 2244, which was amended by the AEDPA, contains important provisions regarding the finality of habeas determinations. We will discuss it in detail in § III.D, below.

6. Section 2255, also amended by the AEDPA, addresses habeas corpus sought by persons in federal custody. We will discuss it in detail in § V, below.

7. Section 2254, also amended by the AEDPA, addresses habeas corpus sought by persons in state custody. We will discuss it in § III, below.

8. The AEDPA added a new chapter to the habeas provisions of Title 28, codified at §§ 2261–66. These provisions apply only to prisoners in state custody subject to the death penalty. We will address these in § III.H, below.

III. Habeas Corpus for State Prisoners

A. Basic Statutory Provisions

1. Section § 2254 governs the issuance of writs of habeas corpus for "a person in custody pursuant to the judgment of a State court." Section 2254(a) provides that the writ may be issued for such a person "only on the ground that he is in custody in violation of the Constitution or laws or treaties of the United States."

2. The AEDPA made significant changes to habeas corpus law in 1996.

3. As noted above, this use of habeas—by which a federal court reviews the legality of a person's confinement by state authorities—raises profound questions of federalism.

B. Statutory Requirement of Exhaustion of State Remedies

1. Section 2254(b) imposes an "exhaustion" requirement on anyone seeking federal habeas concerning state incarceration. That subsection provides that before the writ may issue, one of the following must be true:

    a. "that the applicant has exhausted the remedies available in the courts of the State," or

b. that "there is an absence of available State corrective process," or

c. "circumstances exist that render such process ineffective to protect the rights of the applicant."

2. This exhaustion requirement was originally developed judicially. *Ex Parte Royall*, 117 U.S. 241 (1886). Congress first codified the exhaustion requirement in 1948.

3. The exhaustion requirement serves federalism interests and is "designed to give the State the initial 'opportunity to pass upon and correct' alleged violations of its prisoners' federal rights." *Wilwording v. Swenson*, 404 U.S. 249, 250 (1971).

4. Some early commentators concluded that a state prisoner could never exhaust state remedies, and thus could never seek federal habeas relief, if the state permitted successive applications for post-conviction relief. The Supreme Court rejected this view in *Brown v. Allen*, 344 U.S. 443 (1953), in which it held that the statutory exhaustion principle does not require repetitious applications to the state courts. Specifically, in that case, the petitioner had raised his federal constitutional issues on appeal from his conviction in the state system; he was not then required to request collateral relief from the state courts before seeking federal habeas relief.

5. Exhaustion thus requires that the state prisoner present his federal argument to the highest state court once, either on appeal or collateral attack. This requirement applies even if an intermediate state court of appeals has exercised discretionary review. *O'Sullivan v. Boerckel*, 526 U.S. 838 (1999).

6. The exhaustion requirement is satisfied if the prisoner seeks review by the state's highest court, even if that court refuses to review the matter, or if it reviews the case and fails to discuss the federal issues raised.

7. If a state prisoner combines in one habeas corpus petition both exhausted and non-exhausted claims, the federal court must dismiss the petition. *Rose v. Lundy*, 455 U.S. 509 (1982).

8. The habeas applicant has the burden of showing that she has exhausted state remedies. Failure to do so, of course, results in denial of the petition.

C. Waiver by the State of the Exhaustion Requirement

1. Over the years, the federal courts recognized exceptional circumstances in which the state could be deemed to have waived the requirement of exhaustion. In such rare circumstances, the federal court could decide upon the habeas petition even if the applicant had failed to exhaust state remedies.

2. In 1996, in the AEDPA, Congress for the first time codified the possibility that a state can waive the exhaustion requirement. It permits waiver, however, *only* in one situation: when the state, through its lawyer, "expressly waives the requirement."

   a. Thus, courts are no longer free to determine other circumstances in which the state may be deemed to have waived the exhaustion requirement.

   b. In this and other ways, the AEDPA restricts the availability of federal habeas relief.

D. Review of State Court Findings

1. We saw in § B, above, that the habeas applicant must exhaust state remedies before seeking habeas corpus relief from a federal court. Thus, by the time an applicant brings the question of the legality of his confinement to federal court, a state court probably will have addressed the question on the merits.

2. The question then becomes: what is the effect of the state court determination of the issue of the legality of the applicant's incarceration?

3. Traditional principles of claim and issue preclusion generally do not apply in the case of federal habeas for state prisoners. *See Brown v. Allen*, 344 U.S. 443 (1953).

   a. Thus, the fact that an issue has been determined by a state court does not bar the federal habeas court from determining the question afresh.

   b. Giving preclusive effect to state court findings on the relevant issues would render federal habeas relief meaningless.

4. On the other hand, a federal court is not free simply to ignore state court findings of fact.

a. The Supreme Court established in *Brown v. Allen* that the federal court is to accept state court findings of fact unless there were "unusual circumstances" or a "vital flaw" in the state court proceedings.

b. In addition, in *Townsend v. Sain*, 372 U.S. 293 (1963), the Supreme Court held that a federal court on a habeas petition must re-examine state factual findings if the state court had not afforded the applicant a "full and fair hearing" at trial.

5. These phrases did not provide clear guidance for lower federal courts, leading Congress in 1966 to codify the circumstances in which state court determinations of fact could be reviewed in a federal habeas case. The result, codified at 28 U.S.C. § 2254(d), was that state findings were to be presumed correct unless one of the following conditions was established: (1) the merits of the factual dispute were not resolved in the state proceeding; (2) the state's fact-finding procedure was inadequate to afford a full and fair hearing; (3) "the material facts were not adequately developed at the State court hearing"; (4) the state lacked subject matter jurisdiction; (5) the applicant, an indigent, was not appointed counsel; (6) the applicant did not receive a full and fair hearing; (7) "the applicant was otherwise denied due process of law in the State court proceeding"; or (8) if the federal court concludes that the state court's factual determination "is not fairly supported by the record. . . . "

6. Congress changed this provision dramatically in 1996, in the AEDPA. The relevant provision is now found in § 2254(e)(1).

    a. That section provides that "a determination of a factual issue made by a State court shall be presumed to be correct."

    b. Significantly, the state court determination need not have been made pursuant to "a hearing on the merits," as was required by the 1966 codification.

    c. More significantly, the new statute contains no list of circumstances which will overcome the presumption of correctness.

    d. Rather, new § 2254(e)(1) provides that the applicant "shall have the burden of rebutting the presumption of correctness by clear and convincing evidence."

7. In addition, however, the AEDPA added in § 2254(d)(2) that habeas relief shall be granted if the state decision was "based on an unreason-

able determination of the facts in light of the evidence presented in the State proceeding." It is not clear how this basis for habeas is to be reconciled with the presumption of correctness in § 2254(e)(1).

8. The AEDPA added a significant restriction on habeas for state prisoners in § 2254(d). That section provides that an application for habeas "shall not be granted with respect to any claim that was adjudicated on the merits in State court proceedings" unless the applicant shows either:

   a. That adjudication of the claim resulted in a decision contrary to, or unreasonably applying, clearly established law as determined by the Supreme Court (and by no other federal court), or

   b. That adjudication of the claim resulted in a decision based upon an unreasonable determination of the facts in light of the evidence presented in state court.

   c. The first of these bases clearly establishes that the federal right vindicated must be established by the Supreme Court. The habeas court cannot, therefore, look to lower federal court decisions to determine whether the state court decision is contrary to (or unreasonably applies) "established law."

9. The AEDPA added a provision permitting a federal court to deny habeas corpus on the merits even if the applicant failed to exhaust state remedies. 28 U.S.C. § 2254(b)(2).

10. The AEDPA also added a provision that incompetence or ineffectiveness of counsel—either in state or federal postconviction proceedings—cannot be a basis for habeas relief. 28 U.S.C. § 2254(i).

11. In addition, the AEDPA adds § 2254(e)(2), concerning cases involving an applicant who failed "to develop the factual basis of a claim in State court proceedings." In such a case, the federal court "shall not hold an evidentiary hearing on the claim unless the applicant shows" both:

    a. That her claim relies upon (1) a new rule of constitutional law which was previously unavailable and which the Supreme Court (and no other federal court) made retroactive to cases on collateral review, or (2) a factual predicate that could not have been previously discovered through the exercise of due diligence, *and*

    b. That the facts underlying the claim would establish by clear and convincing evidence that but for constitutional error, no reasonable finder of fact would have found the applicant guilty of the underlying crime.

12. In some cases, the applicant's request for relief in state court will be denied on state procedural grounds, and not on findings of fact. Such cases are addressed in § IV, below.

E. Deprivations Cognizable in Federal Habeas Corpus Proceedings

1. Habeas corpus is a vehicle for reviewing the legality of a state prisoner's conviction and deprivation of liberty. It does not follow, however, that *every* constitutional deprivation can be remedied by federal habeas corpus.

2. The Supreme Court has recognized that at least one constitutional issue cannot be raised on habeas, but only in direct attack and on appeal therefrom. The issue is the exclusionary rule, and a claim that illegally seized evidence was used in the criminal trial in state court.

3. The important case establishing the point is *Stone v. Powell*, 428 U.S. 465 (1976). Specifically, the Supreme Court held that a federal habeas court could not review the claim by a state prisoner that evidence used against him in the criminal trial was illegally seized and should have been excluded from the trial. The reason for barring federal review was that the state court had afforded the criminal defendant "an opportunity for a full and fair" consideration of the claimed illegal seizure.

    a. The Court reasoned that the value of the exclusionary rule is questionable, because, though illegally seized, the evidence may nevertheless be probative, and that while the rule should still apply at trial, its costs did not justify its further use in a habeas corpus proceeding.

    b. According to the Court, the exclusionary rule does not create a personal right in the criminal defendant. Rather, it is a judicial remedy to be employed in the criminal trial and cognizable there and on appeal from the criminal judgment.

    c. The holding was noteworthy because it barred federal review on a question of law, not just a determination of fact by the state court.

    d. Though *Stone* remains vital today, the Court has not provided meaningful guidance on what constitutes "an opportunity for a full and fair" consideration of the issue of illegal seizure of evidence.

4. Justice Brennan dissented and expressed concern that *Stone* presaged "a drastic withdrawal of federal habeas jurisdiction, if not for all grounds of alleged unconstitutional detention, then at least for claims—for example, of double jeopardy, entrapment, self-incrimination, *Miranda's* violations, and use of invalid identification procedures—that this Court later decides are not 'guilt related,' " 428 U.S. at 517–18.

   a. Some commentators also expressed Justice Brennan's concern, that *Stone* marked the beginning of significant restrictions in the availability of federal habeas relief.

   b. For the most part, however, the concerns have not been realized. The Court has not expanded *Stone* beyond the exclusionary rule.

5. Some commentators suggest that the key to *Stone* is that the excluded evidence did not undermine a proper finding of guilt or innocence, because the illegal nature of the seizure did not affect whether the evidence was accurate and probative of guilt. Under this view, habeas review is improper unless the challenged evidentiary ruling might undermine a correct finding of guilt or innocence (e.g., a coerced confession). The Court never articulated this reasoning, however, and in any event it is not clear how such a standard would work in practice.

Example: Applicant seeks federal habeas corpus, alleging that the state court improperly denied his claim of racial discrimination in the selection of the grand jury that issued the indictment. Held: *Stone v. Powell* does not apply to preclude federal review of the state court ruling. *Rose v. Mitchell*, 443 U.S. 545 (1979). If the standard to be employed were whether the constitutional challenge might go to the issue of guilt or innocence, it is difficult to determine whether racial discrimination in the grand jury would meet it.

6. In *Jackson v. Virginia*, 443 U.S. 307 (1979), the Court refused to extend *Stone* to a habeas application claiming that the evidence of conviction in the state criminal trial was constitutionally insufficient.

7. In *Vasquez v. Hillery*, 474 U.S. 254 (1986), the Court reaffirmed its rule that a conviction in a case in which racial discrimination had been found in the selection of the grand jury may be overturned on federal habeas review.

8. In *Withrow v. Williams*, 507 U.S. 680 (1993), the Court refused to extend *Stone* to bar habeas review of a claim that the defendant's confession was obtained in violation of his *Miranda* rights. Even though the *Miranda* claim was addressed by a "full and fair" hearing in state court concerning suppression of the confession, the federal court can address the issue in an application for habeas corpus.

F. **Statute of Limitations and Limitations on Successive Applications for Federal Habeas Relief**

1. The AEDPA imposes a one-year period of limitations on an application by a state prisoner for federal habeas corpus relief. 28 U.S.C. § 2244(d)(1).

   a. The one-year runs from the latest of: (1) the date on which the judgment became final, or (2) the date on which the impediment on filing an application created by state action in violation of the Constitution is removed, or (3) the date on which the constitutional right asserted was recognized initially by the Supreme Court (provided that the Supreme Court (and no other federal court) made the newly-recognized right applicable retroactively), or (4) the date on which the factual predicate of the claim could have been discovered through exercise of due diligence.

   b. The time during which a proper application for state post-conviction review does not count toward the one-year period.

2. The AEDPA also imposes important restrictions on successive applications for habeas relief by state prisoners.

   a. A claim previously presented in a habeas application under § 2254 "shall be dismissed." 28 U.S.C. § 2244(b)(1). Thus, repeat applications are not permitted.

   b. A claim that was *not* presented in a previous habeas application under § 2254 shall be dismissed unless the applicant shows either (1) that the claim relies on a new rule of constitutional law, made retroactive to cases on collateral review by the Supreme Court (and no other federal court), or (2) the factual predicate for the claim could not have be discovered previously through due diligence *and* the facts underlying the claim, if proven and viewed in light of the evidence as a whole, would establish by clear and convincing evidence that no reasonable finder of fact would have found the applicant guilty of the underlying crime. 28 U.S.C. § 2244(b)(2). Thus, the failure to include a claim in a previous application may well result in waiver of that claim.

3. In addition, under the AEDPA, a second or successive application permitted as discussed immediately above cannot be filed in a district court until the applicant obtains an order from the court of appeals authorizing the district court to consider the application. 28 U.S.C. § 2244(b)(3)(A).

   a. The court of appeals will grant the order if the applicant makes a prima facie showing that the standard noted above is satisfied. 28 U.S.C. § 2244(b)(3)(C).

   b. A district court shall nonetheless dismiss the claim unless the applicant demonstrates that she has in fact satisfied the standard noted above. 28 U.S.C. § 2244(b)(4).

   c. The court of appeals' decision, either granting or denying authorization to file a second or successive application, is not appealable and is not subject to review by the Supreme Court by writ of certiorari. 28 U.S.C. § 2244(b)(3)(E).

G. Appellate Review of Federal Habeas Decisions

1. Section 2253 governs appellate review of federal habeas decisions. Before enactment of the AEDPA, a state prisoner could appeal a denial of habeas relief only if she obtained a "certificate of probable cause" from the court of appeals.

2. As amended by the AEDPA, a state prisoner may appeal a denial of federal habeas relief only if "a circuit justice or judge issues a certificate of appealability." 28 U.S.C. § 2253(c)(1)(B).

3. Such a certificate is issued only if the applicant makes a "substantial showing of the denial of a constitutional right." The showing must indicate the denial with specificity. 28 U.S.C. § 2253(c)(2) & (3).

H. Special Provisions for Capital Cases

1. The AEDPA added a new chapter to the habeas corpus provisions of Title 28, codified at §§ 2261–65. They deal with cases involving state prisoners incarcerated "subject to capital sentence."

2. The chapter applies only to federal courts in states which "opt in" to its application by adopting a rule concerning the appointment and compensation of competent counsel for state post-conviction proceedings brought by indigent prisoners whose capital convictions and sentences are upheld on direct appeal by the state's highest court. 28 U.S.C. § 2261(b).

   a. So long as the state has such a rule, the chapter provisions will apply to any state prisoner sentenced to death.

   b. The mechanism set up by the state must provide for entry by a state court of an order either appointing counsel to represent the applicant if she is indigent or finding that the applicant has rejected the offer of counsel (or finding that she is not indigent).

3. Upon the entry of such an order, the order of execution is automatically stayed pending the prisoner's application to a federal court for habeas relief under § 2254.

   a. The stay expires, however, if (1) the prisoner fails to file a timely habeas application, (2) waives the right to file an application, (3) makes the application but fails to make a substantial showing of a denial of a federal right, or (4) the federal court denies habeas relief.

   b. If any of those things has occurred, no federal court may thereafter enter a stay of execution unless the applicant is permitted to file a second application under § 2244(b). *See* § F, above.

4. Section 2263 addresses the timing of the habeas application. Section 2264 addresses the scope of federal review in capital cases. Section 2265 provides specific rules applicable in states that allow a defendant to raise issues on direct appeal that could be raised on collateral attack as well. And § 2266 provides detailed time limits for action by the federal court.

IV. "Abortive State Proceedings"—The Problem of Independent and Adequate State Grounds

A. Background: Case Law Through *Wainwright v. Sykes*

1. In § III.D, above, we discussed the role of the federal habeas court in reviewing determinations of fact made by a state court concerning the applicant's contentions. Here, we address a different scenario: the

applicant lost at state court because she failed to comply with state *procedures* for presenting her claim in state court. This scenario is said to involve "abortive state proceedings."

2. In *Daniels v. Allen*, 344 U.S. 443 (1953), the applicant filed his appeal in the highest court in the state system one day late, and thus failed to appeal the question of the constitutionality of his incarceration to the highest state court. The Supreme Court held that this failure barred the applicant's efforts to seek federal habeas relief.

   a. *Daniels* thus imported the "adequate state ground" doctrine to habeas corpus cases.

   b. The Supreme Court has long applied that doctrine to its appellate jurisdiction to review state court decisions. *See* Chapter 8, § IV.E. It provides that a federal court will not review a federal issue arising in a state case if the state court declined to decide the federal issue because the litigant raising it failed to comply with a legitimate state procedural requirement.

3. The Supreme Court abandoned *Daniels*, however, in *Fay v. Noia*, 433 U.S. 72 (1963). In *Fay v. Noia*, the Court held that a state defendant's failure to comply with state procedural requirements would not preclude federal review of his constitutional claims on habeas corpus unless the defendant had consciously by-passed his state judicial remedies. Thus, inadvertent failure to comply with state procedures would not bar federal consideration of a constitutional challenge, regardless of the merits of the state procedural rule.

4. The Supreme Court turned away from *Fay v. Noia* in *Wainwright v. Sykes*, 433 U.S. 72 (1977). In *Wainwright*, the Court held that a state defendant's failure to raise a contemporaneous objection to the admission of certain evidence precluded Supreme Court review of his claim in a habeas proceeding. This was true even though the defendant's failure to raise the contemporaneous objection was not a deliberate by-pass of a state judicial remedy.

   a. The Court indicated that before the reviewing Court would consider the issue, the habeas applicant must first establish both cause for his failure to object and prejudice from admission of the challenged evidence.

   b. Thus, *Wainwright* moved the focus from whether the applicant was guilty of a "deliberate bypass" of state procedures to whether the applicant can show "cause" for and "prejudice" from his failure.

c. The *Wainwright* Court relied heavily on *Francis v. Henderson*, 425 U.S. 536 (1976), in which the Court had effectively applied the adequate state ground doctrine in habeas corpus, without addressing *Fay v. Noia*.

d. Though the Court in *Wainwright* did not expressly overrule *Fay v. Noia*, it criticized the rule of that case. The Court's comments and holding throw serious doubt on the continued validity of *Fay v. Noia*.

e. The Court finally overruled *Fay v. Noia* in *Coleman v. Thompson*, 501 U.S. 722 (1991), which held that even the right to appeal in state court could be forfeited by a procedural lapse and thus not amenable to federal habeas review.

B. Subsequent Developments

1. In *Engle v. Isaac*, 456 U.S. 107 (1982), the Court held that an applicant's failure to object to a jury instruction at trial barred federal habeas relief related to an error in that instruction. The Court rejected an argument that *Wainwright* should be applied only to errors unrelated to fact-finding at the state criminal trial.

2. In *Smith v. Murray*, 477 U.S. 527 (1986), the Court held that *Wainwright* applies in death penalty cases as well as non-capital cases.

3. In *Reed v. Ross*, 468 U.S. 1 (1984), the Court held that the defendant had shown cause to excuse his failure to raise an issue in state proceedings. The case involved a "constitutional claim so novel that its legal basis is not reasonably available to counsel." *Id.* at 16. The defendant had been tried in state court before the Court had rendered decisions that made his constitutional argument feasible.

4. In *Murray v. Carrier*, 477 U.S. 478 (1986), the Court held that a mistake by the applicant's lawyer at the state trial did not constitute a showing of "cause" under *Wainwright*. To constitute cause, the error must amount to ineffective assistance of counsel, and, under the exhaustion doctrine, the issue must first be presented to the state court.

5. In addition to showing cause, the applicant must also satisfy the "prejudice" requirement under *Wainwright* to avoid dismissal.

a. "Prejudice" must be judged in the context of the overall trial.

b. Moreover, showing of a possible prejudice is not sufficient. The applicant must demonstrate that the mistake "worked to his *actual and substantial disadvantage, infecting his entire trial with error of constitutional dimension.*" *United States v. Frady*, 456 U.S. 152, 170 (1982)(emphasis original).

6. In Chapter 8, § 4.E, we discussed *Michigan v. Long*, 463 U.S. 1032 (1983), which addressed the independent and adequate state ground requirement in assessing Supreme Court appellate jurisdiction. In *Harris v. Reed*, 489 U.S. 255 (1989), the Court extended the "plain statement" requirement of *Michigan v. Long* to habeas corpus cases. In *Lambrix v. Singletary*, 520 U.S. 518, 521 (1997), the Court again pointed out the similarity between the two situations, noting that it has "held that the doctrine applies to bar consideration on federal habeas of federal claims that have been defaulted under state law."

   a. In *Long*, the Court held that an independent and adequate state ground would be found only if the state court expressly indicated its intent to rely on state law.

   b. Thus, under *Harris*, a state procedural default will bar consideration by a federal habeas court *only* if the state court last entering judgment in the case expressly stated that its judgment was based upon a state procedural bar.

   c. The *Harris* decision thus creates a presumption that a state decision is based upon federal law, and thus reviewable in a federal habeas proceeding. The presumption is overcome by a plain statement of reliance on state law.

   d. In *Coleman v. Thompson*, 501 U.S. 722, 735 (1991), however, the Court held that the *Harris* presumption (that the state decision is based upon federal law) applies only in cases in which "the decision of the last state court to which the petitioner presented his federal claims . . . fairly appears to rest primarily on federal law or to be interwoven with federal law."

   e. *Coleman* appears to reduce the number of cases in which federal courts will find a procedural bar to habeas relief, because it permits federal courts to proceed only if the state court opinion can be said to rest *primarily* on federal law or be *interwoven* with it.

f. It is difficult to reconcile *Coleman* with *Harris*, which permitted a federal habeas court to proceed so long as there was no plain statement that the state court based its ruling *only* upon state law.

V. Habeas Corpus for Persons in the Custody of the United States

A. Statutory Provisions

1. Federal habeas relief is available for persons held by a state for an act done under federal authority. 28 U.S.C. § 2241(c)(2). Such cases can be removed to federal court, however, under 28 U.S.C. §§ 1442 and 1442a. Thus, there is little need for federal habeas relief in such situations.

2. Federal habeas relief is also available to test the legality of holding a person in the custody of the United States. 28 U.S.C. § 2241(c)(1).

3. Section 2255 permits a prisoner in federal custody under federal law to make a motion to vacate, set aside, or correct her sentence, based upon various grounds, including that the sentence was imposed in violation of the Constitution or federal statute.

   a. The section sets forth procedures by which the prisoner must make the motion.

   b. The section also provides for a one-year statute of limitations and a limitation on second or successive motions similar to the limitation imposed on state prisoners under § 2244. *See* § III.F, above.

   c. The section also provides that an application for habeas corpus "shall not be entertained" if she did not make the motion noted above or if the court denied the motion, unless the motion was "inadequate or ineffective to test the legality of his detention."

4. For many years, persons in custody of the United States Immigration and Naturalization Service challenged that custody by seeking federal habeas relief. The Illegal Immigration Reform and Immigrant Responsibility Act of 1996 (IIRIRA) largely has removed that use of the writ.

   a. The Supreme Court held, however, that resident aliens subject to deportation because of criminal activity may raise challenges to the IIRIRA in federal habeas proceedings.

b. Moreover, by statute, aliens seized at the border may seek habeas corpus.

5. It is not clear whether suspected terrorists subject to trial in special military tribunals established by presidential order in the wake of the attacks of September 11, 2001 have access to federal habeas relief.

B. Some Specific Issues Concerning Habeas Corpus by Persons in Federal Custody

1. Obviously, the issuance of a writ of habeas corpus from a federal court to a federal officer does not implicate the same federalism concerns encountered when the writ concerns someone in state custody.

2. The writ is of limited utility to persons convicted of federal crimes and in custody of the United States. First, it is generally not available before trial, because of the need to exhaust remedies. Second, after conviction, § 2255, discussed in § A, requires that the prisoner make a motion for relief.

3. Habeas corpus can be employed, however, in a variety of non-criminal situations. For example, it may be used to challenge commitment to a mental hospital operated by the federal government or conscription into the military.

XVI

Federal Common Law

■ ANALYSIS

I. Introduction
II. Sources of and Justification for Common Law
    A. Federal Common Law and the Erie *Doctrine*
    B. Federal Common Law and the Rules of Decision Act
    C. The Reach of Federal Common Law
III. Application of Federal Common Law in Specific Areas
    A. Use of Federal Common Law to Fill Statutory "Gaps"
    B. Federal "Proprietary" Interests
    C. International Relations
    D. Admiralty
    E. Interstate Disputes
    F. Interstate Pollution
    G. Enforcement of Constitutional Rights
    H. Claim and Issue Preclusion Effects of Federal Judgments

I. Introduction

Under the Supremacy Clause of the Constitution, Article VI, cl.2, both federal and state courts are required to apply relevant federal law. Thus, if a federal constitutional or statutory provision is on point, it will govern the resolution of the issue. The Rules of Decision Act, 28 U.S.C. § 1652, seems to provide that state law must govern in all other instances. The *Erie* Doctrine is widely cited for the proposition that state law must govern when no federal provision is on point. But the Supreme Court has made clear that there are narrow areas in which federal courts may make federal common law without violating either the Rules of Decision Act or *Erie*. Principally, such federal common law is permitted either to effectuate a congressional intent or to protect a uniquely federal interest. The situations in which federal common law is employed are fairly well defined, but the reasoning of the case law is often difficult to fathom and results are often hard to reconcile.

II. Sources of and Justification for Federal Common Law

A. Federal Common Law and the *Erie* Doctrine

1. For 96 years, under the authority of *Swift v. Tyson*, 41 U.S. 1 (1842), federal courts determined and applied a "general federal common law." The *Swift* doctrine stood for the proposition that federal courts in diversity of citizenship cases were bound to follow state statutory law, but, with the exception of disputes regarding real property and caselaw construing state statutes, not state common law.

   a. The *Swift* doctrine was rooted in the notion that there is only one true common law, and that the federal courts were authorized to divine what it was. The theory was that the state courts would then be guided by the federal courts' instruction.

   b. The *Swift* doctrine denigrated state court ability to determine the common law. It also was misguided in holding that there was only one true common law. Rather, states may take different approaches on common law issues.

   c. *Swift* led to great confusion, because the common law would be one thing in federal court and a different thing in state court.

2. In *Erie Railroad Co. v. Tompkins*, 304 U.S. 64 (1938), the Supreme Court overruled *Swift*.

a. *Erie* held that *Swift* violated the Rules of Decision Act, 28 U.S.C. § 1652, and the Constitution (apparently the Tenth Amendment, which reserves power to the states). Thus, *Swift* was not only a doctrine of arrogance that created confusion, but was an unconstitutional usurpation of state power.

b. *Erie* held that "[t]here is no general federal common law."

3. Nonetheless, the same day it decided *Erie*, the Supreme Court decided *Hinderlider v. La Plata River & Cherry Creek Ditch Co.*, 304 U.S. 92 (1938), in which it concluded that federal common law controlled the issue of whether an interstate stream must be apportioned between two states. Though *Erie* holds that there is no *general* federal common law, it did not do away with *all* forms of federal common law. Thus, there are circumstances in which the creation of federal common law is appropriate. The Court has not been entirely clear, however, in defining those circumstances or in stating the justifications for federal common law.

4. In a widely-cited concurring opinion in *D'Oench, Duhme & Co. v. Federal Deposit Ins. Corp.*, 315 U.S. 447, 469 (1942), Justice Jackson discussed the propriety of federal common law:

The federal courts have no *general* common law, as in a sense they have no general or comprehensive jurisprudence of any kind, because many subjects of private law which bulk large in the traditional common law are ordinarily within the province of the states and not of the federal government. But this is not to say that wherever we have occasion to decide a federal question which cannot be answered from federal statutes alone we may not resort to all of the source materials of the common law, or that when we have fashioned an answer it does not become a part of the federal non-statutory or common law.

B. Federal Common Law and the Rules of Decision Act

1. The Rules of Decision Act, 28 U.S.C. § 1652, which was interpreted in both *Swift* and *Erie*, provides: "The laws of the several states, except where the Constitution or treaties of the United States or Acts of Congress otherwise require or provide, shall be regarded as rules of decision in civil actions in the courts of the United States, in cases where they apply."

2. On its face the Act appears to preclude the creation of federal common law. The Act seems clearly to provide that state law must govern unless the Constitution (or a treaty) or a federal statute is on point.

3. Though the Supreme Court has never directly ruled on this question, it has occasionally reasoned that the creation of federal common law is designed to fill "gaps" left in federal statutory schemes, implying that the common law development is authorized by an act of Congress.

4. Beyond this, as we explore below, there are cases in which the Supreme Court justifies the employment of federal common law with no grounding in statute, but simply because of a federal interest.

C. The Reach of Federal Common Law

1. Where federal common law is appropriate, the Supremacy Clause dictates that it governs in both federal and state courts. *Banco Nacional de Cuba v. Sabbatino*, 376 U.S. 398, 425 (1964).

2. When a claim arises under federal common law, it invokes federal question jurisdiction under 28 U.S.C. § 1331 (for cases "arising under federal law"). *See, e.g., Illinois v. City of Milwaukee*, 406 U.S. 91 (1972).

3. Congress can override federal common law by legislation. *New Jersey v. New York*, 283 U.S. 336, 348 (1931).

4. The Supreme Court has upheld the use of federal common law in specific substantive areas, occasionally using different justifications. The areas include: (a) cases in which statutory gaps require interstitial federal common law; (b) cases in which the federal government acts in a proprietary role, (c) cases involving international relations, (d) cases involving admiralty, (e) cases involving interstate disputes, (f) cases involving interstate pollution, (g) cases involving enforcement of constitutional rights, and (h) regarding claim and issue preclusion of federal judgments. The areas are not hermetically sealed; a given case may implicate more than one justification for the application of federal common law.

III. Application of Federal Common Law in Specific Areas

A. Use of Federal Common Law to Fill Statutory "Gaps"

1. Occasionally, Congress enacts a general regulatory scheme and provides that the federal courts are to develop rules for effectuating it. The most notable example is *Textile Workers Union v. Lincoln Mills*, 353 U.S. 448 (1957), in which a labor union sued to compel an employer to arbitrate

a dispute under a collective bargaining agreement. Section 301 of the Labor Management Relations Act granted federal subject matter jurisdiction over suits for violations of such contracts, but did not provide applicable rules for determining the dispute. The Supreme Court held that the statute "authorizes federal courts to fashion a body of federal law for the enforcement of these collective bargaining agreements. . . . " 353 U.S. at 451.

2. The Supreme Court has made similar conclusions regarding other federal provisions. *See, e.g., Firestone Tire & Rubber Co. v. Bruch*, 489 U.S. 101 (1989)(courts may develop federal common law regarding rights under ERISA plans).

3. A closely related issue is whether the courts will infer a private right of action when Congress has made certain behavior unlawful but not specifically provided a right to sue. The Supreme Court decisions are not completely consistent, and the recent trend seems to be less hospitable to the argument.

Example 1: Plaintiff sued concerning a merger of a corporation in which he had held stock, allegedly accomplished by use of false and misleading proxy statement. A federal statute provided that "[i]t shall be unlawful" to employ fraud in the use of a proxy statement but did not provide for a private right of action. The Supreme Court concluded that the plaintiff could proceed. A purpose of the statute was to protect investors from deceptive disclosures in proxy materials, "which certainly implies the availability of judicial relief where necessary to achieve that result." *J.I. Case v. Borak*, 377 U.S. 426, 432 (1964).

Example 2: A federal statute provided for criminal penalties for corporations which violated federal election laws. Plaintiff sought to assert a private right of action under the statute. The Supreme Court refused to infer a right of action. It set forth the following factors as relevant to the inquiry: (1) whether plaintiff is one of a class for whose "especial benefit" the statute was passed; (2) whether there is any indication of a legislative intent to allow a private remedy; (3) whether an implied right of action would be consistent with the underlying purpose of the legislation; and (4) whether the claim is one "traditionally relegated to state law, in an area basically the concern of the States, so that it would be inappropriate to infer a cause of action based solely on federal law. *Cort v. Ash*, 422 U.S. 66 (1975).

Example 3: Applying the four-part test from *Cort v. Ash*, the Supreme Court held that there is an implied right of action to enforce Title IX of the Education Amendments of 1972, which prohibits discrimination in education on the basis of sex. *Cannon v. University of Chicago*, 441 U.S. 677 (1979).

Example 4: The Parental Kidnaping Prevention Act requires states to enforce child custody determinations entered in the courts of another state, so long as the judgment is consistent with provisions of the Act. A California court decreed that Husband was to have custody of Child, while a Louisiana court decreed that Wife was to have custody of Child. Husband sued in federal court, and attempted to assert a claim under the Act. The Act did not contain an express right of action, and the Supreme Court refused to infer a right of action. It held that the "context, language, and history of the [Act] make out a conclusive case against inferring a cause of action in federal court to determine which of two conflicting state custody decrees is valid." *Thompson v. Thompson*, 484 U.S. 174, 187 (1988).

4. The Supreme Court appeared for many years to be far more willing to infer a private right of action to enforce constitutional provisions than statutory provisions. As discussed in § G, below, however, more recently the Court has been more reluctant to infer a right of action even as to a constitutional provision.

B. Federal "Proprietary" Interests

1. The federal government often has proprietary interests in matters that end up in litigation. For example, when the United States issues or holds commercial paper, enters a contract, or oversees a regulatory program, by definition, any dispute involves a federal interest. Such interests may be so "uniquely federal" that federal law, including federal common law, will preempt state law.

2. The leading case in this area is *Clearfield Trust Co. v. United States*, 318 U.S. 363 (1943), in which the United States issued a check that was subse-

quently stolen and cashed. The question was what law governed the issue of liability for the stolen funds. The Supreme Court concluded that federal common law applied, and emphasized two points.

    a. First, "[w]hen the United States disburses its funds or pays its debts, it is exercising a constitutional function or power. . . . The authority to issue the check had its origin in the Constitution and the statutes of the United States . . . . . " 318 U.S. at 366–67.

    b. Second, the Court concluded that a uniform federal standard for such issues was necessary to ensure that the federal government's rights and duties were uniform, and did not vary from state to state.

3. Many commentators have criticized *Clearfield*.

    a. First, the doctrine is potentially extremely broad, because every time the federal government does anything, the act presumably "ha[s] its origin in the Constitution and the statutes of the United States." Nothing in *Clearfield* appears to require grounding in some specific federal constitutional or statutory provision.

    b. Second, the Court's expressed concern for uniformity in the interstate commercial dealings of the United States may lead one to question why the government should be any better off than a private interstate commercial enterprise, which routinely must deal with the potential inconsistent application of the laws of different states.

4. *Clearfield* justified resort to federal common law, at least in part, on the need to avoid having the federal proprietary policies subject to different state laws. In addition, federal common law is justified when state law conflicts with federal policy.

Example: State law provided that landowners who sold their property retained underlying mineral rights indefinitely. Because this principle conflicted with a federal interest in protecting migratory birds, as embodied in the Migratory Bird Conservation Act, uniform federal common law governed agreements by which the federal government acquired land from private parties pursuant to the Act. *United States v. Little Lake Misere Land Co.*, 412 U.S. 580 (1973).

5. On the other hand, the fact that federal common law governs an issue does not necessarily require the application of a uniform federal stan-

dard. Though the Supreme Court in *Clearfield* did espouse a uniform federal common law, in other cases it has made clear that it may adopt state law as the federal common law standard.

Example: The Small Business Administration, a federal agency, makes a loan to a Texas family. The family defaults on the note and the SBA forecloses on the mortgage and sues the family for the deficiency. The wife argues that under the Texas doctrine of "coverture," she lacked the capacity to bind herself contractually for the SBA loan. The United States argued that federal common law, rather than Texas law, should apply on the question of the wife's capacity to contract. The Supreme Court held that federal common law governed the issue, but adopted the Texas "coverture" rule as the federal standard. The Court distinguished *Clearfield* because the SBA loan contract was not part of a nationwide scheme, and Texas had a strong interest in applying its own law of domestic relations. *United States v. Yazell*, 382 U.S. 341 (1966).

6. In *United States v. Kimbell Foods, Inc.*, 440 U.S. 715 (1979), the Court reaffirmed the *Clearfield* holding "that federal law governs questions involving the rights of the United States arising under nationwide federal programs." It developed a balancing test, however, to determine whether state law was to be adopted as the federal standard in such cases.

   a. The Court balanced the need for uniformity and the danger that state law would "frustrate specific objectives of the federal program" against "the extent to which application of a federal rule would disrupt commercial relationships predicated on state law."

   b. The underlying tone of the Court's opinion in *Kimbell Foods* indicated it would be rare that state law would *not* be adopted as the federal standard. This view represents a substantial retreat from one of the major justifications for federal common law in *Clearfield*, namely, the need for a uniform federal standard.

7. The Supreme Court may have revitalized the concept of an independent federal common law of "proprietary interests," however, in *West Virginia v. United States*, 479 U.S. 305 (1987). There the Court held that uniform federal common law controlled the issue of a state's liability to the United States for prejudgment interest.

8. In the cases discussed above, the United States or an agency was a party to the litigation. It is conceivable that the Supreme Court will apply federal common law, however, even when neither the United States nor one of its agents is a party to the case, so long as important federal interests are implicated. The Court seems reluctant, however, to reach such a result.

Example 1: A bank sues a private party for conversion of bonds issued by a federal agency. The case invokes diversity of citizenship jurisdiction. Payment on the bonds is guaranteed by the United States. One of the main issues is which party has the burden of proof on the issue of defendant's good faith in receiving the bonds. The Supreme Court held that state law controls the issue. On the other hand, however, federal law controls the issue of whether the bonds could be deemed "overdue." *Bank of America National Trust & Savings Association v. Parnell*, 352 U.S. 29 (1956).

Example 2: Survivors of deceased air passengers bring a diversity of citizenship case against a municipality, arguing that they are third-party beneficiaries of a contract between the municipality and the Federal Aviation Administration. Under the contract, the municipality agreed to maintain activities around the airport compatible with normal aircraft operations—a contract that was allegedly breached by the maintenance of a garbage dump near the airport, which attracted birds that were ingested into the aircraft's engines and causing the crash. The Supreme Court held that the right of one plaintiff to sue third-party beneficiaries and the interpretation of the contract are governed by state, rather than federal, law. *Miree v. DeKalb County*, 433 U.S. 25 (1977).

Example 3: Plaintiff files a libel suit against a former Navy officer because of alleged statements about plaintiff's job performance. The Supreme Court held that whether the defamatory statements were privileged is controlled by federal, rather than state, law, because the case implicates important federal interests. *Howard v. Lyons*, 360 U.S. 593 (1959).

Example 4: The estate of a United States Marine helicopter pilot who drowned when his helicopter crashed filed a diversity of citizenship case alleging, under state tort law, that the defendant, a private company, had defectively designed the emergency escape-hatch system. The defendant invoked the federally-recognized common law "military contractor" defense. The Supreme Court held that the federal common law defense preempted state tort law. *Boyle v. United Technologies Corp.*, 487 U.S. 500 (1988). The Court seemed to establish a two-part inquiry: (1) whether the action involved uniquely federal interests, and, if so, (2) whether there is a significant conflict between the federal interest and state law that would otherwise apply.

Example 5: *Kamen v. Kemper Financial Services, Inc.*, 500 U.S. 90 (1991), involved a shareholder's derivative suit for securities fraud under federal law. The Supreme Court concluded that federal common law permitted the plaintiff to proceed without making a demand on the corporation if the demand was futile. Futility is to be governed by federal law. Because the claim was federal "any common law rule necessary to effectuate a private cause of action under that statute is necessarily federal in character." *Id.* at 98. Because corporate law is an area in which private parties expected their relationship to be governed by state law, however, state law would be adopted as the federal standard; such adoption would not be inconsistent with the federal policy underlying the claim.

9. Moreover, there seems to be some recent movement away from equating federal agencies with the United States. For example, in *O'Melveny & Myers v. Federal Deposit Ins. Corp.*, 512 U.S. 79 (1994), the Supreme Court rejected the argument that federal common law should apply because the FDIC was a party to the litigation. The Court said, bluntly, "the FDIC is not the United States."

   a. *O'Melveny* may indicate a restrictive view toward the use of federal common law in cases involving federal agencies in which their day-to-day operations are not implicated directly.

   b. Some commentators see *O'Melveny* as espousing a significantly restricted view of the availability of the federal common law authority of the federal courts.

C. International Relations

1. In *Banco Nacional de Cuba v. Sabbatino*, 376 U.S. 398 (1964), the Supreme

Court held that common law issues implicating the foreign relations of the United States are to be controlled by federal, rather than state, common law.

    a. Specifically, the decision held that federal common law applies in a diversity of citizenship case to determine whether Cuban expropriation of a shipment of sugar was protected by the "act of state doctrine." Under that doctrine, courts in the United States will not inquire into the validity of a public act of a foreign sovereign committed within its own borders.

    b. Though the claim asserted arose under state law, the Court reasoned that the act of state defense raised issues "that . . . are uniquely federal in nature." *Id.* at 424. It noted that if "state courts are left free to formulate their own rules, the purposes behind the [act of state] doctrine could be as effectively undermined as if there had been no federal pronouncement on the subject." *Id.*

2. Some commentators criticize the use of federal common law in this area because, unlike cases falling under the *Clearfield* heading, there is no conceivable *statutory* basis for authorizing the creation of federal common law.

3. Though the Court recognized the relevance of federal common law in this area, it also acknowledged that ultimately the decisions concerning foreign relations are for Congress and the Executive. Therefore, the political branches may supercede federal common law developed in the field of foreign relations.

D. Admiralty

1. It is well established that federal courts have authority to develop a federal common law of admiralty. The power is thought to derive from the provision of Article III, § 2, extending the federal "judicial power" to "all cases of admiralty and maritime jurisdiction." Thus, admiralty is an area in which the federal courts can espouse federal common law despite the lack of statutory authorization.

2. One may question, however, why the extension of the federal judicial power to such cases logically leads to the conclusion that federal courts possess authority to develop substantive federal common law. After all, the federal "judicial power" also extends to diversity of citizenship cases,

but in *Erie* the Court made clear that federal courts lacked authority to develop substantive common law in cases falling under this jurisdictional heading.

3. Originally, federal court authority to create a federal common law of admiralty did not apply to inland waterways. However, by 1851, the Supreme Court had extended the authority to include these waters.

4. Federal courts do not develop a distinct federal common law standard in every admiralty case. Rather, the Supreme Court has employed a balancing test to decide whether federal common law should supercede otherwise applicable state law. It is not clear how the Court has drawn the line it has in the various cases, which have led to substantial confusion and uncertainty.

Example 1: In *Southern Pacific Co. v. Jensen,* 244 U.S. 205 (1917), the Supreme Court overturned a state workers' compensation award to relatives of a deceased stevedore because use of state law would undermine the uniformity of federal maritime law. This view has since been modified significantly, allowing state law a significant, albeit uncertain, role in the maritime area.

Example 2: The Supreme Court held that state law requiring unemployment compensation contributions from employers of individuals working on navigable waters may be applied, even though the cases could conceivably have been controlled by federal common law. *Standard Dredging Corp. v. Murphy,* 319 U.S. 306 (1943).

Example 3: On the other hand, the Court held that federal common law, rather than state law, applied to a suit brought by a crew member's guest injured onboard a ship berthed in a New York pier. *Kermarec v. Compagnie Generale Transatlantique,* 358 U.S. 625 (1959).

Example 4: The Supreme Court held that Texas law applied to the issue of insurance coverage for a houseboat fire occurring on an inland lake between Texas and Oklahoma, even though the case fell within the federal admiralty jurisdiction. *Wilburn Boat Co. v. Fireman's Fund Insurance Co.,* 348 U.S. 310 (1955).

Example 5: The Court also held, however, that federal common law applied to a diversity suit between a seaman and a shipowner

FEDERAL COMMON LAW

for breach of an oral agreement to assume liability for improper medical treatment. *Kossick v. United Fruit Co.*, 365 U.S. 731 (1961).

Example 6: In *Exxon Corp. v. Central Gulf Lines, Inc.*, 500 U.S. 603 (1991), the Court rejected a *per se* rule excluding agency contracts from admiralty jurisdiction. Instead, "lower courts should look to the subject matter of the agency contract and determine whether the services performed under the contract were maritime in nature." *Id.* at 612.

E. Interstate Disputes

1. In *Hinderlider v. La Plata River & Cherry Creek Ditch Co.*, 304 U.S. 92 (1938), the Supreme Court adopted federal common law to determine how an interstate stream should be apportioned between two states.

2. Federal law must be used to resolve such disputes between states to avoid the friction that would result from choosing one state's law over the other's.

F. Interstate Pollution

1. In *Illinois v. City of Milwaukee*, 406 U.S. 91 (1972) (*Milwaukee I*) a state sued municipalities in a neighboring state regarding their pollution of Lake Michigan. Federal legislation evinced a federal concern with pollution but did not provide the remedy sought by the state. Nonetheless, the Court held that federal common law could provide such a remedy, and that a claim seeking that federal common law relief would arise under federal law and invoke subject matter jurisdiction under § 1331. The Court explained: "[i]t is not uncommon for federal courts to fashion federal law where federal rights are concerned." *Id.* at 101.

2. The federal interest and federal rights were created, according to the Court, by congressional enactment of numerous laws generally concerning pollution of interstate waters.

3. Commentators criticized *Milwaukee I* as authorizing inroads on the Rules of Decision Act by invoking some vague notion of a federal interest or federal right.

4. Congress passed further legislation after the decision in *Milwaukee I*. In *City of Milwaukee v. Illinois and Michigan*, 451 U.S. 304 (1981) (*Milwaukee*

II), the Court held that this further legislation, the Federal Water Pollution Act Amendments of 1972, displaced federal common law. Thus, federal common law could not be created to impose standards more stringent than those imposed by the federal statute.

G. Enforcement of Constitutional Rights

1. In *Bivens v. Six Unknown Named Agents of Federal Bureau of Narcotics*, 403 U.S. 388 (1971), the Supreme Court recognized a private damage remedy for a violation of the Fourth Amendment prohibition against unreasonable searches and seizures, even though the constitutional provision, by its terms, makes no reference to a damage remedy (or any other means of enforcement), and Congress had not provided a statutory remedy.

2. The Court reasoned that "the absence of affirmative action by Congress" did not bar judicial creation of the damage remedy when the Court deemed the remedy an appropriate means of enforcing the constitutional right.

3. More recently, the Court has cut back on the recognition of a *Bivens* action. *Bivens* and the more restrictive recent cases are discussed in detail at Chapter 14, § V.

H. Claim and Issue Preclusion Effects of Federal Judgments

1. The claim or issue preclusive effect of a federal judgment is not addressed by the full faith and credit provision of the Constitution (Article IV § 1) or by the Full Faith and Credit Act (28 U.S.C. § 1738). The issue is to be determined by federal common law.

2. The leading case on this point, *Semtek International, Inc. v. Lockheed Martin Corp.*, 531 U.S. 497 (2001) is discussed in Chapter 17, § II.C.

XVII

Claim and Issue Preclusion in the Federal System

■ ANALYSIS

I. Introduction
II. Full Faith and Credit and Related Common Law Doctrines
   A. Constitutional Provision
   B. Statutory Provision—the Full Faith and Credit Act
   C. Situations Covered by Neither Full Faith and Credit Provision

I. Introduction

In your course in Civil Procedure, you studied the doctrines of claim and issue preclusion, also known, respectively, as res judicata and collateral estoppel. Both doctrines preclude litigation in a second case because a valid final judgment has been entered. That valid final judgment may carry either claim or issue preclusive effect. Claim preclusion prohibits a claimant from asserting the same claim against the same defendant twice. Issue preclusion prohibits re-litigation of an issue that was litigated and determined in an earlier case. Here, we are concerned with the application of claim and issue preclusion when a judgment is entered by a court in a different judicial system from the court that must adjudicate a second case. The problem implicates constitutional and statutory principles of full faith and credit as well as common law principles regarding finality of litigation. For discussion of a related topic, the *Rooker-Feldman* doctrine, *see* Chapter 14, § H.8.

II. Full Faith and Credit and Related Common Law Doctrines

A. Constitutional Provision

1. Article IV, § 1, of the Constitution provides, in part, that "Full Faith and Credit shall be given in each State to the . . . judicial Proceedings of every other State."

2. This provision applies only to cases in state courts, and thus does not apply to proceedings in the federal courts.

    a. It requires the state courts in one state to accord "full faith and credit" to the judgment of the courts of another state.

    b. This generally means that the court of the second state must apply the claim and issue preclusion rules (rules of res judicata and collateral estoppel) of the state that entered the judgment in the first case.

    Example: A state court in Connecticut enters a valid final judgment in a case between P and D. A second case is brought in New Jersey, and the issue is whether the Connecticut judgment has a claim or issue preclusion effect in the case pending in New Jersey. Under the constitutional provision for full faith and credit, the court in New Jersey must apply the claim and issue preclusion rules of Connecticut. This requirement ensures that New Jersey gives the same effect to the judgment that the rendering state, Connecticut, would give it.

B. Statutory Provision—The Full Faith and Credit Act

1. 28 U.S.C. § 1738, known as the Full Faith and Credit Act, provides, in part, that "judicial proceedings" of a "State, Territory, or Possession of the United States" shall have "the same full faith and credit in every court within the United States and its Territories and Possessions as they have by law or usage in the courts of each State, Territory, or Possession from which they are taken."

2. This provision applies not only in the state-to-state situation discussed in § A, above, but in the situation in which the first judgment is entered in a state court and the second case is pending in a federal court.

   a. The federal court is required to give the state court judgment the same "full faith and credit" as would the state court that rendered the judgment.

   b. This generally means that the federal court of the second state must apply the claim and issue preclusion rules (rules of res judicata and collateral estoppel) of the state that entered the judgment in the first case.

   Example: A state court in Connecticut enters a valid final judgment in a case between P and D. A second case is brought in federal court in New Jersey, and the issue is whether the Connecticut judgment has a claim preclusion or issue preclusion effect in the case pending in federal court in New Jersey. Under § 1738, the federal court in New Jersey must apply the claim and issue preclusion rules of Connecticut.

3. The requirement of § 1738—that the federal court give claim and issue preclusive effects to a state court judgment if the courts of that state would—occasionally leads to imponderable questions.

   Example: Doctors sued a professional association in state court, alleging they were denied membership in the association in violation of state law. After the state court entered judgment, the doctors sued the association in federal court, alleging that their exclusion violated federal antitrust laws. The federal antitrust claims invoke exclusive federal jurisdiction, and thus could not have been asserted in the state court case. Nonetheless, the Supreme Court held that the federal court had to determine whether state law of the judgment-rendering state would find that the doctors violated rules of claim preclusion. It's a strange undertaking: the state court must determine whether failure to assert a claim *that could not have been asserted in state court in the first case* meant that a second case—on that claim—should be dismissed under claim preclusion. *Marrese v. American Academy of Orthopaedic Surgeons*, 470 U.S. 373 (1985).

4. The operation of § 1738 may result in the operation of claim or issue preclusion to preclude litigation of issues within the exclusive jurisdiction of the federal courts.

   Example: A plaintiff class action in state court in Delaware asserted state-law claims arising out of a tender offer and corporate acquisition. The class action was settled on terms that included a release of any federal claims concerning the tender offer and acquisition. The settlement was approved by the Delaware courts and resulted in entry of a valid final judgment. Some of the class members filed a second case in federal court, asserting that the tender offer and acquisition violated federal securities laws. Such claims invoke exclusive federal jurisdiction and could not have been asserted in the Delaware state court proceeding. Nonetheless, the Supreme Court held that because Delaware law would ascribe claim preclusive effect to the class settlement judgment, a federal court must do so also. Thus, class members who did not opt out were barred from asserting their federal claims in federal court. The Supreme Court emphasized that § 1738 required this result and that federal securities law did not repeal the application of the full faith and credit provision. *Matsushita Elec. Indus. Co. v. Epstein*, 516 U.S. 367 (1996).

5. Courts refuse to hold that a federal statute supersedes the requirement of § 1738 unless the statute clearly states the congressional desire to supersede its operation.

   a. Federal securities laws did not supersede, even partially, the operation of § 1738; the state court judgment releasing federal claims that would have invoked exclusive federal jurisdiction was entitled to full faith and credit. Nothing in the federal law evinced a congressional intent to contravene the rules of preclusion or to prevent state court litigants from voluntarily releasing federal claims in approved settlements. *Id.*

b. 42 U.S.C. § 1983, which allows suits to vindicate federal rights violated under color of state law (*see* Chapter 14), does not repeal the Full Faith and Credit Act. Thus, federal courts must provide issue preclusive effect to state judgments in suits brought in state court under § 1983. *Allen v. McCurry,* 449 U.S. 90 (1980).

c. A federal court in a § 1983 suit must give res judicata effect to a state judgment, even on issues which could have been raised in an earlier state court proceeding but were not. *Migra v. Warren City School District Board of Education,* 465 U.S. 75 (1984).

d. Similarly, Title VII of the 1964 Civil Rights Act, prohibiting discrimination in employment, does not repeal the Full Faith and Credit Act. *Kremer v. Chemical Construction Corp.,* 456 U.S. 461 (1982).

C. Situations Covered by Neither Full Faith and Credit Provision

1. Neither the constitutional nor the statutory provisions for full faith and credit applies when the initial judgment is entered in *federal* court. Both apply to define the credit due a judgment entered by a *state* court.

2. Nonetheless, the courts have clearly established that a second court—state or federal—must apply federal claim and issue preclusion law if the first judgment was entered by a federal court in a federal question case. *Heck v. Humphrey,* 512 U.S. 477, 488 n.9 (1994)("State courts are bound to apply federal rules in determining the preclusive effect of federal-court decisions on issues of federal law.").

3. A more difficult issue is whether a second court must apply federal claim and issue preclusion law if the first judgment was entered by a federal court in a diversity of citizenship case. Lower courts split on the issue, with some applying federal preclusion law and some applying preclusion law of the state in which the federal court entering the judgment sat.

4. The Supreme Court addressed this issue in *Semtek International, Inc. v. Lockheed Martin Corp.*, 531 U.S. 497 (2001). A federal court in California, exercising diversity jurisdiction, entered a judgment in favor of the defendant on the basis of the California statute of limitations. Plaintiff brought a second case in state court in Maryland, which had a longer statute of limitations, and the question was whether the case should be dismissed under claim preclusion. The specific issue was whether a dismissal on the basis of the statute of limitations was "on the merits," which is a requirement for the application of claim preclusion.

a. Federal Rule of Civil Procedure 41(b), concerning involuntary dismissals, provides that all such dismissals are to be treated as "on the merits" unless they were based upon jurisdiction, venue, or indispensable parties. Because the dismissal in *Semtek* was based upon none of those, the defendant argued that the dismissal was "on the merits" and claim preclusive.

b. The Supreme Court held that Rule 41(b) simply states a rule for determining whether a case can be re-asserted in the federal courts, and does not embody preclusion doctrine.

c. Instead, federal common law governs the effect of a judgment entered by a federal court exercising diversity of citizenship jurisdiction.

d. Although federal common law governed the question, the Supreme Court, noting that there was no need for national uniformity on this question, held that the federal common law would apply the law of the state in which that federal court sat. Because California law provided that a dismissal based upon the statute of limitations was not "on the merits," the judgment of the federal court in California did not carry claim preclusive effect.

e. The Supreme Court in *Semtek* can be accused of having it both ways. On the one hand, it held that federal common law will govern the question of the preclusive effect of a judgment entered by a federal court. On the other, it held that the federal common law will adopt state law as its content, unless there is some reason not to. Thus, the Court retains the flexibility to adopt state law on preclusion in such cases when it wants to and to ignore it when it feels there is a justification.

REVIEW QUESTIONS (PART III; CHAPTERS 9–17)

True or False Questions

1. **T or F** When Congress is silent on the issue of whether state courts shall have jurisdiction to enforce claims created by a federal statute, it is presumed that state and federal courts have concurrent jurisdiction.

2. **T or F** Congress may condition a state's participation in federal programs on the state's waiver of Eleventh Amendment immunity.

3. **T of F** The doctrine of *Younger v. Harris* applies only to ongoing state criminal proceedings.

4. **T or F** When the federal government exercises one of its constitutional powers, any issue arising in a suit concerning the exercise of those powers that is not controlled by statute is to be decided as a matter of federal common law.

5. **T or F** The Constitution requires a federal court to give full faith and credit to a valid final judgment of a state court.

6. **T or F** Under all forms of abstention, the plaintiff may ultimately return to federal court for a final adjudication.

7. **T or F** A state prosecution may be removed to federal court pursuant to the civil rights removal statute if the state prosecution will preclude the defendant from enforcing any federal right.

8. **T or F** Congress may abrogate the Eleventh Amendment immunity of states directly only by legislation passed under § 5 of the Fourteenth Amendment.

9. **T or F** Under *Ex Parte Young*, a federal court may enter an order having an adverse impact on the treasury of a state, so long as the order is prospective in nature.

10. **T or F** A federal court may issue an injunction prohibiting someone from instituting litigation in state court without satisfying one of the exceptions of the Anti–Injunction Statute.

11. **T or F** Though generally state courts are obligated to adjudicate suits under federal law, the Supreme Court has recognized "valid excuses" which allow the state courts to decline jurisdiction of such suits.

12. **T or F** Though § 1983 is silent as to whether a federal court can issue an injunction against state court proceedings, the Supreme Court held that it constitutes an "expressly authorized" exception to the Anti–Injunction Statute.

13. **T or F** The "in aid of jurisdiction" exception to the Anti–Injunction Statute has been read broadly to permit federal courts to enjoin parallel state court cases and thus avoid overlapping *in personam* litigation in the state and federal courts.

14. **T or F** Because § 1983 is an "express" exception to the Anti–Injunction Statute, a federal court may issue an injunction against state court proceedings whenever the equitable requirements for an injunction are satisfied.

15. **T or F** A plaintiff who alleges that federal law enforcement officers burst into her home without a warrant and subjected her home to an illegal search and seizure in violation of the Fourth Amendment may sue the officers in their individual capacity under § 1983.

16. **T or F** A plaintiff who alleges that municipal law enforcement officers burst into her home without a warrant and subjected her home to an illegal search and seizure in violation of the Fourth Amendment may sue the officers in their official capacity and may sue the municipality which employed them.

17. **T or F** Section 1983 cannot be used to vindicate a claim that officers acting under color of state law violated the plaintiff's state law rights.

18. **T or F** In a habeas corpus proceeding in federal court, in which a state prisoner challenges her confinement, the federal court is free to ignore state court findings of fact whenever the federal court disagrees with the state court's findings based upon the record.

19. **T or F** Under current habeas corpus doctrine, a state prisoner's failure to satisfy a state procedural basis for asserting her claim in state court will bar federal habeas relief only if the prisoner deliberately bypassed the state remedy.

20. T or F Plaintiff is a prisoner in state court. If she sues under § 1983 for deprivation of federal rights, she is not required to exhaust state remedies, but if she seeks federal habeas, she must exhaust state remedies.

Essay Question

A tenured public school teacher was fired for teaching the use of birth control devices in a high school sexual education class. The firing was based upon a state statute providing that a tenured teacher may be removed for "teaching matter not in the best interests of the students." The statute provides that the initial removal decision is to be made by the school principal, and that an appeal may be taken to an administrative review board, consisting of several state-appointed educators. The review board's decision, according to the statute, may receive very limited judicial review in the state courts.

Instead of pursuing the state statutory procedure, the teacher filed suit in federal district court, challenging the state statute as a violation of his first amendment right of free expression because it was unconstitutionally vague. He seeks an injunction, ordering the principal to reinstate him. The lawyer for the principal asserts that the federal court should abstain on grounds of *Pullman*, *Burford* and *Younger* abstention. Discuss how the court should rule on each of these contentions.

*

APPENDIX A

Answers to Review Questions

■ PART I (CHAPTERS 1–3)

1. **False.** The plaintiff has not suffered injury in fact, which is a prerequisite for standing. *See* Chapter I, § 4.B.

2. **False.** Because the plaintiff has actually been threatened with prosecution, there is a live controversy. The plaintiff need not wait until the prosecution has actually been filed to bring a federal court challenge to the constitutionality of such a prosecution. The case is fit for judicial decision and it would cause hardship on the individual to withhold judicial consideration of the issue. *See* Chapter 1, § V.B.

3. **True.** The political question doctrine does not apply to questions concerning the constitutionality of *state* governmental action, which is what is involved in this question. The doctrine applies only to political questions involving the *federal* government. Thus, the case can proceed. It is not barred by the political question doctrine. *See* Chapter 1, § VII.A.5.

4. **False.** However broad Congress's Article III power may be, it can be limited by other provisions of the Constitution, particularly those contained in the

amendments. The law in question would clearly violate the Due Process Clause of the Fifth Amendment, which is held to incorporate an equal protection component. Thus, a statute denying certain groups access to the federal courts would be unconstitutional. *See* Chapter 2, § VI.A.

5. False. Though the Supreme Court's existence is mandated by Article III, its appellate jurisdiction is granted subject to Congress's power to impose regulations and make exceptions. *See* Chapter 2, § II.A & B and § V.A.

6. True. The principle of separation of powers has been construed to mean that even though Congress may exclude the jurisdiction of the Article III federal courts completely, it may not undermine their integrity by ordering them to act in an unconstitutional manner. *See* Chapter 2, § VI.C.

7. False. The Supreme Court has viewed administrative agencies simply as adjuncts to the Article III federal courts. Because the ultimate judicial power remains in an Article III court, adjudication by administrative agencies does not run afoul of constitutional limitations. *See* Chapter 3, § IV.B.

8. True. Though the Supreme Court has not addressed this specific question, it has held that the political question doctrine will be invoked to prevent a federal court from possibly embarrassing the executive branch in the conduct of foreign policy. *See* Chapter 1, § VII.C.2.

9. False. An organization's special interest in an area is an insufficient basis on which to establish standing. To have standing, a plaintiff must have suffered some injury in fact. On the facts of this question, there is no such injury. *See* Chapter 1, § IV.A.

10. True. Though the mootness doctrine is said to derive from the Article III requirement of a "case" or "controversy," the Supreme Court has on occasion developed exceptions, largely because of the public interest in having the legal issue resolved. *See* Chapter 1, § VI.B.

11. True. Under the holding of *Crowell v. Benson*, the principle of separation of powers dictates that some Article III court have final power to rule upon constitutional questions. While the case has been much undermined, that is largely because the case concerned property rights, which are not accorded as much weight today as they were at the time of the decision. The general principle remains sound. Note, however, that the Article III review of constitutional facts need not be *de novo* review. *See* Chapter 3, § III.C.7 and § IV.B.2.

12. False. While there is language in *McCardle* which seems to justify broad congressional power over the Supreme Court's appellate jurisdiction, the Court there also emphasized that Congress had not totally removed all procedural avenues to obtain Supreme Court review. The Court reaffirmed the principle in *Felker v. Turpin*, 518 U.S. 651 (1996). *See* Chapter 2, § V.B.

13. False. Though the Due Process Clause has usually been construed to require an independent forum prior to the deprivation of property or liberty, it has never been construed to require any level of appellate review. *See* Chapter 2, § VI.B.3.

14. False. Although three justices in *Tidewater* accepted this view, a majority of the Court rejected it. *See* Chapter 2, § VII.D.2.

15. True. Such a practice would violate the "case or controversy" requirement of Article III. *See* Chapter 1, § III.A.

Essay Question

Proposal 1: Of all the proposals, this is the most clearly unconstitutional. While Article III may grant Congress power to limit federal court jurisdiction, it says nothing about congressional authority to employ its jurisdiction-curbing authority to overrule Supreme Court constitutional determinations. Under *Crowell v. Benson*, the courts, independent of political pressures, must make the final determination of the meaning of constitutional provisions.

Proposal 2: Under traditional thinking, this proposal would be constitutional. It is widely thought that, because Congress need not have created lower federal courts, it may abolish them. Therefore, the thinking goes, Congress may take the lesser step of limiting the jurisdiction of the lower federal courts. Similarly, Congress is thought to have broad power under the Exceptions Clause of Article III to regulate the Supreme Court's appellate jurisdiction. The due process right to an independent forum is not violated, because the state courts remain available. However, certain modern theories, such as the "essential functions" thesis, would, if accepted, render the proposal unconstitutional.

Proposal 3: Such a statute would be unconstitutional, because it deprives all judicial fora of their function as enforcer and interpreter of the Constitution and constitutional rights.

Proposal 4: This statute poses difficult questions concerning the interrelation of due process and the principle of separation of powers. Traditionally, the courts have assumed that while due process requires an independent adjudicator, such independence need not include the Article III protections of judicial tenure and salary. Thus, it is conceivable that a non-Article III legislative court could meet the due process requirement of independence. While of course such a court does not meet the requirement of Article III independence, it is questionable whether that Article can be construed to *require* the use of an Article III court. *Crowell v. Benson* does seem to require such a result (or at least the use of state courts), but the basis in Article III for such a position has never been fully explained.

■ PART II (CHAPTERS 4–8)

1. False. While the operative language of the statutory and constitutional provisions are identical, Supreme Court has interpreted the statutory language more narrowly than that of the Constitution. The relatively narrow construction of the statute avoids inundation of the federal courts with federal question cases. *See* Chapter 4, § II.A. and § III.

2. False. Each claim in federal court must invoke a basis of federal subject matter jurisdiction. The claim against D–1 invokes federal question jurisdiction. The claim against D–2 does not invoke federal question jurisdiction (because it arises under state law) and does not invoke diversity of citizenship jurisdiction (because P and D–2 are citizens of the same state). Nonetheless, the claim against D–2 arises from the same transaction as the federal question claim against D–1 and thus invokes supplemental jurisdiction under 28 U.S.C. § 1367(a). Nothing in that section limits its application to exclusive federal question cases. *See* Chapter 6, § IV.B.

3. False. Section 1367(a) grants supplemental jurisdiction to the full extent of Article III in all cases. However, § 1367(b) cuts back on that grant in diversity of citizenship cases. Thus, the exercise of supplemental jurisdiction is narrower in diversity of citizenship cases than in federal question cases. The restrictions on supplemental jurisdiction in diversity cases were imposed in an effort to avoid overruling the complete diversity rule. *See* Chapter 6, §§ IV.B & C.

4. False. In establishing the complete diversity requirement in *Strawbridge v. Curtiss*, Chief Justice John Marshall failed to make clear whether he was construing the constitutional or the statutory provision concerning diversity of citizenship. More recently, however, the Supreme Court has made it absolutely clear that the requirement is a matter of statutory (and not constitutional) construction. As such, it can be overturned by Congress. *See* Chapter 5, § III.A.

5. True. By statute, 28 U.S.C. § 1332(c)(1) a corporation is deemed to be a citizen of the states in which it is incorporated and the one state in which it has its principal place of business. Because most corporations incorporate in only one state, and because there can never be more than one principal place of business, a corporation generally is a citizen of, at most, two states. *See* Chapter 5, § III.C. On the other hand, as recently as 1990, in *Carden v. Arkoma Associates*, the Supreme Court refused reaffirmed the longstanding rule that an unincorporated association partakes of the citizenship of all its members. Thus, for example, if a partnership had members who are citizens of all 50 states, the partnership would be deemed a citizen of all 50 states. *See* Chapter 5, § III.D.

6. **False.** The Supreme Court has held that certain matters falling within the Court's original jurisdiction may be adjudicated by the lower federal courts. *See* Chapter 8, § III.

7. **False.** While the Supreme Court's refusal to review non-federal *substantive* bases for a state decision is based upon the desire to avoid making an advisory opinion, the *procedural* branch of the "independent and adequate state ground" doctrine is based upon grounds of comity and federalism. *See* Chapter 8, § IV.E.

8. **True.** Under the "collateral order" doctrine of *Cohen v. Beneficial Industrial Loan Corp.*, the Court has authorized appeals that could not be deemed technically "final," because the case in the state court has in no way been completed. Also, in *Cox Broadcasting Corp. v. Cohn*, the Court described certain categories of cases in which appeal could be taken in which the appealed order could not be considered "final." *See* Chapter 8, § IV.D.

9. **False.** There are two significant problems with this statement. First, the "legal certainty" test does not apply to the plaintiff. She need not show to a legal certainty that her claim meets the amount in controversy. Rather, after the plaintiff makes a good faith allegation that her claim meets the requirement, the burden is on the defendant to show "to a legal certainty" that the plaintiff *cannot* recover that much. *See* Chapter 5, § IV.B. Second, 28 U.S.C. § 1332 requires that the amount in controversy *exceed* $75,000. The question says "$75,000 or more." That is wrong, because a claim for exactly $75,000 does not meet the statutory requirement. *See* Chapter 5, § IV.A.

10. **Unclear.** The Supreme Court decision in *Zahn v. International Paper Co.* requires that each member of the class claim more than $75,000. On the other hand, the supplemental jurisdiction statute, § 1367, has been interpreted to abrogate that requirement and to permit the class to proceed if the class representative's claim exceeds $75,000 (regardless of the value of the other class members' claims). Presently, five courts of appeals (the Fourth, Fifth, Seventh,

Ninth, and Eleventh Circuits) have held that the statute abrogates *Zahn*. Three other courts of appeals (the Third, Eighth, and Tenth Circuits) have held that *Zahn* continues to apply. *See* Chapter 6, § IV.F.

11. True. The starting point is the general rule that the defendant can remove a case to federal court if the case invokes federal subject matter jurisdiction. *See* Chapter 7, § III.B. This case fails to invoke any basis of federal subject matter jurisdiction, however, and therefore is not removable. It does not invoke diversity of citizenship jurisdiction because P and D are citizens of State A. *See* Chapter 5, § III.A. It does not invoke federal question jurisdiction because P's claim does not arise under federal law. The federal issue is injected into the case only by P's anticipation of a federal defense. Under the "well-pleaded complaint rule," the case does not arise under federal law and does not invoke federal question jurisdiction. *See* Chapter 4, § III.B.

12. False. Again, the general rule is that the defendant can remove a case to federal court if the federal court would have subject matter jurisdiction over the case. This case does invoke diversity of citizenship jurisdiction, because the plaintiff is of diverse citizenship from the defendant and the amount in controversy exceeds $75,000. *However*, this general rule is subject to significant exceptions. One exception, under 28 U.S.C. § 1441(b), is that a case cannot be removed on the basis of diversity of citizenship jurisdiction if any defendant is a citizen of the forum state. Here, the defendant, D, is a citizen of State B, which is the forum state (the state in which the case was brought). Thus, even though the case would satisfy diversity of citizenship jurisdiction if originally brought in federal court, it cannot be removed. *See* Chapter 7, § D.2.

13. False. The case invokes *neither* alienage nor diversity of citizenship jurisdiction. First, note that the amount in controversy requirement for either diversity or alienage would be met, because the claim exceeds $75,000. *See* Chapter 5, § IV.A. Second, however, an alienage case must be between an alien and a citizen of a state in the United States. *See* Chapter 5, § II.B.4. Though P is an alien, D is *not* a citizen of a state. To be a citizen of a state, a U.S. citizen must be domiciled in that state. *See* Chapter 5, § III.B. D is not domiciled in a state at all, so is not a citizen of a state. (D is also not an alien; she is still a citizen of the U.S.) Third, a diversity of citizenship case must be between citizens of different states of the United States. Here, neither P nor D is a citizen of a state of the United States. *See* Chapter 5, § III.A.

14. False. Under the principles of aggregation, when a case is brought by one plaintiff against one defendant (as in this Question), the plaintiff may add together ("aggregate") all claims that she has against the defendant, even if the claims are unrelated factually, transactionally, and legally. So in this case, the amount in controversy exceeds $75,000 and the plaintiff is of diverse citizenship from the defendant. Thus, the case invokes diversity of citizenship jurisdiction. *See* Chapter 5, § IV.C.

15. False. The well-pleaded complaint rule requires that the federal ingredient be part of the *plaintiff's claim*–in other words, not part of an anticipated defense (as in Question 11 above) or an affirmative defense raised by the defendant. In *Holmes Group v. Vornado Air Circulation*, 535 U.S. 826 (2002), the Supreme Court made clear that this rule applies as well to defendant's counterclaims. Thus, even if the defendant asserted a counterclaim that clearly arose under federal law, it would not invoke federal question jurisdiction. The plaintiff's claim alone must do so. *See* Chapter 4. § III.B.7.

Essay Question

1. There is no federal subject matter jurisdiction over Claim 1. Federal courts have limited subject matter jurisdiction. The two principal types of cases which federal courts can hear are diversity of citizenship and federal question cases.

For diversity of citizenship jurisdiction, all plaintiffs must be of diverse citizenship from all defendants and the amount in controversy must exceed $75,000. Here, the claim against both defendants fails to invoke diversity of citizenship jurisdiction for two reasons. First, the claim is for $55,000, and thus does not exceed $75,000, as required by 28 U.S.C. § 1332. Second, all parties are citizens of State A. the facts indicate clearly that P is a citizen of State A. The defendants are corporations. Under § 1332(c)(1), a corporation is a citizen of the state in which incorporated and the state in which it has its principal place of business. The facts indicate that both Monster and Goliath are incorporated and have their PPB in State A. There is no diversity.

To invoke federal question jurisdiction under § 1331, the case must "arise under" federal law. The claim here appears in P's well-pleaded complaint–it is not an anticipated defense. The question is whether the federal ingredient in the claim is sufficiently important to the claim to invoke federal question jurisdiction. The Supreme Court has embraced differing tests for this element. One, set forth in *American Well Works*, is whether federal law created the cause of action. Here, however, state law created the cause of action, so the case does not invoke federal question under that test. Under *Smith*, the test is whether the right to relief depends upon the construction of federal law. Arguably, that is so here, because the statute invites courts to look at what behavior constitutes a violation of *federal* antitrust law.

On the other hand, in *Merrell Dow* the Court seems to have stated a nebulous "federal interest" standard, indicating that federal question jurisdiction might exist for state-created claims when some important issue of federal law is presented. In the present case, ultimately all that is at stake are matters of state law. No federal statute is directly in point, since the statute in question has an impact only upon *intrastate* commerce—an area which Congress is not constitutionally empowered to regulate. Moreover, federal law did not create a private right of action for intrastate cases. Since interpretation of the state law can have no effect on any federal interests, there is no justification for the invocation of federal court power. This is so, even though the state has chosen to incorporate the federal standard by reference.

2. There is no federal subject matter jurisdiction over Claim 2. First, there is no diversity of citizenship jurisdiction over this claim because P and Monster are citizens of the same state. Second, there is no federal question jurisdiction over this claim because the claim is based upon common law (state) fraud. Finally, there is no supplemental jurisdiction over this claim for two reasons. First, supplemental jurisdiction is appropriate only when some claim in the same case invokes a basis of federal subject matter jurisdiction. Here, as discussed in Part 1, the first claim fails to invoke subject matter jurisdiction. Second, supplemental jurisdiction is invoked under § 1367(a) only by a claim that shares a common nucleus of operative fact with a claim that does invoke federal subject matter jurisdiction. Thus, even if Claim 1 did invoke federal question jurisdiction, supplemental jurisdiction would not attach to Claim 2 because it is factually unrelated to Claim 1 and thus cannot satisfy the "common nucleus" test.

■ PART III (CHAPTERS 9–17)

1. True. This is the rule of *Claflin v. Houseman*. It should be noted, however, that under *Claflin*, this presumption may be rebutted in an individual case, as has happened in the case of suits to enforce the federal antitrust laws. *See* Chapter 9, § III.A.

2. False. The Supreme Court initially upheld this "constructive waiver" notion. The leading case for the proposition was *Parden v. Terminal Railway*. More recently, however, it has rejected the concept. Today it is clear that *Parden* is overruled and that constructive waiver has no role to play regarding Eleventh Amendment immunity. *Florida Prepaid Postsecondary Education Expense Bd. v. College Savings Bank. See* Chapter 10, § VI.D.

3. False. The *Younger* doctrine started in such instances, and still has its greatest force in the area of ongoing state criminal proceedings. Nonetheless, the

Supreme Court used *Younger* to prevent federal judicial interference with certain state civil proceedings in *Pennzoil Co. v. Texaco, Inc. See* Chapter 13, § V.A & B.

4. **True.** This is the rule of *Clearfield Trust,* which, though criticized, has never been overruled. It is important to note, however, that while technically federal common law is always applied in those cases, today the Supreme Court will often choose to adopt state law as the federal common law standard. *See* Chapter 16, § III.B.

5. **False.** It is true that a federal court must give full faith and credit to a state court judgment, but the Constitution does not compel that result. The constitutional full faith and credit provision requires a *state* court to give full faith and credit to the valid final judgment of another state's court. It is the full faith and credit *statute* (not the Constitution), § 1738 that requires a *federal* court to give full faith and credit to a state court judgment. *See* Chapter 17, § II.A & B.

6. **False.** This is true of *Pullman* abstention; the *England* procedure, by which the federal court stays pending litigation in state court, applies without question in *Pullman* abstention. *See* Chapter 11, § VII.A. It may also be true in *Colorado River* abstention, in which the action may be stayed in federal court pending return from state court. *See* Chapter 11, § VI.A.6. In *Thibodaux* abstention, though the Supreme Court upheld a stay of federal proceedings, it is not clear that there is any issue left for the federal court to litigate. *See* Chapter 11, § V.B.3. But in *Burford* abstention, the statement in Question 6 clearly is not true. The federal court dismisses the case, and the parties go to the state system for ultimate adjudication. *See* Chapter 11, § IV.B.7.

7. **False.** The civil rights removal statute is limited to federal rights of racial equality. *See* Chapter 14, § VI.B.

8. **True.** Though for many years it was not clear that Congress was so limited, now it is clear that it may abrogate Eleventh Amendment immunity *only* under § 5 of the Fourteenth Amendment. *Seminole Tribe of Florida v. Florida. See* Chapter 10, § VI.B. Remember, however, that legislation under that provision does not automatically abrogate Eleventh Amendment immunity. Congress must (1) expressly indicate its intent that states be amenable to suit in federal court and (2) tailor the statute to remedy a particular constitutional violation; the Court talks of this second point as the requirement for "congruence and proportionality." *See* Chapter 10, § VI.C.

9. **True.** So long as the various requirements of *Ex Parte Young* are satisfied, the fact that the state must expend funds to satisfy an equitable order

does not make the order invalid. Relief requiring state expenditures, such as those in *Milliken v. Bradley* (requiring state officials to desegregate schools), are acceptable if ancillary to prospective equitable orders. *See* Chapter 10, § IV.C.

10. True. The Anti–Injunction Statute applies only when state court proceedings are already underway. Thus, it does not apply at all to limit a federal court's power to enjoin someone from instituting suit in state court. Because the prohibition of the statute does not apply, the federal court need not satisfy one of the exceptions to the operation of the statute. As long as the equitable requirements for an injunction are satisfied, the court may enter it. This was the holding in *Dombrowski v. Pfister*. *See* Chapter 12, § II.B.6.

11. True. The Court has recognized two such "valid excuses," though the theoretical bases for them is unclear. First, if the state court is of limited subject matter jurisdiction and cannot hear the claim, notwithstanding its federal nature, the state court need not enforce the federal claim. Second, if the state court would dismiss under the doctrine of *forum non conveniens*, it need not entertain the federal claim. *See* Chapter 9, § IV.B.

12. True. This is the holding of *Mitchum v. Foster*. The case stands for the proposition that Congress can invoke the "expressly authorized" exception to the Anti–Injunction Statute without specifically referring to that statute. The Court has had difficulty applying *Mitchum* more recently, and it seems likely that the Court will not lightly find "express" authorization so readily in other circumstances. *See* Chapter 12, § III.A.

13. False. Despite arguments by commentators that the "in aid of jurisdiction" exception be extended to avoid overlapping federal and state *in personam* litigation, the Supreme Court has interpreted the exception narrowly. Generally, it applies to permit injunctions against state cases only in *in rem*, *quasi-in-rem*, and other cases involving attachment of property by the federal court. *See* Chapter 12, § III.B. Though some lower courts have expanded use of the exception, the expansion has been limited, and it clearly does not permit federal courts to enjoin overlapping *in personam* cases in the interest of avoiding duplicative litigation.

14. False. Though the Anti–Injunction Statute does not restrict the federal court's power in this regard, the doctrine of "Our Federalism," embodied in *Younger v. Harris*, does. *See* Chapter 13, § II.B. That case stands for the proposition that a federal court may not enjoin state court proceedings absent exceptional circumstances, such as bad faith or harassment. *See* Chapter 13, § III.C & D.

15. False. Section 1983 may be used to sue persons who violate the plaintiff's federal rights under color of *state* law. Here, the officers allegedly violated her rights under color of *federal* law. Thus, they cannot be sued under § 1983. *See* Chapter 14, § III.E. The plaintiff in this situation may proceed against the officers by asserting a *Bivens* claim, which is available for violations under color of federal law. *See* Chapter 14, § V.

16. False. The officers may be sued only in their individual capacities, not in their official capacities. *See* Chapter 14, § III.D.4. Officers in their official capacities are not considered "persons" under § 1983, which officers in their individual capacities are "persons" under the statute. The municipality cannot be held liable under the doctrine of *respondeat superior*, but can be liable only if the deprivation was the result of some official policy or custom of the municipality. *See* Chapter 14, § III.D.5.

17. True. Section 1983 can be used only to vindicate certain *federal* rights. Deprivation of state-law rights does not fall within the statute. *See* Chapter 14, § III.F.

18. False. The federal courts have always been more deferential to state fact-finding than the standard stated in this question. Under recent revisions to § 2254 under the Antiterrorism and Effective Death Penalty Act, a state court factual determination is "presumed to be correct" and can be ignored only if the applicant can rebut that presumption "by clear and convincing evidence." *See* Chapter 15, § III.D.6. Another section of the AEDPA, however, authorizes habeas if the state decision was based upon an "unreasonable determination of the facts in light of the evidence presented in the State proceeding." *See* Chapter 15, § III.D.7. It is not clear how these two provisions are to interact, but each clearly requires more deference to the state court findings than the standard mentioned in this question.

19. False. While this was true under *Fay v. Noia*, it is no longer good law in light of *Wainwright v. Sykes*. *See* Chapter 15, § IV.A.

20. True. There is no exhaustion-of-state-remedies requirement under § 1983. *See* Chapter 14, § III.B.3. (The Prison Litigation Reform Act does require exhaustion of administrative remedies by *federal* prisoners proceeding under a *Bivens* claim. *See* Chapter 14, § V.D.1.) In contrast, the state prisoner who seeks federal habeas must exhaust state remedies before proceeding in federal court. *See* Chapter 15, § III.B. *See also* Chapter 14, § II.D.

Essay

1. *Pullman Abstention.*

The argument in support of *Pullman* abstention here is that the state statute is inherently ambiguous and therefore the state courts should be given the opportunity to construe the statute narrowly to avoid the constitutional issue.

Arguably, however, *Pullman* abstention should not be followed. The fact that the state statute may be unconstitutionally vague does not mean that it is "ambiguous" for purposes of *Pullman* abstention. The vagueness does not mean that the statute lends itself to two constructions, one of which would render it unconstitutional. Moreover, the case involves the exercise of first amendment free speech rights, where the delay in ultimate vindication of the federal right may increase the chilling effect.

On the other hand, many federal judges might wish to provide the state court the opportunity to narrow the statute.

2. *Burford Abstention.*

At least a plausible argument could be made to support the applicability of *Burford* abstention to this case. The issue of public education is a matter of great importance to the state, and, as in *Burford*, the state has established a complex network of administrative and judicial review. On the other hand, a federal court could decide that *Burford* should be limited to truly complex matters of state law, and not apply to cases in which the central issue will be a matter of federal constitutional law.

3. *Younger Abstention.*

Younger abstention traditionally was applied to cases of state criminal prosecutions. The Supreme Court has invoked it, however, in certain state civil proceedings implicating important state interests. In the present case, the federal interference would not be with an ongoing *judicial* proceeding of any kind, but rather one that is—at least at now—administrative. Though state judicial review is provided, it is only after the administrative process is completed, a point which may unduly delay vindication of first amendment rights. While the basic assumption of the *Younger* doctrine is that state *courts* are constitutionally and historically capable of enforcing federal rights, the same cannot be said of state administrative agencies.

In *Middlesex County Ethics Committee v. Garden State Bar Association*, the Supreme Court held that *Younger* barred federal injunctive relief against a state attorney disciplinary proceeding which had been challenged on first amendment grounds. The Court did note the important state interest involved, which arguably renders the case relevant to this one. The case might be distinguished, however, because the Court emphasized the "unique relationship" between the administrative ethics committee and the state supreme court, which appointed and supervised it. This seemed to indicate that the case is limited to such instances of close judicial and administrative interaction, a view confirmed in *Hawaii Housing Authority v. Midkiff*.

APPENDIX B

Model Examination

QUESTION 1

In response to concern over what some people consider undue interference by the federal judiciary in the operation of federal prisons, Congress has enacted and the President signed into law the Judicial Prison Review Act of 2004. The Act provides:

> **Section 1.** No federal district court may review the constitutionality of decisions by federal prison officials regarding the confinement or discipline of prisoners.
>
> **Section 2.** Any prisoner may seek review of a decision by federal prison officials in the Federal Prison Review Board, which is to be comprised of three individuals, appointed by the President and confirmed by the Senate, who sit at the discretion of the President.
>
> **Section 3.** Decisions of the Federal Prison Review Board are not subject to review in any federal court.

Write a memorandum discussing the constitutionality of the Act.

QUESTION 2

P, a citizen of Illinois, filed suit in federal district court in a proper venue against two defendants: X, who is a citizen of Venezuela, and Y Corp., which is incorporated in Delaware. P's claim is based upon state law and she claims that X and Y Corp., as joint tortfeasors, caused her personal injuries of $100,000. Y Corp. has its headquarters in Chicago, Illinois, where it makes corporate decisions. It manufactures all of its products in Tucson, Arizona.

X asserted a counterclaim against P. The counterclaim arose from the same transaction as that alleged by P in her complaint. The counterclaim is based upon state law. X claims damages under that claim of $55,000. In addition, Y Corp. asserted a counterclaim against P. Its counterclaim also arose from the same transaction that P alleged in her complaint. Y Corp.'s claim against P arises under federal law.

X and Y Corp. then move to dismiss the entire case for lack of subject matter jurisdiction. Assume that the motion is timely, because subject matter jurisdiction can be raised at any time during the proceedings.

The district court held (1) that P's claims against X and Y Corp. failed to invoke federal subject matter jurisdiction, but that (2) it had subject matter jurisdiction over the case because Y Corp.'s claim against P invoked federal question jurisdiction, and (3) that X's counterclaim against P failed to invoke federal subject matter jurisdiction.

Write a memorandum discussing the correctness of each of the district court's rulings.

QUESTION 3

A filed suit against B in state court under state unfair competition law. Both A and B are citizens of the same state. B answered, arguing that its alleged unfair competition was justified by its interest in protecting its federally issued patent.

The state court denied defendant's motion for summary judgment, holding that because the federal courts have exclusive jurisdiction over patent cases, it lacked authority to rule upon the relevance of defendant's patent as a justification for its actions. Under state law, interlocutory appeals can be taken directly to the state supreme court. B took such an appeal to the state supreme court, which affirmed the lower court's decision. B then sought review in the United States Supreme Court, which agreed to hear the case and reversed the state courts' conclusion that they could not take into account the relevance of B's patent.

Write a memorandum considering the correctness of each judicial ruling.

ANSWER TO MODEL EXAMINATION

QUESTION 1

All conceivable constitutional objections to the Act flow either from Article III or from the fifth amendment's due process clause.

ARTICLE III

The clear impact of the Act is to exclude the Article III federal courts (including the Supreme Court) from review of significant constitutional issues. Under traditional thinking, Congress need not vest the federal judicial power in any Article III court. It need not vest the judicial power in the lower federal courts, because Article III expressly allowed Congress not to create lower courts, and in light of this power it has been assumed that Congress could abolish such courts. If Congress has power to abolish them, the argument proceeds, it has power to take the lesser step of curbing their jurisdiction. The argument that Congress could exclude Supreme Court appellate jurisdiction turns on the "exceptions" clause of Article III, which allows Congress to make exceptions to the Supreme Court's appellate jurisdiction.

There are several arguments, however, that would preclude all or part of Congress' action. Most suspect is the congressional limitation of Supreme Court jurisdiction. The "exceptions" clause has never received a definitive interpretation, and certain commentators have argued that Congress may not make exceptions to the Court's jurisdiction which interfere with performance of its "essential functions." Though there is little linguistic or historical basis to support such a thesis, if accepted it would invalidate Congress' exclusion of Supreme Court appellate jurisdiction.

Other commentators have adopted a type of "floating" essential functions thesis—a theory that states that since Article III provides that the federal judicial power "shall be vested," the Article requires that *some* federal court (*either* the Supreme Court *or* a lower federal court) exercise the judicial power. Under this theory, the Act is invalid because it removes *both* lower court *and* Supreme Court jurisdiction. However, these theories have never received judicial acceptance.

In *Crowell v. Benson*, the Supreme Court did indicate that separation-of-powers principles dictate that the judiciary have the final say on the meaning of the Constitution, but it is not clear whether that requirement could not be satisfied by *state* court review. The issue of state court review is also relevant to the due process concern, and will be discussed under that heading.

DUE PROCESS

Due process has been construed to require the provision of an independent forum for the adjudication of constitutional rights. At least in regard to actions of the federal government, state courts—who are bound to enforce the Constitution through the Supremacy Clause—meet this independence requirement. However, under the doctrine of *Tarble's Case*, state courts may not be allowed to directly control the actions of federal officials.

If the rule of *Tarble* were held applicable even when the federal forum has been congressionally closed (which was not the case in *Tarble* itself), it is conceivable that the Act's exclusion of federal judicial review would be unconstitutional. The question would then come down to whether the newly created review board could satisfy due process. However, if the limit of *Tarble* on state court jurisdiction were to fall, then the requirements of due process and the separation-of-powers considerations of *Crowell* would be satisfied.

■ QUESTION 2

1. *P's claims against X and Y Corp.* Because P's claims against X and against Y Corp. are based upon state law, and not federal law, they cannot invoke federal question jurisdiction. They can, however, be brought in federal court if they satisfy the requirements of diversity of citizenship or alienage jurisdiction.

For either diversity of citizenship (28 U.S.C. § 1332(a)(1)) or alienage (28 U.S.C. § 1332(a)(2)) jurisdiction, the amount in controversy must exceed $75,000. In determining the amount in controversy, a plaintiff may not aggregate separate claims against multiple defendants. Here, however, the claims against the two defendants allege liability as "joint tortfeasors." With allegations of joint liability, the amount in controversy is the amount of the claim against them. Here, that claim is for $100,000. Thus, it exceeds $75,000 and satisfies the amount in controversy requirement.

In addition to the amount in controversy, alienage jurisdiction requires suit between a citizen of a state in the United States and a citizen of a foreign country. The claim by P against X satisfies this requirement, because P is a citizen of Illinois and X is a citizen of Venezuela. Thus the district court was erroneous in concluding that it lacked subject matter jurisdiction over P's claim against X.

In addition to the amount in controversy, diversity of citizenship jurisdiction requires suit between citizens of different states. This statutory requirement is interpreted to mean that every plaintiff must be of diverse citizenship from every defendant. Here, again, P is a citizen of Illinois. Y Corp., because it is a corporation, under 28 U.S.C. § 1332(c)(1), is a citizen of both the state of its incorporation and the one state in which it has its principal place of business. Y Corp. is incorporated in Delaware, so is a citizen of that state, which is diverse from P.

But if Y Corp.'s principal place of business is in Illinois, it will be a co-citizen of P, and thus diversity of citizenship jurisdiction will fail. To determine a corporation's principal place of business, some courts look to the headquarters, where corporate decisions are made. For Y Corp., that place is Chicago, from which we would conclude that Y Corp. is a citizen of Illinois and thus that there is no diversity between it and P. But other courts emphasize the place of operations, which is where the corporation does most of its activity. Here, that would be where Y Corp. has its sole manufacturing plant, in Arizona. If this is the principal place of business, there would be diversity between P and Y Corp. Most courts use headquarters as principal place of business only if the corporation's business is far-flung among multiple states. Here, Y Corp. undertakes all of its manufacturing in Arizona. Under these facts, most courts would conclude that the place of activities—Arizona—constitutes the principal place of business. Thus, the district court probably erred in concluding that there was no diversity of citizenship jurisdiction over P's claim against Y Corp.

2. *Y Corp.'s counterclaim against P.* There is no question that Y Corp.'s counterclaim against P invokes federal subject matter jurisdiction. Specifically, it invokes federal question jurisdiction under 28 U.S.C. § 1331. The citizenship of the parties and the amount in controversy are irrelevant. The claim invokes federal question jurisdiction, and thus could be asserted in the pending case by P against X and Y Corp. which, as we discussed above, invoked both alienage and diversity of citizenship jurisdiction.

The district court concluded, however, that the original claims by P did not invoke federal subject matter jurisdiction. It then claimed that it had jurisdiction over the suit under federal question jurisdiction because the counterclaim invoked federal question jurisdiction. In this holding, the court was wrong. In *Holmes Group v. Vornado Air Circulation*, 535 U.S. 826 (2002), the Supreme Court held that a counterclaim arising under federal law cannot invoke federal subject matter jurisdiction in a case in which the plaintiff's claims did not invoke federal subject matter jurisdiction. Stated another way, federal question jurisdiction can be invoked only in a well-pleaded complaint, which does not include a counterclaim.

Thus, the district court was wrong to hold that the counterclaim could give it federal question jurisdiction over the case. But, as discussed in part 1, the court was also wrong in concluding that P's claims against X and Y Corp. failed to invoke federal subject matter jurisdiction. Because they did, Y Corp.'s counterclaim can be asserted in the pending matter because it invokes federal question jurisdiction.

3. *X's counterclaim against P.* X's counterclaim against P arises under state law, and thus fails to invoke federal question jurisdiction under 28 U.S.C. § 1331. Federal question jurisdiction attaches only to claims that arise under federal law. X's counterclaim against P also fails to invoke alienage jurisdiction under 28 U.S.C. § 1332(a)(2). Though it is brought by a citizen of a foreign country (X) against a citizen of a state of the United States (P), and thus satisfies that requirement for alienage, it does not satisfy the amount in controversy requirement. For alienage jurisdiction, the claim must exceed $75,000. X's claim does not, because it is for $55,000. Thus the district court was correct insofar as it concluded that there is no *independent* basis of federal subject matter jurisdiction over X's counterclaim.

But the counterclaim does invoke supplemental jurisdiction. That form of jurisdiction permits the assertion in federal court of claims that do not satisfy an independent basis of federal subject matter jurisdiction such as federal question, diversity of citizenship, or alienage. 28 U.S.C. § 1367(a) grants supplemental jurisdiction to claims that involve a common nucleus of operative fact as a claim that invokes federal subject matter jurisdiction. Here, the facts make clear that X's counterclaim arises from the same transaction as P's claims against X and Y Corp. We demonstrated in part 1 above that those claims invoked federal subject matter jurisdiction. Thus, § 1367(a) grants supplemental jurisdiction to X's counterclaim.

Section 1367(b) removes supplemental jurisdiction in cases in which the original basis of jurisdiction is § 1332, which, as we saw in part 1, is the case here. But § 1367(b) removes supplemental jurisdiction only over certain types of claims asserted by plaintiffs. X's claim is asserted by a defendant, so the restriction on supplemental jurisdiction found in § 1367(b) does not apply here, and the claim can be asserted in federal court under supplemental jurisdiction. Thus, ultimately, the district court was wrong in concluding that there was no subject matter jurisdiction over X's counterclaim against P.

■ QUESTION 3

1. *State Court Power to Adjudicate the Patent Defense:* The state courts were incorrect and the Supreme Court correct on the issue of state court power to adjudicate the federal patent claim. While it is true that under 28 U.S.C. § 1338 federal jurisdiction for suits under the patent laws is exclusive, the Supreme Court

held in *Lear, Inc. v. Adkins* that state courts much adjudicate defenses under the patent laws. This is because the opposite conclusion would threaten enforcement of federal patent law policy.

2. *Appealability:* 28 U.S.C. § 1257 allows Supreme Court review of only *final* decisions of the state's highest court. Since the state supreme court here reviewed a denial of a summary judgment motion, its decision could not be deemed "final" in any technical sense of the term.

Though the Court has recognized a number of exceptions to the strict finality requirement, particularly in *Cox Broadcasting Corp. v. Cohn,* none of those exceptions applies to this case. Therefore the Supreme Court incorrectly agreed to review the state supreme court's decision.

*

APPENDIX C

Glossary

A

Abstention. A judge-made doctrine authorizing federal courts to relinquish jurisdiction over an action in favor of the state courts in order to further important interests of federalism. The doctrine is sub-divided into specific categories. *See Pullman* Abstention, *Burford* Abstention, *Thibodaux* Abstention, *Colorado River* Abstention, and *Younger* Doctrine.

Adequate State Ground Doctrine. A judge-made principle that prevents the Supreme Court from reviewing a state court decision when the decision is premised, at least in part, on grounds of state law, so that even if the Supreme Court were to alter the disposition of the federal issue in the case, the result would remain the same.

Alienage Jurisdiction. A form of federal subject matter jurisdiction for cases between a citizen of a foreign country and a citizen of a state of the United States and the amount in controversy exceeds $75,000. 28 U.S.C. § 1332(a)(2).

Ancillary Jurisdiction. A judge-made doctrine allowing a federal district court to exercise jurisdiction over claims that lack an independent basis of subject matter jurisdiction, such as federal question or diversity of citizenship jurisdiction. The concept is now subsumed under the generic principle of supplemental jurisdiction, which is codified at 28 U.S.C. § 1367.

Anti–Injunction Act. A federal statute providing that a federal court may not enjoin state proceedings unless expressly authorized by Congress, or where necessary in aid of its jurisdiction, or to protect or effectuate its judgment. 28 U.S.C. § 2283.

Appeal. Review of the decision of a lower court by a higher court.

Article I Courts. *See* Legislative Courts.

Article III Courts. Federal courts whose judges receive the protections of salary and tenure provided by Article III of the Constitution. Matters heard by them include the following types of cases: those arising under the Constitution and the laws and treaties of the United

States, those to which the U.S. is a party, and those between states and between citizens of different states.

B

***Burford* Abstention.** A form of judge-made abstention that authorizes a federal court to defer to a state's review system when the subject matter is better adjudicated under a complex regulatory scheme and concerns predominantly local factors in sensitive areas of state concern.

C

Certification. A procedure, authorized by state law, allowing a federal court to submit unsettled issues of state law to a state's highest court for determination while retaining jurisdiction over the action. This procedure can be used instead of abstention, but certification is not available in all states.

Certiorari. A statutorily-provided means of obtaining Supreme Court review. The Supreme Court uses its discretion in choosing whether to review a lower court's proceedings. The votes of four Justices are required. A denial of certiorari by the Supreme Court is not a decision on the merits.

Civil Rights Removal. A statute, 28 U.S.C. § 1443, authorizing the removal of a case from state to federal court in any of the following circumstances: 1. where a person has been "denied or cannot enforce" a civil right of equality in a state court; 2. where a person is being sued or prosecuted for performing "any act under color of authority derived from any law providing for equal rights;" or 3. where a person is the subject of suit for refusing to perform an act that would be inconsistent with a law providing for equal rights. The denial clause has been narrowly construed to permit removal only when a state statute or constitutional provision invades a federal civil right, or when a federal statute immunizes from prosecution the very conduct for which a person is being prosecuted.

Claim Preclusion. The principle that a final judgment by a court of competent jurisdiction is an absolute bar to a subsequent action involving the same cause of action between the same parties or their privies.

Collateral Estoppel. *See* Issue Preclusion.

***Colorado River* Abstention.** A category of judge-made abstention under which a federal court may in extreme circumstances abstain due to concurrent state judicial proceedings in order to avoid harassment of the parties or duplication of effort.

Comity. The notion that the federal system will operate best if the states are allowed to perform their legitimate functions without undue interference from federal courts. Federal judicial deference to state courts. This principle was used in part to justify the *Younger* doctrine.

Complete Diversity. The requirement that the federal courts exercise the diversity of citizenship jurisdiction only when *all* plaintiffs are citizens of different states from *all* defendants. Developed originally by Chief Justice Marshall in *Strawbridge v. Curtiss*, the rule was held in 1967 to derive from the diversity statute, rather than Article III, allowing Congress to modify the rule if it so desires. The Federal Interpleader Act is an example of congressional provision for only "minimal" diversity (i.e., *at least* one plaintiff is a citizen of a state different from the state of *at least* one defendant).

Concurrent Jurisdiction. A situation in which tribunals of more than one system have jurisdiction over a case. For example, the federal and state courts have concurrent jurisdiction in diversity of citizenship actions.

Constitutional Facts. A constitutional doctrine, deriving from separation-of-powers principles, that provides that the Article III federal courts are not bound by an administrative agency's findings of facts when such findings have constitutional implications. Though today the federal court may not conduct a *de novo* proceeding to make its own findings regarding such facts, it still is supposed to make an independent inquiry on the basis of the preexisting record.

D

Declaratory Relief. A procedure allowing a litigant to seek a binding decision to settle a controversy prior to engaging in conduct which may lead to legal liability. The procedure is authorized in federal court by federal statute. However, the procedure is limited by the constitutional requirement of case or controversy.

Diversity of Citizenship Jurisdiction. A form of federal subject matter jurisdiction in which the case is between citizens of different states and the amount in controversy exceeds $75,000. 28 U.S.C. § 1332(a)(1).

Domicile. A human being's one true, fixed, permanent location. It is established by a person's physical presence in a place combined with the subjective intent to make it her permanent home. Though a person may have more than one "residence," she cannot have more than one domicile at a time.

E

***England* Procedure.** A procedure, devised in *England v. Louisiana St. Bd. of Medical Examiners,* providing that after a federal court has referred issues of state law to a state court under *Pullman* abstention and the state court has adjudicated the state law issues, a litigant has the right to return to federal court for adjudication of federal constitutional issues.

***Erie* Doctrine.** A principle, derived from *Erie Railroad Co. v. Tompkins,* governing whether a federal court in a diversity of citizenship case must apply state law to determine an issue. In *Erie,* the Court held that the federal courts are bound by the constitutional limits of Congress' power to prescribe statutory law for such suits and by the statutory limits prescribed for the courts by the Rules of Decision Act and the Rules Enabling Act.

Exceptions Clause. A provision of Article III authorizing Congress to make exceptions and regulations to the Supreme Court's appellate jurisdiction.

Exhaustion of Remedies. This doctrine requires that relief must be sought in one forum before entering another. Exhaustion of state administrative or judicial remedies may be required before a federal court will adjudicate a case. A state criminal defendant must exhaust his state judicial remedies before obtaining federal habeas corpus relief. The Supreme Court has held, however, that generally a federal civil rights plaintiff, suing under 42 U.S.C. § 1983, need not first exhaust state administrative or judicial remedies.

Expressly Authorized Exception. An exception to the bar of the Anti–Injunction Act providing that a federal court may issue an injunction to stop litigants from proceeding in a state court when such an injunction has been expressly authorized by an act of Congress. 28 U.S.C. § 2283. Courts have found such an authorization in such laws as the Securities Exchange Act and the Civil Rights Act, 42 U.S.C. § 1983.

F

Federal Common Law. A body of decisional law developed by the federal courts. The application of this body of common law is limited by the *Erie* doctrine and by the Rules of Decision Act, which provides that except for cases governed by the Constitution, the treaties of the United States, or acts of Congress, federal courts are to apply state law. Areas in which federal common law have been developed include federal "proprietary" interests, admiralty and foreign relations.

Federal Question Jurisdiction. A form of federal subject matter jurisdiction for cases arising under federal law. 28 U.S.C. § 1331.

Final Judgment. A decision that terminates the action. An appeal to a higher court must ordinarily be from a final judgment.

Forum Non Conveniens. The discretionary power of a court to decline jurisdiction when, in the interest of justice, the action should proceed in another forum. This power is usually used when another forum would be more convenient for the parties because the parties, witnesses, or evidence is located in that forum.

Full Faith and Credit. The enforcement of one jurisdiction's law or judgments in the court of another forum. Under the Constitution, a state must give the judgment of a court of another state the authority that would be accorded it by the courts in the state in which the judgment was rendered. Under the Full Faith and Credit Act, 28 U.S.C. § 1738, the federal courts must recognize the judgments of state courts.

H

Habeas Corpus. A writ used to test the legality of a person's detention by the government, but not to determine his innocence or guilt. It is a Latin expression meaning "you have the body."

I

"In Aid of Jurisdiction" Exception. An exception to the Anti–Injunction Act authorizing a federal court to issue an injunction to stay litigants from proceeding in a state court where such an injunction is necessary in aid of the federal court's jurisdiction. 28 U.S.C. § 2283. This exception has generally been limited to cases which are *in rem*, in which the federal court has acquired jurisdiction of the subject property prior to the state court action.

Injunction. An equitable remedy which prohibits a party from performing a particular act. Injunctions may be either temporary or permanent.

Issue Preclusion. A rule that provides that when an issue of fact or mixed law and fact has been decided in a previous action brought under a different cause of action between the same parties or their privies, it cannot be relitigated.

J

Johnson Act of 1934. A statute providing that federal district courts cannot enjoin an order issued by a state administrative body affecting rates charged by a public utility. 28 U.S.C. § 1342.

Judicial Review. The principle that courts may examine the constitutionality of the actions of the executive and the legislative branches of government. Courts will decline to rule on those issues which are purely political questions. *See* Political Question.

Jurisdictional Amount Requirement. The dictate that a case may be heard in federal court only if the dispute involves a specified amount in controversy. The most important such requirement is found in 28 U.S.C. § 1332, which requires that diversity of citizenship and alienage cases involve an amount in excess of $75,000, exclusive of interest and costs.

L

Legal Certainty Test. The test for determining whether the amount-in-controversy requirement is met. It provides that the amount claimed in the complaint will control unless it appears to a "legal certainty" that the claim could not be for more than $75,000.

Legislative Courts. Federal courts whose judges lack constitutional protections for salary and tenure. Congress forms such courts not under its authority in Article III, but usually under its authority under Article I and the "necessary and proper" clause. Congress has the power to make all laws necessary to execute such courts' functions, and it may require such courts to perform non-judicial activities. Examples of legislative courts include are the Territorial Courts, the Tax Court and the local courts of the District of Columbia.

M

Manufactured Diversity. The improper or collusive creation of diversity of citizenship for the sole or primary purpose of obtaining federal court jurisdiction. Such a practice is prohibited by 28 U.S.C. § 1359.

Mootness. The principle that when the matter in dispute has already been resolved, there is no actual controversy that would be affected by a judicial decision, and federal courts will not exercise their jurisdiction. Though federal courts will not hear any case that has been mooted, they may exercise their jurisdiction when the behavior is likely to recur but to continually evade review.

O

Our Federalism. *See* comity. *See Younger* Doctrine.

P

Pendent Jurisdiction. A judge-made doctrine allowing a federal district court to exercise jurisdiction over claims that lack an independent basis of subject matter jurisdiction, such as federal question or diversity of citizenship jurisdiction. The concept is now subsumed under the generic principle of supplemental jurisdiction, which is codified at 28 U.S.C. § 1367.

Pendent Party Jurisdiction. The exercise of supplemental jurisdiction to allow a federal court to hear a claim over which there is no independent basis of subject matter jurisdiction and which is by or against a party as to whom no claim has an independent basis of subject matter jurisdiction. The concept is codified in 28 U.S.C. § 1367(a), which grants supplemental jurisdiction to the full extent of Article III and, in its last sentence, makes clear that this grant applies to claims involving additional parties. This statute overruled the result in *Finley v. United States* and other cases in which the Supreme Court had refused to permit pendent parties jurisdiction.

Political Question. The principle that a federal court will refuse to decide issues which it determines are committed to other branches of the government by the Constitution, or for which no judicially discoverable and manageable standards can be found, or where judicial determination may create enforcement difficulties or institutional conflicts.

***Pullman* Abstention.** The judge-made doctrine that a federal court may stay a case involving a federal constitutional question to give the state courts the opportunity to interpret an ambiguous state law which can be construed in a manner which will render it constitutional, although unconstitutional constructions are also possible. *See also England* Procedure.

R

Removal. The process authorizing a case to be transferred from state to federal court before a final decision occurs. *See also* Civil Rights Removal.

Res Judicata. *See* Claim Preclusion.

Ripeness. The principle that the federal courts require an actual, present controversy, and therefore will not act when the issue is only hypothetical or the existence of a controversy merely speculative.

Rules of Decision Act. A statute that provides that state law shall be regarded as the rules of decision in a federal court unless the federal Constitution, a treaty of the United States, or an act of Congress otherwise requires or provides. 28 U.S.C. § 1652.

S

Standing. The principle that only one with a tangible and legally protectible interest has the capacity to obtain judicial resolution of a controversy. The plaintiff must be able to show that she has suffered or will suffer actual injury and that there is a causal nexus between the injury suffered and the conduct complained of. A taxpayer who challenges the constitutionality of a federal action must establish a logical link between his status as a taxpayer and the type of federal action she is challenging. She must also prove that there is a nexus between her "status and the precise nature of the constitutional infringement alleged." *Flast v. Cohen*, 392 U.S. 83 (1968). Within the limits of the case-or-controversy requirement of Article III, Congress may grant an express right of action to those who would otherwise meet these requirements. *See* Third–Party Standing.

State Sovereign Immunity. The principle that there can be no legal action against a state unless it has consented to the suit. The doctrine has a common law basis and, to an undefined extent, may have received some level of constitutional protection in the Eleventh Amendment. Congress may abrogate a state's Eleventh Amendment protection under § 5 of the Fourteenth Amendment. In addition, a state may waive its Eleventh Amendment protection, either expressly or by litigation conduct.

Supplemental Jurisdiction. The authority of the federal courts to hear claims that do not satisfy an independent basis of federal subject matter jurisdiction, such as federal question or diversity of citizenship. The concept is codified in 28 U.S.C. § 1367. Section 1367(a) grants supplemental jurisdiction to the full extent of Article III, which codifies the result in *United Mine Workers v. Gibbs*. That case permitted such jurisdiction over claims sharing a "common nucleus of operative fact" with a claim that invoked an independent basis of federal subject matter jurisdiction. The last sentence of § 1367(a) provides that the grant applies even as to claims involving additionally joined parties and intervenors, thus establishing the propriety of what had been called "pendent parties jurisdiction." Section 1367(b), however, imposes significant restrictions on the grant of supplemental jurisdiction, which apply only in cases brought in federal court under § 1332, which includes diversity of citizenship. Section 1367(c) provides discretionary grounds on which a court with supplemental jurisdiction might decline to exercise it.

Supremacy Clause. Article VI, clause 2 of the Constitution, providing that the Constitution, treaties and laws of the United States are the "supreme law of the land; and the Judges in every State shall be bound thereby, any thing in the Constitution or laws of any State to the contrary notwithstanding."

T

Tax Injunction Act of 1937. A statute that mandates that federal district courts not interfere with the assessment or collection of any state tax where a plain, speedy and efficient remedy is available in the state courts. 28 U.S.C. § 1341.

Taxpayer Standing. *See* Standing.

***Thibodaux* Abstention.** The judge-made principle that a federal court has the discretion to abstain to allow state courts to decide difficult issues of public importance that, if decided by the federal court, could result in unnecessary friction between state and federal authorities.

Third-Party Standing. The assertion of one individual's right by another. Traditionally, third-party standing has not been allowed in federal court. On occasion, however, the practice is allowed, to protect important interests that might otherwise be undermined. The classic example of such a case involves the First Amendment overbreadth doctrine, which allows an individual who could constitutionally be prosecuted for his conduct to challenge a statute on its face because it reaches constitutionally protected, as well as unprotected conduct.

V

Venue. The particular place within a judicial system in which a court may adjudicate a cause of action. In the federal courts, the term refers to the federal district in which suit is brought. The venue statute for civil actions in federal district courts is 28 U.S.C. § 1391, which, generally, allows plaintiff to lay venue in any federal district in which all defendants reside or in which a substantial part of the claim arose.

W

Well–Pleaded Complaint Rule. The principle that the federal courts have federal question jurisdiction only when the plaintiff's complaint, properly drawn, establishes the presence of a controlling issue of federal law. Though the general federal question statute, 28 U.S.C. § 1331, makes no explicit reference to the requirement, the Supreme Court has construed the statute to impose the requirement.

Y

***Younger* Doctrine.** The principle, developed by the Supreme Court in *Younger v. Harris* and other cases, that federal courts should not interfere with an on-going state criminal proceeding, either by injunction or declaratory relief, unless the prosecution has been brought in bad faith or as harassment. The *Younger* doctrine has also been applied in civil actions where the state is a party and important state substantive goals are implicated.

APPENDIX D

Text Correlation Chart

Federal Courts: Black Letter Series	R. Clinton, R. Matasar & M. Collins, Federal Courts: Theory and Practice (1996)	D. Currie, Federal Courts: Cases and Materials (4th ed. 1990)	D. Doernberg & C.K. Wingate, Federal Courts, Federalism and Separation of Powers (2d ed. 2000)	R. Fallon, D. Meltzer, & D. Shapiro, Hart & Wechsler's The Federal Courts and The Federal System (4th ed. 1996)	H. Fink, L. Mullenix, T. Rowe, Jr., & M. Tushnet, Federal Courts in the 21st Century (2d ed. 2002)	P. Low & J. Jeffries, Jr., Federal Courts and the Law of Federal–State Relations 4th ed. 1998)	C. Wright & J. Oakley, Federal Courts: Cases and Materials (10th ed. 1999)
PART ONE: FEDERAL COURTS & POLITICAL BRANCHES OF THE FEDERAL GOVERNMENT							
I. Problems of Judicial Review	991–1081	6–98	22–139	67–293	1–182	331–448	4–157
II. Congressional Power to Regulate Federal Jurisdiction	33–166	98–113, 128–38	140–95	348–87	184–252, 909–27, 948–49	213–264	—
III. Legislative Courts	28–32, 167–246	114–28	277–324	387–444	909–48, 950–55	265–330	—
PART TWO: THE STRUCTURE OF FEDERAL COURT JURISDICTION							
IV. Federal Question Jurisdiction	297–387	139–74	196–276	878–948, 982–93	309–74	450–56, 459–76	77–157
V. Diversity of Citizenship and Alienage Jurisdiction	413–536	227–309	—	1521–57, 1567–77	375–425	476–97	158–241
VI. Supplemental Jurisdiction	537–583	188–200, 251–60	—	962–73, 1558–66	427–47	457–59, 497–502	—

Federal Courts: Black Letter Series	R. Clinton, R. Matasar & M. Collins, Federal Courts: Theory and Practice (1996)	D. Currie, Federal Courts: Cases and Materials (4th ed. 1990)	D. Doernberg & C.K. Wingate, Federal Courts, Federalism and Separation of Powers (2d ed. 2000)	R. Fallon, D. Meltzer, & D. Shapiro, Hart & Wechsler's The Federal Courts and The Federal System (4th ed. 1996)	H. Fink, L. Mullenix, T. Rowe, Jr., & M. Tushnet, Federal Courts in the 21st Century (2d ed. 2002)	P. Low & J. Jeffries, Jr., Federal Courts and the Law of Federal–State Relations 4th ed. 1998)	C. Wright & J. Oakley, Federal Courts: Cases and Materials (10th ed. 1999)
VII. Removal Jurisdiction	585–605	183–85, 260–67	—	948–62, 1615–31	449–80	1186–1206	242–300
VIII. Supreme Court Jurisdiction	28–32, 495–502, 1355–1455	320–26, 573–607	836–941	294–347, 492–655, 1636–1714	959–1001	72–117, 539–76	325–54, 748, 776–841
PART THREE: FEDERAL COURTS, FEDERALISM, AND THE STATES							
IX. State Courts and Federal Power	247–295	176–83, 185–88, 421–32	878–81	444–91, 951–53, 1185–89	955–57, 1003–18	32–72, 888–905	355–63, 383–88, 495–551
X. CHAPTER 10	1081–1153	433–52	559–695	1041–1105	253–86	809–888	—
XI. Abstention	623–36, 1228–57	485–14, 556–68	712–37, 790–835	1222–1336	820–43	577–610	422–49
XII. The Anti–Injunction Statute	605–23, 1207–28	514–28	697–712	1189–1222	844–75	631, 668–83, 825	364–83
XIII. "Our Federalism:" The Doctrine of *Younger v. Harris*	1259–1303	528–56	738–92	1256–1308	820–43	610–68	449–94
XIV. Actions to Vindicate Federal Civil Rights	815–931, 984–88, 1153–1206	379–425, 452–55, 474–84	464–558	847–877, 954–62, 994–1041, 1105–1184, 1513–15, 1516–20	286–308, 472–80, 1008–1014	173, 180–212, 849, 906–1167, 1186–1206	389–421
XV. Habeas Corpus	931–90	608–54	388–405, 942–1061	1337–1467, 1516–20	1019–84	686–808	495–528
XVI. Federal Common Law	388–412, 697–814, 1347–54	220–26, 327–79	325–463, 878–81	656–743, 744–877, 973–81	481–586, 875–908, 1015, 1018	2–31, 118–80, 502–38	552–639
XVII. Claim and Issue Preclusion in the Federal System	1315–47	—	—	1468–1520	1003–1018	1167–86	529–51

APPENDIX E

Table of Cases

Abbott Laboratories v. Gardner, 65, 67
Ableman v. Booth, 227, 228
Adler v. Board of Education, 64, 67
Agua Caliente Band of Cahuilla Indians v. Hardin, 240
Air Courier Conference v. American Postal Workers Union AFL–CIO, 61
Alabama Public Service Commission v. Southern Ry. Co., 260
Alden v. Maine, 25, 236, 249
Aldinger v. Howard, 166, 167, 169, 169
Allegheny County v. Frank Mashuda Co., 27, 263, 264, 265
Allen v. McCurry, 319, 375
Allen v. Wright, 57, 58
American Const. Co. v. Jacksonville, T. & K.W. Ry. Co., 209
American Fire & Cas. Co. v. Finn, 186
American Ins. Co. v. 356 Bales of Cotton, 101, 102, 103
American Well Works Co. v. Layne & Bowler Co., 129, 130
Ames v. Kansas, 180
Ankenbrandt v. Richards, 156, 157
Arizona v. New Mexico, 195
Arizonans for Official English v. Arizona, 271
Arkansas v. Farm Credit Services of Cent. Arkansas, 281
ASARCO Inc. v. Kadish, 64

Association of Data Processing Service Organizations, Inc. v. Camp, 53, 60
Atlantic Coast Line R. Co. v. Brotherhood of Locomotive Engineers, 276
Avco Corp. v. Aero Lodge No. 735, 183

Bakelite Corporation, In re, 95, 96, 104
Baker v. Carr, 73, 74, 76
Banco Nacional de Cuba v. Sabbatino, 360, 369
Bank of America Nat. Trust & Sav. Ass'n v. Parnell, 365
Bank of United States v. Deveaux, 146
Barber v. Barber, 156
Barnett v. Baltimore & O. R. Co., 225
Bartlett v. Bowen, 90
Battaglia v. General Motors Corp., 90
Bennett v. Spear, 53, 56, 62
Bivens v. Six Unknown Named Agents of Federal Bureau of Narcotics, 34, 35, 325, 370
Blatchford v. Native Village of Noatak and Circle Village, 249
Board of County Com'rs v. Brown, 310
Board of Regents v. Tomanio, 317
Board of Trustees of University of Alabama v. Garrett, 250
Boerne, City of v. Flores, 249

Boyle v. United Technologies Corp., 366
Breard v. Greene, 196
Brillhart v. Excess Ins. Co., 268
Briscoe v. LaHue, 322
Brown v. Allen, 343, 344, 345
Brown v. Western Ry. of Ala., 227
Buckley v. Fitzsimmons, 322
Burford v. Sun Oil Co., 26, 27, 255, 259, 260, 261, 262, 263, 266, 269
Bush v. Lucas, 329
Bush v. Palm Beach County Canvassing Bd., 207

California v. Grace Brethren Church, 282
California v. Texas, 194
California, United States v., 86
California Bankers Ass'n v. Shultz, 66
Camp v. Arkansas, 206
Cannon v. University of Chicago, 362
Carden v. Arkoma Associates, 149
Carlson v. Green, 328
Chapman v. Barney, 148
Chapman v. Houston Welfare Rights Organization, 313
Chappell v. Wallace, 329
Charles Dowd Box Co. v. Courtney, 220
Chicago, R. I. & P. Ry. Co. v. Martin, 179
Chicago & Southern Air Lines v. Waterman S. S. Corp., 1

413

Chick Kam Choo v. Exxon Corp., 280
Chisholm v. Georgia, 22, 86, 236, 238
City of (see name of city)
Claflin v. Houseman, 219
Clarke v. Securities Industry Ass'n, 60, 61
Clearfield Trust Co. v. United States, 39, 362, 363, 364, 367
Clinton v. Jones, 330
Cohen v. Beneficial Indus. Loan Corp., 200
Cohens v. Virginia, 254
Coleman v. Thompson, 353, 354, 355
Colorado River Water Conservation Dist. v. United States, 27, 255, 260, 265, 266, 267, 268, 269, 287
Commercial Trust Co. v. Miller, 75
Commodity Futures Trading Com'n v. Schor, 107
Commonwealth of (see name of Commonwealth)
Pennsylvania v. West Virginia, 194
Cort v. Ash, 362
Cory v. White, 239
Costarelli v. Massachusetts, 199
Cousins v. Wigoda, 75
Cox Broadcasting Corp. v. Cohn, 201
Crowell v. Benson, 8, 106, 108, 109, 110, 111

Daniels v. Allen, 352
Davidson v. Cannon, 315
Davis v. Passman, 328
Davis v. Scherer, 323
DeFunis v. Odegaard, 68
Dellmuth v. Muth, 249
Dennis v. Higgins, 313
Dennis v. Sparks, 312, 320
Deposit Guaranty Nat. Bank, Jackson, Miss. v. Roper, 71
Dice v. Akron, C. & Y. R. Co., 226
District of Columbia Court of Appeals v. Feldman, 319, 372
D'Oench, Duhme & Co. v. Federal Deposit Ins. Corporation, 359
Dombrowski v. Pfister, 30, 31, 277, 289, 290
Donovan v. City of Dallas, 283
Doran v. Salem Inn, Inc., 294
Doremus v. Board of Ed. of Borough of Hawthorne, 64
Douglas v. City of Jeannette, 289

Douglas v. New York, N.H. & H.R. Co., 225
Dragan v. Miller, 157
Duhne v. New Jersey, 193
Duke Power Co. v. Carolina Environmental Study Group, Inc., 57
Durousseau v. United States, 103
Dynes v. Hoover, 103

Edelman v. Jordan, 239, 244, 251
Eisentrager v. Forrestal, 83
England v. Louisiana State Bd. of Medical Examiners, 26, 28, 269, 270
Engle v. Isaac, 353
Erie R. Co. v. Tompkins, 38, 358
Estelle v. Gamble, 313
Everson v. Board of Education, 64
Ex parte (see name of party)
Exxon Corp. v. Central Gulf Lines, Inc., 369

Fair Assessment in Real Estate Ass'n, Inc. v. McNary, 282
Farrar v. Hobby, 316
Fay v. Noia, 37, 352, 353
Faysound Ltd. v. United Coconut Chemicals, Inc., 143
Federal Election Com'n v. Akins, 55, 62
Federal Radio Commission v. General Electric Co., 95
Federated Dept. Stores, Inc. v. Moitie, 182
Felker v. Turpin, 88
Fenner v. Boykin, 289
FERC v. Mississippi, 225
Finley v. United States, 15, 165, 166, 167, 169
Firestone Tire and Rubber Co. v. Bruch, 361
Fiske v. Kansas, 208
Fitzgerald v. Racing Ass'n of Central Iowa, 208
Fitzpatrick v. Bitzer, 249
Flast v. Cohen, 63
Florida v. Thomas, 203
Florida Dept. of Health and Rehabilitative Services v. Florida Nursing Home Ass'n, 247
Florida Prepaid Postsecondary Educ. Expense Bd. v. College Sav. Bank, 25, 250

Ford Motor Co. v. Department of Treasury of State of Indiana, 240, 241
Forrester v. White, 322
Frady, United States v., 354
Franchise Tax Board v. Construction Laborers Vacation Trust for Southern California, 128
Francis v. Henderson, 353
Freeman v. Howe, 163
Friends of the Earth, Inc. v. Laidlaw Environmental Services (TOC), Inc., 70

Garcia v. San Antonio Metropolitan Transit Authority, 224
Georgia v. Rachel, 332, 334, 335
Georgia Railroad & Banking Co. v. Redwine, 281
Gerstein v. Pugh, 248, 292
Gibson v. Berryhill, 292
Gilligan v. Morgan, 75
Glidden Co. v. Zdanok, 96, 104, 105
Goldwater v. Carter, 74
Gonzaga University v. Doe, 34, 315
Graham v. Connor, 313
Gratz v. Bollinger, 305
Green v. Mansour, 246
Greenwood, City of v. Peacock, 336
Gulf Offshore Co. v. Mobil Oil Corp., 220

Hafer v. Melo, 308
Hagans v. Lavine, 131
Hans v. Louisiana, 22, 237, 238
Harlow v. Fitzgerald, 323, 330
Harman v. Forssenius, 257, 258
Harris v. Reed, 354, 355
Harris County Com'rs Court v. Moore, 270
Hawaii Housing Authority v. Midkiff, 258, 259, 298
Heck v. Humphrey, 375
Henry v. Mississippi, 205, 206
Hepburn & Dundas v. Ellzey, 98, 142
Herb v. Pitcairn, 203, 224
Hess v. Port Authority Trans–Hudson Corp., 236
Hicks v. Miranda, 31, 294
Hinderlider v. La Plata River & Cherry Creek Ditch Co., 359, 369
Hobson v. Hansen, 95
Hodgson v. Bowerbank, 98, 136

Holmes Group v. Vornado Air Circulation, 124, 126
Honig v. Doe, 70
Hope v. Pelzer, 324
Houston, City of v. Hill, 271
Howard v. Lyons, 265
Howlett By Howlett v. Rose, 223, 304
Huffman v. Pursue, Ltd., 32, 295, 296
Hurn v. Oursler, 163, 164, 165
Hutto v. Finney, 245

Idaho v. Coeur d'Alene Tribe of Idaho, 244
Illinois v. City of Milwaukee, Wis., 193, 194, 360, 369
Ingraham v. Wright, 314
In re (see name of party)
I.N.S. v. St. Cyr, 93

Jackson v. Virginia, 348
Jacobellis v. Ohio, 109
J.A. Olson Co. v. City of Winona, 147
J.I. Case Co. v. Borak, 361
Jimenez–Angeles v. Ashcroft, 85
Jinks v. Richland County, S.C., 16, 173
Johnson v. Mississippi, 333
Jones v. Alfred H. Mayer Co., 305
JPMorgan Chase Bank v. Traffic Stream (BVI) Infrastructure Ltd., 136, 139
Juidice v. Vail, 297

Kalina v. Fletcher, 322
Kamen v. Kemper Financial Services, Inc., 366
Keller v. Potomac Electric Power Co., 95
Kelly v. United States Steel Corp., 147
Kenosha, Wis., City of v. Bruno, 309
Kentucky v. Dennison, 193
Kenyon v. Hammer, 207
Kermarec v. Compagnie Generale Transatlantique, 368
Kerotest Mfg. Co. v. C–O–Two Fire Equipment Co., 283
Kimbell Foods, Inc., United States v., 364
Kimberlin v. Quinlan, 318
Kimel v. Florida Bd. of Regents, 249, 250
Klein, United States v., 6, 91, 92

Kline v. Burke Const. Co., 279
Kohn v. Central Distributing Co., 281
Kossick v. United Fruit Co., 369
Kramer v. Caribbean Mills, Inc., 158
Kremer v. Chemical Const. Corp., 375
Kroll v. Finnerty, 132

Lambrix v. Singletary, 354
Lapides v. Board of Regents of University System of Georgia, 240, 241, 247, 308
Lear, Inc. v. Adkins, 222
Leatherman v. Tarrant County, 318
Lehman Bros. v. Schein, 271
Leiter Minerals, Inc. v. United States, 276
Little Lake Misere Land Co., Inc., United States v., 363
Local No. 438, Const. & General Laborers' Union v. Curry, 200
Lockerty v. Phillips, 81
Louisiana Power & Light Co. v. City of Thibodaux, 27, 27, 255, 263, 264, 265
Louisville, C. & C.R. Co. v. Letson, 146
Louisville & N.R. Co. v. Mottley, 126
Lugar v. Edmondson Oil Co., Inc., 311, 312
Lujan v. Defenders of Wildlife, 53, 56, 62
Lujan v. National Wildlife Federation, 54
Lusby v. T.G. & Y. Stores, Inc., 311
Luther v. Borden, 73, 74
Lynch v. Household Finance Corp., 304

Maestri v. Jutkofsky, 322
Maine v. Thiboutot, 304, 315
Marbury v. Madison, 1, 49, 50, 86, 97, 192
Markham v. Allen, 157
Marrese v. American Academy of Orthopaedic Surgeons, 374
Martin v. Hunter's Lessee, 82, 222
Maryland v. Louisiana, 194
Massachusetts v. Mellon, 62
Mathews v. Eldridge, 314
Matsushita Elec. Indus. Co., Ltd. v. Epstein, 374
McCardle, Ex parte, 5, 5, 87, 88, 89, 114

McClung v. Silliman, 229
McKnett v. St. Louis & S.F. Ry. Co., 226
Memphis Community School Dist. v. Stachura, 316
Mercantile Nat. Bank at Dallas v. Langdeau, 200, 219
Meredith v. City of Winter Haven, 255
Merrell Dow Pharmaceuticals Inc. v. Thompson, 129, 130, 131
Mesa v. California, 122, 185
Metropolitan Life Ins. Co. v. Taylor, 128, 183
Michigan v. Long, 207, 354
Middlesex County Ethics Committee v. Garden State Bar Ass'n, 298
Migra v. Warren City School Dist. Bd. of Educ., 319, 375
Milliken v. Bradley, 245
Milwaukee, City of v. Illinois and Michigan, 369
Minneapolis & St. L.R. Co. v. Bombolis, 227
Miree v. DeKalb County, Ga., 365
Mississippi, United States v., 237
Missouri ex rel. Southern Ry. Co. v. Mayfield, 225
Mistretta v. United States, 97
Mitchum v. Foster, 29, 277, 278, 288, 289
Mondou v. New York, N.H. & H.R. Co., 222
Monell v. Department of Social Services of City of New York, 33, 167, 309
Monroe v. Pape, 33, 307, 309, 310, 313
Monterey, City of v. Del Monte Dunes at Monterey, Ltd., 318
Moor v. Alameda County, 309
Moore v. Chesapeake & O. Ry. Co., 130
Moore v. New York Cotton Exchange, 163
Moore v. Sims, 297
Morrison v. Olson, 96
Moses H. Cone Memorial Hosp. v. Mercury Const. Corp., 267, 268, 269
Murdock v. Memphis, 203
Murphy v. Hunt, 69
Murphy Bros., Inc. v. Michetti Pipe Stringing, Inc., 187
Murray v. Carrier, 353
Murray v. City of Onawa, Iowa, 317

Napier v. Preslicka, 318
Nashville, C. & St. L. Ry. v. Wallace, 51
National Credit Union Admin. v. First Nat. Bank & Trust Co., 61
National Labor Relations Board v. White Swan Co., 209
National League of Cities v. Usery, 224
National Mut. Ins. Co. v. Tidewater Transfer Co., 98, 142
Navarro Sav. Ass'n v. Lee, 149
NCAA v. Tarkanian, 312
Nelson v. Keefer, 152
Nevada v. Hall, 238
Nevada, United States v., 196
Nevada Dept. of Human Resources v. Hibbs, 250
New Jersey v. New York, 360
New Orleans Public Service, Inc. v. Council of City of New Orleans, 262, 299
Newport, City of v. Fact Concerts, Inc., 310
New York v. Ferber, 60
Nixon v. Fitzgerald, 330
Nixon, United States v., 75, 76
NLRB v. Nash–Finch Co., 276
Noble v. Bradford Marine, Inc., 179
Northern Pipeline Const. Co. v. Marathon Pipe Line Co., 106, 107, 108, 111, 113

O'Callahan v. Parker, 104
O'Donoghue v. United States, 95
Ohio v. Johnson, 207
Ohio v. Wyandotte Chemicals Corp., 87, 195
Ohio Civil Rights Com'n v. Dayton Christian Schools, Inc., 299
Oklahoma Packing Co. v. Oklahoma Gas & Elec. Co., 275
O'Melveny & Myers v. F.D.I.C., 366
Osborn v. Bank of United States, 120, 121, 123, 162
O'Sullivan v. Boerckel, 343
Owen v. City of Independence, Mo., 241
Owen Equipment & Erection Co. v. Kroger, 171
Owens v. Okure, 318

Pacific Gas and Elec. Co. v. State Energy Resources Conservation & Development Com'n, 66
Padelford, United States v., 91
Palmore v. United States, 105
Parden v. Terminal Ry., 251
Parratt v. Taylor, 314
Parsons Steel, Inc. v. First Alabama Bank, 281
Patsy v. Board of Regents of State of Fla., 239, 298, 307
Pennhurst State School & Hosp. v. Halderman, 243
Pennsylvania v. Muniz, 207
Pennsylvania v. Ritchie, 202
Pennsylvania v. Union Gas Co., 248
Pennsylvania v. West Virginia, 194
Pennzoil Co. v. Texaco, Inc., 32, 297
Plaut v. Spendthrift Farm, Inc., 92
Port Authority Trans–Hudson Corp. v. Feeney, 246
Porter v. Nussle, 319
Powell v. McCormack, 76
Principality of Monaco v. Mississippi, 237
Puerto Rico Aqueduct and Sewer Authority v. Metcalf & Eddy, Inc., 237
Pulliam v. Allen, 322

Quackenbush v. Allstate Ins. Co., 263
Quern v. Jordan, 240, 245, 246

Radio Station WOW v. Johnson, 200, 201
Railroad Commission of Tex. v. Pullman Co., 26, 27, 28, 255, 256, 257, 259, 263, 264, 265, 266, 269, 270, 271
Raines, United States v., 58
Raygor v. Regents of University of Minnesota, 170, 174
Reed v. Ross, 353
Reetz v. Bozanich, 258
Regents of the University of California v. Doe, 241
Reno v. American–Arab Anti-Discrimination Committee, 85
Reno v. Catholic Social Services, Inc., 65
Rivet v. Regions Bank of Louisiana, 182
Rizzo v. Goode, 297, 298

Robertson v. Seattle Audubon Soc., 92
Robertson v. Wegmann, 317
Rockefeller v. Court of Appeals Office, Tenth Circuit Judges, 325
Roe v. Wade, 69
Rogers v. Alabama, 204
Rooker v. Fidelity Trust Co., 319, 372
Rose v. Lundy, 343
Rose v. Mitchell, 248
Rosewell v. LaSalle Nat. Bank, 281
Royall, Ex parte, 343
Ruhrgas AG v. Marathon Oil Co., 180
Runyon v. McCrary, 305

Samuels v. Mackell, 288, 293
Saucier v. Katz, 324
Scheuer v. Rhodes, 241
Schlesinger v. Reservists Committee to Stop the War, 54, 62
Schultea v. Wood, 318
Schweiker v. Chilicky, 329
Scot Typewriter Co. v. Underwood Corp., 147
Seminole Tribe of Florida v. Florida, 25, 244, 248
Semmes Motors, Inc. v. Ford Motor Co., 283
Semtek Intern. Inc. v. Lockheed Martin Corp., 40, 370, 375, 376
Sh.A. ex rel. J.A. v. Tucumcari Mun. Schools, 324
Shamrock Oil & Gas Corp. v. Sheets, 179, 180
Shaw v. Murphy, 313
Sheldon v. Sill, 81
Shoshone Mining Co. v. Rutter, 129
Sierra Club v. Morton, 54
Simon v. Eastern Kentucky Welfare Rights Organization, 56
Sioux Nation of Indians, United States v., 91
Skelly Oil Co. v. Phillips Petroleum Co., 120
Smith v. Kansas City Title & Trust Co., 129, 130
Smith v. Murray, 353
Smith v. Wade, 316
Smith v. Washington, 155
Snyder v. Harris, 154
Sosna v. Iowa, 71
South Carolina v. Katzenbach, 86

TABLE OF CASES 417

Southern Pac. Co. v. Jensen, 368
Southern Pac. Terminal Co. v. Interstate Commerce Commission, 69
Standard Dredging Corporation v. Murphy, 368
Stanley, United States v., 329
State Farm Fire & Cas. Co. v. Tashire, 141
State of (see name of state)
Steffel v. Thompson, 31, 293, 294
St. Joseph Stock Yards Co. v. United States, 109
Stone v. Powell, 36, 347, 348
St. Paul Mercury Indem. Co. v. Red Cab Co., 151
Strauder v. West Virginia, 333, 334
Strawbridge v. Curtiss, 140, 141, 143, 169
Students Challenging Regulatory Agency Procedures (SCRAP), United States v., 53
Stump v. Sparkman, 321
Sullivan v. Little Hunting Park, Inc., 205
Sun Printing & Publishing Ass'n v. Edwards, 138
Supreme Court of Virginia v. Consumers Union of United States, Inc., 322, 323
Supreme Tribe of Ben Hur v. Cauble, 150, 175
Suter v. Artist M., 315
Swift v. Tyson, 358, 359
Syngenta Crop Protection, Inc. v. Henson, 181

Tafflin v. Levitt, 220, 221
Tarble, In re, 21, 228, 229, 230
Tennessee v. Davis, 185
Tenney v. Brandhove, 320
Testa v. Katt, 223, 225
Texas v. White, 74
Textile Workers Union v. Lincoln Mills, 122, 360

Thomas v. Union Carbide Agr. Products Co., 107, 108
Thompson v. City of Louisville, 199
Thompson v. Thompson, 362
Toucey v. New York Life Ins. Co., 275, 280
Townsend v. Sain, 345
Trafficante v. Metropolitan Life Ins. Co., 55, 62
Trainor v. Hernandez, 296
Turner v. Bank of North America, 83

United Airlines, Inc. v. McDonald, 71
United Mine Workers v. Gibbs, 15, 16, 163, 164, 165, 166, 167, 168, 173
United Public Workers of America v. Mitchell, 67
United States v. _____ (see opposing party)
United States Parole Commission v. Geraghty, 68, 71

Valley Forge Christian College v. Americans United for Separation of Church and State, Inc., 52, 55, 61, 62, 63
Vasquez v. Hillery, 348
Vendo Co. v. Lektro–Vend Corp., 278
Verlinden B.V. v. Central Bank of Nigeria, 121
Virginia v. Rives, 333, 334
Virginia v. West Virginia, 194

Wainwright v. Sykes, 37, 206, 352, 353
Warth v. Seldin, 51, 53, 55, 58, 61
Watson v. Buck, 292

Welch v. State Dept. of Highways and Public Transp., 251
West Virginia v. United States, 364
White v. Fenner, 83
Wilburn Boat Co. v. Fireman's Fund Ins. Co., 368
Will v. Calvert Fire Ins. Co., 267
Will v. Michigan Dept. of State Police, 249, 308
Williams v. United States, 104, 105
Wilson v. Garcia, 317, 318
Wilton v. Seven Falls Co., 268
Wilwording v. Swenson, 343
Wisconsin v. Constantineau, 258
Wisconsin v. Pelican Ins. Co., 86
Withrow v. Williams, 349
Wooley v. Maynard, 31, 294, 295
Wright v. Roanoke Redevelopment and Housing Authority, 315
W.T. Grant Co., United States v., 70
Wyatt v. Cole, 320
Wyoming v. Oklahoma, 195

Yazell, United States v., 364
Yellow Freight System, Inc. v. Donnelly, 221
Yerger, Ex parte, 88
Young, Ex parte, 23, 24, 242, 243, 244, 245, 248
Younger v. Harris, 30, 31, 32, 287, 289, 290, 291, 292, 293, 295, 296, 297, 298, 299

Zablocki v. Redhail, 261, 295
Zahn v. International Paper Co., 154, 155, 174, 175
Zucht v. King, 198

APPENDIX F

Index

ABSTENTION
See also "Our Federalism"
Generally, 254
"Administrative Abstention," 260
Burford Abstention, 259–263
Certification to State Court, 270–271
Colorado River Abstention, 265–269
England Doctrine, 269–270
Overview of Abstention Doctrines, 255
Procedural Aspects of Abstention, 269–271
Procedure in *Pullman* Abstention, 269–270
Pullman Abstention, 256–259
Sources of the Doctrine, 254–255
Thibodaux Abstention, 263–265

ADJUNCTS TO ARTICLE III COURTS
See also Legislative Courts
Generally, 109
Administrative Agencies, 109–111
Bankruptcy Courts, 111–112
Magistrate Judges, 112

ADMINISTRATIVE AGENCIES
See Adjuncts to Article III Courts

ALIENAGE JURISDICTION
See Diversity of Citizenship Jurisdiction

AMOUNT IN CONTROVERSY FOR DIVERSITY & ALIENAGE JURISDICTION
Generally, 150
Aggregation of Claims, 153–155
Assessment of, 151–153
Class Actions, 154–155
Equitable Relief, 155–156
"Good Faith" Test, 152–153
"Legal Certainty" Test, 151–153
Rationale, 150

ANTI-INJUNCTION STATUTE
See also "Our Federalism"
Generally, 274
Background, 274–277
Exceptions, 277–281
"Expressly Authorized" Exception, 277–278
"In Aid of Jurisdiction" Exception, 278–280
Injunction by a Federal Court of Federal Proceedings, 282–283
Injunction by a State Court of Federal Proceedings, 283
Injunctions of Federal Judicial Proceedings, 282–283
Johnson Act of 1934, 282
Other Statutory Restrictions on Federal Injunctions, 281–282
"Relitigation" Exception, 280–281
Statutory Provision, 274
Tax Injunction Act of 1937, 281–282

ARISING UNDER JURISDICTION
See Federal Question Jurisdiction

ARTICLE I COURTS
See Legislative Courts

BANKRUPTCY COURTS
See Adjuncts to Article III Courts

BIVENS CLAIMS
See Federal Civil Rights

CIVIL RIGHTS
See Federal Civil Rights

CIVIL RIGHTS REMOVAL
"Authority" Clause, 331
Background, 330–332
"Denial" Clause, 331, 332
"Equal Rights" Interpreted, 332–333
Modernly, 334–336
Narrow Interpretation, 332–333
"Refusal" Clause, 331
State Statutes vs. State Practices, 333–334, 336
Statutory Provision, 330–332

CLAIM PRECLUSION & ISSUE PRECLUSION IN THE FEDERAL SYSTEM
See also Federal Common Law
Generally, 372
Civil Rights Cases, 375
Effect of Federal Court Judgments, 375–376
Exclusive Jurisdiction of Federal Court, 373–374
Federal Diversity Cases, 375–376
Federal Question Cases, 375
Full Faith and Credit Constitutional Provision, 372–373
Full Faith and Credit Statutory Provision, 373–375
Situations Not Covered by Either the Constitution or Statutory Provision, 375–376

COLLATERAL ESTOPPEL
See Claim Preclusion & Issue Preclusion in the Federal System

CONCURRENT JURISDICTION
Definition of, 218
Presumption of, 219–221
State Law Obligation to Adjudicate Federal Claims, 222–227
State Law Obligation to Utilize Federal Procedures for Federal Claims, 226–227
"Valid Excuse" Doctrine, 223–226

CONGRESSIONAL POWER OVER JURISDICTION
See also Legislative Courts
Generally, 79–81
Constitutional Limitations, 89–94
Lower Federal Courts, 81–85
Madisonian Compromise, 81
Supreme Court, 85–89
Vesting Article III Powers in Article I Courts, 101–109
Vesting Non–Article III Powers in Article III Courts, 94–98

DECLARATORY JUDGMENT ACT
Federal Question Jurisdiction, 127–128
Relation to Abstention, 268
Well–Pleaded Complaint Rule Applicable, 127–128

DIVERSITY OF CITIZENSHIP JURISDICTION & ALIENAGE JURISDICTION
See also Amount in Controversy in Diversity & Alienage Jurisdiction
Generally, 135
Amount in Controversy, 150–156
Citizenship Determinations, 143–150
Citizenship of Class, 150
Citizenship of Corporations, 146–148
Citizenship of Decedents, 149
Citizenship of Human Beings, 143–146
Citizenship of Incompetents, 149
Citizenship of Minors, 149
Citizenship of Non-Incorporated Associations, 148–149
Citizenship with Representatives, 149–150
Collusive Joinder, 157–158
Complete Diversity Rule, 140–143
Constitutional Basis, 135–136
Domestic Relations Exception, 156–157
Exceptions, 156–157
Minimal Diversity, 140–142
Permanent Resident Alien Proviso, 137–138
Policy Rationale, 138–140
Probate Exception, 156–157
Statutory Basis, 136–138

DOMESTIC RELATIONS EXCEPTION
See Diversity of Citizenship Jurisdiction & Alienage Jurisdiction

ELEVENTH AMENDMENT IMMUNITY
See Sovereign Immunity

EXCLUSIVE JURISDICTION
Definition of, 218
Doctrine of Implied Exclusivity, 219–221
State Court Adjudication in Exclusive Jurisdiction Matters, 221–222

FEDERAL CIVIL RIGHTS, ACTIONS TO VINDICATE
Generally, 303
Absolute Immunity from § 1983 Cases, 321–323
Attorney's Fees, 316–317
Bivens Claims, 325–330
Bivens Claims: Limitations on, 327–329
Bivens Claims: Procedure, 329–330
Civil Rights Removal, 330–336
Civil Rights Statutes, 303–306
Contrast with Habeas Corpus, 304–305
Defendant Must be a "Person", 308–310
Defendant Must have Deprived Plaintiff of a Federal Right, 312–315
Defendant Requirements, 308–315
Deficiency of § 1983, 317
Deprivations under Color of Federal Law, 325–330
Equitable Remedies, 316
Exhaustion of State Remedies, 307, 318–319, 329–330
Federal Actors, 325–330
Fundamental Rights, 313–315
"Good Faith" Immunity from § 1983 Cases, 321, 323–325
Heightened Pleading Requirements, 318
Immunity from § 1983 Cases, 320–325
Implied Constitutional Rights of Action, 325–329, 362
Judicial Immunity, 321–322
Juror Immunity, 322
Jury Trial, 318
Legislator Immunity, 322–323
Litigation issues, 317–319
Litigation under § 1983, 306–319
Non–Fundamental Rights, 313–315
Plaintiff as Citizen or Person within US Jurisdiction, 308
Plaintiff Requirements, 308
Presidential Immunity, 330
Prison Litigation Reform Act impositions, 318–319
Prosecutorial Immunity, 322
Punitive Damages, 316
Qualified Immunity from § 1983 Cases, 321, 323–325
Remedies, 316–317
Rooker-Feldman Doctrine, 319
Statute of Limitations, 317–318
"Under Color" of "State Law," 308, 310–312
Witness Immunity, 322

FEDERAL COMMON LAW
See also Claim Preclusion & Issue Preclusion in the Federal System
Generally, 358
Admiralty, 367–369
Application, 360–370
Claim Preclusion, 370
Constitutional Rights, 370
Erie Doctrine, 358–359
Federal Proprietary Interests, 362–366
Implied Statutory Remedies, 361–362
International Relations, 366–367
Interstate Disputes, 369
Interstate Pollution, 369–370
Issue Preclusion, 370
Justification for, 358–360
Reach of Federal Common Law, 360
Rules of Decision Act, 359–360
Sources of, 358–360
Statutory Gaps, Use to Fill, 360–362
Swift Doctrine, 358–359

FEDERAL JUDGES
Constitutional protection of, 49

FEDERAL QUESTION JURISDICTION
Generally, 120
Articulated-and-Active-Federal–Policy Theory, 122–123
"Cause of Action" Test, 129
Constitutional Basis, 120–123
Declaratory Judgment Act, 127–128
Effect on Removal, 128–129
"Federal Interest" Test, 130–131
Greater–Includes-the-Lesser Theory, 122

Policy Rationale, 123
Protective Jurisdiction, 121–123
Scope of Statutory Grant, 129–132
Statutory Basis, 123–132
Well–Pleaded Complaint Rule, 125–129

HABEAS CORPUS
Generally, 339
Abortive State Proceedings, 351–355
"Adequate State Ground" Doctrine, 351–355
Appellate Review of Federal Habeas Decisions, 350
Background, 339–340
Capital Cases, 350–351
"Cause and Prejudice," 352–354
Concept of Habeas Corpus, 339–340
Current Statutory Provisions, 340–342
"Deliberate Bypass" of State Procedures, 353–354
Deprivations Cognizable in Federal Habeas Proceedings, 347–349
Exhaustion of State Remedies, 342–343
Exhaustion of State Remedies: Waiver, 344
Federal Custody, 355–356
History of the Writ, 340
In State Court, 227–229
Origins of the Writ, 340
Persons in Custody of the United States, 355–356
"Plain Statement" Requirement, 354–355
Review of State Court Findings, 344–347
State Court Findings, 344–347
State Prisoners, 342–349
Statute of Limitations, 349
Successive Petitions, 349–350
Waiver of Exhaustion Requirement, 344

IMPLIED CONSTITUTIONAL REMEDIES
See Federal Civil Rights

IMPLIED STATUTORY REMEDIES
See Federal Common Law

INTERPLEADER
See Statutory Interpleader
See also Rule Interpleader

ISSUE PRECLUSION
See Claim Preclusion & Issue Preclusion in the Federal System

JUDICIAL REVIEW
Generally, 49–50
See also Justiciability

JURISDICTION
See also Justiciability
Alienage Jurisdiction, 133–158
"Case or Controversy" Requirement, 50–51
Congressional power over, 77–112
Diversity of Citizenship Jurisdiction, 133–158
Federal Question Jurisdiction, 120–132
Removal Jurisdiction, 177–188
Supplemental Jurisdiction, 159–175
Supreme Court Jurisdiction, 189–209

JUSTICIABILITY
Generally, 49
Advisory Opinions, 50–51
Mootness, 67–71
Political Questions, 71–76
Ripeness, 65–67
Standing, 51–64

LEGISLATIVE COURTS
See also Adjuncts to Article III Courts
Generally, 100
Constitutional authorization for, 101
Distinguish from Article III Courts, 100
Jurisdictional limitations, 101–109
Military Courts, 103–104
Private Rights, 106–109
Public Rights, 106–109
Territorial Courts, 102–103

LOWER FEDERAL COURTS
Congressional power over, 81–85
Constitutional authorization for, 79

MAGISTRATE JUDGES
See Adjuncts to Article III Courts

MILITARY COURTS
See Legislative Courts

MOOTNESS
See Justiciability

"OUR FEDERALISM"
Generally, 287
Background, 287–289
Civil Proceedings, 296–297
Early Cases, 289
Exceptions, 291–292
Future vs. Ongoing Prosecutions, 292–295
Historical Development, 289–292
Modernly, 290–291
Non–Judicial State Action, 297–299
Post–Trial Intervention, 295
Relationship to the Anti-Injunction Statute, 288–289

State Administrative Actions, 298–299
State Executive Actions, 297–298
State Legislative Actions, 299
Timing Issues, 292–295

POLITICAL QUESTIONS
Generally, 71–72
Application, 74–76
Factor Approach, 73–74
Modernly, 73–74

PRIVATE RIGHTS
See Legislative Courts

PUBLIC RIGHTS
See Legislative Courts

REMOVAL JURISDICTION
Generally, 178
Availability, 178–179
Civil Rights Removal, 185, 330–336
Diversity Jurisdiction, 183–185
Federal Officer Removal, 185, 230–231
Federal Question Jurisdiction, 128–129, 181–183
Jurisdiction Required, 179–180, 181
Notice of Removal, 186
Principles of, 178–180
Procedure for Removal and Remand, 186–188
Remand, 178, 187–188
Specialized Grants, 185–186
State Court Lacks Jurisdiction, 180
Statutory Grant, 180–181
Timing of Removal, 187
Venue, 179

RES JUDICATA
See Claim Preclusion & Issue Preclusion in the Federal System

RIPENESS
See Justiciability

ROOKER-FELDMAN DOCTRINE
See Federal Civil Rights

SOVEREIGN IMMUNITY
Generally, 235
Avoidance of, 242
Background, 235–237
Congressional Abrogation, 247–252
Constructive Waiver, 247, 250–251
Definition of "State", 240–242
Direct Congressional Abrogation of Immunity, 247–250
Doctrine of *Ex Parte Young*, 242–246
Eleventh Amendment, 236
Exceptions to Immunity, 237–238
History, 235–237
Indirect Congressional Abrogation of Immunity, 247, 250–251
Interpretation of the Eleventh Amendment, 237–242
Municipalities, 241
Waiver, 246–247

STANDING
Generally, 51–52
Causation, 52, 56–57
Constitutional Requirements, 52–58
Injury in fact, 52–56
In the Supreme Court, 64
Prudential Limitations, 58–62
Redressability, 53, 56–57
Taxpayer Standing, 62–64
Third-party Standing, 58–60

STATE COURTS AND FEDERAL POWER
Generally, 217
Adjudication of Federal Matters, 219–222
Concurrent Jurisdiction, 218–221
Constitutional presumptions, 217
Doctrine of Implied Exclusivity, 219–221
Exclusive Jurisdiction, 218, 221–222
Federal Officers in State Court, 227–231
Injunctions, 229–230
Mandamus, 229–230
Obligation to Adjudicate Federal Claims, 222–227
Obligation to Utilize Federal Procedure for Federal Claims, 226–227
"Valid Excuse" Doctrine, 223–226
Writs of Habeas Corpus, 227–229

STATUTORY INTERPLEADER
Minimal Diversity Requirement, 141–142

SUPPLEMENTAL JURISDICTION
Generally, 160
Ancillary Jurisdiction, 162
Class Actions, 174–175
Definition of, 162
Discretionary Decline, 172–173
Diversity Cases, 170–172
Historical Development of, 162–168
Pendent Jurisdiction, 162
Policy Issues, 160–161
Problems with Application, 174–175
Restrictions, 170–172
Statute Generally, 168

Statute's Passage, 167–168
Statutory Grant of Jurisdiction, 168–170
Terms, 162
Tolling Provision, 173–174

SUPREME COURT
Appellate Jurisdiction, 80, 87–89, 196–209
Congressional power over, 85–89
Constitutional authorization for, 79
Constitutional grant of jurisdiction, 191–194
Exceptions Clause, 80, 87
Independent and Adequate State Ground Doctrine, 203–208
Jurisdiction Generally, 191
Original Jurisdiction, 80, 85–87, 194–196
Review of Courts of Appeals' Decisions, 208–209
Review of State Court Decisions, 198–208
Review of State Court Decisions: Findings of Fact, 208
Review of State Court Decisions: Highest State Court, 199
Review of State Court Decisions: The Final Judgment Rule, 199–203
Writ of Certiorari, 196–197

TERRITORIAL COURTS
See Legislative Courts

WELL-PLEADED COMPLAINT RULE
See Federal Question Jurisdiction